THE ZONDERVAN 2014
PASTOR'S
ANNUAL

AN IDEA & RESOURCE BOOK

T. T. CRABTREE

ZONDERVAN®

ZONDERVAN.com/
AUTHORTRACKER
follow your favorite authors

ZONDERVAN

The Zondervan 2014 Pastor's Annual
Copyright © 1993, 2013 by Zondervan

Requests for information should be addressed to:
Zondervan, *Grand Rapids, Michigan 49530*

Much of the contents of this book was previously published in *Pastor's Annual 1994.*

ISBN 978-0-310-493952

Printed in the United States of America

13 14 15 16 17 18 19 20 /DCI/ 22 21 20 19 18 17 16 15 14 13 12 11 10 9 8 7 6 5 4 3 2 1

CONTENTS

MISCELLANEOUS HELPS

CONTRIBUTING AUTHORS

Morris Ashcraft	P.M.	March 2, 9, 16, 23, 30
Tal D. Bonham	A.M.	November 2, 9, 16, 23
Tom S. Brandon	P.M.	October 5, 12, 19, 26
		November 2, 9, 16, 23
James E. Carter	P.M.	January 1, 8, 15, 22, 29
T. Hollis Epton	A.M.	October 5, 12, 19, 26
David R. Grant	A.M.	November 30
		December 7, 14, 21, 28
	P.M.	January 5, 12, 19, 26
		February 2, 9, 16, 23
		Funeral Meditations
James G. Harris	P.M.	April 6, 13, 20, 27
James F. Heaton	A.M.	August 31
		September 7, 14, 21, 28
Howard S. Kolb	P.M.	July 6, 13, 20, 27
		September 28
Lowell Milburn	P.M.	May 4, 11, 18, 25
		June 1, 8, 15, 22, 29
E. Warren Rust	P.M.	November 30
		December 7, 14, 21, 28
Chester L. Smith	A.M.	July 6, 13, 20, 27
		August 3, 10, 17, 24
	P.M.	August 3, 10, 17, 24, 31
		September 7, 14, 21
Fred M. Wood	A.M.	January 5, 12, 19, 26
		February 2, 9, 16, 23
		March 2, 9, 16, 23, 30
		April 6, 13, 20, 27
B. W. Woods		Messages on the Lord's Supper
		Messages for Children and Young People

PREFACE

Favorable comments from ministers who serve in many different types of churches have encouraged me to believe that the *Pastor's Annual* provides valuable assistance to many busy pastors as they seek to improve the quality, freshness, and variety of their pulpit ministry. To be of service to fellow pastors in their continuing quest to obey our Lord's command to Peter, "Feed my sheep," is a privilege to which I respond with gratitude.

I pray that this issue of the *Pastor's Annual* can be blessed by our Lord in helping pastors to plan and produce a preaching program that will better meet the spiritual needs of the congregation to which they are called to minister.

This issue contains sermons by several contributing authors who have been effective contemporary preachers and successful pastors. Each of these authors is listed with his sermons in Contributing Authors. I accept responsibility for those not listed there.

This issue of the *Pastor's Annual* is dedicated to the Lord with a prayer that he will bless these efforts to let the Holy Spirit lead us in preparing "A Planned Preaching Program for the Year."

T. T. Crabtree

JANUARY

■ Sunday Mornings

The theme for the morning messages for January is "The Life and Works of the Lord Jesus." Use this series to introduce your people anew to the Person, the power, the purpose, and the presence of the Christ who lived, who died, and who victoriously rose from the dead.

■ Sunday Evenings

The Sunday evening theme this month is "Great Texts from 1 John." With love and wisdom, the apostle of love dealt with the problems that plagued our Lord's followers during the first century of the Christian era. His message is relevant for our Lord's disciples in this century as well.

■ Wednesday Evenings

"The Bible Speaks to Our Condition" is the theme for all of this year's Wednesday evening services. I suggest that the pastor lead his people in a daily devotional reading of one chapter each day. This theme grows out of the conviction that Bible study can be the listening side of the experience of prayer. It is more important that we hear what God has to say than it is that he hear what we have to say.

If this program is followed, every seventh chapter in sequence will serve as the scriptural basis for the time of prayer, meditation, spiritual renewal, and rededication on Wednesday evenings.

The theme passage for January is "All scripture is given by inspiration of God, and is profitable for doctrine, for reproof, for correction, for instruction in righteousness: That the man of God may be perfect, thoroughly furnished unto all good works" (2 Tim. 3:16–17).

WEDNESDAY EVENING, JANUARY 1

Title: The Bible Speaks to Our Condition

Scripture Reading: Matthew 2

Introduction

The apostle Paul declared, "All scripture is given by inspiration of God, and is profitable for doctrine, for reproof, for correction, for instruction in righteousness" (2 Tim. 3:16). If we are to grow as the children of God, it is essential that we read God's Word. God will speak to our condition if we will read his Word in a prayerful, responsive attitude.

Someone has said, "An apple a day will keep the doctor away, and a chapter a day will keep the devil away." This proverb is probably an oversimplification of both our health and spiritual needs. However, there is a fundamental truth in this proverb that commands serious thought.

A prayerful reading of God's Word enhances the listening side of the prayer experience, for God will speak through his Word to those who have an inclination to listen. A thoughtful, careful, prayerful reading of a chapter a day, each day through the new year, will bring untold blessings into the life of each reader.

Let us let God speak to us through Matthew 2.

I. Wise men sought the Savior (Matt. 2:1–10).

Magi from the East, students of the stars, came seeking the Savior. From whence did these wise men come? How far had they traveled? How much did they know about the Messiah's star? It is impossible for us to answer these and many other questions. The important thing is that they came seeking the Savior.

We use the highest wisdom that humans can exercise when we seek a deeper knowledge and a more intimate acquaintance with the Savior who came to die for our sins. He alone can deliver us from the tyranny of evil. He alone can lead us into abundant life. He alone can give us victory over death. He alone can lead us into the eternal home of God.

Let each of us seek him with the same diligence with which the wise men sought him.

II. The wise men worshiped the Savior (Matt. 2:11–12).

When the wise men found the Christ child, they fell on their knees before him in worship. They gave him gifts of gold, frankincense, and myrrh.

A. *Gold is an appropriate gift for a king.* Jesus was born to be a king. He wants to rule not by force but through love. He reigns in the hearts of those who love him. We all need to crown him King of our hearts.

B. *Frankincense is the gift for a priest.* In temple worship at the time of sacrifices, the sweet perfume of frankincense was used. Jesus was to be our High Priest. It is he who has given us access into the very presence of the holy God.

C. *Myrrh is a gift for one who is to die.* It was used to embalm the bodies of the dead. Christ came into the world to die for our sins.

As the wise men gave of their best, we would be wise to give our very best for the service of Christ.

III. Piety does not guarantee immunity from trouble (Matt. 2:13–18).

Why the innocent suffer and the righteous experience trouble has always been a mystery. We will never have a satisfactory answer to this question as long as we walk the ways of humanity.

There is no question concerning the innocence and righteousness of Joseph and Mary. They were within the will of God. By virtue of their being in the will of God, they found themselves to be the objects of the hostility of an evil king who sought to bring about their destruction.

Much of the evil and suffering that the innocent and the righteous experience is due to no fault or sin on their part. The devil is responsible for much of our suffering. The wickedness and carelessness of others brings about suffering.

Should we find ourselves innocent victims of tragedy as did the parents of the children in Bethlehem, we must look to God for grace and strength to bear the agony of our misfortune.

Piety does not provide us with immunity from suffering. We must not permit ourselves to lose our faith in the goodness of God if tragedy should befall us or someone very dear to us.

IV. The purpose of our God (Matt. 2:19–23).

Behind everything that is recorded in Matthew 2, we need to see the plan and purpose of God. Repeatedly the inspired writer refers to the fulfillment of prophecy.

God had been at work through the centuries to accomplish his redemptive purpose. In the fullness of time, he sent forth his Son to be our Savior, Lord, Teacher, and Friend.

God continues to be at work in the various congregations around the world seeking to communicate the good news of his love for people, even while they are in the midst of sin and rebellion.

God is at work to accomplish his purpose in our homes. He wants to help us with the responsibilities involved in marriage and the raising of our families.

God is at work in individual hearts, seeking to deliver from the tyranny of evil and lead into a life of devoted service.

Conclusion

Have you been listening? Did you let God speak to your heart through the verses of Matthew 2? He wants to speak with you. He will speak to your condition if you will listen.

SUNDAY MORNING, JANUARY 5

Title: Jesus Grew

Text: "Jesus increased in wisdom and stature, and in favour with God and man" **(Luke 2:52).**

Scripture Reading: Luke 2:40–52

Hymns: "Higher Ground," Oatman

"I Am Thine, O Lord," Crosby

"I Am Resolved," Hartsough

Offertory Prayer: Our Father, this is the first Sunday of the new year. We stand on the threshold of new opportunities, but we also feel the responsibility of new obligations. You have led us in the past, and we face the future with full assurance of your guidance in the days ahead. We thank you for open doors, and we pray for faith to enter them in your strength. Today we bring fresh resolve concerning the stewardship of our lives. Help us to recognize that a part of that stewardship is the bringing of our tithes and offerings. We ask your blessings on each gift, each giver, and each cause that we support through our giving. Accept our gifts and use them to spread the gospel of your grace. We pray in Jesus' name. Amen.

Introduction

There is very little material in the New Testament concerning Jesus from the time of his birth until the beginning of his ministry. A few scattered passages tell of the days immediately following his birth. Matthew records Jesus' parents' flight with Jesus into Egypt and their return. Luke tells of Jesus' presentation in the temple and of the response of Simeon and Anna.

Two silent periods confront us concerning Jesus' life. The first is from the time his parents "came and dwelt in a city called Nazareth" (Matt. 2:23) after they returned from Egypt until the time Jesus visited the temple at the age of twelve. The other silent period is from his return to Nazareth, where Luke says, "He went down with [his parents] ... and was subject unto them" (Luke 2:51) until he presented himself to John for baptism at the age of thirty.

What kind of life did Jesus live during these days? Many apocryphal stories and fantastic legends have come down to us concerning these periods, especially when he was between the ages of twelve and thirty. Most of them have been rejected as untrustworthy. The truth is that we just do not know. Reliable records are not available. Two statements of Luke give us the best clue. Immediately after Luke records the return of Jesus from Jerusalem following his presentation in the temple, he says, "The child grew, and waxed strong in spirit, filled with wisdom: and the grace of God was upon him" (Luke 2:40). Luke then tells of the visit of Jesus and his parents to Jerusalem and concludes this account by saying, "Jesus increased in wisdom and stature, and in favour with God and man" (v. 52).

In speaking of the growth of Jesus, we are not implying either imperfection or immaturity. We are speaking only of the finiteness of his human nature. He was divine, to be sure, but he was also human and experienced normal human growth. The inexperience of childhood progressed in a normal way to wider knowledge and clearer self-consciousness. As Jesus' capacity increased, his ability to grow and comprehend increased. There were no pauses nor sinful elements mingled in his growth. His powers were neither deformed nor unduly developed. His growth means merely that he had no failings in his childhood but was taught by life as well as by Scripture and communion with the Father. The silence of Scripture is as eloquent as if it were vocal with reference to Jesus' early years. Jesus' innocence grew into holiness and did so naturally without attracting attention to itself. The world did not hate him as a child, for he did not yet, except perhaps by his unconscious example, testify against it concerning its evil deeds. On this first Lord's Day of the new year, we consider Jesus' growth as an example for growth in every area of our lives.

I. Jesus grew physically.

Strong bodies are useful for giving our best in God's service. Of course, we have seen outstanding examples of people with disabilities who have concentrated on their work and had amazing success in spite of limited physical abilities. These, however, are glorious exceptions to the rule. Our bodies are the temple, or the dwelling place, of God's Spirit; therefore we need to be as health conscious as we possibly can. The New Testament gives every indication that Jesus had a vigorous physical constitution. His work schedule was remarkably full. He naturally became tired, but there is no indication that he had limited physical capacities. On the contrary, he often performed tasks that showed he was a man of great physical strength. The early years of our lives set the pattern for physical strength or the lack of it in the mature years. Boys and girls who are called on to work hard in the growing years of life may grumble at the time, but later they realize what a privilege they enjoyed. Jesus worked in the carpenter shop. He took care of his body, and in the years to come, he was able to use it in his work to God's glory.

II. Jesus grew mentally.

God warns us many times about the folly of trusting human wisdom, but this does not mean that he is opposed to our intellectual growth. Nowhere does the Bible place a premium on ignorance. God gave us a mind, and he expects us to develop it through study. All other things being equal, the best-trained Christians will be the most effective ones. The boy Jesus must have spent many hours reading the Old Testament scrolls and the writings of the learned men. It is not possible for us to know when he first gained what scholars call his "messianic consciousness," but we are sure that early in his life his human nature found perfect fellowship with his divine nature and he understood his true mission. During the early days, his consciousness of divine sonship was real but as yet undeveloped. He was not merely a "childlike" God in whom growth was impossible. He was truly human in mind and lived under all the limitations common to humans in the mental realm. He therefore had to study in order to grow. He is our example for intellectual achievement. If the Son of God grew mentally, those of us who seek to follow in his steps should take seriously academic development and utilize it to the glory of God.

III. Jesus grew socially.

There is, of course, a danger in striving for popularity. We must not become a "chameleon" and adjust to whatever moral color prevails with the crowd. Christians must always stand for their convictions and be firm in their decisions for right conduct. On the other hand, however, we must hold our standards with a sweet spirit. This means we must learn to get along with people. Christians should not make others feel miserable in their presence. They should make others feel relaxed and happy. If we will cultivate the art of making people enjoy our company, we can grow in the "graces" of social life and, at the same time, lead people

15

to respect our Christian principles. People enjoyed having Jesus in their midst. He was invited to their social gatherings. He was "at home" among them without compromising his convictions concerning God and his redemptive purposes.

IV. Jesus grew spiritually.

It was Jesus' personal fellowship with the Father that enabled him to face life victoriously. Our relationship with God is established through the new birth. Our fellowship comes through growth in things of the spirit. The public life of Jesus had its roots in his private and personal walk with the Father. His bright faith, optimistic outlook, and confidence in God's power to transform others came because he maintained spiritual growth through personal communion in prayer, Scripture study, and constant striving to know God's will and do it. We can be born physically only once, but we can grow physically. We can be born spiritually only once (John 3:16), but we can grow day by day in things of the Spirit as we feed on God's Word and seek to follow his purpose for our lives.

Conclusion

Jesus' growth and our growth may be different in some ways, but in many ways it is exactly the same. Jesus possessed two complete natures—the divine and the human. His two natures did not mingle into one with the divine predominating; they remained separate. His human nature could therefore grow. Born-again Christians also have two natures. The old nature is still with us, but the new nature imparted in the conversion experience is also a reality. Our whole being *must* grow if our lives are to be happy and victorious. If we do not press ahead, we fall back. We are not divided into separate compartments but are one personality. As we grow in each area, life will become meaningful to self, helpful to others, and pleasing to God.

SUNDAY EVENING, JANUARY 5

Title: Life in Him

Text: "For the life was manifested, and we have seen it, and bear witness, and shew unto you that eternal life, which was with the Father, and was manifested unto us" (**1 John 1:2**).

Scripture Reading: 1 John 1:1–10

Introduction

John was an old man when he wrote 1 John and likely outlived the other apostles. These are the words of an inspired writer who was the most intimate companion of our Lord in the days of his earthly ministry.

First John is a book for Christians in general, and "Life in Him" is the theme of the book. Eternal life is not only endless existence; it is the life of God revealed in Jesus Christ and shared by all who put their trust in him. Believers possess a new life, and the source of that life is God, accessed by faith and grounded in goodness and love.

I. The relationship to that life (1 John 1:1–4).

A. *Life in Jesus is through the Word.* In John 1:1 Jesus is called the Word. He is the living Word who possesses this life in eternal fellowship with God. The phrase "from the beginning" in 1:1 shows the infinity of Jesus and goes back behind the incarnation to the eternal purpose of God.

Three of the human senses are used, and their tenses show the reality of Christ's humanity and the qualifications of John to write. "We have heard" and "we have seen" portray continuous action. "We have touched" portrays repetition. John made contact with Jesus time and again.

B. *Life is properly manifested.* John said he had experienced life in Christ and now testified of it to his readers. His testimony is valid because of his experience (1:2). John goes further and says that "you" (meaning all) can have eternal life too. This divine life is fellowship with other believers and with God. The basic idea of fellowship is to have things in common, so the specific idea in this passage is sharing life in Christ through the Holy Spirit.

C. *There is real joy in this fellowship and in proclaiming it.* True joy comes from fellowship with God, and the joy is overflowing when it is shared with others.

II. This life is manifested in our conduct (1 John 1:5–10).

Believers do three things:

A. *We proclaim the message (1 John 1:5).* The word "declare" in the King James Version means to give a report. Believers tell what Christ has done for them and can do for others.

B. *We walk in the light (1 John 1:6–7).*

C. *We tell the truth about sin.*

III. A fuller discussion of these thoughts is seen in an emphasis on the negative and positive.

A. *There is the allegation that one has fellowship with God while walking in darkness (1:6).* The idea of walking refers to conduct or character. God is light. Light is a symbol of splendor and purity. It is that which illuminates our lives. Since God is light, it is not possible to have fellowship with him while walking in darkness.

1. Walking in darkness means to pursue daily tasks without reference to the will of God. It means living according to worldly standards and seeking selfish goals. It means excluding the light that is God.

2. Walking in the light is living a righteous life. Righteousness is doing the will of God. This can be done only when we are in fellowship with God and one another.

B. *There is the claim that one has no sin, and John opposes this (1:8).* The words "no sin" are in reference to no guilt or no principle of sin.
   1. A person is shown that all are guilty of sin and responsible for it. One is not to deny it or seek to explain it away.
   2. The sinner is shown what to do with sin: confess it. To confess means to agree with God. The sinner says to God, "I agree with you; I am a sinner."
C. *There is the claim that one has no sin, and this makes God a liar (1 John 1:10).*
   Many verses in the Bible specifically point out that all have sinned (e.g., Rom. 3:23). The message of the Bible is that humans are sinful and that God has provided salvation for them in Jesus Christ.

Conclusion

True life—really living—is fellowship with God, which is possible through faith in Jesus Christ. The deepest source of joy is found in Christian service, and the highest form of service consists in bringing others into fellowship with the Father through Jesus Christ.

My appeal to you who do not have this life is to accept Jesus as your personal Savior now and enter into eternal life with him. My appeal to you who are Christians is to surrender your life to him in Christian service.

WEDNESDAY EVENING, JANUARY 8

Title: The Bible Speaks to Our Condition
Scripture Reading: Matthew 9

Introduction

Through the inspired Word of God, we can hear God speaking to the deepest needs of those who look to him for guidance and help. Only as we listen to his Word can we become equipped to do his work.

Matthew 9 contains material that could command our attention for a week rather than for a single day. It gives us a picture of the movement and the ministry of our Lord as he met the needs of those about him. As we study this chapter, we can see that he was very busy ministering to others. His heart was compassionate, and he gave himself completely to ministering to the various needs of others.

Matthew reveals in this chapter that our Lord was involved almost constantly in controversy with those who disagreed with his ministry and with his method of doing things. The Pharisees, representing the religious establishment of that day, were his harshest critics. It is interesting to note that our Lord did not let this controversy and disagreement cause him to swerve from his purpose. Neither did he let vicious attacks embitter him and cause him to retaliate. We see our Lord giving himself unreservedly to his task and refusing to yield before the opposition of his critics.

"Jesus Christ is the same yesterday and today and forever" (Heb. 13:8 NIV).

If the Christ was concerned during his earthly life about the suffering of those around him, we can be certain that he is moved with compassion as our eternal Lord. He will minister to us with sympathy and power.

I. The Lordship of Christ.

In Matthew 9 we have an outstanding display of the lordship of our Lord.

A. *We see Jesus as the Lord over disease (9:1 – 7).*

B. *We see Jesus as the Lord over life (9:9).* He issued a call that was to claim the life of Matthew for his service. Matthew gave up a profitable position using his pen to keep tax accounts in order that his pen might be used to write the first gospel.

C. *We see Jesus as Lord over death (9:18 – 26).*

D. *We see Jesus as Lord over blindness (9:27 – 31).*

E. *We see Jesus as Lord over the demonic (9:32).* Christ is the Lord over the greatest foes that we face. He wants to give us victory over the enemies that would defeat or destroy us. He is worthy to be the Lord of our lives and of all that we are and have.

II. The importance of faith.

Matthew 9 speaks dramatically of the importance of faith as the human response that opens the door for God's power to do its work.

A. *The faith of the paralytic and his friends brought both forgiveness and the restoration of health (9:1 – 7).*

B. *The faith of the grief-stricken ruler made possible our Lord's restoration of his daughter to life (9:18 – 19).*

C. *The faith of the woman who suffered from a hemorrhage for twelve long years brought healing to her body (9:20 – 22).*

D. *The faith of the two blind men who were seeking their sight was rewarded by Christ (9:27 – 30).*

The refusal to believe in Jesus Christ places limitations on his power to change lives and circumstances that would defeat us.

The Christ of the gospel of Matthew is the Christ whom we should be worshiping today as Lord. We need to trust him as we face the painful problems of life so that he might work miraculous changes in us and through us.

III. The purpose of prayer.

Matthew 9 provides us with many examples that disclose the nature and purpose of prayer.

In this chapter, we discover that prayer is a dialogue between a needy believer and an all-sufficient Lord. It is a dialogue in which there is communication between ordinary human beings and the unique Son of God.

The chapter opens with a paralytic and his friends petitioning the Savior for the return of health. Jesus responded by granting forgiveness of sin along with the restoration of health.

There is a divine side to the experience that we call prayer, for we hear our Lord making a request to one who sat in a tax collector's booth. Matthew answered the prayer of our Lord and became one of his devoted followers.

The ruler came petitioning the attention, time, and power of our Lord on behalf of his daughter. Our Lord responded by graciously granting his request.

The poor woman, without a word but with an outstretched hand, requested help. And our Lord responded to her prayer even in the midst of a multitude.

The chapter closes with a word from the Lord to the effect that we are to enter into dialogue with the Father God concerning where and when we are to labor in the fields that are white unto harvest. Our Lord is not suggesting that we rebuke God or overcome his reluctance to send laborers into those fields. Instead, he is saying that each of us should report for duty and listen to the divine instructions in order that we might know what part of the harvest field God would have us labor in.

Conclusion

Let us spend some time listening to what God would say to us through this tremendous chapter from Matthew's gospel.

SUNDAY MORNING, JANUARY 12

Title: Jesus Was Baptized

Text: "This is my beloved Son, in whom I am well pleased" (**Matt. 3:17**).

Scripture Reading: Matthew 3:1 – 17

Hymns: "My Faith Looks Up to Thee," Palmer

        "Down to the Sacred Wave," Smith

        "O Happy Day," Doddridge

Offertory Prayer: Our Father, the Father of our Lord and Savior, Jesus Christ, we have come this morning to worship you. We see about us the glories of your handiwork in nature, and we see the beauty of your holiness in many lives that have been transformed by your grace. We thank you for the privilege of telling others the story of God's redeeming love in Jesus Christ. We bring our offerings that your work might be carried on both near and far. Our gifts are a symbol of our love for you, but they are more: Our gifts are a practical way in which we demonstrate our love and concern. Accept our gifts and use them in a way that is pleasing to you. Bless us that we may be a blessing. We pray in Jesus' name. Amen.

Introduction

The subject of baptism has divided Christendom across the centuries. It would be popular perhaps to ignore this event in the life of Jesus when sketching the main events from his birth to his crucifixion and resurrection. Such a course of action, however, would cause us to omit one of the most significant happenings in the life of our Savior. Regardless of the disagreements, we would be spiritually poorer if we ignored a fair and honest look at the baptism of Jesus. We shall seek to profit from the lessons it brings to us.

I. John's call to baptism.

There is no more colorful picture in all the Bible than that of John the Baptist calling his fellow Israelites to repentance. There was no compromise in his message. He was not interested in statistics. When the Pharisees and Sadducees flocked to him, he warned them, indicating his lack of faith in their sincerity. He was interested in the kind of living that produced fairness and compassion in daily person-to-person relationships.

The Jews were already familiar with one kind of baptism — that of initiating a proselyte to their religious faith. John's baptism introduced a new element. His was a baptism of repentance. There was no institutional church at that time into which members were received on profession of faith. The kingdom of God was about to be introduced to the world in a new and unique way by the Messiah, the Son of God himself. John was sent to call the people to repentance and prepare them for the coming of the Lamb of God who would take away the sin of the world.

John recognized his role. He never tried to go beyond it or to usurp the dignity and prestige that belonged to the Savior. Later, when his devotees began to leave him to follow Jesus of Nazareth, his only reply was, "He must increase, but I must decrease" (John 3:30).

Another example of John's loyalty to Christ was his insistence that his baptism would be replaced by a greater one. He was not minimizing his own ministry, nor was he in any way deemphasizing water baptism when he insisted that the one following him would baptize "with the Holy Ghost, and with fire." The point was that where John had his limitations, the Messiah would possess perfect insights and be able to evaluate properly and judge fairly with reference to moral and spiritual conduct.

II. The baptizing of Jesus.

There is something sweet and tender in the relationship between John and Jesus. At first John was reluctant to baptize Jesus. We cannot be sure that he understood everything about Jesus at the moment. Perhaps it was later, after the baptism and after Jesus returned victoriously from Satan's temptations in the wilderness with a glow of triumph on his face, that John realized the full truth. But as he looked into the face of the one making request for baptism, he immediately recognized the spiritual superiority of this man standing before him. John's reasoning was that if either of the two was to baptize the other with a repentance baptism, he should be baptized by Jesus. The quiet insistence of the Galilean, however, won John over completely, and he baptized Jesus.

The theological questions that arose because of later events in the history of the developing Christian faith were not present at the Jordan River that day. Later Paul, in writing to the Romans, saw much more in baptism than might have been seen by the most observant follower of John on the banks of the Jordan when Jesus came "up straightway out of the water." Paul saw baptism as a symbol of the believer's death and burial of the old life and resurrection to a new one (Rom. 6:4). He saw it further as a picture of the bodily resurrection at Christ's second coming. We must remember, however, that Paul lived on the other side of the historical event at Calvary. The disciples of Jesus refused to believe, until the very end, that Jesus was going to die. They thought in terms of an earthly kingdom in spite of Jesus' insistence to the contrary. The people standing with John and Jesus by the Jordan were incapable of understanding all of the teaching that was implicit in this beautiful symbolic act.

Why was Jesus baptized? It certainly was not because he was a sinner and needed to repent. He was identifying himself with the repentance baptism of John, not personally repenting of sin. The Bible teaches consistently that Jesus was entirely without sin. Jesus was putting his stamp of approval on a good act. He was dedicating himself to the ministry and message of John because this preaching represented the highest and best in the Judaism of that day. Jesus was about to enter into the public arena of proclamation and service for God. He would take the people where they were spiritually and lead them to where he wanted them to arrive in understanding the true nature of God's kingdom. For Jesus, baptism was a dedication as he began his work. He spoke of it as an act "to fulfill all righteousness."

III. God's approval of the act.

The opening of heaven was a supernatural act. It was for the benefit of Jesus, but we learn from John 1:32 that John the Baptist saw it also. We cannot tell from the record whether anyone other than these two saw and heard. In John 12:28 the people heard a sound from heaven, which they thought was thunder, but they were not able to distinguish the words. Similarly, at the conversion of Saul on the Damascus road, the people with him saw the light and heard a sound but were not able to distinguish the words. The expression "descending like a dove" may refer to either a dove's form or a dove's manner of descending. Most scholars believe that some bodily form was present, although certainly the gentleness of the dove is emphasized. The point here is that God was pleased with his Son. This act of dedication by identification with the work of John the Baptist was commended by the heavenly Father.

Baptism is important. If it were not, Jesus never would have insisted that John baptize him. The water does not "wash the sin away," but the act contains a great message. Some groups in history have perverted this doctrine by an overemphasis of it or a misinterpretation of it. This, however, is no excuse for one to avoid participation in a beautiful and meaningful experience that was accepted by Jesus and later included in his great commission to his disciples as he sent them out to evangelize the world (Matt. 28:19–20). Baptism is a part of God's redemptive plan. It speaks a definite message to the new convert. It further enables him to speak a clear-cut confession to the world. God said concerning Jesus at his baptism, "This is my beloved Son, in whom I am well pleased."

Conclusion

Various groups within Christendom hold varying viewpoints concerning baptism. This is unfortunate and has at times led to sharp words between people who should love one another in Christ. The difficulty began early in the history of Christianity. Some attached a saving value to baptism that is unwarranted by Scripture. Some changed the form for their own convenience. Within a few centuries, most of the Christian world had eliminated the part of baptism that symbolizes the burial and resurrection. This is most unfortunate.

It is doubtful that the Christian world will ever be reunited in form on this meaningful observance. We can, however, be reunited in spirit. Baptism is for believers, for those who have had a personal experience of salvation in Jesus Christ and wish to confess to the world their identification with Christ. Some feel more deeply about the form of baptism than others and are very militant in their views. Whatever our persuasion concerning the form of baptism, we are not justified in being unchristian in attitude toward those who disagree with us.

The important thing concerning baptism is that it speaks of repentance, death to the old life and identification with the new. Unless one has had an experience of regeneration, he or she can go down into the baptismal waters a dry lost person and merely come up a wet lost person. It is our experience with Christ as Savior that makes baptism meaningful and valid in God's sight.

Jesus was baptized. He did not feel himself above this experience. He believed it contained a vital part of God's message to the world. The early Christians likewise practiced it and incorporated it into the requirements for the fellowship of believers.

SUNDAY EVENING, JANUARY 12

Title: Fellowship in Him

Text: "Anyone who claims to be in the light but hates a brother or sister is still in the darkness. Anyone who loves their brother and sister lives in the light, and there is nothing in them to make them stumble" **(1 John 2:9 – 10 NIV).**

Scripture Reading: 1 John 2:1 – 11

Introduction

The Expositor's Greek Testament gives a title of the introductory portion of this Scripture as "The Remedy for the Sins of Believers" ([Grand Rapids: Eerdmans, 1956], 5:172). Part of this passage does deal with the remedy, but the total passage deals with Christian fellowship — fellowship with God and with others. The remedy for sin makes this possible.

John uses the term "little children" in verse 1 advisedly and with a tender tone. He is an old man and regards his readers as "little children." This was a phrase of Jesus, as is seen in John's gospel (13:33). John assumes this tone because he is about to give them a warning, and he desires to remove the sting and disarm the opposition.

I. Fellowship in God as it relates to sin (1 John 2:1–2).

A. *John exhorts believers to live above sin (2:1).* John had no patience with professional perfectionists (1:8–10), but he had even less patience with loose lives.

In dealing with these concepts, he points out two dangers. One is, since it is impossible to live without sin, why strive after holiness? The argument is that such effort is useless; sin is an abiding necessity. The other danger is to say, why dread falling into sin since it is so easy to escape? We may sin with light hearts since we have the blood of Jesus Christ to cleanse us.

John writes that he is not trying to discourage his readers in their pursuit of holiness or to embolden them in sinning, but on the contrary, to warn them to stay away from sin. To avoid sin, we must take two measures—(1) walk in the light and (2) confess past sins.

B. *Believers have a twofold provision for sin (2:1–2).* The words "we have" in verse 1 are a present active indicative that indicates continuous reality. The first provision is found in an advocate as verse 1 mentions. The word *advocate* means "to call by the side of, to render assistance." An advocate champions the cause or pleads the case. Jesus does not plead one's innocence nor adduce extenuating circumstances; rather, he acknowledges one's guilt and presents his victorious works as grounds for acquittal.

The second provision is found in the word "propitiation" in verse 2. This word means to appease and render favorable. It means to gain or regain favor. It means to make complete satisfaction for a wrong.

II. Fellowship in God is determined by the knowledge of a believer (1 John 2:3–6).

The tense of the verb *know* (2:3) is continuous—one keeps on knowing.

A. *We know God if we keep his commandments (2:3–4). The Expositor's Greek Testament* translates this verse "and herein we get to know that we know Him—if we observe His commandments" (5:174). This knowledge is proof of our propitiation and advocacy.

There are two ways to look at this: first, one gets to know by keeping; and second, when one knows, one keeps. Knowledge of God, or fellowship with him, is tested by obedience to the divine commands. For one to profess to know Jesus and not obey him is a contradiction according to verse 4.

B. *We know God when love is perfected (2:5).* The redeeming love of God has attained its end in the person who observes God's Word. This is to love

24

one's enemies so that they might become born again. We need to love sinners as God loves them. This is forgiving love.

C. *We know God if we abide in him (2:6).* Evidence of abiding in Christ is walking with him. This is another verb that displays continuous action. Walking in him is a conformation of one's life to Christ's. Believers become like Christ by imitating him.

III. Fellowship in God is seen in the light of Christians (1 John 2:7 – 11).

A. *The nature of light is love.* Love is an inevitable test of fellowship with God. Light keeps people from stumbling. Love destroys the desire to hurt and seeks good. A person who hates lives in darkness. Hate shuts out light and thus hinders knowledge of where one goes and destroys fellowship.

Nothing is so blind as hatred. It insulates people from their own faults and from the virtues of others. It keeps them in ignorance of moral peril and indifferent to the consequences of deeds. No one who lives under the power of hatred or who fails to obey the impulse of love can claim fellowship with God, for God is love.

B. *The commandment to love is made new in Jesus.* It is new in time, standard, and motive.

Those who are walking in the light revealed in Christ will not only do what is right in refraining from sin but will also keep the great commandment of love that Christ gave and himself fulfilled.

Conclusion

The greatest life we can have is that of fellowship with God. All believers are to resist sin and walk close to God. But when we commit sin, it is adequately covered in Jesus Christ. Turn to him in faith. Resist evil and test your fellowship by how and whom you love.

WEDNESDAY EVENING, JANUARY 15

Title: The Bible Speaks to Our Condition

Scripture Reading: Matthew 16

Introduction

The events and conversations recorded in Matthew 16 focus on a pivotal point in the life and ministry of our Lord. Here we read that his opposition was becoming more aggressive. Pointed personal questions provoke recognition and confession of his messiahship. He talked about the establishment of his church and its undying nature. For the first time, he speaks plainly concerning his death and resurrection, which is a fulfillment of Old Testament prophecy. The chapter closes with a declaration concerning his ultimate glory.

A prayerful study of this chapter will speak to our present condition.

I. Our motive is highly important (Matt. 16:1–8).

Those who came to our Lord with selfish and malicious motives did not receive an open and direct reply to their questions or a favorable answer to their prayers.

If we are to enter into dialogue with the eternal God, we must do so with an open mind and a heart ready to do his will.

II. Daily bread in abundance (Matt. 16:9–10).

As Jesus warned his disciples concerning the erroneous teachings of the Pharisees and the Sadducees, he reminded them of the manner in which God provides for our material needs. He reminded them of how provisions had been made for the multitudes in a time of need and asked, "How many baskets did you fill?" God provides in excess of our needs. He provides for us adequately and gives us a surplus. Our God provides for us in a liberal and generous manner rather than in a stingy manner (James 1:5).

III. Divine truth is revealed truth (Matt. 16:13–17).

The real truth about God and life cannot be discovered by the unaided human intellect. The real truth about God is revealed to those who earnestly seek to know him and to be responsive to his will (1 Cor. 2:14). Peter was earnestly seeking to come to a deeper understanding of the nature and purpose of our Lord. God, according to his own purpose of grace, opened the mind and heart of Peter and let him grasp the truth that Jesus of Nazareth was indeed the Messiah, the Son of God in human flesh.

It is wonderful to sit at the feet of great teachers and to read the books of outstanding writers. The greatest privilege we have is that of letting God reveal to us his truth as it speaks to our condition.

IV. The peril of false thinking (Matt. 16:22–23).

How can one be so open to the truth in one moment and so far from the truth in the next? Peter could speak a word of warning to each of us at this point. In one moment, he was open to a fresh revelation from God. He was granted insight to understand who Jesus really was. From this pinnacle of spiritual insight, we find him descending to the valley of being totally wrong in his understanding concerning the purpose of God in Jesus Christ.

If the thoughts of humans and the purpose of Satan could take command of the mind of the apostle Peter, you and I should be alert to the same dangers. We must not make the fatal assumption that because we have been right about one thing that this guarantees that we will always be right about other things.

If Satan could infiltrate the mind of Peter, he can infiltrate our minds and cause us to think thoughts and accept ideas that are erroneous and harmful. We need to be on guard against believing "the doctrine of the Pharisees and the Sadducees" and accepting the false teachings of Satan.

V. Profits that do not evaporate (Matt. 16:24–28).

Our Lord was a life investment counselor. He extended an invitation for his disciples to follow him in a life of faith and faithfulness. He warned them against living a life of selfishness that produces perishable profits.

He encourages us to find abundant life by losing our life in service to God and to others. He also encourages us to take the long look and to live with the ultimate values of an eternal kingdom foremost in our minds and actions.

Conclusion

Let us search our hearts and look at our motives. Let us trust God to provide adequately for us through the day. Let us open our minds and wills to receive divine truth and to avoid the false way that leads to disappointment. What can we do for his glory today?

SUNDAY MORNING, JANUARY 19

Title: Jesus Overcame Temptation

Text: "For we have not an high priest which cannot be touched with the feeling of our infirmities; but was in all points tempted like as we are, yet without sin" **(Heb. 4:15).**

Scripture Reading: Luke 4:1–13

Hymns: "Stand Up, Stand Up for Jesus," Duffield

"Yield Not to Temptation," Palmer

"May God Depend on You?" Martin

Offertory Prayer: Our Father, we approach you as redeemed children of God by faith in Jesus Christ. Part of the Christian life is the bringing of our offerings, and we do so gladly. We count it not merely a duty but a privilege to bring the tithe into the storehouse that God's work may be carried on both here in our own church and through our mission outreach to the uttermost parts of the earth. Help us to give and to find joy in giving. Accept our gifts and use them in a way that will glorify your name and take the message of your Son to many who need him. In our Savior's name we pray. Amen.

Introduction

It is after moments of spiritual ecstasy that we are most prone to temptation. This is because there is a tendency to relax our discipline and feel we have reached spiritual maturity. Jesus did what we should do when we feel a crisis arising. He went into a place of solitude for prayer and meditation. It was time for him to begin his life's work, and he needed to listen to the voice of God and set his goals in perfect harmony with the purposes of his Father for him.

There is no need for a meticulous discussion as to whether the temptations were literal or Jesus fought the battle purely within his soul. God is not limited in his means nor his methods. The Bible teaches clearly the existence of a personal devil—an adversary. Unless we are absolutely prejudiced against the supernatural, we can accept without any problem the personal appearance of the evil one.

The matter of whether Jesus could have sinned is also one that should not greatly concern us. Of course, he could have sinned. If he could not, his whole temptation experience is a sham and the recording of it is useless. Jesus had two natures—human and divine. He could have forfeited his right to be the Savior if he had not disciplined himself to obedience. Jesus' desert experience was more, however, than a departure for "devotions." It was a necessary confrontation with Satan at the beginning of Jesus' ministry in order that certain basic issues would be settled. God's Spirit "led" Jesus into the wilderness. The verb has the significance of "drive" and thus indicates a strong compulsion. He was literally thrust into personal encounter with the one who was head of the dark kingdom of evil.

What kind of Messiah would Jesus of Nazareth be? The crowds would endeavor to force him into their mold and place an earthly crown on his head. Jesus therefore had to come face to face with the options offered by the ungodly forces of the universe and make his choice. He had to meet temptation in every area of his personality and decide that the "short-cut" through favor with people would never bring long-range approval from either God or humanity. Every temptation that is possible for humans to experience may be categorized in one of the three offered by Satan.

I. The temptation of appetite.

The seclusion of Jesus and the consequent communion with God produced an ecstasy that helped to master the flesh. There are recorded cases in history that verify the ability of high emotion to hold physical wants in abeyance. Everyone, however, must "come to earth" again and feel the reality of physical hunger. Jesus was no exception. There is nothing either right or wrong with hunger. It is independent of all moral considerations. It is, however, how humans satisfy physical cravings that determines whether they have sinned against God. The suggestion of Satan seemed innocent enough. Jesus, however, saw the bait wound skillfully over the barbed hook. He tore it away and disclosed the sharp point. He refused to claim special privileges because of his unique relationship to God. He had come to be the Savior, and this meant identifying himself with his fellow humans. They were not able to command stones to be made bread. If he claimed special privilege or preferential treatment, he would not be playing the game fairly, and that would be sin. The Redeemer must be spotless. This meant he must refuse to claim a way of escape from personal problems and needs that was not open to every human. He was to be a burden bearer. He could not do this by separating himself from his own burdens. If he were to share the lot of his fellow humans, he had to be content to live as they lived.

All of us meet this temptation every day. It may not have to do with stones and bread, but it has to do with the passions that incite us to satisfy the cravings of our flesh by illegitimate means. The cry of the flesh is normal, but it must not be satisfied in abnormal ways. We must have disciplines in life. God has put certain guidelines in our personal relationships, and we ignore these at our peril. In the garden of Eden, the woman saw that the Tree of the Knowledge of Good and Evil was "good for food." This means it appealed to the lust of her flesh. How many homes are broken today because one marriage partner has sought to satisfy the cravings of the flesh in a way that violated faithfulness to his or her companion! Or perhaps the passion was satisfied in the premarital years but the blot of remorse lingers and clouds the marriage relationship. How many bodies have been impaired for life because the lust of the flesh was satisfied with that which at the last "bites like a snake and poisons like a viper" (Prov. 23:32 NIV)! Every physical drive that is allowed to run uncontrolled threatens future happiness.

The physical is not only subservient to the spiritual, it is dependent on it. Fleshly needs must be satisfied in ways that are in harmony with spiritual principles. People need bread. They cannot live without it, but it must be supplied through processes approved by God and that recognize that nourishment has a divine reference as well as a human one.

II. The temptation of avarice.

Matthew and Luke reverse the order of the second and third temptation. It seems more logical that Luke's account renders the events as they occurred for two reasons. First, Luke made it clear in his introduction that he was writing an "orderly account" (1:3). Second, this temptation to materialism is still related somewhat to the physical, for it involved the "lust of the eye" while the third temptation was much subtler, involving the "pride of life." Thus the first two temptations were direct while the third was more indirect (yet perhaps far more appealing than even the first two).

Does Satan have the power to offer the kingdoms of his world? The Faust theme has been predominant in literature. Man *can* sell out to the devil and enjoy temporary success.

III. The temptation of ambition.

In the garden of Eden, the woman saw that the tree was "to be desired to make one wise" (Gen. 3:6), while John speaks of this aspect of temptation as "the pride of life" (1 John 2:16).

It is this desire for sophistication that is perhaps the subtlest temptation of all today. It is not enough to have well-fed bodies and a comfortable bank account. People want to be looked up to and worshiped as though they are gods. Some of the things people do today in order to seem prestigious would be amusing if they were not so tragic.

If Jesus had jumped from the pinnacle of the temple, people would have considered him outstanding. They would have fed his ego and surely looked up to him as a god of some kind. But Jesus was not in the business of having his vanity satisfied. He had a message to deliver, and he wanted people to follow him in deeds of kindness and service.

This third temptation was the hardest of all, for Satan even offered Scripture that seemed to prove his position. It is easy to find Scripture that seems to justify our position when we want something badly enough. Those who classified the seven deadly sins arranged them in correct order—at least when they put pride at the top of the list!

Conclusion

How did Jesus overcome temptation? Being tempted is not sin. It is how we react to the temptation that counts. Jesus gave us the perfect example when he met Satan's attack with the written Word of God. Facing each of the temptations, he quoted from the marvelous career-climaxing messages of Moses as recorded in the book of Deuteronomy. It is impossible to overemphasize the importance of being familiar with Scripture. There is a school of thought today that minimizes memorizing lest we let it become a mechanical thing and lose the meaning. This is, of course, always a danger in the amassing of facts, but we should not "throw out the baby with the bathwater." The solution is not to quit memorizing Scripture but rather to be sure we understand the meaning as we commit the words to our mind and heart. A professor years ago insisted that large portions of Scripture be memorized by his students. A woman years later testified that the Scriptures she memorized in that Bible class had been the most valuable learning during her entire four years of college. She said she found herself, in times of crisis, referring again and again to verses that she committed to memory.

The way to be victorious in temptation is not merely to clench one's fist, grit one's teeth, and stomp one's foot in defiance against the tempter. It is rather to be so saturated with the Word of God that one lives in a living fellowship with God. This way of life will allow one to rise above the temptation. The attractions that Satan offers will simply have no appeal.

Jesus was here on his Father's business. So are we, and we, too, must be about the things of our Father. Perhaps then we can understand the words of Thomas A. Edison, "I am not bothered with temptation. I stay too busy."

SUNDAY EVENING, JANUARY 19

Title: Childhood in Him

Text: "I write unto you, little children, because your sins are forgiven you for his name's sake" **(1 John 2:12)**.

Scripture Reading: 1 John 2:12–29

Introduction

"The Apostle has been setting forth searching truths and is about to make an exacting claim; and here he pauses and with much tenderness reassures his readers: 'I am not addressing you as unbelievers or casting doubt upon the sincerity of your faith. On the contrary, it is because I am assured thereof that I am writing this letter to you and wrote the Gospel which accompanies it'" (*The Expositor's Greek Testament* [Grand Rapids: Eerdmans, 1956], 5:177).

I. The writer sets forth the conditions of childhood (I John 2:12–14).

A. *Before John establishes the conditions of becoming children of God, he explains why he is writing.* His reasons are fourfold: (1) to encourage further achievements, (2) to caution against temptation, (3) to urge believers to live righteously and to manifest love, and (4) to warn against perilous allurements of the world. These things are not to be done to become a Christian but because the believer has already enjoyed fellowship with God and is seeking a closer relationship and all the privileges that this fellowship allows.

B. *Now John sets forth the conditions of childhood.* These conditions are forgiveness, knowledge, faith, and abiding in the Word of God. A discussion of these conditions is found in the way John addresses his readers.

1. The term "little children" in verse 12 refers to believers in general. John writes of forgiveness here as the initial and fundamental experience of believers. It is the supreme need of every soul and is the absolute condition for fellowship with God.

2. The term "fathers" here is used to portray maturity. The evidence of maturity is seen in the knowledge of the Father. It dates back to the beginning.

   Knowledge is made possible through Jesus Christ and is the very essence of eternal truth. It increases in its depth and fullness by the experiences of life, by the pressure of problems, by the stress of sorrows, and by the changes and mysteries of the passing years.

3. The term "young men" is used to describe the strong. They are strong in faith because the Word of God abides in them. They have overcome the evil one.

4. Since all believers become Christians the same way, the terms "children," "father," and "young men" are all-inclusive, and each statement applies to all others.

II. The writer sets forth the manifestations of childhood (I John 2:15–17).

A. *A negative idea is presented to emphasize the positive, namely, a love for the world.* A love for the world is not in keeping with believers in Christ. The world is the unbelieving men and women. It is the society of the unspiritual and godless. A Christian is not to covet the world. Three terms are used to describe the world: "lust of the flesh," "lust of the eyes," and "pride of life."

   If anyone keeps on loving these things — the world — the love of the Father is not in that person. Besides that, these things are temporary; they pass away.

B. *The real manifestation of true childhood is seen in a love for the Father.* Children born of God do the will of the Father.

III. The writer sets forth a contrast between true children and those who claim to be God's children (1 John 2:18).

A. *A negative is presented to emphasize the positive.* Crises will arise and adversaries of Christ, antichrists, will deceive. They are a nuisance party. True children will not be deceived.

Neither will true children fall away (2:19). By falling away, persons prove that they never shared the real life and fellowship of the Christian community.

This is one of the most important doctrines of the church. It is clear that these people had been members of the visible church; they had fulfilled the outward requirements for church membership, but although it was from the fellowship that they went out, they were not of them. This reminds us that more than outward membership in the visible church is required if one is to be a member of the body of Christ. Also, we must not expect that the visible church will always be composed entirely of true believers.

True children will not deny the Father and the Son (2:22). One cannot be a believer in Christ as Savior and then deny the incarnation and the filial relation of humans to God. The term "Christ" in verse 22 is the Son of God, the Eternal Word, of whom John writes.

B. *The positive is now contrasted with the negative.*
1. True believers have been anointed by the Holy Spirit (2:20–21). This is the unction of the Holy One.
2. True believers confess the Father (2:24). It is only as people receive Christ that they become children of God (John 1:12); thus, if Christ is resisted—not confessed—it is evident they are not his children. They do not recognize God as Father. Belief is thus shown to be a touchstone of character; it is a test of life. It is more than an intellectual assent to truth. It has its moral elements as well, and it consists in submission to a Being who is holy and divine. It is a spiritual experience made abiding by the indwelling Spirit of God.
3. True believers abide in Christ (2:24, 28). That which is heard as is mentioned in verse 24, is the gospel message of Jesus Christ. As people abide in Christ, they become confident. This abiding results in obedience, and this is the greatest manifestation of childhood.

Conclusion

The greatest experience one can have is to become a child of God by being born again. If you have never received Christ as Savior and been forgiven of your sins, this is the time to do it. This is also a good time to examine your life and see how you manifest your relationship with God.

WEDNESDAY EVENING, JANUARY 22

Title: The Bible Speaks to Our Condition

Scripture Reading: Matthew 23

Introduction

How can this chapter, which begins with a warning against the example of the scribes and Pharisees (Matt. 23:1–12) and continues with an announcement of seven woes upon these civic and religious leaders of the nation of Israel (vv. 13–36), be profitable for the people of God in our day? The Holy Spirit did not lead Matthew to write this chapter merely to preserve a historical record of the controversy our Lord had with those who were plotting to bring about his death. However, as we study this chapter in its historical context, we will be able to properly apply its message to our own lives and circumstances in the present.

Our Lord is unchanging in his nature, his desires, and his denunciations. We can discover the will of our Lord by examining that which he approved in contrast to that which he denounced. We can be certain that if an attitude of mind or an ambition of life brought displeasure to him then, it would do so today.

Two major pictures of our Lord in Matthew 23 have significance for the present.

I. Christ the critic.

Our Lord was no killjoy (John 3:17). He was critical only of that which was hurtful, destructive, and negative. His denunciation of evil was but the backside of his love. He could not condone that which was destructive and at the same time be genuinely concerned about the welfare of people.

This passage reveals Christ as a radical critic who was dealing drastically with the malignancy that was destroying the nation and hindering it from fulfilling God's purpose. Let us examine our own lives in the mirror of his criticism of the scribes and Pharisees.

A. *Christ criticizes profession without practice (23:3).*

B. *Christ criticizes unwillingness to share the burdens of others (23:4).*

C. *Christ criticizes wrong motivation for religious service (23:5).* The applause of our contemporaries is not an adequate and proper motivation for religious services. While it is important that we stand high in the opinion of others, we must not be guilty of taking a public opinion poll before we take a stand on moral issues.

D. *Christ criticizes an attitude of judging success in terms of a position of prominence rather than in terms of service rendered to the needy (23:6–11).*

E. *Christ criticizes hypocrisy (23:13–15).* Repeatedly our Lord denounces pretense, sham, and phoniness. He uses terms such as "hypocrites," "blind guides," "fools," and a "generation of serpents."

33

Hypocrites are those who deliberately pretend to be something they aren't. There is a difference between failing to be fully Christian and being something on the outside that does not represent the inward reality.

F. *Christ criticizes the hindering of others from entering the kingdom of God (23:13).*

G. *Christ criticizes basic dishonesty in relationships with God and others (23:16–22).*

As we listen to our Lord criticize attitudes, actions, and ambitions of these religious leaders, it makes us tremble as we examine our own minds and motives in the presence of God.

II. Christ the compassionate one (Matt. 23:37–39).

Christ was at the end of his earthly ministry. The events in this chapter describe his final encounter with the civic, religious, and political leaders who were plotting to bring about his death. They had rejected him as their Messiah and Lord. Our Lord responded with tears of compassionate grief as he beheld the city and addressed it with a broken heart.

A. *Our Lord was weeping because of what his people were missing and would continue to miss.*

B. *Our Lord was weeping because of the foolishness and the hard-heartedness of these people who had turned away from their only hope of salvation.*

C. *Our Lord was weeping because of the calamity that was going to befall his nation and his capital city.*

Conclusion

The words recorded in Matthew 23:37 are some of the saddest to be found in all of the Bible. They reveal the heartbreak of our Savior. He addresses his nation with these sad, pathetic words: "Ye would not." Let it not be said concerning us, "Ye would not" do the will of God.

SUNDAY MORNING, JANUARY 26

Title: Jesus Called People

Text: "Come and see" (**John 1:39**). "Follow me, and I will make you fishers of men" (**Matt. 4:19**).

Scripture Reading: John 1:35–51; Matthew 4:18–22

Hymns: "Jesus Calls Us," Alexander

"O Master, Let Me Walk with Thee," Gladden

"Footsteps of Jesus," Slade

Offertory Prayer: Eternal God, our heavenly Father, we are grateful that we are not our own but have been bought with a price. We are thankful that this price was not corruptible things such as silver and gold but was the Lamb slain from the foundation of the world. We rejoice in the blessings that are ours because we are members of God's redeemed family. We stand amazed in your presence

34

because of your great love for us. We know that we are not all we should be, but we are grateful for the privilege of seeking to grow in grace and in further knowledge of you. The offerings we bring this morning are testimonies of our love for you. We desire, through our financial gifts, to have a part in your work at home and around the world. Thank you for every cause that is supported by the gifts we bring. We ask your blessings upon all who are serving in your name and trumpeting the message of Christ on this Lord's Day. Receive our gifts as expressions of our dedication. Use our gifts in constructive ways to tell the message of God's redeeming love in Jesus to those who do not know him. May this service be a means of renewing our lives in dedication to you. May we make fresh resolves this morning concerning the living of our lives, and may we go forth from God's house today to put these resolves into practice. We pray in Jesus' name. Amen.

Introduction

It is not easy to harmonize the four Gospels with reference to the early ministry of Jesus. Most scholars, however, agree that Jesus had a short ministry in Judea before he went into Galilee for an extended preaching tour. In all probability, Jesus went back to Galilee briefly after his baptism and immediately returned to Jerusalem for the Passover. While he was in Galilee, he performed his first miracle as recorded in John 2. John 3, including the visit of Nicodemus to Christ, records events that occurred after Jesus returned to Jerusalem. After a brief ministry in this area, he returned to Galilee through Samaria, where he met and led to saving faith the woman at the well of Sychar. He then began his major ministry in Galilee as recorded by Matthew, Mark, and Luke.

Thus we have the record of Jesus, immediately after his baptism, calling several disciples to himself, including Andrew, Peter, Philip, and Nathaniel. Later we find that in Galilee he called Peter and Andrew once more. The first call, as recorded in John's gospel, was for them to accept him as a person. It is not incorrect to say this was a "call to salvation." The call that came to them in Galilee was a call to leave their work and be full-time followers of him. Both of these calls were important. There is a twofold sense in which he calls us today.

I. Christ's call to us to receive him personally.

John's gospel is preeminently the gospel concerning the personhood of Jesus Christ. It was written to set forth with clarity and certainty that Jesus was the divine Son of God. This is the emphasis of the gospel from the first chapter until the last. John's gospel records that after Jesus was baptized he began to attract some of John's followers to himself. John seems to have had only one purpose — that of calling people to repentance. Jesus had a deeper goal — to draw people to follow him for further instruction in doing the will of God. John declared Jesus to be the "Lamb of God, which taketh away the sin of the world" (John 1:29). After John's declaration, some of John's followers began to leave him and follow Jesus.

35

The disciple Andrew immediately recognized Jesus as the Messiah. He went and told his brother, Simon, and brought him to Jesus. The next day, Jesus found Philip and called Philip to himself. Philip found Nathaniel. An interesting conversation developed between Nathaniel and Jesus, and Nathaniel made a great confession concerning Jesus. He called him, "the Son of God ... King of Israel" (John 1:49).

What was happening? One by one these men were being brought to Jesus. They would later form the nucleus of his twelve disciples. First of all, however, they had to believe in him as a person.

Today if we would serve God, we, too, must accept the personhood of Jesus Christ. We cannot do his work effectively unless we accept him as Savior. As we survey the contemporary scene, we become aware that too many people are trying to do the works of Jesus without believing in him. It is necessary for us to decide once and for all what we believe concerning the deity of Christ and his complete equality with God as we begin our service for him.

II. Christ's call to us for dedication and service.

The scene changes! Jesus is no longer in Judea. He is now in Galilee. He is beginning his active ministry.

One thing we should note about Jesus' relationship with John the Baptist is that he gives us a beautiful example in ministerial ethics. Jesus did not begin an extensive ministry until John the Baptist was off the scene. One of the most significant verses to be found in the Bible is that which says, "Now after that John was put in prison, Jesus came into Galilee, preaching the gospel" (Mark 1:14). Jesus did not want to overshadow John and hence would not begin his active, public ministry until John had gone into forced retirement.

The first thing a good leader does is to try to find good followers. This is in order that he may train them to carry on his work in the event he must step aside. As Jesus began his active ministry, he sought for leaders. Where would he find them? The best answer was some of those whom he had met and won to himself in Judea while John was preaching. Some of John's early followers became some of Jesus' most faithful disciples.

The record does not tell us what Peter and Andrew did from the time they met Jesus in Judea until he called them by the Sea of Galilee for full-time service. We presume they carried on their work according to their customary business habits. Perhaps they had spoken often of Jesus since meeting him. Probably they wondered if they would see him again. The seed had been sown, however, and when Jesus called them, they were ready to respond without question.

How like life this is! Although we should accept Jesus as complete Lord of our life in the initial salvation experience, many times we wait a season before we understand the full implications of complete surrender to his will for us. There are amazing examples of people who are saved and called to preach at the same moment, but these are the exception. Most of us go through a period of evaluation and establishment of priorities. Many God-called preachers will confess that their call to the ministry was a far greater emotional "tug" than their conversion experience.

Perhaps they were converted as a child and the experience was a quiet and peaceful one—although very meaningful. On the other hand, their call to full-time service was a deep struggle of the soul concerning the commitment of a full life.

The fact that the disciples immediately left their nets and followed Jesus indicates two things. First, Jesus possessed a tremendous personal appeal. Second, the previous experience with Jesus in Judea had left its imprint on them and they were now ready to follow him wherever he would lead.

III. Each call is distinctive.

In every encounter between a person and God, the individual personality is respected. No two calls come exactly alike. Some are diametrically opposite from others. In some cases, two calls may have some similarities, but there are still differences that make each person's call a unique one. With some calls, the emotions may be stirred greatly. There may be great sins that have separated a person from God, and the call to salvation is the call to forsake those sins. In some experiences of salvation, however, it is the still small voice that whispers winsomely and invites to the Savior. The sin element is, of course, present in every conversion experience, but it is not articulated as much in some as in others.

The call to service likewise differs. Peter and Matthew were poles apart. One was a fisherman and the other a tax collector. Yet each heard the voice of Jesus in his own way and each responded according to his background, temperament, and lifestyle. We should never try to force another person into the mold of our own exact experience. Our task is to witness concerning the claim of Jesus on life and let the Holy Spirit minister in his own way so that the hearer may respond in a way that is consistent with his or her own personality.

Conclusion

God's call comes continuously. We can reject the call, but we cannot ignore it. Indecision is a form of refusal. Yet God remains ever pleading for us to come to him and accept his will for our lives.

The greatest discovery we will ever make is to find what God wants us to do. The greatest goal we will ever attain is that of accomplishing the purpose that he has for us in this world. The first call comes to everyone for the same purpose—for personal salvation. Each one of us needs to be saved from our sins and become a new creature in Christ. The second call may vary in intent as well as in method. God calls some people into full-time Christian work, such as being a preacher or missionary. Although most of us are not called to full-time ministry in such a way that we depend on Christian people for financial support, there is still a sense in which we are in full-time service for the Lord. Our business is the Lord's business. We may have a trade, retail business, or profession to pay our expenses, but we all are called to be full-time Christians.

As long as there are lost people in the world who need to be saved and saved people who need to be trained, we have a mission from the Lord. The same Christ who called Peter, Andrew, James, John, Matthew, and Philip is calling twenty-first-century people to himself. Let us never turn a deaf ear to the Master's call!

SUNDAY EVENING, JANUARY 26

Title: Dignity and Destiny in Him

Text: "Beloved, now are we the sons of God, and it doth not yet appear what we shall be: but we know that, when he shall appear, we shall be like him; for we shall see him as he is" **(1 John 3:2)**.

Scripture Reading: 1 John 3:1–4

Introduction

In the first two chapters of 1 John, the Christian life has been presented under the figure of divine fellowship. In chapter 3, it is presented as a result of a divine birth. In the earlier chapters, salvation is presented as what Jesus wrought—propitiation and advocacy. In this chapter, it is presented as an amazing expression of God's love. First John 2:29 introduces the idea, and it is elaborated on in the following verses.

I. The Bible presents salvation as something of divine dignity (1 John 3:1, 2).

The dignity of being in Christ is a present as well as future possession.

A. *This divine dignity finds its basis in our being children of God.* The word "children" draws attention to community of nature rather than rights and privileges. Verse 2 adds to verse 1 in that Christians are not only *called* "sons of God" but *are* sons of God. To be born of him is to be a partaker of the divine nature. First Peter 1:4 says it is an inheritance that is imperishable, undefiled, unfading, and kept in heaven. John, in his gospel (3:5–6), says that regeneration moves one from the sphere of the flesh into the sphere of the Spirit. Second Corinthians 5:17 says that anyone in Christ Jesus is a new creature.

B. *This divine dignity is a product of God's love.* Love follows and vitalizes new life. Love bestows on people something of God's nature and thereby installs believers as members of God's family. Love grants to all who believe a change of moral nature, a new disposition, and a spiritual experience. Love is concerned for the highest good. It is not concerned that believers simply be saved from suffering and loss, but that they might live as children of God. This love is not something inherent in human nature but is due wholly to the love of God. The believer's dignity is not only based on being a child of God and is a product of God's love, but is also a gift of God (Eph. 2:8–9).

II. The dignity the believer possesses presents a dilemma (1 John 3:1).

A Christian is not ostensibly different from other people, but the world did not recognize Jesus as the Son of God, so they do not know God as Father. God is the potential Father of all people by creation, but those who believe in Christ are children of a heavenly birth and are real children of God.

The true fatherhood of God is never fully appreciated until one draws near to him through Christ, and the brotherhood of humanity will never be realized until people find the Father through Jesus Christ.

38

Those who reject Christ should never expect to understand or be expected to understand the followers of Christ. Thus the world has no sympathy with the motives and aims and character of the church of God.

Believers do not know all of what they shall be, but they know that their destiny is to conform to the image of God.

III. The destiny of a Christian is to be like the Son of God (1 John 3:2).

To be like the Son is a blessed hope that concerns the character, disposition, and moral nature that were transformed and made perfect (Matt. 5:8). It also includes the transformation of the body, which is to be conformed to the body of his glory (2 Cor. 3:18).

To be like Jesus in the life to come, we must practice that likeness now by imitating him here on earth. This imitation is shown in pure living and is a result of the new birth. We are not content to live in sin when we know God.

IV. The duty of a Christian is a concern along with his dignity and destiny (1 John 3:3).

The word translated "hope" in verse 3 literally means "rest" in him. That is, rest in God as Father. Luke 5:5 is a good example. It means relying on the Word of God, and Christ is the Living Word.

The word *purifieth* in verse 3 denotes purity maintained with effort and fearfulness amid defilements and allurements. One who is purified is free from contamination (Ex. 19:10; John 11:55; Acts 21:24, 26). It is a personal inner cleansing of the heart (James 4:8), of the soul (1 Peter 1:22), of the self (1 John 3:3), and of one's word (Phil. 2:12).

Conclusion

Those who are not children of God lack the dignity that humanity's Creator intended for them. Those who are not Christians will never reach the destiny planned for them by God, and neither will they be able to perform the divinely ordained duty. If you do not know Jesus Christ as your Savior now, accept him and become what he wants you to be.

WEDNESDAY EVENING, JANUARY 29

Title: The Bible Speaks to Our Condition
Scripture Reading: Mark 2

Introduction

A daily study of the Word of God will provide us with the instruction we need for living a righteous life. We need a proper attitude toward our Lord and a proper understanding of life with its opportunities and responsibilities. We need the insight and the encouragement of divine instruction every day. Let us open our minds and hearts and listen as God speaks to our condition through Mark 2.

This chapter reveals our Lord as being a very busy man, sharing the good news of God's kingdom and ministering to the needs of those about him. He was the center of attention. It was impossible for him to hide from the people. There was a magnetism about the personality and teachings of our Lord that attracted large crowds to him.

I. Christ the Great Healer (Mark 2:1–12).

There are three different features of this account that deserve our attention.
A. *The helpless man.* The man was a paralytic and therefore unable to move from one place to another. Evidently there was some connection between his disease and his sin.
B. *The helpers.* At least four men were concerned about bringing the helpless man to the Great Healer. They did so at great inconvenience and with much persistence.
C. *The hinderers.* Some were very critical of our Lord, and they were hinderers. The crowd that thronged about our Lord hindered the four from bringing the helpless man to him in the most direct manner.

In the world today, there are many helpless ones who need helpers who can bring them to Christ the Great Healer. Let us make certain that we are not among the hinderers.

II. Sharing the Good News (Mark 2:14–17).

Our Lord treated each person with dignity. He did not discriminate on the basis of race, religion, culture, or profession. Levi, better known as Matthew, was a despised publican in the service of the Roman occupational forces. Jesus loved him and wanted to redeem him. He extended an invitation to Levi, and the tax collector responded affirmatively and became Matthew the apostle and writer of Scripture. In these words, we have a picture of the response of a redeemed individual who was eager to share the good news of his salvation experience with his friends. How natural that Levi should gather all of the publicans together in his house for a banquet with Jesus as the guest of honor. Matthew was eager for these other publicans to learn what he had learned about Jesus and to experience what he had experienced.

Matthew was using a natural method for sharing the Good News with his friends. His method was appropriate and effective. He gave proof of the genuineness of his relationship to Jesus Christ by immediately becoming concerned that others might come to know Christ as he did. Each of us could make a similar response and be a tremendous blessing to our friends who do not yet know Jesus as Savior.

III. The joy of our Lord and his disciples (Mark 2:18–20).

Sculptors and artists have given the world a false concept of the Messiah. Instead of his being a melancholy individual, our Lord was characterized by a radiant personality that attracted people to him and caused them to give him their undying loyalty.

When the enemies of our Lord inquired concerning why he and his disciples did not fast, he described himself as a bridegroom and his disciples as guests at a wedding feast. Bridegrooms and their guests were happy, lighthearted, delightful individuals to be around.

A long, sad face is a poor advertisement for what it is like to be a Christian. Christ came to make joy possible and to give us a faith to sing about (John 15:11).

IV. The purpose of the Sabbath (Mark 2:23–28).

Our Lord was in constant controversy with the religious leaders of his day concerning the proper use of the Sabbath. Their traditions and laws had caused the Sabbath to become a blight rather than a blessing. Our Lord insisted that the Sabbath was made for the good of humanity. He did not look upon it as being a ritualistic requirement that people must observe in order to earn God's favor.

The Sabbath was intended as a day of rest. People were not made as machines of perpetual motion. They must have relief from the grind and the struggle of labor to restore the vital energies of life.

Jesus used the Sabbath to relieve suffering. He insisted that one should always do what was right on the Sabbath.

Conclusion

On the Lord's Day, the modern follower of Christ should spend some time in rest, some time in worship, and some time in service. To ignore the day set apart by the Lord is to deny our spiritual nature and to expose our children to the perils of secularism and materialism.

The Sabbath was made for the good of humanity. We should make certain that it is used in a manner that will produce good in our own lives and in the lives of others.

FEBRUARY

- ## Sunday Mornings

  Continue with the theme "The Life and Works of the Lord Jesus."

- ## Sunday Evenings

  Continue with the theme "Great Texts from 1 John."

- ## Wednesday Evenings

  "An apple a day keeps the doctor away, and a chapter a day keeps the devil away" is a common proverb. Continue to emphasize the habit of reading one chapter each day in order to let the Bible "speak to your condition."

SUNDAY MORNING, FEBRUARY 2

Title: Jesus Taught Regeneration

Text: "Ye must be born again" (**John 3:7**).

Scripture Reading: John 3:1–18

Hymns: "Since Jesus Came into My Heart," McDaniel

            "Ye Must Be Born Again," Sleeper

            "Come, Thou Fount of Every Blessing," Robinson

Offertory Prayer: Our God and our Father, help us to recognize the privileges that come to us from your gracious hand. Give us the wisdom to use the opportunities of our lifetime during the lifetime of our opportunities. May we never be too busy with the trivial to do those things that are eternal. May the relationship that we have in Christ produce a daily fellowship that enables us to meet problems victoriously. We pray that God's majesty and power may inspire us to give our best in faithful service. As we bring our tithes and offerings, may we do so in the spirit of gratitude. May we see beyond the narrow walls of self to a world that needs the gospel of Christ and therefore give joyfully and generously. We pray in Jesus' name. Amen.

Introduction

Finding a more moral man in all Judea than Nicodemus would have been a difficult task. He was an outstanding leader among the Jews. Perhaps he came to Jesus by night because of fear of what others would say, or perhaps both he and Jesus were so busy that they met by appointment. His opening words were designed to pay respect to Jesus. The reply of Jesus in verse 3 is, if not sharp, certainly straight to the point. There are three stages in the conversation between these two men. First, they spoke face-to-face. Next, they challenged each other mind to mind. Finally, they discussed heart to heart.

I. The nature of the new birth.

The transformation that comes when Christ enters our lives cannot be explained. Neither can it be analyzed completely. It can, however, be visualized. There are three distinct results. First, there is a *divine* change. The new birth is not a product of human ability or effort, nor is it to be explained in terms of reformation. God acts on our hearts and does a work that causes our attitudes to change. The change is a *complete* one, affecting every part of our personalities. This does not mean that we become sinless, but it does mean that we have surrendered completely to God's will. The new birth is also *secure*. God is unchanging and will not change his feelings toward us. Only we can turn away from him; he will never turn away from us. There are two distinct births in our lives—the physical and the spiritual. We become a member of our earthly families through physical birth. We become members of God's family through spiritual birth.

II. The necessity for the new birth.

Our sinful human nature makes it essential that we be born again. We have no righteousness of our own. We must be justified on the basis of Christ's atonement. When we trust completely in Jesus as Savior, God accounts it to us as righteousness, but he does more. God's Holy Spirit gives us a new nature. Jeremiah prophesied concerning the change God would work in the hearts of people when he spoke of a new covenant. He said, "I will put my law in their inward parts, and write it in their hearts; and will be their God, and they shall be my people" (Jer. 31:33). Ezekiel prophesied, "A new heart also will I give you, and a new spirit will I put within you" (Ezek. 36:26). It is necessary to have a new heart and a new nature because our natural state is enmity against God. In Romans 3:10–18, Paul presents a mosaic concerning sin. He selects quotations from the Old Testament to show that every part of our personalities has been affected by our transgressions. Everyone stands equally guilty before God, because when we are guilty of one sin, we are guilty of all (James 2:10).

III. Negotiator of the new birth.

Throughout all of the Bible, God's Holy Spirit is represented as the agent in salvation. People are convicted of sin by the Holy Spirit. Jesus said that the Holy Spirit "will reprove the world of sin ... because they believe not on me" (John 16:8–9). People are regenerated through the work of the Holy Spirit as they are brought through repentance and faith into a right relationship with God through Jesus Christ. Through the Holy Spirit, we become conscious of our adoption into the divine family. He becomes the pledge of our final redemption as he forms Christ in us as the hope of glory. His work brings us from a sinful state of alienation from God to a right relationship with God through a redemptive experience.

43

IV. The now of the new birth.

As Jesus and Nicodemus discussed the new birth, Nicodemus became profoundly interested. He asked, "How can these things be?" Jesus replied with a simple illustration from the life of Moses. The Israelites, while en route from Egypt to Canaan, had been the victim of fiery serpents. The situation became acute, and Moses prayed to God. He was told to place a brass serpent on a pole and put it up outside the camp. Those who would go and look at the serpent would be healed. Jesus told Nicodemus that the Son of Man would be lifted up in the same way, and whoever placed faith in him would have eternal life. Jesus used the expression that meant "lifted up on a cross for execution" and referred to his coming crucifixion.

The closing verses of the conversation between Jesus and Nicodemus reflect the urgency of the Master's appeal. There are two good reasons for coming to Jesus in the "now" of life. First, we do not know when we will die. To pass from this world unprepared to meet God in eternity is a fearful thing. To come to the Savior now is wise, for it is the only safe path to pursue. Second, the sooner one comes to Christ, the sooner a life of abundance and joy will begin. Of course, one who is still lost does not know of this abundance and joy but should receive the testimony of others who have found happiness in surrendering to Jesus. Today is the day that salvation is available, and today is the day that salvation should be appropriated. The new birth is God's way of turning sinful people into new people in Christ Jesus.

Conclusion

We do not cease to be sinners when we become Christians. The new birth gives us a new nature, but the old nature is still present. In Romans 7, Paul describes the eternal conflict between the old nature and the new nature within the saved person. The new birth, however, does give us a new affection and a new desire. People who have been born again have one great goal. They wish to serve Jesus and please him in every action of life. The judicial act in salvation is justification. The dynamic act is regeneration, or being born again. Both take place when one has a genuine experience of salvation. Justification has to do with a person's guilt before God. The new birth relates to the change in attitude and therefore to the change in our activity. One of our pioneer preachers, George Whitefield, used to preach over and over on "Ye must be born again." One day a woman asked him, "Why do you preach so much on that passage?" He replied, "Because, ma'am, ye must be born again."

SUNDAY EVENING, FEBRUARY 2

Title: Obligation in Him

Text: "No one who lives in him keeps on sinning. No one who continues to sin has either seen him or known him" **(1 John 3:6 NIV)**.

Scripture Reading: 1 John 3:5–10

Introduction

In the previous verses of 1 John, John has pointed out such things as life in Christ, fellowship in Christ, childhood in Christ, and dignity and destiny in Christ. In the verses under consideration, John points out the obligations that arise out of such relationships. After a person has been begotten of God—born again—some obligations are involved.

I. All sin has its origin in the devil (I John 3:8).

The devil has been a sinner from the beginning, and those who imitate him become his spiritual children.
   A. *This sin is lawlessness (3:4).* The law is the revelation of God's will, the Father's requirement for his children. Sin is the operation of the will in defiance of the law of God. It is the refusal to live in accordance with the revealed standards of right and wrong. Lawlessness and sin are interchangeable terms.
   B. *This sinfulness is a true manifestation of the true self (3:10).*

II. All sin has its remedy in the Son of God (I John 3:5).

The mission of Christ—his coming into the world—was to provide a remedy for sin. Christ was manifested to take away sin (3:5). In the lives of all people, there is an eternal conflict between Jesus and Satan, but victory over Satan is certain. The purpose of Jesus' incarnation was to take away sin—past, present, and future. Jesus was qualified to do this because he had no sin in him.

The nature of this removal is found in the words "take away." It means to lift up and carry away (John 1:29). It is complete expiation wrought by Christ on Calvary.

The word "destroy" in verse 8 is used metaphorically as loosening an obligation or bond.

III. The obligation in Christ is to live righteously (I John 3:6–7, 9).

The word *righteousness* simply means right living, doing what is right. Here then is the true obligation in Christ. It is to live rightly according to the standards of God. The tenses of the verbs in verses 6, 7, and 9 are continued action verbs. The one who has the habit of sin and keeps on doing it shows that he is not a true child of God. Verse 9 says that the child of God does not have the habit of sin. He does not keep on sinning. Verse 6 points out that the one who keeps on abiding in Christ does not keep on sinning. The reverse is also true; that is, the one who keeps on sinning—lives a life of sin, not mere occasional acts of sin—has not seen the Father. The habit of sin is proof that one has no vision or knowledge of Christ. From all of this, it is understandable that if people are Christians, they will do what is right. If they are children of God, they are obligated to resemble him in righteousness.

IV. This obligation shows a major contrast.

Sin in all its forms is the very antithesis of that which is in Christ. Sinfulness and a Christian profession are incompatible, and the Christian must never grow complacent in his attitude toward sin. A life of sin is proof that one is a child of the devil and not of God (John 8:33–39). Truth and falsehood, good and evil, right and wrong, God and the devil are irreconcilable opposites. So are sin and holiness, lawlessness and righteousness opposites. Sin is doing wrong, and righteousness is doing right.

Conclusion

The most wonderful thing that can ever happen to a person is to become a child of God. The greatest achievement of a child of God is to become righteous like God. I plead with you to surrender your all to Jesus Christ for cleansing of sin. Resist the devil, and he will flee from you. Draw close to God, and he will draw close to you. Then assume the obligation that is yours in him.

WEDNESDAY EVENING, FEBRUARY 5

Title: The Bible Speaks to Our Condition

Scripture Reading: Mark 9

Introduction

The psalmist prayed, "Open thou mine eyes, that I may behold wondrous things out of thy law" (Ps. 119:18). Only the Spirit of God can open up our minds to understand the Scriptures. Our Lord opened up the Scriptures so that his disciples could understand the nature and the necessity of his death and resurrection (Luke 24:45). As we develop and maintain the habit of reading at least one chapter of the Bible each day, we need to do so with the awareness that we must let God speak through his Word if this spiritual exercise is to be truly profitable.

Let us try to let God speak to us through Mark 9.

I. The purpose of spiritual retreats (Mark 9:2–8).

Repeatedly our Lord took his disciples and went aside to a private place for prayer, rest, and instruction. The experience described in these verses was unique. It occurred some six months before our Lord's death. Luke's gospel tells us that our Lord took Peter, James, and John and went up into a mountain to pray (Luke 9:28). As our Lord communed with his Father, he was transfigured before them. His humanity slipped into the background, and the disciples with him saw a manifestation of his deity. The *shekinah* glory of the eternal God was upon his countenance. He entered into dialogue with Moses and Elijah, representing the Law and the Prophets concerning his forthcoming death. Our Lord was strengthened and encouraged for the ordeal that confronted him. The voice from heaven identified and confirmed him as the Son of God and gave specific instructions to the apostles concerning their response to him.

This experience was not understood by Peter, James, and John at the time. It was a part of their training that could be understood only after Jesus' death and resurrection and the coming of the Holy Spirit on the day of Pentecost. In this retreat on a mountaintop with their Lord, the apostles were given some new truth about God and some new instructions for their own lives.

Each of us needs to find a place and a time for a retreat into solitude that we might listen and hear what God would say to us.

II. Suffering in the valley (Mark 9:14–29).

We must beware lest we envy those who have mountaintop experiences with God. We need to be on guard lest we interpret our own mystical experiences with God in terms of something merely to enjoy.

At the foot of the Mount of Transfiguration there was a distressed father who in his agony was seeking help for his demon-possessed and epileptic child. On previous occasions, the disciples had cast out demons (Mark 6:13). In this situation, however, the nine who remained at the foot of the mountain were powerless and unable to help.

The desperate father brought his plea to the Lord. He spoke of the necessity of faith and prayer for miracles to take place. The father spoke for most of us when he pled, "Lord, I believe; help thou mine unbelief" (Mark 9:24).

We need to utilize all of the trust we have as we face the needs of those who suffer in the world's valleys, highways, and byways today.

III. Only those who serve are truly great (Mark 9:33–37).

The apostles of our Lord were very human at the point that they were motivated by low and selfish motives much of the time like the rest of us. They were seeking for position, power, prestige, and comfort.

Our Lord rebuked them for their self-centeredness and declared that if they would find greatness in the kingdom of God, they must deny themselves and give themselves unreservedly to meeting the needs of others.

Kingdom greatness is not determined by how high our position is or by how many people we have supervision over. Kingdom greatness is to be thought of in how many people we serve and bless and help.

Let each of us make certain that we serve others today instead of seeking to be served by others.

IV. Tolerance is essential (Mark 9:38–41).

For some strange reason, human nature causes us to want others to conform to our own pattern and our own way of thinking and serving. Our Lord rebuked the attitude of narrow exclusiveness that required that everyone march to the same tune.

Our God is not limited to one individual or congregation to accomplish his work. Let us be thankful that God does not wait for us to attain perfection or conformity in every respect to his will before he works miracles through us.

V. Faithful discipleship involves radical surgery (Mark 9:42–50).

How are we to interpret this passage of Scripture? Must we interpret every phrase of it in a very literalistic way? How many people do you know who have only one hand, one foot, or one eye? Did our Lord mean that we should literally place our hand on a chopping block and cut it off? Was he suggesting that we amputate one of our legs? Was he demanding that we gouge out one of our eyes? He who restored the withered hand and made the lame to walk and gave sight to the blind would never literally expect us to cripple ourselves in this manner.

Our Lord is commanding in the strongest words that could be used that we deal drastically with those attitudes, affections, appetites, ambitions, or actions that would lure us away from the way of the cross. He is saying that we must not tolerate evil in our lives. He is suggesting that we walk the high road of self-discipline and dedication to the will of our God.

Conclusion

No one can draw aside and do our praying for us. No one can go down into the valley of human suffering and render the service that we are capable of rendering. If we are to find true significance in life, we will find it through the pathway of the cross that involves humility, the denial of selfish desires, the toleration of those who do things a bit differently from the way we would, and by a continual program of voluntary self-discipline and dedication.

Read the chapter again and let God speak to your heart.

SUNDAY MORNING, FEBRUARY 9

Title: Jesus Gives New Meaning to Life

Text: "But whosoever drinketh of the water that I shall give him shall never thirst" (**John 4:14**).

Scripture Reading: John 4:1–26

Hymns: "'Tis So Sweet to Trust in Jesus," Stead

"I Heard the Voice of Jesus Say," Bonar

"My Faith Looks Up to Thee," Palmer

Offertory Prayer: Our Father, we are grateful that you know far more about us than we know about ourselves. We are thankful that you are more concerned about us than even we are concerned about ourselves. We are grateful that because of your insight into us you are able to provide for our needs. We make mistakes when we try to plan our lives without you. We can be our best only when we are in the center of your will. This morning we come to you with our problems and ask for your guidance. We come with our weakness and ask for your strength. We come with our needs and ask for your fullness. We come with our gifts of money and ask that you will accept these gifts and use them in the furtherance of your work. Help us to realize that the gift without the giver is bare and thus to dedicate not only our possessions but our influence, our enthusiasm, our loyalty, and all that we are in the work of your kingdom. We pray in Jesus' name. Amen.

Introduction

John 4 closely follows the chronology of John 3. Jesus had spent a brief time in Judea and was now ready to go into Galilee for a lengthy ministry. How would he go? If he had followed the traditional route, he would have gone to Jericho and crossed eastward over Jordan into Perea and gone north until he passed Samaria and then cut back westward across the Jordan into Galilee. In this way, he would have bypassed the Samaritan country. This half-breed race was despised by the Jews. Because of their prejudice, they would not even pass through the country of the Samaritans, much less associate with them.

The compulsion that caused Jesus to go through Samaria was twofold. First, the disciples must learn a great lesson. They must be made to realize that God loves all people without distinction as to race or ethnic background. Second, Jesus knew there would be a woman at Sychar who needed the Living Water. He wanted his disciples to witness God's grace extended in saving power to a hated Samaritan.

I. The approach of Jesus.

Because the woman had some deep personal problems, Jesus felt that it was best to deal with her alone. He chose an opportunity while his disciples were gone away into the city to buy food. He made it his business to be at a place where the woman would come; he waited by the well.

Jesus did not use a direct approach. Some people can be approached in this manner, but others must be approached indirectly. Jesus realized the woman would quickly become defensive. In the first place, she was a Samaritan. She would be suspicious of any Jew who sought conversation with her. Second, she had deep moral problems and therefore would be slow to become interested in spiritual things, especially when such interest would involve coming face-to-face with her sin.

Jesus' simple request was that she give him a drink of water. Few, if any, women would be unwilling to do such a small favor for a weary traveler.

II. The answer of Jesus to opposition.

It is not possible for us to know the attitude with which the Samaritan woman spoke the words in verse 9. Some feel she spoke sharply to Jesus, being enraged that he would dare to make a request of her. Others feel that the words represent one weary of life and defeated in spirit, being surprised that a Jew would be willing to socialize with her especially in view of her background, which she probably thought everyone knew.

Jesus' answer in verse 10 was designed to stir curiosity and interest. He probably felt that the woman would recognize the spiritual overtones of the statement. The woman's answer reveals that she did not yet fully appreciate the significance of Jesus' words. Jesus' answer in verses 13 and 14 contained further spiritual implications, but it is doubtful that she completely understood his message. Her reply in verse 15 still seems a bit shallow, although we cannot be certain at this point.

Jesus recognized the necessity of bringing the woman face-to-face with her sin. This is the significance of his statement that she call her husband. It worked! It gave Jesus a springboard from which to confront her with her former life and even her present one. The woman then tried to change the subject by starting an argument over religion. Jesus, however, continued to press his point.

III. The announcement of his messiahship.

A controversy had existed for many years between the Jews and Samaritans concerning the proper place of worship. The Samaritans were half-breeds. The race had been formed after Assyria captured the northern kingdom. They were a mixture of the lower elements of the Assyrians and Israelites. The Samaritans, however, insisted that they were the true descendants of Abraham. They had their own version of the Pentateuch. Their worship place was Mount Gerizim, and they refused to recognize Jerusalem as the true place for religious ceremonies.

Before identifying himself, Jesus realized the necessity of presenting to the woman the true nature of worship. It is not forms, ceremonies, or institutions that bring one to God. One must discover God through a spiritual experience. As Jesus presented this truth to her, she seemingly was not able to grasp the full significance of it. She dismissed it with a casual, "I know that Messiah is coming. When he comes, he will explain everything to us" (v. 25 NIV). This gave Jesus the perfect opportunity to announce to her exactly who he was. He had paved the way by his unique approach. Now she was face-to-face with a decision.

IV. The attitude of the woman.

We have no record concerning the woman's reply to Jesus. The scene is interrupted by the coming of the disciples. Obviously they recognized that an important conversation was taking place, for no one asked Jesus why he was talking with the woman. They must have sensed that he was discussing spiritual matters. John resumes the narrative concerning the woman in verse 28. The woman was, no doubt, very much impressed with Jesus, for she left her water pot and went into the city to tell the men of her discovery. These were, in all probability, men who knew her well. A great transformation must have come to remove her inhibitions toward religion. It should be pointed out, however, in fairness to the woman, that throughout the entire story she seems to have a religious background. She knew of Jacob. She was informed concerning the worship habits of the Samaritans and the Israelites. She also knew that the Messiah was coming. What led her into a life of sin, we are not told. We are only given an account of the one who transformed her life.

Conclusion

Although the Samaritan woman was familiar with Scripture, she did not know about divine grace. Her broken life had affected her attitude and perhaps caused her to be cynical of anyone who spoke concerning spiritual matters. Only grace can bring forgiveness. When we are presenting the gospel message of grace, we should seek the best time to approach the individual and should also be tender and gentle in making an appeal. God's grace accommodates itself to the temperament of each individual. One of the most convincing proofs of God's ability to forgive is the change that comes to individuals when they experience divine grace. To see a life made anew is indeed a miracle. True conversion comes from a power greater than any human effort or ability.

From this story we learn that all things are possible through God's divine grace even if the difficulty seems insurmountable. The story of Nicodemus (last Sunday) shows us that there are no people so good that they do not need a new birth. And today's story teaches us that there are no people so sinful that they cannot be changed through a new birth.

The sequel to the story should not be overlooked. Jesus gave an object lesson to his disciples concerning values. There is a place for physical food. The disciples had gone into the city to secure nourishment for their bodies. Jesus used this encounter with the Samaritan woman to teach them that our lower desires in life must be subordinated to the higher ones. Jesus never neglected the claims of the body. In fact, he worked miracles to supply people with food. He insisted, however, that the highest duty of man is not to attend to the desires of the body but to do the will of God. The hunger of his soul for the spiritual experience of leading the woman to new life was greater than his physical fatigue or appetite. The joy that came with this experience brought him inspiration. He glowed with inward spiritual energy as he explained to his disciples where they would find their greatest joy.

SUNDAY EVENING, FEBRUARY 9

Title: Assurance in Him

Text: "And hereby we know that we are of the truth, and shall assure our hearts before him" **(1 John 3:19)**.

Scripture Reading: 1 John 3:11 – 24

Introduction

In 1 John 2:7 – 11, the apostle John reiterates the old commandment as not only the paramount duty of believers but the evidence of their sonship. He said that the evidence lies in doing righteousness. He defines righteousness as loving the brethren.

First John 3:1 – 10 applies to the test of righteousness. Here is applied the test of love. John regards love as an obvious test. He declares that the whole message of the life and character of Christ is a message of love. These verses (vv. 11–24) point out that the Christian's whole duty is summed up in the obligation to exercise love.

I. Love is manifested toward one another (I John 3:11–18).

A. *This love is a natural result of sonship, but it is also a commandment (3:11–13).* Hate, envy, and jealousy have no part in one's true Christian nature of love. Cain is used as the example (v. 12). Those who are motivated by hate are still in a state of spiritual death. They have not been born of God; they are not children of God (v. 14).

   A lack of love is an indication of one who is still in the death of sin, being, in fact, a murderer; for the essential part of being a murderer, at least from the divine point of view, is the inward attitude of which the outward deed is but the expression.

B. *This love is a testimony of a believer's experience of grace—the new birth (3:14–18).* The words "we know" in verse 14 are so located in the original language as to make them emphatic. This is in contrast to the unregenerate world. The words "passed from" in verse 14 mean to pass over from one place to another; to migrate out of death into life. The believer does this while here on earth. Verses 14, 16, and 18 give a positive affirmation of love. Jesus is the example. By dying he showed a divine love toward people who had sinned against him and his Father. The practice of love, therefore, can be broadly described in terms of the imitation of Christ.

   The Christian's love is not manifested in words alone, but in deeds. It is seen in warm words accompanied by warm deeds. It is the willingness to surrender that which has value in one's own life to enrich the life of another (3:14, 18). It is shown in daily living.

   Verse 17 points out the negative. If one closes his heart to the needs of others, God's love does not abide in him.

C. *This love is identified with the world.*

II. The Christian's assurance is seen in a free conscience (I John 3:19–24).

Verse 19 may be translated, "In the presence of God, we shall have confident assurance because God understands us."

A. *The conditions of a free conscience are to believe in him (3:23), love one another, and abide in him.* Believing in Christ is the summary of all his commandments (Mark 12:28–31). To believe in the name of Christ is to believe in all that he is. Christians abide in God and God in them through the Holy Spirit (John 14:10; 17:21, 23). Believers remain in him only as they imitate the example of Christ. This is seen as believers are loyal to the gospel.

B. *The conscience is free because the Lord frees it, and this is a contrast to the believer's own freedom (3:20–21).* Human beings in their own weakness will condemn themselves. *Condemn* means "to know something against." We know our failures, and they rise up to condemn us. This challenge may come from within or from without. But the most serious is the doubt in the heart. The wonderful thing, though, is that our own hearts are not the final judge (1 Cor. 4:4–5). When sin is confessed, the Lord removes it and no longer holds it against us. He is greater than the human heart, and he links omniscience with love and sympathy. He is bigger and final, and when he forgives, we have assurance in him.

This is not a claim to sinlessness, but a claim to a consciousness of fellowship with God.

C. *When the conscience is free, the Christian can be assured of answered prayers (3:22).* There are no limitations to prayer, but the one praying must completely surrender to God's will (Mark 11:24; Luke 11:9). The answer may not always be in the form expected, but it will be best.

To pray in the name of Jesus is to pray in virtue of union with him. That union is love and obedience in which Christ's love and obedience to the Father are reproduced in the Christian through faith.

Conclusion

There is nothing that produces insecurity like a lack of assurance. Uncertainty with God is our greatest frustration. Hear the words of this passage, believe in God, abide in him, pray in him, and love in him, and then you can walk with assurance — assurance of being his child, assurance of being forgiven, assurance of a free conscience.

WEDNESDAY EVENING, FEBRUARY 12

Title: The Bible Speaks to Our Condition

Scripture Reading: Mark 16

Introduction

The last chapter of the gospel of Mark contains the account of the events surrounding the resurrection of our Lord. It makes mention of several appearances of our Lord to various disciples and groups of disciples.

When the risen Christ first appeared to Mary Magdalene, she did not recognize him (John 20:14). The two travelers between Jerusalem and Emmaus were blind to the true nature of the person who joined them for their journey homeward (Luke 24:16, 31). As we read this account of our Lord's resurrection, we could pray as did the psalmist, "Open my eyes that I may see wonderful things in your law" (Ps. 119:18 NIV).

I. "He has risen!" (Mark 16:6 NIV).

The angelic announcement concerning the resurrection of Jesus Christ was truly the best news that has ever fallen upon the ears of humanity. All believers need to enter into the heritage that is theirs by virtue of the fact that Christ is alive.

53

A. *The resurrection was a dramatic declaration of the victory of Jesus Christ over sin, death, the grave, and all of the forces of evil.* We worship and serve a triumphant Christ.
B. *By Jesus' conquest of death and revelation of the reality of immortality, he gave to his disciples a hope and a faith in victory over death and the grave.*
C. *By Jesus' conquest of death, he was raised to a position of authority.* He was granted authority to both invite and command his disciples to share the significance of his redemptive achievements with a needy world.

We need to respond to the great truth announced by the messenger who spoke to the women when they visited the Lord's tomb.

II. "He is going ahead of you" (Mark 16:7 NIV).

The resurrection of our Lord was to have continuing significance for his disciples. It provided for them the abiding presence of their living Lord who was to be their companion along the road of life.

A. *Jesus goes before us as our Teacher.* The other Gospels relate how our Lord continued to teach his apostles following his resurrection. He sought to help them understand the prophecies that had predicted his death and his triumphant resurrection. Our Lord continues to be heaven's authoritative Teacher for us today.
B. *Jesus goes before us to provide guidance.* The Christ of history wants to be the Christ of our personal experience. He wants to provide us with light for all of the dark mysteries of life in the present (John 8:12). Today we need to follow him in faith and obedience.
C. *Jesus goes before us to provide for our needs.* Out of the abundance of his grace, he will minister to our needs in whatever circumstances we find ourselves. He is the Christ who fed the multitudes to the extent that there was a surplus. We can trust him for what we need today.

III. Our continuing commission (Mark 16:15).

Our Lord did not intend for the commandment he gave his disciples to cease with them. It was an imperative with future significance for every follower of the way of the cross.

Each of us is in a process of going about from place to place. In our going about from place to place, we are to announce the Good News. The phrase "preach the gospel" is not to be limited to a formal worship service with a minister behind the pulpit. It really means that each of us in our daily walk is to be engaged in communicating the good news of God's love as we have experienced it in Jesus Christ.

We are to continue to share this good news until every creature on the face of the earth has had the privilege of either accepting or rejecting Jesus Christ as Lord.

Conclusion

How have you related to this great commission? Have you professionalized it and let it apply only to the clergy? Have you internationalized it and applied it only to those who are vocational foreign missionaries?

Each of us must put ourselves in the middle of this continuing commission if Christianity is to be relevant for us and helpful to others.

SUNDAY MORNING, FEBRUARY 16

Title: Jesus Loved People and Believed in Them

Text: "When he saw the multitudes, he was moved with compassion on them" **(Matt. 9:36)**.

Scripture Reading: Matthew 9:35–38

Hymns: "Send the Light," Gabriel

"Tell Me the Story of Jesus," Crosby

"Jesus Calls Us," Alexander

Offertory Prayer: Our Father, we need a closer walk with you. Help us to know that it will not come to us accidentally nor incidentally. Make us willing to accept the disciplines of life that lead us closer to you. Help us to be willing to take the initiative in self-sacrifice as we dedicate ourselves completely to your purposes for us. Help us to recognize that we are incomplete until we have laid our all on the altar. Give us both the grace and the knowledge to grow toward your likeness. May we find your presence more real each day as we give ourselves more completely. Forgive us where we have sinned and strengthen us where we are weak. Let our love for you be unreserved. Help us ever to live in the light of the glorious gospel of our Lord and seek to make him known to others. Bless us as we bring these tithes and offerings and use them for your redemptive purposes in the world. We pray for Jesus' sake. Amen.

Introduction

Matthew's gospel is mainly topical. Much of his material is grouped under certain subjects. Jesus' great Galilean ministry lasted at least eighteen months. It would have been virtually impossible to have recorded every event. Chapters 8 and 9 of Matthew's gospel record representative episodes in the life and ministry of Jesus during the early part of the Galilean ministry.

Jesus kept a busy schedule. No person living today maintains such a rigid discipline or reaches out to touch the lives of more people. Yet Jesus was always ready to lend a helping hand to anyone regardless of need or social status.

In chapters 8 and 9, we see Jesus healing a leper, healing a centurion's servant, healing the mother-in-law of Simon Peter, and casting out demons from those who were possessed with them. While he was at rest in a boat, a mighty storm arose on the Sea of Galilee. Jesus rebuked the wind and the sea, and there was a great calm. Jesus went to the other side of the Jordan and cast demons out of two men. He came back west of the Jordan and healed a paralyzed man. He called a man named Matthew to follow him. He healed a woman who had a problem with hemorrhaging for twelve years, and he healed the daughter of one of the rulers of the city. Two blind men followed him, and he healed them. He cast demons out of a mute man. Everything he did was to help the lives of people physically, mentally, and spiritually.

The close of chapter 9 gives a summary of everything Jesus did. He engaged in a threefold ministry—teaching, preaching, and healing. This is still a part of the basic Christian message and ministry. When Jesus took time to view the people, it brought a sense of pathos to his soul. The tenderness of his heart caused him to identify with them and make their suffering become a part of his own. He then uttered a command to his followers to "get into the action" and use their talents to help spread the message of God's kingdom and help heal humanity's spiritual hurt. These verses bring to us a threefold picture of the Master as he viewed the multitudes.

I. He saw confusion.

If any people in the world have ever been confused as to their state of life and ultimate security, it was the Jewish people of Jesus' day. They had been in bondage, with the exception of a few years, to a foreign power since the days of the Assyrian and Babylonian Empires. They had been kicked up and down the field of international politics like a football. False messiahs had arisen, and they had gone after them. The book of Acts (5:36–37) tells of two leaders who had arisen and deceived the people. They had come to the place where they did not know whom they could trust or to whom they could turn. They were confused.

Their world was not unlike our day. We too live in a day when it is difficult to know what the real issues are in national life. Our political life is definable in simple terms. One party is in, and the other wants in now. Militarily, we are confused. Some feel we should seek peace by preparing a strong defense against possible aggression. Others believe we should disarm completely and immediately, and thus show others our good faith. Economically, we are in a state of confusion. Most of us, unless we have suffered a recent reverse, have more material possessions than we have ever had in our lives. Yet there is more uncertainty and anxiety concerning our economic situation as we look to the future than we have ever had in the history of our nation. In the realm of morals, we are equally perplexed. Convictions that we have held as necessary to life itself have been given up in favor of a permissive approach that justifies anything. The black-and-white distinctions have faded to a dull gray with nothing being really wrong—that is, if we can get away with it! Sin consists in getting caught, not in performing the wicked deed.

II. Jesus felt compassion.

As Jesus viewed the spiritual confusion of these people as well as their other needs, he was stirred within the recesses of his soul. All suffering humanity comes within the orbit of Christ's interest. Jesus was aware that many of the people had been disappointed in life, and it crushed his heart. To see one without an aim or purpose causes any sensitive person to feel deeply. The word *compassion* means literally "suffering with" and is one of the most meaningful words in our language.

One of our greatest needs today is for people who are strong enough to be leaders and yet tender enough to feel deeply concerning the deficiencies of others. Jesus was and is such a person. No one ever possessed such a drive and dynamic in his personal life. Yet no one was more sympathetic with people who could not keep up with his pace. Jesus knew of the scattered world that had lost the sense of its oneness, and it grieved him because the Father never intended such a situation to develop in the beautiful world he created.

The godlessness of our day is enough to bring a shock of concern to any person who is spiritually sensitive. If life is to be worth living for the multitudes, there must be courageous people possessed with the love of God in Jesus Christ who will minister to their needs and point them to the one who can make their lives anew.

Jesus saw with the eye of God, and he felt with the heart of both God and humanity. We associate the word *pity* with the idea of divinity, but the word *compassion* actually belongs to divinity incarnate. One of the tragedies of our day is that we can walk the streets of our towns and cities and never feel one touch of emotion when we see people who are torn, weary, without a Shepherd, and without hope in this world or in the one to come. It is only the compassionate love of Christ in us that can motivate us for effective Christian service. Jesus not only loved people, but he also believed in them. The crowd would have looked at Matthew and not been impressed that he had spiritual potentiality. Jesus saw him and realized immediately that here was a man who could become one of his inner circle and write a book concerning his life. Jesus let Matthew know that he saw good in him. The good came forth and developed under the teaching of the Savior. It was compassion that led Jesus to think Matthew had possibility for growing.

III. Jesus gave a commission.

One thing we must never forget: if you excite emotions that are intended to lead people to action, the action should follow. If it does not, the emotion without the proper action will make the heart grow much harder than it was in its previous condition. An old truism says, "Impression without expression leads to depression."

Jesus pointed the group to the possibilities for service. He pictured these opportunities as a harvest that is truly plenteous but with only a few laborers. The injunction of Jesus was that we should pray for the Lord to thrust forth laborers into the harvest. Jesus realized that if people will pray sincerely concerning a need, they will eventually offer themselves to meet that need. It is quite significant that the next chapter tells of how Jesus called his Twelve and sent them out to witness concerning him. It is unfortunate that there is a chapter division at this point. Actually, the calling of the Twelve follows immediately upon the statement of Jesus that we are to pray that the Lord would send forth laborers into the harvest.

Conclusion

How much do you really care about people? Does it really matter to you that hearts are broken, lives are torn, hopes have been blighted, and many people are living without a sense of direction in life? Jesus cared. He did not set up an office in Capernaum with a shingle outside of it that said, "Jesus of Nazareth. Office Hours 9 to 5. May Be Seen by Appointment Only." He went where the people were. He made it his business to be at the very place Zacchaeus was in order that he might win Zacchaeus to faith in himself. The best way to lead people to higher aims and ideals for their lives is to believe in them. If we make people think that we do not have faith in them, they will never feel a compulsion to rise above mediocrity. If, on the other hand, we let them know that we feel they have infinite possibilities, they will do their very best to live up to our hopes and dreams for them. With the tremendous pressures that are in the world today, Christian people cannot afford to become complacent. We must think as Jesus thought, feel as he felt, and work as he worked to God's glory and the helping of lost and defeated humanity.

SUNDAY EVENING, FEBRUARY 16

Title: Knowledge in Him

Text: "Hereby know we that we dwell in him, and he in us, because he hath given us of his Spirit" **(1 John 4:13).**

Scripture Reading: 1 John 4:1–21

Introduction

It is noticeable in 1 John that the work of the Holy Spirit is related almost exclusively to the imparting of faith. Therefore, belief in Jesus Christ is related to the presence and work of the Holy Spirit. Chapter 4 opens with the assurance that one is a child of God based on confession inspired by the Holy Spirit.

I. Knowledge is imparted by the Holy Spirit (I John 4:1–6).

A. *False spirits lead seekers astray (4:3, 5).* Some victims fall easily to spiritualistic humbuggery. This is the work of false spirits known as the spirits of antichrist. These antichrist spirits are in the world now and can be recognized by their failure to acknowledge that Jesus came to earth in the flesh (4:3).

In verse 5, these antichrists are characterized. They are spoken of as prating. The world listens to those who speak in its own language. The false prophets and the world are in perfect union. The false prophets have gone out and left the church and joined the society of the godless and unbelieving. They claim to be spiritual—that is, Christian. They claim to be divinely inspired, but in reality they are of the devil.

B. *The Holy Spirit testifies to the truth (4:2–4, 6).* The Holy Spirit testifies about the incarnation, which is the real test that Jesus is the Christ. The crucial test is their attitude toward him. He also overcomes false testimonies (4:4). The faithful (not false) are God's delegates bearing their Master's commission and continuing his warfare (John 20:21), and they have shared his victory. This comes through the working of the Holy Spirit.

The faithful can claim final victory over false prophets, and the reason lies in God, who abides in them (3:20, 24). God is greater than Satan, who is in the world, the prince of the world (John 12:31; 14:30), the god of this age (2 Cor. 4:4).

The Holy Spirit accentuates the Christian testimony (4:6). "We know" in verse 6 is for emphasis in the sentence. This is in sharp contrast with the false prophets and the world. Christians know because they are in tune with the infinite God. The reason sermons are inspiring or dull is because both the preacher and hearer are in continuous contact with God or because they are not. Christians know by personal experience, and there is no reason for them to be duped by the spirit of error.

II. Knowledge is manifested by love (I John 4:7–12).

A. *God is the source of love.* Love is the divine nature, and those who love have been made partakers of the divine nature (2 Peter 1:4). By the practice of love, they get to know God more and more.

It is true that God is love, but love is not God; they are not interchangeable. Not every manifestation of love, kindness, benevolence, or sacrifice is a sign of a new birth or of being a child of God. Godly love is sure to result in confidence toward God and love toward humanity.

B. *Because God is love and so loves, the believer ought to love also (4:9–12).* The incarnation is the supreme manifestation of the love of God. This love was manifested that humanity might receive life. This life is eternal. It is present and in harmony with the true order of things. God's children must have this love, for it is their nature. This love is an indication of God indwelling his children.

III. Knowledge is proved by Christian witnessing (I John 4:13–21).

A. *He has given the Spirit so that the ones who believe in him may know and witness (4:13–14).* Believers are the sphere in which the love of God operates. The gift of God is proof of fellowship with him. The witness is that Christ is the Savior of the world (4:14). Jesus is unseen, and it is the business of Christians to make him visible. Christians are to him now what he was to the Father in the days of his flesh.

B. *Witness is born in confession (4:15).* This is a confession born of persuasion. This conviction implies fellowship with God. A confession of the deity of

Jesus Christ implies surrender and obedience and not mere lip service (1 Cor. 12:3; Rom. 10:6–12). Confession is proof of fellowship with God. It follows experimental and confident trust.

C. *Believer's are filled with a love that casts out fear and instills confidence (4:17–21).* Love is a heavenly visitant sojourning with the believer. It has been carried to its end when believers are like Jesus and are his visible representatives. It casts out fear of judgment and establishes right relations. Fear does not exist in real love. It harbors no fear and no dread.

Conclusion

The Bible teaches that believers are indwelt by the Holy Spirit. The passage here teaches that the Holy Spirit imparts knowledge, which is manifested by love and is proved by Christian witnessing.

People need to examine themselves to make sure the Holy Spirit is in control of their lives and that this control is seen in their relationships with fellow humans.

Right now, will you make a total surrender to Jesus Christ for salvation and to the Holy Spirit for power?

WEDNESDAY EVENING, FEBRUARY 19

Title: The Bible Speaks to Our Condition

Scripture Reading: Luke 7

Introduction

As we read God's Word each day, we need without exception to pray, "Open my eyes that I may see wonderful things in your law" (Ps. 119:18 NIV). Luke 7 is something more than an unrelated collection of incidences in the life of our Lord. Seemingly, the inspired writer is trying to help his readers understand the nature and the scope of the ministry of Jesus. This chapter begins with the healing of a Gentile military officer's slave and concludes with the forgiveness of the sins of a prostitute. Between these two extremes we can get a small picture of the range of our Lord's ministry to the needs of humanity.

I. Gentiles are the object of our Lord's concern (Luke 7:1–10).

Jesus did not belong exclusively to the Jewish race. His concern was not limited to the needs of Jews.

This first incident in Luke 7 reveals that our Lord included those outside of Israel in the scope of his compassionate concern. Here we see that our Lord revealed his authority over disease at a distance. He did not have to be present and place his hand on a sick person for healing to occur.

The Gentile military officer was a man of both faith and humility. He believed in the authority of Jesus and at the same time did not feel worthy to approach Jesus personally.

We would experience more of the power of our Lord if we expressed both faith and humility toward him.

II. Concern for a grieving widow (Luke 7:11 – 17).

With compassionate eyes, our Lord looked upon the distressed condition of a grieving widow who was following the body of her son to the place of burial. Our Lord was moved with compassion toward her and utilized his power and his authority over death to restore her son, to comfort her heart, and to provide for her future.

If Christ is the same yesterday, today, and forever, we can be assured that he suffers with us in our suffering and grieves with us in our grief. Ultimately, the family of faith will be reunited.

This incident reminded the people of the actions of Elijah (1 Kings 17:17 – 24) and Elisha (2 Kings 4:21 – 37). The people believed that Jesus was a prophet sent from God.

III. A ministry of mercy contrasted with a ministry of military might (Luke 7:18 – 23).

John the Baptist found himself imprisoned by Herod (Luke 3:20). It was natural for him to be eager to have an authentic word from Jesus concerning his ministry. Perhaps John the Baptist was eager for our Lord to assert his messiahship and exercise some of the popular concepts of what the Messiah would do. Perhaps John was hoping that Jesus would raise an army and rescue him from the discomfort and despondency of imprisonment. We can sympathize with John.

Our Lord replied to the inquiry of John's disciples by describing the nature of his ministry in terms of its being a ministry to the blind, the lame, the lepers, the deaf, the dead, and the spiritually bankrupt (Luke 7:22). Jesus' performance was in line with his messianic platform as announced earlier (Luke 4:18 – 19). We need to be certain that our expectations of the Lord are in harmony with the purpose of his ministry lest we be caused to stumble and fall.

IV. The response of a fickle people (Luke 7:31 – 35).

Jesus contrasted the reactions of the crowd to the ministry of John the Baptist and to his ministry. He revealed how fickle and how changeable they were. Consequently, many of them missed the blessings of God because they responded neither to the ministry of John nor to the ministry of our Lord. Each of us needs to beware lest we miss what God has to offer us.

V. The all-inclusiveness of our Lord's love (Luke 7:36 – 50).

A. *Our Lord's concern for Pharisees.* Most of us have categorized the Pharisees as those who were completely beyond the range of our Lord's concern because they were his foes and critics. But a close study of the Gospels will reveal that our Lord was concerned about reaching them with the message of his love. Repeatedly we find him eating with them and in conversation with them. They needed a Savior, so he offered them God's love.

B. *Concern for a prostitute.* This passage is a compressed account of the events that took place during a dinner in a Pharisee's home. This sinful woman sensed a concern and an attitude of acceptance in Jesus that caused her to respond to him in faith. She expressed her gratitude for his forgiveness in a spontaneous and extravagant, and at the same time, very appropriate manner. Because of her deep awareness of full forgiveness, she loved much. Likewise, the proof of our experience of forgiveness will be indicated by our expression of gratitude to our Lord.

Conclusion

How grateful are we to our Lord? How do we express our affection for him? Is it possible that we are like the self-righteous Pharisee who felt no need for forgiveness?

The woman trusted Christ. She experienced forgiveness. Forgiveness produced love. Love demanded self-expression. This she did by anointing Jesus' feet, a most appropriate thing to do in that day. Genuine love will find an appropriate avenue for expressing itself.

SUNDAY MORNING, FEBRUARY 23

Title: Jesus Taught Us How to Pray

Text: "Your Father knoweth what things ye have need of, before ye ask him" **(Matt. 6:8)**.

Scripture Reading: Matthew 6:5–15

Hymns: "What a Friend We Have in Jesus," Scriven

"Did You Think to Pray?" Kidder

"Near to the Heart of God," McAfee

Offertory Prayer: Our Father, we are citizens of heaven, but we live on earth. We lie exposed to the rough storms and troubles of temptation. We must live day by day with those who are not in sympathy with your purposes in this world. Help us to overcome our own cowardice, negligence, and indifference. Give us the strength to discipline our wills, cultivate our minds, and harness our powers. As the crises of life arise, make us equal to them. Deliver us from the sin of shrinking from our responsibilities. Give us faith in the greatness of life and in the adequacy of Christ as we march into the future. Help us to live by faith, but give us always the strength to show our faith by our good deeds. As we bring our tithes and offerings today, make us mindful that this is as much a part of the worship service as the praying, the reading of your Word, and the preaching from the pulpit. You have blessed us in many ways. We return to you a portion of that which you have given to us. We invest it in the work of your kingdom. Use this money to your glory and make us witnesses of your grace through our gifts. We pray for Jesus' sake. Amen.

Introduction

Jesus' work was not all activity and service. He was also a teacher. He recognized the need to instruct the people in order that they could carry on his work and live by his principles after he had gone. This was especially true of his disciples. Before Matthew took two chapters to outline the Galilean ministry in miniature, he told of Jesus' great "Sermon on the Mount." The fact that portions of it are repeated elsewhere in the ministry of Jesus in no way reflects on the integrity or the unity of Matthew 5–7. Speakers often repeat themselves on other occasions. This sermon was delivered near the beginning of Jesus' ministry in order to set forth the guidelines of living for those who would follow him.

The middle chapter of the three is, in many ways, the heart of the sermon. Jesus began this section with a warning against an ostentatious display of one's good deeds. He then immediately applied the same principle to prayer. We are not to pray in order to be seen by people. We are praying to God and should realize this both in our method of praying and in the words that we use in our prayers.

I. The command to pray.

Jesus prefaced one of his parables with the statement that "men ought always to pray, and not to faint" (Luke 18:1). This is more than a suggestion that spiritual power is available for those who wish to have it. Jesus is making clear that a supreme obligation of the Christian life is to be constantly in prayer. In the Sermon on the Mount, however, Jesus makes it clear that this does not mean we are to pray on the street corner to be seen by people. Paul's exhortation to "pray without ceasing" (1 Thess. 5:17) is in harmony with Jesus' command. Neither does Paul, however, mean that we are to make ostentatious display of our personal communication with the Father. To be constantly in prayer means we are always to be attuned to the will of God and always in such a frame of mind that he can speak to us, and we can in turn be responsive to any word he may have for us on a given occasion. An outstanding preacher of another generation was once asked what it means to be filled with the Holy Spirit. He replied, "It means to be extremely God conscious in one's life." Some may feel this is an oversimplification, but the full truth is certainly implicit in the words of the great minister. Likewise, to be constantly in prayer means to be always in a frame of mind that puts us in perfect fellowship with the Father. Prayer is an act, of course, but it is also an attitude—a way of life that recognizes God's presence and stands always ready to submit to his leadership. We can take further action after we have prayed, and we should, but until we have prayed concerning a matter, it is doubtful we can do anything effective concerning it.

Prayer has been called "the lost word" in the Christian life. This is not an overstatement. Our powerlessness is often, if not always, due to our prayerlessness.

The greatest people on earth today are those who have a proper prayer life. This does not mean those who talk about prayer or those who say they believe in prayer or even those who can explain prayer. The greatest people are those who *take time to pray*. It is not easy. The circumstances of life press in and seek to claim our priorities. We must put prayer first in our lives, and that means *taking time* from other things in life's schedule and giving that time to prayer. Those who pray are those who are doing the most for God in winning souls, in solving problems, in leading churches to renewal, and in supplying both people and money for the mission field. God reaches lost people in this earth through the willingness of his born-again children to witness. It needs to be emphasized again and again, however, that God can only do with a person's life what a person allows him to do. A large part, if not all, of our personal surrender to God's will is directly proportionate to our personal prayer life.

II. A pattern for prayer.

Matthew 6:9–13 is often erroneously called "The Lord's Prayer." Rather it is a "model" prayer. If we are actually looking for a "Lord's Prayer," we probably should consider Jesus' prayer in John 17:1–26, because these words are literally a prayer of Jesus in the garden of Gethsemane. The words of Jesus in the Sermon on the Mount are not meant as a prayer for us to repeat word for word and thus substitute as a prayer. This does not mean it is wrong to repeat this prayer in a worship assembly, but it should never be repeated mechanically as a substitute for our own personal prayer. There are values, of course, in repeating it in a worship service, but the greatest value is that it should serve as a model or guideline for the kind of praying in which we should engage.

Jesus addressed his prayer to the Father and began with a reverent honoring of the Father's name. This is important, for one's name stands for his character. We cannot be irreverent toward a person's name without minimizing if not actually blaspheming the personal characteristics of the one whom the name represents. It is important that we constantly keep a high regard for the name of our God. The Jews reverenced the name of Jehovah. They were so afraid, at one time in their history, that they would use his name lightly and irreverently that they refused to speak the sacred name but rather substituted another word for it. This was probably an overemphasis, but the lesson comes to us forcefully. We must honor the person to whom we pray.

The kingdom of God is both present and future. It exists today as a spiritual reality. It will come to full consummation when our Lord comes again. There is nothing inconsistent with praying for his kingdom to come in the hearts of people on earth even though we know that it will never come completely until Jesus returns personally. The kingdom of God now is the rule of God in the hearts of people. As we pray, we need to ask God to help each of us individually to let his will be done in our lives now even as it shall be done in the day when the kingdoms of this world become the kingdom of our Lord. God's will is being done now in heaven. We should pray for it to be done on earth now as we grow in grace and the knowledge of his will and as we are more surrendered to his purposes for us.

There is nothing wrong in praying for our temporal needs. The suggestion of this petition, however, is that God should give us day by day the things we need rather than giving us several years' supply in advance. The Israelites, during their wilderness wanderings, were given manna for their sustenance. It is significant, however, that they were given only enough each day for that day's needs. A part of prayer is faith. Faith means living "one day at a time" and being perfectly willing to trust God for future needs as we try to do his will in the "todays" of our life.

In verse 12, Jesus made it clear that there is a relationship between our willingness to forgive others and our personal forgiveness by the Father. This is not inconsistent with the doctrine of the atonement or justification by faith. It rather suggests that the truly born-again person will be one with a forgiving spirit. Earlier in the Sermon on the Mount, Jesus said, "Blessed are the merciful: for they shall obtain mercy" (5:7). Those who are unwilling to forgive those who have sinned against them should reexamine the genuineness of their own personal salvation experience.

The words concerning temptation do not mean that God may lead us into temptation and that we are asking him to not do so. James (1:13–14) makes it very clear that God does not tempt any person. James says, "But every man is tempted, when he is drawn away of his own lust and enticed." The petition in the model prayer is paraphrased by Phillips, "Keep us clear of temptation, and save us from evil."

The model prayer ends on the same note on which it begins. The Father is great. His sovereignty must be recognized and his character respected. He is the one who rules now, will rule always, and because of his moral purity, *must* rule. To him, all praise and all honor are due now and forever.

Conclusion

One who prays constantly and according to the guidelines set forth by Jesus will be a person with a spiritual dynamic. As we adore him, his characteristics will unconsciously be reproduced in our own lives. People become what they love. When they find delight in fellowship with the divine, they become more like the divine. When they wrestle with God in prayer, they will find themselves becoming equipped to wrestle with the problems of the world. True prayer is hard work. We do not necessarily need immense and commanding powers of thought in order to pray, but we do need to bring that which we have to God in an immense and powerful way if we are to learn the secret of spiritual strength. The greatest and grandest subject in the universe is the infinite God. When we have been in fellowship with him, we shall go out prepared for the problems of life. George Truett once said, "The closet with the closed door is the trysting place for power. Men and women who come from it, come with faces that shine, with visions that inspire and with power that shakes the world."

SUNDAY EVENING, FEBRUARY 23

Title: Faith in Him

Text: "Everyone who believes that Jesus is the Christ is born of God, and everyone who loves the father loves his child as well" **(1 John 5:1 NIV)**.

Scripture Reading: 1 John 5:1 – 12

Introduction

In today's Scripture reading, we find that the life God imparts to his children is tested by righteousness, love, and belief. The passage also points out the close relation between the three elements of the Christian life; love is shown by righteousness, and righteousness is secured by faith, thus the title of our lesson, "Faith in Him."

I. Faith is the condition of salvation (I John 5:1).

Faith has three components—knowledge, belief, and trust. It is not merely intellectual conviction, but full surrender to Jesus Christ as Lord and Savior.

The object of faith is Jesus Christ. The term *Christ* refers not only to the redeeming work of Jesus, or to his anointing by the Spirit of God for that work, but more specifically to his divine nature as is seen in verse 5—"the Son of God."

The person who so believes is a child of God, but one who does not believe has no right to the name Christian, for to deny this truth is to manifest the spirit of antichrist. John presents "belief" as the absolute proof that one is a child of God.

II. Faith results in love and obedience (I John 5:1 – 3).

There are two commandments of God.

A. *The first commandment is love—love God and love the children of God.* Love is the natural expression of the new life imparted by God. It is defined as keeping the commandments of God.

B. *The second commandment is obedience.* Obedience is a proof of love. The commandments of God are not grievous (5:3)—that is, they are not irksome. God's standards of obedience are high, but believers are given the Holy Spirit so that they may keep them. The commandments are not hard to obey, for God gives the grace we need for fulfillment, even though effort is required.

III. Faith overcomes the world (I John 5:4).

The world is in opposition to God. The world's maxims, principles, ideals, and spirit are all contrary to God's will and antagonistic to the spiritual life.

God gives believers victory through their faith. "Overcome" can be found twice in verse 4. The first time it is a continuous action, thus a continuous victory because it is a continuous struggle. One keeps on overcoming the world. The second time it indicates victory over one temptation at a time.

Jesus won the victory over the world (John 16:33), and God in believers

66

(1 John 4:4) gives them the victory. The faith is not in human merit but in God and in what Jesus Christ has done. This power is operative only in believers.

Christians will face conflict, but victory is assured. The energy imparted by God is mightier than that of the world. The believers' weapon is faith.

IV. Faith has some witnesses (1 John 5:7–10).

A. *The strongest witness of faith is the Holy Spirit (5:7).* The Holy Spirit testified to Jesus at his baptism (Matt. 3:16–17; Mark 1:9–11; Luke 3:21–22). Jesus was baptized with the Holy Spirit (Matt. 3:1; Mark 1:8; Luke 3:16). Acts tells that the Holy Spirit was poured out on the apostles (Acts 2:33).
B. *Another witness is seen in the water and the blood (5:8).* It is commonly believed that the water is referring to the baptism of Jesus and the blood to his death. In these two, Jesus is manifested as the Savior of the world.
C. *The third witness is the human witness (5:9).* The conditions for a legal, valid witness are found in Deuteronomy (19:15), Matthew (18:16), John (8:17; 10:25), and 2 Corinthians (13:1). The human witness is a valid one.
D. *The fourth witness is human experience (5:10).* Those who believe on the Son of God have the witness in themselves. Those who believe on Christ come to possess a deepening consciousness that he is the divine Savior. They are cleansed and pardoned. They have peace, power, and victory.

V. Faith results in the possession of eternal life (1 John 5:11–12).

Belief in Jesus Christ is a sign that one has experienced the new birth and is a child of God.

Eternal life is quality as well as duration. It is life like God's or the life of God. It is a present possession and is eternal in duration. Duration is less prominent than the moral character. Eternal life is the very life of God, manifested in Christ—thus, a life like that of Christ.

Conclusion

The one greatest thing a human being can do is exercise faith in Jesus Christ and receive eternal life. If you have never done that, then you are urged to do so right now. I invite you to bow your head, confess your sin, receive Jesus as your Savior, and receive God's life.

WEDNESDAY EVENING, FEBRUARY 26

Title: The Bible Speaks to Our Condition
Scripture Reading: Luke 14

Introduction

The habit of studying a chapter of the Bible each day gives us an opportunity to have eyes that are open to see wonderful things in God's Holy Word. The chapter suggested for this date closes with the phrase "Whoever has ears to hear, let them hear" (Luke 14:35 NIV). This is an imperative. We are not only to hear, but we are to heed that which God communicates to us through his precious Word.

I. The priority of the law of love (Luke 14:1–6).

In the days of our Lord, the ritual and traditions associated with the Law of Moses took precedence over all other considerations. In this incident in which our Lord healed a man on the Sabbath, he declared by his actions that the law of love takes precedence over all other customs, traditions, or accepted interpretations of the law of God. The Pharisees believed that the Sabbath should be observed negatively in terms of doing no labor and positively in terms of resting and feasting. The Sabbath was made for man and was intended to be a continual reminder that God was his Creator, Redeemer, and Sustainer. By healing the sick man on the Sabbath, our Lord was saying that the expression of genuine goodwill must never be restricted to a particular time or place.

II. Humility leads to honor (Luke 14:7–14).

Our Lord spoke to those who had been invited to the feast concerning the fact that selfishness and disregard for others disqualifies one for the place of honor at God's banquet table. He points out that in the practice of hospitality we should not restrict ourselves to an exclusive circle of self-serving friends but that we should become concerned about the unfortunate, the needy, and the helpless. He says that service to those who cannot return the favor will be remembered by the Father God on the day of resurrection.

III. Beware of making excuses (Luke 14:15–24).

Our Lord warned those who considered themselves to be inside the circle of God's favor against the peril of making excuses for themselves that would lead to exclusion from the favor of God. Something in the nature of people causes them to have an inflated concept of their own piety and acceptability in the sight of a holy God.

It is always possible to find excuses for neglecting to respond to the invitations that come from God to his people. We need to beware lest we rationalize and exclude ourselves from some experience with God when his invitations come to us. These invitations usually come in the form of a command. Every command is linked to a promise. To make foolish excuses for not obeying God's invitations or God's commands is to deny ourselves the privilege of experiencing the fulfillment of his promises.

IV. The demands of discipleship (Luke 7:25–33).

Our Lord never offered any easy, cheap, convenient way to achieve success. While salvation may be the free gift of God's grace, being a disciple requires faithful discipline.

The passage under discussion is not teaching that we must hate instead of love. Rather, we have here an example of the use of hyperbole, which is common among Middle-Easterners as they seek to speak in the strongest words possible to convey an important truth. Our Lord is declaring that if one would be his disciple, then the claims of this discipleship must have priority over all personal relationships, interests, and ambitions. Followers of Christ must have no competing loyalties.

Our Lord is commanding that potential disciples count the cost of discipleship before beginning the journey. And those of us who claim to be disciples must examine the quality of our "followship."

Conclusion

As you read Luke 14, do you have ears that hear? Do you have a heart that is open and receptive? Are you willing to begin to do as our Lord taught that we should? Not to do so is to discredit the cause of Christ, and it is to place ourselves in the category of salt that has lost its saltiness.

MARCH

- ## Sunday Mornings

  Continue with the theme "The Life and Works of the Lord Jesus."

- ## Sunday Evenings

  The theme for the Sunday evening messages is "The Biblical Doctrine of the Forgiveness of Sin." These messages were provided by Dr. Morris Ashcraft, who authored a book titled *The Forgiveness of Sins* (Nashville: Broadman, 1972).

- ## Wednesday Evenings

  Continue with the theme "The Bible Speaks to Our Condition." The theme verse for the month is "But his delight is in the law of the LORD; and in his law doth he meditate day and night" (Ps. 1:2).

SUNDAY MORNING, MARCH 2

Title: Jesus Was Dedicated to Duty

Text: "And it came to pass, when the time was come that he should be received up, he steadfastly set his face to go to Jerusalem" (**Luke 9:51**).

Scripture Reading: Luke 9:43–56

Hymns: "Jesus Calls Us," Alexander

              "O Jesus, I Have Promised," Bode

              "Our Best," Kirk

Offertory Prayer: Our Father, you are a merciful God. Grant that we may ever seek the constant aid of the Holy Spirit that we may follow each day of our lives after those things that build us up in Jesus Christ. We praise you and bless you because of your great power and goodness. You have given us the ability to work and to earn money. We come now to bring our tithes and offerings to you. Our gifts represent our lives. May we recognize that the giving of money is not only symbolic but is actually the giving of our lives, for it has taken hours of our lives to earn the money. We give these offerings to you because we love you and we wish to have a part in your work around the world. Use these gifts to advance the work of your kingdom in the hearts of people. Most of all, use us individually and collectively as instruments of your grace and your peace to touch the lives of people and bring them to a knowledge of you. We pray these things in Jesus' name. Amen.

Introduction

The greatest part of Jesus' ministry was in Galilee. Matthew and Mark major on Jesus' Galilean ministry, which lasted at least eighteen months and may have been interrupted by brief visits to Jerusalem.

Luke, however, majors on the last period of Jesus' ministry of approximately six months, consisting of a "later Judean ministry" and followed by a "Perean ministry" before the days in Jerusalem immediately preceding his death.

In Luke 9:51, we find the "watershed" of Jesus' ministry. This verse identifies the time that Jesus left Galilee as a sphere of operations and turned southward — a decision that set him squarely on his journey to the cross. In all probability, the material in Luke 9:51 – 18:14 is parallel with John 7:2 – 11:54. Also, three passages in John (7:2ff.; 11:17 – 18; 12:1) correspond to the three times that Luke speaks of Jesus' going to Jerusalem (9:51; 13:22; 17:11). As said before, Jesus may have come back for a brief period in Galilee and joined the pilgrims coming to Jerusalem, but Luke 9:51 presents Jesus' great decision to leave Galilee as the major field of ministry and set his face toward Jerusalem and toward his death.

I. Jesus had one great mission in life.

Although our Savior was a great teacher, this was not his primary mission. He indeed taught the crowds, and he spoke as no other man has ever spoken. His wisdom was far greater than anyone who had ever come to the world or has ever come since his day. Jesus used some material that existed, but he gave his individual touch to it. He spoke with authority — not as one merely reciting the opinions of others. Likewise, Jesus worked miracles. He did supernatural things to help those who were weak and needy and also to show his power. Every part of the Savior's life was a blessing to others and an example of how people should live.

Yet the mission of Jesus from the beginning was to die. He did not come so much to preach the gospel as he came in order that there might be a gospel to be preached. Everything in his ministry pointed toward his passion. It was necessary for him to live a perfect life so that he might be the Lamb of God without spot or blemish. The life itself, however, was not the sin offering. The Scriptures do speak of our "being saved by his life," but this does not refer to the initial experience in salvation by which we become justified in God's sight through the death of the Savior. It refers to the process of growth whereby we are saved daily from the "power" of sin rather than to the original experience in which we are saved from the "penalty" of sin. It is the death of Jesus that makes atonement for sin and makes it possible for us to find redemption through his blood. This was the overarching purpose of Jesus' life, and his mind was on the cross from the beginning of his ministry.

II. The time for decision.

One of the most important things we face in life is our decision as to *when* we shall do a thing. Jesus felt it was necessary to have an extended ministry in Galilee before his final clash with the religious authorities at Jerusalem. If Jesus had stayed in Galilee, he never would have been crucified. He was so popular in Galilee that the people wanted to make him a king. They wanted to force him to become a political messiah and lead them in rebellion against the Roman government. Jesus sought during his entire Galilean ministry to instruct the people in this section of Palestine concerning the spiritual nature of God's kingdom. At certain periods, he withdrew with his disciples for special "in-depth seminars." The first came when he felt that he had instructed them sufficiently and must leave them on their own. He wisely stayed away from a lengthy sojourn in Judah (where Jerusalem was located) during this period of instructing the common people in Galilee. The visits there to the religious feasts were brief. His premature death would have interfered with the plan the Father had for him. Timing is very important in one's life, and Jesus had the exact time planned when he would leave Galilee and concentrate on the provinces of Judah, Perea, and later the city of Jerusalem itself.

III. Dedication means complete surrender to a cause.

Once Jesus set his face toward Jerusalem, he never looked back. Although he realized it meant his death, we see in his decision the "completed surrender of a spotless soul." Everything that happened subsequent to Luke 9:51 was under the influence of the cross. Throughout the rest of the gospel, we are reminded that the destiny of Jesus was Jerusalem, where he would confront the religious leaders. There Jesus would be rejected and put on the cross. Jesus accepted the divine imperative under which God had placed his life. He did it voluntarily. God was in charge of his life, and he was completely surrendered to the Father's purpose for him. Jesus was not a helpless victim of circumstances. He made the choice deliberately. He was fully aware of all that was involved, but he also knew that by giving his life he would in reality realize it most completely. This is the true meaning of dedication. In the Old Testament, the word *dedicate* or *consecrate* comes from a root that means "to cut off" and has the further meaning of "to separate for a special purpose." This is the true nature of dedication. When we are dedicated to God, we are cut off from the rest of the world and separated completely unto him for holy living and unselfish service.

There are many illustrations of true consecration. One of the best illustrations is that of the words of General Pershing, commander of the American troops, to General Foch, commander of the Allied forces in World War I. Pershing brought his forces to Foch and said, "Our men, our equipment, our supplies are yours to use as you wish." What a change we would see in the world if every Christian would surrender to God completely and say, "My time, my talents, my money, my enthusiasm—all that I have is yours to be used completely in your service."

Conclusion

How dedicated are you? Robert E. Lee insisted that the word *duty* is the most sublime word in our language. He once said, "You can never do more than your duty. You should never wish to do less." We must always realize, of course, that the highest motive in service is love. We should seek to serve Christ because it is a privilege, not because it is our ironclad duty. We should, nevertheless, find a joy in doing our duty. We should come to love to do those things that we should do. In this way, love and duty are blended into one beautiful action. The doing of our duty is similar to learning how to obey the rules. The obeying of rules is, likewise, not the highest form of Christian living. We should seek to live on such an exalted level of Christlikeness that we act superior to the law and have no need for laws or rules. There is, however, a great value in learning to obey the rules and also to do our duty. These approaches to life deepen character. When we fail to do our duty or to obey the rules, we find ourselves deteriorating in our personal growth. On the other hand, the doing of duty and the obeying of rules contributes to the development of a great personality. We should always let love be our supreme motivation, but we should find joy in the simple doing of our duty.

SUNDAY EVENING, MARCH 2

Title: The Keys of the Kingdom

Text: "And I say also unto thee, That thou art Peter, and upon this rock I will build my church; and the gates of hell shall not prevail against it. And I will give unto thee the keys of the kingdom of heaven: and whatsoever thou shalt bind on earth shall be bound in heaven: and whatsoever thou shalt loose on earth shall be loosed in heaven. Then charged he his disciples that they should tell no man that he was Jesus the Christ" **(Matt. 16:18–20).**

Scripture Reading: Matthew 16:13–20

Introduction

Jesus used many bold figures in teaching the disciples. They remembered these striking expressions, parables, and figures and repeated them many times in their own witnessing. Some of these expressions, which have come to us in the New Testament, are difficult to interpret. One such passage relates to the "keys of the kingdom."

One well-known interpretation of this passage suggests that Simon Peter and his successors were endowed with the authority from Jesus Christ to open or close the doors of heaven by their control of the church and its sacraments. I believe that this passage has to do with the church and with the forgiveness of sins, but not in the authoritative sense. I also am convinced that this expression conveys a very significant message regarding the church and the forgiveness of sins.

I. The rock.

The "rock" on which the church is built is the confession of faith in Christ and Christ's acceptance of the confessor. In the passages before us, we have the great confession at Caesarea Philippi. In response to Jesus' question, Peter, whose name means rock, confessed to Jesus, "Thou art the Christ, the Son of the living

God." Thereupon Jesus responded, "Blessed art thou Simon Bar-jona: for flesh and blood hath not revealed it unto thee, but my Father which is in heaven. And I say also unto thee that thou art Peter, and upon this rock I will build my church." The rock is not the man Simon Peter, nor is the church built upon a man. When Peter confessed his faith that Jesus was the Christ and Christ accepted Simon Peter on the basis of that confession, the foundation was laid for the church. In short, Jesus said, "I can build my congregation of the faithful on this foundation."

II. The church.

The church is not primarily an institution; the church is the community of the people of God gathered into a fellowship by the mutual experience of faith in Jesus Christ. In the New Testament, the word *church* is used in several ways. The two most significant ones designate the church in its universal sense and the church as a local body. In the first sense, "the church" includes all Christians of all ages. This idea is prevalent in Ephesians and Colossians. It is the "people of God," the "body of Christ," and the "fellowship of the Holy Spirit." By far the most frequent use of the word *church* has to do with local congregations.

III. The churches.

Wherever the early Christian missionaries went preaching the Word, communities of the faithful originated. These are the "churches." Each of these churches is a genuine manifestation of "the church." In Matthew 18:15–35, Jesus establishes the connection between forgiving sins, the church, and "binding and loosing." In that passage, the spirit of the church is seen in Jesus' statement "Where two or three are gathered together in my name, there am I in the midst of them."

IV. Binding and loosing.

"Binding and loosing" refer to the church and to the forgiveness of sins. We have noted that in Matthew 16:19 Jesus promises "the keys of the kingdom" and then says, "Whatsoever thou shalt bind on earth shall be bound in heaven; and whatsoever thou shalt loose on earth shall be loosed in heaven." In Matthew 18:18, Jesus repeats the identical statement after he has instructed Christians in the settlement of disputes among themselves. In verse 20, he speaks of the church as the place where "two or three are gathered together in my name." Then Peter asked (v. 21), "Lord, how oft shall my brother sin against me, and I forgive him?" This seems to leave no doubt as to the meaning of the keys of the kingdom and the binding and loosing. If any doubt remained, it would have been removed by Jesus' statement after his resurrection, "And when he had said this, he breathed on them and said to them, 'Receive the Holy Spirit. If you forgive the sins of any, they are forgiven; if you retain the sins of any, they are retained'" (John 20:22 RSV).

V. The forgiveness of sins.

In the passages cited, the contexts and specific statements require us to understand what Jesus intended by the "keys of the kingdom." The binding and the loosing have to do with the forgiveness of sins.

Does this mean that the church forgives sins? Not in the sense that the church authoritatively or arbitrarily forgives or retains sins. However, it does mean that the church knows about God's forgiveness and proclaims the message of the forgiveness of sins. Since the church proclaims the promise of forgiveness, it does "open the door" for people to enter into the kingdom of heaven. On the other hand, if it fails to proclaim the Christian message of forgiveness, people remain outside the kingdom. When Jesus said that the actions of his people are binding in heaven, he meant that the decisions made in these congregations in response to the message of forgiveness are eternally binding. In short, when we preach the gospel and offer the forgiveness of Jesus Christ, people make decisions that determine eternal destiny.

This interpretation of the keys of the kingdom as the forgiveness of sins is consistent with other New Testament teachings; the interpretation of sheer authority is not consistent with the New Testament. For instance, in the immediate context of this statement (Matt. 18:1–4), when the disciples asked, "Who is the greatest in the kingdom of heaven?" Jesus replied by calling a small child to him and by indicating that the greatest is the humblest. On another occasion, when an ambitious mother specifically requested that her two sons be given priority in Jesus' organization, he expressly refused the request and prohibited such "exercise" of "authority" as was later claimed for Simon Peter. Jesus said, "You know that the rulers of the Gentiles lord it over them, and their great men exercise authority over them. It shall not be so among you; but whoever would be great among you must be your servant, and whoever would be first among you must be your slave; even as the Son of man came not to be served but to serve, and to give his life as a ransom for many" (Matt. 20:25–28 RSV). It is unthinkable that Jesus intended to imply that the keys of the kingdom and the binding and the loosing should be tied to any view of the authority or the primacy of Peter, his successors, or an institution that would claim to admit or exclude people from heaven. The passages involved do relate the church to the forgiveness of sins through its faithful proclamation of the message of Jesus Christ.

Conclusion

Jesus said to us in the church, "I give you the keys." Will you faithfully proclaim the gospel of forgiveness so that people may enter the kingdom?

WEDNESDAY EVENING, MARCH 5

Title: The Bible Speaks to Our Condition

Scripture Reading: Luke 21

Introduction

With eyes open for truth and with ears attuned to listen to God, let us approach this great and perplexing chapter from Luke's gospel.

The events described and the teachings recorded in Luke 21 come from the last week of our Lord's life. The events described follow his triumphal entry into Jerusalem and precede his arrest, trials, and crucifixion by a matter of hours.

I. Commendation for a spirit of sacrifice (Luke 21:1–4).

Our Lord was watchful as the people made their contributions to the temple treasury. He beheld the manner and the motive behind their gifts. Without criticizing the rich who came giving generously, he highly commended the widow who gave sacrificially. He was particularly impressed with the fact that she gave to the extent that there was nothing remaining for her.

What attitude does our Lord have toward our spirit of giving? How much sacrifice is involved in our giving?

II. The danger of being deceived (Luke 21:5–9).

In all ages, people have been subject to deception. We can be deceived by others, by the devil, and by ourselves. Our Lord warned his disciples against the peril of listening to false messiahs.

III. On a collision course with catastrophe (Luke 21:10–24).

This particular passage is difficult for the casual reader to understand. Our Lord uses apocalyptic language to communicate truths to his disciples that were easier for them to understand than for the modern reader. Apocalyptic language was used by Hebrew sages and prophets to express their hopes and dreams for a divine, dramatic manifestation of God's work, particularly in a time of national stress. Often Jewish prophets and writers used apocalyptic terminology to describe the ultimate consummation of the ages.

The verses under consideration deal both with the catastrophe that Jerusalem faces and with the final windup of human history. Because our Lord is speaking about both of these events, the casual reader may be confused. However, several thoughts and impressions come through clearly as we read this passage.

A. *Disciples of our Lord are always exposed to trouble.* These were facing the possibility of imprisonment and persecution from both the Jewish authorities and from pagan kings and governors (Luke 21:12).

B. *A time of testimony (Luke 21:13–15).* Whatever life brings, followers of Christ should look for opportunities to give verbal testimony of their experience with Jesus Christ. God will bless their efforts. We should trust the Holy Spirit for leadership when the opportunity occurs.

C. *Enduring faithfulness leads to ultimate victory (Luke 21:19).* There will be trouble along the way. Persecution or injury may be our lot. Our ultimate security is with God. The faithful will be rewarded even if martyred.

D. *Jerusalem was to be destroyed (Luke 21:20–24).* Israel rejected their Messiah and God's plan for their national life. Instead of being a missionary force among the nations of the world, Israel had retreated into narrow, nationalistic exclusiveness. Israel refused to be a channel through which the

76

message and grace of God could reach the world. By their rejection of God's plan, they chose a pathway that was leading to disaster.

IV. Victory belongs to the Lord (Luke 21:25–28).

In apocalyptic language, our Lord spoke of the consummation of history. In a time when the nation was being threatened by the power of Rome, the followers of Christ were to recognize that above and behind it all, the Lord would rule sovereign and supreme.

V. Be alert and ready (Luke 21:29–36).

The overwhelming impression that comes through this passage is that each disciple of the Lord Jesus should live each day in readiness for the final victorious return of Jesus Christ. We should not be overly concerned about the day-by-day events that precede his coming. We should concentrate on being faithful and obedient and let God take care of the ultimate outcome.

VI. In the presence of God and among the people (Luke 21:37–38).

At night our Lord drew aside that he might go into his Father's presence. In the early morning, our Lord went among the crowds to be their Teacher, Comforter, Healer, and Guide.

Conclusion

If we would face the trials and trouble and fears of the present, we need to spend time in the presence of our Father God. Each day we should find a place of retreat and solitude in order that we might let God speak to our condition.

SUNDAY MORNING, MARCH 9

Title: Jesus Changed People's Lives

Text: "Zacchaeus stood, and said unto the Lord; Behold, Lord, the half of my goods I give to the poor; and if I have taken anything from any man by false accusation, I restore him fourfold" **(Luke 19:8)**.

Scripture Reading: Luke 19:1–10

Hymns: "Stand Up, Stand Up for Jesus," Duffield

"Since I Have Been Redeemed," Excell

"Standing on the Promises," Carter

Offertory Prayer: Our Father, we are grateful that we know you are with us in every circumstance of life. We pray that you will help us to recognize our dependence on you, on your saving help, on your guidance, and on your forgiveness. Help us now as we bring our tithes and offerings to you to rejoice in the privilege of giving. We ask your blessing on all the causes our gifts support. Bless your servants who are laboring in places that are difficult or dangerous. Use our gifts in the proclamation of your gospel, and use us as personal witnesses for Christ in the place where we live. We pray these things in Jesus' name. Amen.

Introduction

The last six months of Jesus' ministry were busy days for him. As was pointed out last week, Luke's gospel majors on this period. Luke 9:51 through 18:14 contains the record of events that occurred during this time. The parallel section John 7:2–11:54 records the happenings in this same period. Although it cannot be irrefutably established, in all probability the material beginning with Matthew 19:1 and Mark 10:1 occurred in this latter part of Jesus' ministry after he left Galilee as a sphere of operations. Luke records much more of this latter period of Jesus' activities than Matthew or Mark because they major on the Galilean ministry. The fact that some of Jesus' words seem to be repetitions of things he said during his Galilean ministry does not reflect on their integrity. It is inconceivable that Jesus would not have repeated himself on numbers of occasions as he taught, for he met people with similar problems and questions. Jesus touched the lives of many people during this last six months of his ministry. Perhaps the most significant of all, however, was his visit to Jericho. Luke's gospel tells of a blind man who cried for mercy and how Jesus restored his sight. Immediately following this account, we have Zacchaeus's life-changing story.

I. The money-mad man.

Zacchaeus was a tax collector. Tax collectors were perhaps the greediest of all the Jews. The Roman government had a system of farming out tax-collecting privileges. They would select a Jew and give him the authority to collect taxes in a district. Anything he collected over the stipulated fee to the Roman government would belong to him. Naturally, this encouraged greed on his part, and therefore the temptation was to be overbearing with his fellow countrymen. Zacchaeus, as a publican, or tax collector, was no doubt one of the most unpopular men in Jericho. He must have been a lonely man, as the people surely had ostracized him from their social lives. One writer suggests with creative imagination that perhaps Zacchaeus lived in the last house on a dead-end street and that he had a large fence or hedge around his home. It was strictly private, for no one ever came to see him.

II. The man with lonesome longings.

Surely Zacchaeus wanted a better life. No one could have remained happy under such conditions. In the early stages of greedy money hoarding, a person may believe he is securing happiness. Later, however, he realizes that the things of true value in life are not material. Zacchaeus had undoubtedly heard that those who came in contact with Jesus went away changed. Perhaps Zacchaeus thought to himself that he, too, would find a new life if he saw Jesus. Curiosity was probably one motive in Zacchaeus's climbing the tree to see Jesus, but he also had a higher motivation. Perhaps someone had told him about the woman who had merely touched Jesus' garment and was healed. Zacchaeus may have reasoned that if Jesus could do that, something similar might happen if he climbed the sycamore tree and saw Jesus as he passed. When a person is in desperate circumstances, he will "grab at any straw" he thinks can help him. Life was crowding in on Zacchaeus, and he followed the only course he knew to guarantee a personal glimpse of Jesus and perhaps a glance or even a word in return from the one who had changed the lives of so many people.

III. The Savior's sudden statement.

How surprised Zacchaeus must have been when Jesus spoke his name! But how much more surprised he was at the words that followed! Jesus was going to Zacchaeus's house for a visit! Luke does not tell us many of the details that we would love to know. The short man hurrying down the tree must have made some of the people laugh unless they were among those who were filled with jealousy at the personal attention Jesus was showing to Zacchaeus. Although the text does not state the fact definitely, we gain the impression that Jesus had a meal with Zacchaeus.

When did the change in Zacchaeus occur? Was it the minute he saw Jesus and obeyed his voice? Was it as they walked along the way toward Zacchaeus's home? Was it as they broke bread together and Jesus led the family in prayer? Was it as they sat together in Zacchaeus's home and talked about spiritual things and the possibility of a new start for this one who had messed up his life so badly? We do not know when the change came, but we do know that it came!

IV. The meaning of conversion.

Salvation is more than an external transaction regarding God and a human being whereby the latter has a new standing with the Lord. When people are truly converted, change takes place in every area of their lives. They become new creatures in Christ Jesus. The things they once loved they begin to hate. The things they once despised they begin to love. They have a new sense of values. Their priorities are different. Their very reason for living changes. Zacchaeus revealed by his testimony that a transformation had taken place. He began with an act of benevolence — he would give half of his possessions to the poor. To the Jewish people, nothing indicated godliness more than one's willingness to help those who were underprivileged. Zacchaeus's second evidence of conversion was his willingness to make restitution where he had wronged his fellow Jews. The Mosaic law only required that a person restore twofold, but Zacchaeus went far beyond the command. We have no way of knowing what a "dent" this put in Zacchaeus's personal fortune. It could have taken most of his material net worth. There is no evidence that Jesus required him to make such a strong statement of his intention. It could be that Jesus, however, pointed out to him the necessity for stripping himself of that which had come to be his god — personal wealth. Jesus made an even greater demand on the rich young ruler. God does not require all believers to make such a radical distribution of their earthly possessions. There are many whose besetting sin is in another realm. Before people can experience true conversion, however, they must look at themselves honestly and turn over to Jesus their entire lives. This involves a surrender of anything and everything that stands between themselves and complete commitment to Christ.

V. A reaffirmation of Christ's mission.

Verse 10 contains Jesus' words, not Luke's comment. This occasion gave our Savior a marvelous opportunity to give a comprehensive statement concerning his ministry. There is probably no finer summary of Jesus' purpose in coming to the world than these words. Jesus came to save, but he did more. He came to seek those whom he would save. Our Master is always taking the first step toward the sinner. He took the first step when he went to the cross of Calvary. He takes other steps toward sinners long before they move toward him. Through the Holy Spirit, he leads friends to witness to the lost. He leads people to write tracts, build church buildings, and make personal visits and many other avenues of approach to lost humanity. This is Jesus "seeking" the lost today. How marvelous to know that the Savior is still at work! No one is too sinful for him. He loves us all. We should remember, however, that although he does love us, we must be willing to make radical changes in our lives and attitudes as a manifestation of our sorrow for sin and genuine repentance. We must not be merely sorry that we are caught in our sinning; we must be sorry enough for sin that we will forsake it. We will never live perfect lives, for this is impossible. Even after we become Christians, we are still human beings. The Master came, however, to put within us a new heart and a new spirit. Zacchaeus, after this experience, could have testified in the words of the songwriter, "No one ever cared for me like Jesus." Jesus came to earth because he loved and because his Father loved. God continues to love us today, and his greatest desire is that lost people repent of their sins and turn in saving faith to Jesus Christ.

Conclusion

Can a human life be changed? Some say that once the pattern of life is set, nothing can be done about it. The message of Jesus Christ says that human life is the one thing that can be changed. The stars are fixed in their courses. The laws of nature are immutable. Humankind's free will, however, guarantees their ability to make choices that alter their outlook, attitude, and way of life.

SUNDAY EVENING, MARCH 9

Title: The Church as the Community of Forgiveness

Text: "Therefore, as God's chosen people, holy and dearly loved, clothe your-selves with compassion, kindness, humility, gentleness and patience. Bear with each other and forgive whatever grievances you may have against one another. Forgive as the Lord forgave you" **(Col. 3:12–13 NIV)**.

Scripture Reading: Colossians 3

Introduction

The church is a community of the "forgiven." People may join a church only if they come through the door of the forgiveness of sins. All people have sinned against God and have thereby suffered estrangement from him. God's call to repentance is a call for people to come back to him; people do this only by accepting God's gracious forgiveness. It goes without saying that we Christians should have real joy in the acknowledgment that when we were in sin, Christ forgave us. This witness constitutes one of our strongest appeals to those who have not yet been forgiven.

I. A church is a community of "forgiving" people.

In the Sermon on the Mount, Jesus said, "For if you forgive men their trespasses, your heavenly Father will also forgive you; but if you do not forgive men their trespasses, neither will your Father forgive your trespasses" (Matt. 6:14–15 RSV). On another occasion, Jesus was asked how many times a Christian should forgive an offending person. There was an old adage that a righteous person might forgive someone as much as seven times in a day. Jesus required his followers to forgive not seven times in a day, but seventy times seven times (Matt. 18:21; Luke 17:3).

It is also important to recognize the role of forgiving in the Christian life. It is universally acknowledged that Christians, regrettably, sin after conversion (1 John 1:9). But when they do, Christ forgives them, and they mutually sustain each other by forgiving one another (Eph. 4:32; Col. 3:13). When Christians worship, they confess their sins and accept forgiveness. If Christians are genuinely true to their nature, it may be said of them, "Behold how they forgive one another!"

II. The church is committed to a ministry of forgiveness.

In the writings of Paul, forgiveness is the same as reconciliation, and he refers to the church as having the "ministry of reconciliation" (2 Cor. 5:18). The church exercises the ministry by proclaiming "the message of reconciliation" (v. 19). As the church proclaims this message, and as its members live the example of forgiving, they show estranged sinners the gracious forgiveness of God.

III. As Christ's body on earth, the church is concerned for people.

The church heals its own members by forgiving them, and it restores people to healthy human relations by forgiveness. When the church forgets its ministry of healing by forgiveness and clamors over principles instead of witnessing to people, it abandons its task. All around us there are people burdened down to the point of collapse by guilt for their own sins. Families are divided; individuals are crushed; institutions are torn by controversy. The only cure for these situations is for the persons to forgive one another. The church knows how to forgive and proclaims the message of forgiveness.

Conclusion

Men and women without faith in Jesus Christ live their lives in lostness. Believers who know God's forgiveness and who will share God's message of forgiveness stand as their only hope. When the church is faithful in its ministry of proclaiming forgiveness, it opens the door of heaven.

WEDNESDAY EVENING, MARCH 12

Title: The Bible Speaks to Our Condition

Scripture Reading: John 4

Introduction

Today's chapter is one of the great chapters of John's gospel of love. The events of this chapter had a profound effect on the lives and ministry of the apostles. By these words and events, our Lord was speaking to his apostles and to his future followers. John, the writer of this gospel, under the inspiration of the Holy Spirit, selected these events that help prove that Jesus is indeed the Christ and that people can find eternal life through faith in him.

I. The scope of our Lord's loving concern.

Very few chapters in the New Testament reveal the scope of our Lord's concern for all people as does this chapter.

A. *Loving concern for the Samaritans (John 4:4–42).* The revolutionary nature of our Lord's love is revealed in his experience with a Samaritan woman who had a very low moral standard, even among the Samaritans. Our Lord entered into dialogue with this woman who was ostracized by Jews because of her sex, race, and religion. He was eager to make available to her the fountains of living water from which she could quench the thirst of her soul.

It was not because of a desire to make a hasty trip from Judea to Galilee that our Lord decided to go through Samaria (4:4). Rather, he deliberately went through this area that was avoided by orthodox Jews in order that he might register divine concern for a disenfranchised people.

B. *Loving concern for Jewish people (John 4:43–45).* Christ was returning from Jerusalem to Galilee. He was genuinely concerned about his nation and about the people whom God had chosen to be the instruments of his redemptive love.

C. *Loving concern for Gentiles (John 4:46–54).* The text does not declare that the officer was a Gentile, but it implies such. Perhaps he was very sympathetic toward the Jewish faith and the Jewish people. He had heard about Jesus. He felt a desperate need for the help of the Christ and came searching and pleading for his assistance. In response to the Gentile official's plea for mercy and assistance, our Lord revealed his concern and performed a miracle of healing.

Our Lord's love crossed all natural and artificial barriers that normally separate people. If we are to be his true followers today, we must have a universal concern for the needs of all people.

82

II. The spirituality of worship (John 4:21–24).

We should not assume that places dedicated to prayer and worship were considered to be unimportant by our Lord. However, in his conversation with the Samaritan woman, he emphasized that worship is the response of the heart to God rather than merely going to a place and observing certain rituals or ceremonies.

Our Lord declared that God is Spirit and that they who worship him must worship him in spirit and in truth.

Genuine worship is a spiritual response to a spiritual God. As the instrument of the Spirit, the body with all of its faculties is to be put at God's disposal.

We can rejoice in the fact that God is accessible to us in all places, at all times, and under all possible circumstances. God is not limited to a specific place and to a particular time. He is always present and always available to those who will worship him in spirit and in truth.

III. The joy of the harvest (John 4:35–42).

Our Lord used terminology that was appropriate to his listeners. Here he speaks in terms of people in need of the grace of God as being compared to a harvest field ready to be harvested. He emphasizes the perennial nature of the spiritual harvest.

Jesus saw the Samaritan people as people who were hungry for and eager to respond to the good news of God's universal love.

Some serve as sowers and others serve as reapers. In the end, God will reward each according to his or her labors. The spiritual harvest will have eternal significance for those who labor in the fields for the Lord.

IV. The avenue of faith (John 4:46–54).

In this miracle of healing, our Lord emphasized the necessity of faith in the person, the presence, and the power of God. Our Lord responded to the deep sense of need and to the faith the official focused on him.

The Lord revealed his power to heal at a distance without being present to actually touch the body of the one who has sick.

As a result of the man's faith, Christ was provided an avenue through which he could work, not only upon the man's son, but also within his household.

When Jesus returned to Nazareth, he was unable to do many mighty works because of the unbelief of the people. This is perhaps the explanation for the failure of so many of us today. We either refuse to believe or we neglect to believe in the promises and in the power of our Lord.

Conclusion

A survey of the Bible and a consideration of Christian history will reveal that the spiritual giants who have walked across the stage have been men and women who out-believed their contemporaries. Through this great chapter, God encourages us to have a greater faith.

SUNDAY MORNING, MARCH 16

Title: Jesus Founded His Church

Text: "Upon this rock I will build my church; and the gates of hell shall not prevail against it" **(Matt. 16:18)**.

Scripture Reading: Matthew 16:13–18

Hymns: "The Church's One Foundation," Stone

"Faith of Our Fathers," Faber

"I Love Thy Kingdom, Lord," Dwight

Offertory Prayer: Our Father, you have taught us that our hearts will be where our treasures are. Give us, therefore, the divine grace and the personal wisdom to lay up our treasures in heaven in order that our interests on earth may be in spiritual things. By your generosity, we have received all that we have. Help us to use the things that have been entrusted to our care in a way that may make us more truly your servants. May we ever hold before our minds the truth that as you have blessed us so we should seek to be a blessing to others. May our gifts be used here in our own church and to the uttermost part of the world for the building up of your kingdom in the hearts of people. We pray in Jesus' name. Amen.

Introduction

During Jesus' Galilean ministry, he took his disciples on several retreats away from the thronging crowds. The purpose of the retreats was twofold. First, the disciples need physical rest. Second, Jesus desired to instruct them more thoroughly in order that they could carry on his work after he left.

One of those retreats was as far away as Caesarea Philippi, quite a number of miles north of the Sea of Galilee and not far from Mount Hermon, the probable site of the transfiguration, which occurred a few days later. Jesus had been with the disciples for some time now, and he wished to know how much they understood concerning his nature. His first question was a general one. He probably was not as much interested in knowing what the multitudes thought of him as he was in knowing how the disciples felt and how they interpreted the ideas of the masses. The first question paved the way for the more intimate second question.

Simon Peter had a way of speaking first whether he knew the correct answer or not. This time, however, he was exactly right. Jesus assured him that his answer had not come on the basis of human knowledge. It was revealed to him by the Father—and for a particular purpose. Jesus used it as the basis on which to instruct his disciples more clearly and to give them a foundation for evangelization.

I. The foundation of the church.

Peter said that Jesus was the "Christ, the Son of the living God." The word *Christ* means "Messiah," or "Anointed One," and this means that Simon Peter

84

was recognizing Jesus as the one whom God had promised to send to his people. But Peter said more. He identified the Messiah as the Son of God. There was not complete agreement among all Jews concerning the coming Messiah. There was not even a unanimous understanding among the people that the Messiah would necessarily be equal with the Father. As there are various ideas and understandings of the Scripture today concerning the second coming of Jesus, there were various ideas concerning the first coming of Jesus, based on interpretations of Old Testament passages. Simon Peter's statement, however, rang loud and clear: Jesus of Nazareth was the Son of God. Implicit in his statement are all the later teachings we have concerning the complete equality of the Son with the Father and the complete deity of the Savior. It was indeed a marvelous confession!

Jesus said that he would build his church on the fact that he is the Son of God. There have been various understandings as to the exact meaning of Jesus' words. Some have felt that Jesus made a play on words in his statement. *Peter* means "rock" in the Greek language. Some have suggested that the difference in the two Greek words used for rock in the text means that Jesus was saying to Peter that he is a "movable" type of rock, but he (Jesus) is the solid Rock that cannot be moved. There may be a basis in the text for such an interpretation. Others have felt that Jesus meant that he would build his church on Peter's confession or even on Peter's faith and therefore on the faith of others who would come along with and after Peter in accepting this truth. Whatever shade of interpretation we give to the confession, one thing is certain: the church of Jesus Christ is built on the fact of his complete deity and his equality with God the Father. Jesus was born of a virgin and possessed a unique nature, and although he identified himself with man, he was nevertheless God in the flesh.

The church is built on this truth, and when any local congregation minimizes it, the truth of Scripture is compromised. Unless a church believes in the deity of Christ, it will seek to win the lost in vain. When a church falters on this truth, it is not long before the church is compromising in other areas. It is important that every minister and every teacher maintain the fundamental truth about Jesus—he is the Son of God.

II. The nature of the church.

The word translated "church" comes from a Greek word that means literally "called out," and this is the true nature of Christ's church. It is composed of those who have been called out from sin and the world and have been made new people in Jesus Christ. This same word is translated "assembly" in Acts 19:41.

The church consists of born-again believers. When Jesus spoke of his church in this passage, he was speaking, of course, in terms of a concept. There were no buildings or church organizations as we know them today. It was later that people gathered themselves together in local congregations and constituted assemblies known as churches. In the New Testament, we read of the "church at Corinth" or the "church at Ephesus" or "the churches at Galatia." These churches were visible bodies and consisted of born-again people. The ideal for our churches today is that every member of each local assembly be a born-again Christian. No one should be admitted to membership in a local body unless he or she has had a genuine experience of regeneration. There have been times in the history of Christianity when people were required to tell of their personal experience with Christ in salvation before they were admitted to membership in the local church. Unfortunately, some congregations have been more lax and have failed many times to require or even to emphasize the new birth experience as a prerequisite to membership in the local group. If we follow such a practice, we lose our influence with nonbelievers.

There are a few places in the New Testament where the church is spoken of in a general institutional sense rather than as a local body. This is similar to the way in which we speak of "the Christian home" in America. Each Christian home in America is a separate entity even though we speak of "the Christian home" in our nation. Likewise, our churches today are local, visible bodies even though we sometimes speak of the church in a general sense.

Some people speak of "the church universal," meaning all saved people regardless of their affiliation, or lack of it, with a local congregation. This is sometimes spoken of as the "universal" church, or the "catholic" church. Protestants today speak of the "holy catholic church," while the Roman Catholic Church speaks of their church as the "Roman" Catholic Church. The expression "kingdom of God" may also be used to refer to the universal body of saved believers. Many people believe this is a better expression to describe the invisible body of believers.

Whatever terminology we use to describe the church, we should remember that the church is composed of people who have had a personal experience with Jesus. The words "called out" signify that those who comprise Christ's church are different from the world. Christ has forgiven their sins, and their lives should reflect this change.

III. The promise to the church.

Jesus gave a great assurance to his church. He said, "The gates of hell shall not prevail against it." Many have seen this passage as Jesus' promise that the church will never go out of existence. It will remain until his second coming. This may be what Jesus meant in this passage, but there is another possible interpretation. When the church goes on the offensive, the forces of hell will not be able to withstand the onslaught of Christian people banded together in militant action. In other words, the church is not on the defense. The church is marching under the orders of Christ. The combined forces of evil will not be able to resist this onward march. This interpretation magnifies the conquering power of the church under the leadership of the Holy Spirit in today's world.

Conclusion

Are you a member of Christ's church? Have you had an experience with him that has caused a transformation in your life? You should belong to a local congregation and invest your talents in the work of Christ through that church. No church is perfect. This is because churches are made of people, and no people are without fault. Your life will be better, however, if you will find a place of service in a local congregation with fellow believers.

Joining a local church does not bring personal salvation. Salvation comes only through an experience with the Savior. There is great value, however, in being associated with other Christians in a local body. If you are not a church member, will you give serious consideration to belonging to a church? This is, of course, on the condition that you have been saved. If you have not been saved, your first step is to receive Jesus as personal Savior.

Those who are church members should give loyalty to the church where they belong. To move from one church to another Sunday after Sunday does not deepen one's life nearly as much as finding a place of service in one church and being loyal to that church. This does not mean that there are not legitimate times when we can visit other churches. On the whole, however, our loyalty should be to the congregation where we hold our membership.

SUNDAY EVENING, MARCH 16

Title: The Keys of the Kingdom: A Blessing and a Burden

Text: "And I will give unto thee the keys of the kingdom of heaven: and whatsoever thou shalt bind on earth shall be bound in heaven: and whatsoever thou shalt loose on earth shall be loosed in heaven" **(Matt. 16:19)**.

"Verily I say unto you, Whatsoever ye shall bind on earth shall be bound in heaven: and whatsoever ye shall loose on earth shall be loosed in heaven" **(Matt. 18:18)**.

"Whose soever sins ye remit, they are remitted unto them; and whose soever sins ye retain, they are retained" **(John 20:23)**.

Scripture Reading: Matthew 16:13–20

Introduction

Each one of us who has faith in Jesus Christ knows the joy of being forgiven. We recall the burden of sin and the guilt that hung on our consciences. Then someone witnessed to us about the promise of Jesus Christ and we came to know the forgiveness of our sins. Liberation from bondage resulted in a joy unspeakable. To be forgiven is to live a life of blessing.

I. The blessing of the keys.

A. *Sharing forgiveness.* It would be difficult to exaggerate the blessing of being able to share this message and promise of God with others who are burdened by sin. Along the route of our pilgrimage, we meet many people who are burdened down by their sin but who come to experience the joy we know merely by our witnessing to them. Can you imagine a greater blessing than to be in a position such as this—a position in which we can share the unsearchable riches of Christ so freely? This is what it means to have the "keys of the kingdom."

To be able to forgive another is a tremendous blessing. There are people who live their lives under the severe burden of a grudge. There are those who fool themselves into saying, "I forgive him, but I cannot forget." To remember the sins of another is to refuse to forgive that person. The person who does not forgive an offender will live in bondage and bitterness. To forgive another is to get rid of those shackles and be free.

B. *Forgiveness cures sin.* Along the journey we meet people whose lives are distorted by sin. Sometimes the life that is distorted has also distorted that of a family and other relationships. When we faithfully witness for Jesus Christ to such persons, we may see the complete transformation of their lives and the resultant transformation of their families. The Christian senses a joy comparable to that of a physician who by using his or her skills restores a sick person to health. In our case, however, the transaction is eternal. It is a blessing beyond description to be able to witness to such a person; this is the legitimate use of the keys.

II. The burden of the keys.

But it also follows that the possession of the keys imposes a tremendous burden. Those of us who know the forgiveness of God are under the burden of sharing that good news with others by our teaching, witnessing, and forgiving. To know the forgiveness of God and to refuse to share it with others is an unspeakable crime.

Since we do know the message of forgiveness and have the assurance that God will forgive sinners, we are under the burden of having to be faithful to that witness, available to those who need forgiveness, and sensitive to those people around us. In short, this means that we are "not our own" but that we belong to Christ. Therefore we must give ourselves as he gave himself.

Possession of the keys may tempt some people to be presumptuous. If this is so, a word of warning should be sufficient. When we meet in our churches to pray, sing, worship, and hear the Word of God, we need to be reminded that we are holding the keys of the kingdom of heaven. The decisions are binding in heaven. These decisions are made in response to the church as it witnesses about God's forgiveness. When the church is faithful in its witness, it actually opens the doors for people to enter into God's presence.

When people who are mentally or emotionally ill go to a psychiatrist, they receive the best treatment the psychiatrist can give. However, they must often be sent back into the situation that produced their illness in the first place. In the church, however, we surround new Christians with brothers and sisters who love and know how to forgive. In that context, they can recover from their sin and grow into strong people. There is no setting in the world like that of Christian fellowship in which people can be made whole.

Conclusion

Jesus says to us in the church, "I give you the keys of the kingdom of heaven. If you are faithful in your ministry, the door is open and they will enter. What will you do?"

WEDNESDAY EVENING, MARCH 19

Title: The Bible Speaks to Our Condition

Scripture Reading: John 11

Introduction

When John wrote his gospel, he was inspired by the Holy Spirit to select certain great events in the life of our Lord that indicated something unique about the nature and purpose of the Lord Jesus Christ (John 20:30). Each of the great miracles was something more than a miraculous event; each taught a lesson. They were designed to reveal something to the hearts of people concerning Jesus Christ and God's great purpose in and through his life and ministry.

Besides our Lord's death and resurrection, perhaps the most significant sign concerning our Lord is the raising of Lazarus from the dead.

I. A disclosure of the power of the Son of God (John 11:4, 25–26, 40–44).

In this great chapter, we are confronted with mystery and miracle. There is no way to explain this event except on a supernatural level. Christ revealed his lordship over physical death and his power to restore physical life. He did this to declare that he also had power to impart the gift of eternal life.

II. The creation of faith (John 11:15, 45).

Our Lord used the death of his friend Lazarus as an occasion to deepen the faith of his disciples and to create faith in the hearts of those who did not yet have faith.

Without faith, it is impossible to please God. Without faith, we face life with human resources alone. Without faith, we hesitate to attempt to do anything above and beyond what common sense would dictate.

Our Lord recognized that we needed faith in the greatness and goodness of our God. Through this miracle of raising Lazarus, he would strengthen our faith in both the goodness and power of our Lord.

III. The devotion of a disciple (John 11:16).

In the midst of this great chapter is a verse that reveals the devotion of a disciple that could be easily overlooked by the casual reader. Thomas, who is often criticized because of his doubts, here reveals the depth of his devotion and the extent of his loyalty. He recognized the danger our Lord would be facing if he returned to Bethany, yet he was willing to face that risk with the Lord, even if it meant a tragic death. He encouraged the other disciples to join with him as he journeyed with the Lord into dangerous territory. Are we willing to risk our lives out of devotion and loyalty to our Lord?

IV. The sorrow of the Savior (John 11:35).

One of the most beautiful pictures of our Lord to be found in all of the Holy Word is in these two words that make up the Bible's shortest verse. Our Lord wept in the midst of their sorrow and agony. We are not going too far when we assume that he weeps with us when we weep and suffers with us when we suffer. He is a compassionate Savior.

V. The victory of life over death (John 11:43).

Jesus teaches that instead of living to die, by divine grace we die to begin really living. Lazarus's restoration to physical life is but a prophecy of our resurrection to an eternal life that will never end. The body will perish, but the spirit will continue to live in a new body that will not be subject to disease or death (John 11:25–26; 1 Cor. 15:49–57).

Conclusion

Through this miraculous event, our Lord speaks to us today and helps us overcome our fear of death. He seeks to relieve our anxiety about those who have entered death ahead of us. He assures us that life, rather than death, is permanent.

SUNDAY MORNING, MARCH 23

Title: Jesus Is Coming Again

Text: "This same Jesus, which is taken up from you into heaven, shall so come in like manner" (**Acts 1:11**).

Scripture Reading: Acts 1:1–11

Hymns: "Praise Him! Praise Him!" Crosby

"He Lives on High," McKinney

"We'll Work Till Jesus Comes," Mills

Offertory Prayer: Our heavenly Father, we bow our heads and our hearts in your presence to remind ourselves again that we are dependent on you not only for the necessities of life but for life itself. You have been our dwelling place in all generations. You have been our help in years that are gone. You are our hope for days yet to come. We are yours today, and we must give every moment to you. This is the part of the service where we bring our tithes and offerings that the work of Christ might be carried on here in our own congregation, among our own people, and through our mission causes to the ends of the earth. Bless those today who are serving Christ in places that are difficult, and be in a very special way with those who are serving where it is dangerous. May we feel a kinship this morning through our gifts with everyone who is proclaiming the saving name of Christ to those who do not know him. We pray these things in Jesus' name. Amen.

Introduction

Although Jesus had discouraged his followers from expecting a temporal kingdom, the idea was so deeply ingrained in them that they could not forget it. After his resurrection, Jesus was seen by them for forty days. He showed by many infallible proofs that he was alive, and he spoke to them of things pertaining to God's kingdom. The final question recorded as coming from the disciples to Jesus was an inquiry concerning the restoration of the Jewish monarchy. Jesus gave them a mild reprimand. The Father has the future planned, and we are not to worry ourselves with that which he has reserved for himself. The true task of the believer is to be a witness for Christ, beginning where he is and reaching out as far as his influence and resources will carry him. The disciples were promised a visit of enabling power to assist them in the proclamation of the gospel message.

As he finished speaking, while they were still watching, Jesus was taken up into heaven. The onlookers stood by in wonderment, and two heavenly messengers spoke to them. Their words consisted of a firm declaration that Jesus would return to earth in the same way he ascended into heaven. Nothing is clearer or plainer. Jesus of Nazareth ascended in the flesh. It is true that he had a glorified body, but he was the Jesus whom they knew. This same Jesus is going to return. This message has found itself being proclaimed over and over through the centuries. It is the hope of Christian people for vindication in this world of sin.

I. The fact of Christ's coming.

Christianity was revealed to the world in a historical situation. Likewise, it will be consummated within a historical framework. Spiritual truth has been brought to the world within the context of historical fact. The vehicle by which the message is brought contains accurate information regarding the environment in which the message lived and came to fruition.

The return of Jesus to earth is not something about which people speculated and believed *should* happen. It is that which God, through his divinely inspired Word, has said *will* happen. God's Word makes it abundantly clear. One has only to look at books such as Matthew (24:30, 44), Luke (21:25, 27), 1 Thessalonians (1:10; 3:13; 4:16–17; 5:1–2, 6), 2 Thessalonians (1:7–10; 3:5), Hebrews (9:27–28), and 2 Peter (3:10–14) to see that God's Word is clear on the subject.

It is significant that there has recently been a renewed emphasis of, and interest in, the return of the Lord. The Second Coming has always been prominent in fundamentalist circles, but this revival of interest is present among many modern liberal and neoorthodox writers as well. The blessed hope of Christ's coming is being seen by more and more people as the only hope for our confused and troubled world. Human ingenuity has failed to solve the world's problems, and many thoughtful people are coming to the conclusion that although we still need to work to solve our problems in everyday living, the only permanent solution will be God's intervention by the sending of Jesus Christ back to the world to consummate history.

II. The purpose of Christ's coming.

The return of Christ to earth will reveal his infinite glory and majesty. In the days of his flesh, he often limited himself and did not express the fullness of his divine glory. At his second appearance, however, every eye shall see him in the fullness of the divine majesty that is his as the second person of the Trinity.

At his coming, he will receive his saints. We shall be caught up in the clouds and forever be with him. At that moment, the dead in Christ shall receive their new glorified bodies. Those who are living at the time of his coming will be transformed immediately and be given their glorious bodies. The redeemed family of God shall be received unto Jesus and shall "ever be with the Lord" (1 Thess. 4:17).

At Jesus' coming, he will reject unbelievers. It will be a time for judgment for those who refused to receive him as personal Savior. The Bible says that the ones whose names are not written in the Lamb's Book of Life will be cast into a lake of fire. Eternal punishment awaits all who refused to submit themselves to Jesus as Lord.

III. The nearness of Christ's coming.

There are many signs that the coming of Christ will be soon. The Jews have been restored to their homeland and are now once more a nation. Although there are various ideas concerning the program of events at the coming of Jesus, one thing is clear: the second coming of Jesus is always very closely associated with the return of the Jews to their homeland. They are now there! The nations of the world have divided themselves on the basis of whether they are pro-Israel or anti-Israel. All of this seems to be pointing to a great battle in which Israel will be the central figure.

Moral and spiritual conditions have deteriorated as the Bible writers predicted would happen immediately before the coming of Jesus. Of course, the world has always offered enticements to people, and in every generation there have been those who turned away from God. In this day, however, it seems we have unparalleled falling away from godly living. This age of permissiveness has come upon us with a force that leaves us baffled as to how we can contend with it. Wickedness in high places threatens our national life. The same is true with other nations.

There is a turning away from sound doctrine as the Bible predicted would occur. People have little or no interest in spiritual things. They follow clever and cunningly devised fables and leave the Word of God. A return to paganism in the midst of a sophisticated society shocks those who believe in the integrity of God's written Word.

It looks as though the coming of Christ is near. Every sign points toward it.

IV. Preparation for Christ's coming.

There is only one way to be saved. The door of mercy is open now. Christ stands as our Counselor. He will intercede for us if we will turn ourselves over to him in complete surrender and trust. The preparation for his coming is to "repent of sin and trust in Christ as personal Savior." This is the only way to be safe in that day when he will come again. If we receive him as Savior, we will be one of those who join him in the sky at his coming. We will have transformed bodies. If we are in graves as those asleep in Christ, we will be awakened by the trumpet sound and be immediately raised up with new and glorified bodies. If we remain until his coming and are saved, our earthly bodies will be transformed that they might become like his glorious body (Phil. 3:21).

Conclusion

There are many schools of thought with reference to the program that shall occur at the coming of Christ. There is no possible way in one sermon to harmonize all of these various interpretations. The Bible is clear, however, beyond the shadow of a doubt on one thing: Jesus is coming again. He is coming personally, visibly, in the same manner he left and for the purpose of revealing his glory, receiving his saints, and rejecting unbelievers.

The business of Christians is to wait, witness, and work until Jesus comes. Lost people need to repent before the day of judgment comes. Jesus is Savior now, but if he is rejected, his presence will be a terror to those who have ignored his plea of grace.

Non-Christians should not be disturbed about the order of events that will occur at Jesus' coming. There always have been disagreements among sincere Christians concerning events that will take place at Christ's second coming, and there always will be until he comes again. The wise course is to trust Christ as Savior now. In-depth Bible study concerning this and other subjects should be a part of Christian growth, but becoming a Christian by receiving Jesus as Savior is a priority.

Sunday Evening, March 23

Title: The Forgiving Father

Text: "It was meet that we should make merry, and be glad; for this thy brother was dead, and is alive again; and was lost, and is found" **(Luke 15:32)**.

Scripture Reading: Luke 15

Introduction

Luke records four of Jesus' parables in chapter 15 of his gospel. These parables tell about a lost animal, lost money, and two lost sons; but they are primarily speaking about the seeker, who turns out to be God. For instance, the parable is not so much about a prodigal son as it is about the forgiving Father.

I. The four parables speak of God the Father.

A. *The lost sheep.* It seems somewhat dangerous that a shepherd would leave ninety-nine sheep in the wilderness while going after one sheep that had strayed away. However, this is the nature of shepherds who feel responsible for their sheep. Upon finding the sheep, there is a period of rejoicing by the shepherd and his neighbors. The parable teaches that there is joy in heaven when a sinner repents and is brought back to the fold of God.

The lost sheep, with no sense of direction, is completely helpless while it is lost. Nevertheless, in spite of its innocence in straying and its helplessness in being lost, it is in great danger until someone finds it. This parable speaks of the nature of God who goes seeking after his lost creatures and rejoices upon restoring them to the fold. It also implies something of our missionary task in the church, that of seeking the lost for God.

B. *The lost coin.* The coin was lost by the carelessness of someone else. However, it is just as lost as if it bore responsibility for its own condition. It can do nothing until someone looks for it. It may be that many people are lost because of the carelessness of someone else; it is certain that many people can be saved only when someone else begins searching for them.

This little story portrays the nature of God as one who goes searching for the lost until he finds them and then rejoices over them when they repent.

C. *The lost son.* The prodigal son was lost by his own choice. He demonstrates disobedience, disrespect, and willful turning from God. He exhibits the waste of his talents and resources, the dissipation of his family name and respect, the shame of sinful existence, and the desperation of being lost. He also comes to know the betrayal of his sinful friends, but he remembers the nature of his father and is thereby motivated to return.

The father is the main character of the story. He is portrayed as strong and loving. He waits for, understands, forgives, receives, and restores the son, and rejoices over his return.

D. *The older brother.* The older brother was lost, too, but he didn't know it. Actually, he was farther from his father than the prodigal son who journeyed to a distant land. Nevertheless, he deluded himself with external evidence in his futile attempt to prove his faithfulness to the father. The older brother was unwilling to forgive his younger brother. He showed his lack of filial loyalty in that he would not rejoice with the father at having another opportunity to make a man out of the younger son.

The older brother represented the critics of Jesus on this occasion who considered themselves the elect of God but who were very unforgiving toward the sinners about them. It is also possible that this parable may indicate to us that the forgiveness of God does not mean that the personal relationships fractured by our sins are automatically and immediately mended.

These parables teach clearly the nature of God as heavenly forgiving Father.

They portray that people may be lost in various ways, but they are saved only when someone searches for them or motivates their return to God. The parables teach that God cares for his own and searches for them. They teach that God freely forgives and restores sinful people when they do return. They portray the great joy in heaven when sinners repent.

II. The Father forgives our sins.

A. *Forgiveness is personal.* In biblical faith, sin is a personal act against God, and sins are personal acts against other human beings. The result is estrangement from the person against whom the sin is committed. Forgiveness is the personal act of removing that sin and restoring the broken relationship.

Consequently, forgiveness must never be thought of as a legal transaction. It is not a bargain, a truce, or a settlement. It is rather a personal act that involves the will and the feelings of one person toward another. The judge on the bench may exercise leniency within the guidelines spelled out by the law, but he does not forgive the criminal. The criminal has not sinned against the judge. There is no personal relationship broken or to be mended between the criminal and the judge. The judge represents the law and the court. This is an entirely different situation from that which we know in forgiveness.

B. *Forgiveness removes the barrier of sin.* Explaining how forgiveness does this is not easy. The sin becomes a reality and is like a barrier between the persons involved. With time the barrier appears to get larger. In most instances, one cannot return to undo the damage done by sin. Time moves on. Consequently, the only way to destroy this barrier is to will it out of existence. In short, a person can decide that it will no longer remain as a barrier between him and another. He wipes it out; he destroys it; he forgets it. This is precisely what God does with reference to our sins.

C. *Forgiveness is reconciliation.* Sin separates people from God and people from people. Forgiveness brings them back together. Forgiveness reestablishes the harmony that was broken. It is always an extremely personal and human act. It is *reconciliation,* one of the most beautiful New Testament words for salvation. It portrays salvation not as something one gets but rather as a relationship with God into which one enters by faith in Jesus Christ. Forgiveness in the New Testament always includes the reconciliation of the parties involved. It can never be reduced to a decision to tolerate or endure.

D. *Forgiveness is restoration.* When the prodigal son returned home, the father restored him to his original place as a son and as a member of the family. Sin had disrupted all of that. In sin a person falls from God and is cast out of Eden. In forgiveness a person is restored to God and to the relationship that had been lost.

People are tempted to see forgiveness in terms of less than full res-

95

toration. We should guard against this compromise. Forgiveness is not probation; it is restoration.

III. The Father's forgiveness is free but costly.

A. *God forgives us freely.* The New Testament abounds with reminders that our salvation is a gift of God, the result of his grace freely given. Sinners stand before God with empty hands; they have nothing to bring to him with which to secure the forgiveness of their sins.

In most instances, there is nothing we can do to undo the damage caused by our sins. Our evil deeds have happened; they are irrevocable. They go on having their influence long after we have ceased to remember them. It is unthinkable that we could repay the damage or that we could undo the wrong we have done. Forgiveness is the gracious act of God in which he freely erases the record of our sins and gives us a free new start in life.

B. *But forgiveness involves the cost of the cross.* Salvation was not free to God; it cost the life of his Son, Jesus Christ. Somehow in the mystery of God, only in the cross do we see our sin in all of its evil and God's grace in all of its majesty. At the foot of the cross, we meet God. In our rejoicing at the greatness of his redemption, let us not be ungrateful for the tremendous price that Jesus Christ paid for our reconciliation.

C. *Forgiveness may not remove all the costs of our sin.* The prodigal son squandered a fortune, disgraced his family name, and violated his own conscience; the cost of his acts could not be recovered. Sin always comes at a very high price and continues to collect interest from those who engage in it. The prodigal son could rejoice in the freeness of his father's forgiveness; however, he could not reclaim the years the locusts had eaten.

D. *God's forgiveness may not cover the cost of personal injury to others.* Many people who know God's forgiveness of their sins cannot understand why other people will not so readily forgive them. Admittedly, we should forgive others when they repent, but many people will not do so. Sinners, although they enjoy the forgiveness of God, must often live with the lack of forgiveness from those against whom they have sinned.

The older brother is a glaring example of the cost of the younger brother's sin. The older brother would not accept him back as freely as did the father. Now the younger brother would live with the ill will from the brother against whom he sinned. In time perhaps the older brother would forgive him as genuinely as the father did; in the meantime, the younger brother would be painfully aware of the cost of his sin.

Conclusion

The Christian faith proclaims a message of forgiveness to the entire world. On the basis of Jesus Christ's life, death, and resurrection, we extend to you this day the promise of forgiveness. He has authorized us to offer you free forgiveness for your sins. There is no need for you to carry your sins any longer; God will forgive you; he will remove the burden from your back. God is eager to forgive your sin just as the father is eager to forgive his son and have him back at home. God will not charge you for forgiveness; but remember that your sin goes on exacting a dreadful price for each day you exist within it.

WEDNESDAY EVENING, MARCH 26

Title: The Bible Speaks to Our Condition

Scripture Reading: John 18

Introduction

When we ask God to speak to us through John 18, we need to be aware that this chapter describes the events that took place on the night before our Lord's crucifixion. It is an awesome experience to solemnly read of our Master's march toward his cross. With humility, sorrow, joy, and gratitude, we should contemplate the spirit of sacrifice that possessed our Savior as he came to these moments in his life.

This is a chapter characterized by an unusual number of great questions.

I. The questions of Jesus.

    A. *A question repeated to the soldiers (18:4,7).*

    B. *A question directed to Peter (18:11).*

    C. *A question to the high priest (18:19–21).*

    D. *A question directed to the servant of the high priest (18:23).*

    E. *A question directed to Pilate (18:34).*

II. The questions directed toward Peter.

    A. *The question of a maid at the door (18:17).*

    B. *The question of one standing by the fire (18:25).*

    C. *The question of the servant of the high priest (18:26).*

III. The questions of Pilate.

    A. *A question to the Jewish officials (18:29).*

    B. *A question concerning Jesus' kingship (18:33).*

    C. *A sarcastic question (18:35).*

    D. *A pointed question to Jesus (18:35).*

    E. *A searching question directed to Jesus (18:37).*

    F. *A very important question (18:38).*

    G. *A question to the angry mob that was seeking to crucify Jesus (18:39).*

Conclusion

One cannot read this chapter without being impressed with the calm, compassionate courage of our Lord Jesus as he approached the hour when he was to suffer for our sins. It would appear that instead of our Lord being on trial, Annas, Caiaphas, and Pilate, the Jewish and Roman officials, were the ones really on trial. He was determined to register the degree of God's great love for sinners and succeeded beyond power of words to describe.

This chapter contains the record of Peter's threefold denial of a knowledge of the Lord. Perhaps he was frightened. Perhaps he was hoping to rescue his Lord. Our Lord knew of Peter's peril and had predicted Peter's disgraceful denials (John 13:36–38). Our Lord was to give Peter a threefold opportunity to reaffirm his love following his resurrection (John 21:15–17).

We face the peril of following in the train of Peter's denial. If we live unworthy lives and claim to be disciples of our Lord, we are denying the power of his presence in our lives. We deny him when we are unfaithful to the highest and to the best to which the divine Spirit calls us. We deny a transforming experience with him when we remain silent in the midst of humanity's need for the Good News. We deny him when we do not give ourselves in positive obedience to the Great Commission.

As the Lord forgave Peter and utilized him, so the Lord wants to forgive us and use us to be a blessing to others.

SUNDAY MORNING, MARCH 30

Title: Jesus Went a Little Farther

Text: "And he went a little farther" **(Matt. 26:39)**.

Scripture Reading: Matthew 26:36–46

Hymns: "Trust and Obey," Sammis

"Did You Think to Pray?" Kidder

"Close to Thee," Crosby

Offertory Prayer: Our Father, we bring to you our grateful praise that in every circumstance of life you are present with us. You have made us. Your Son has redeemed us. Your Holy Spirit is our Comforter and Energizer. As we bring our money to you, we are expressing our gratitude for blessings that have been sent to us. Your mercies are so great that they cannot be numbered. We are showing our interest in the work of your kingdom and investing ourselves in bringing others to a saving knowledge of you. We pray that these gifts may help others to proclaim boldly the message of Christ—the joy of receiving him as Savior and the folly of refusing his call. May these gifts be used to convert unbelievers; to give strength to the weak, health to the sick, and rest to the weary; and to make the world a better place in which to live because the message of Christ has been proclaimed. We pray these things in Jesus' name. Amen.

Introduction

Jesus' life was filled with interesting and meaningful incidents. John's gospel says, "Jesus did many other things as well. If everyone of them were written down, I suppose that even the whole world would not have room for the books that would be written" (21:25 NIV). In a series of messages on the life of Jesus, therefore, it is necessary to be selective about the material.

The last week of Jesus' life was spent in and around the city of Jerusalem. He made his headquarters in Bethany at the home of Mary, Martha, and Lazarus. He made arrangements to eat the Passover in the upper room of a home. After the meal was finished, he went with his disciples to the garden of Gethsemane for prayer.

This was a time of deep emotion for our Savior. He warned the disciples that they would be embarrassed that night because of him. Simon Peter insisted that he would never be offended because of Jesus, but Jesus cautioned him that he would deny his Master three times before the cock crowed. Some of the greatest spiritual truth in the Bible is found in the Gethsemane experiences of our Lord.

I. Jesus had an inner circle.

All great leaders have a few men who are close to them. In a sense, the Twelve were Jesus' "select group," but in an even greater sense, it was Peter, James, and John who understood their Master best. These three went with him into the house when he raised Jairus's daughter from the dead. These same three accompanied Jesus on the Mount of Transfiguration where they viewed Moses and Elijah and Jesus in their glorified bodies.

Often in a church it is necessary for the pastor to have "key members" who help him in a most significant way. This does not mean the pastor is playing favorites, although he may sometimes be accused of it, but it means rather that there are always certain people who are more receptive to suggestions and seem to possess keener insight into God's work. Peter, James, and John were being trained for greater service. Two of them became outstanding evangelists after the ascension of Jesus.

II. Jesus identified with the sins of the world.

The Bible says that Jesus spoke of his soul as being "exceeding sorrowful, even unto death" and asked these three to stay at a certain spot and watch with him. He had already left eight of them at a spot near the entrance to the garden. It is difficult for us to realize the burden that was on the heart of Christ. He knew the significance of the night. He knew that he would be arrested shortly and that the next day he would be crucified. Nevertheless, he was more concerned about his followers than he was about himself. He had already said to them earlier, "Let not your heart be troubled" (John 14:1). There is a great lesson for us here. When we think constantly of our own distresses, they become greater. The best way to forget our own problems is to help others in the sharing of their burdens. Our burdens disappear when we help others. Paul tells us, "Carry each other's burdens, and in this way you will fulfill the law of Christ" (Gal. 6:2 NIV).

III. The secret of it all—go a little farther.

Of course, these words in Matthew's gospel refer to geographical distance. Jesus left a group of eight in one place, a group of three in another place, and went deeper into the garden. We are doing no violence to the Scripture when we lift this phrase out and give it an even deeper meaning. Every part of Jesus' ministry was "going farther" than anyone else.

A. *Jesus went farther in his interpretation of the Law.* Many scholars have pointed out that very little in Jesus' teaching was entirely new. Almost all of his sayings have parallels or near parallels in the Old Testament. It was not the newness of the material but the freshness of interpretation that made Jesus stand out as a teacher with authority. He did not merely recite the interpretations of the rabbis. He gave his own meaningful exposition of the Law. He breathed a spirit into it that far surpassed anyone who had gone before him. We are not to obey in the letter of the Law, according to Jesus, but in the sweetness and reasonableness of spirit. Murder is more than an action; it is an attitude. The same is true of adultery and of all the other commandments concerning human relationships. Out of the heart the mouth speaks, and from the heart come the issues of life.

B. *Jesus went a little farther in his refusal to retaliate.* Throughout all of his ministry, Jesus recognized that God's kingdom could be extended in the hearts of people only by unselfish love. He refused to take issue with the Roman government who ruled the Jews at this time. He would not fulfill the popular Jewish notion of a politically oriented Messiah by leading a revolt against the Roman establishment. He insisted that we are to love our enemies, bless those who curse us, and pray for the ones who despitefully use us. In the garden of Gethsemane, he demonstrated this spirit: Judas, who had already left the Twelve, came with a great multitude to take Jesus away for trial and later for crucifixion. Peter drew his sword and struck a servant of the high priest, but Jesus rebuked him with the warning, "They that take the sword shall perish with the sword" (Matt. 26:52). And going even farther, he healed the servant.

C. *Jesus went a little farther in his concern for a lost world.* This was the fundamental point of Jesus' ministry! He came to be our Savior by going to the cross. From the beginning of his ministry, he saw the act on Calvary by which he would redeem humankind. Every part of his earthly activity pointed to this solemn and serious hour. Jesus has left us an example of concern for the lost that should inspire full commitment to this cause. The dedication of our Lord calls for our own dedication and discipline to live in such a way that we may lead others to the Savior.

The winning of lost people is not an elective in the Christian's curriculum; it is a required course. The Lord's one purpose in his ministry was to find people and win them to himself. No sacrifice was too great for him, and nothing should stand in our way of making soul-winning the first priority in daily living. We should take advantage of every contact and, indeed, should seek to make contacts that will give us opportunity to give testimony to the lost. Only as Christians are willing to follow the Master's example of going "a little farther" in this area will our rapidly deteriorating world find redemption and salvation from the ills that threaten our extinction.

Conclusion

How far do you go? Those who go farther in every category of life make the great contributions to humanity. Those laboring in the scientific laboratory go far beyond the point of duty. The business executive who arrives at his office early to chart the work for the day long before the "paid staff" comes in is the one who builds a great organization. The teacher who spends extra time with a child who needs help in order to bring him up to a normal level or with an exceptionally talented child in order to make him a leader is the one who is truly great in his or her field. The joys of life are present for those who give themselves beyond measure. The person who lives merely by the "What do I *have* to do" rule never finds real fulfillment. When Phillips Brooks, the great New England clergyman, was being buried, someone said to his brother, "If Dr. Brooks had just held himself back and not pushed himself so hard, he might have lived longer." His brother replied, "Yes, but if he had done that, he wouldn't have been Phillips Brooks." This does not mean that we ought to "burn out" prematurely, but it does mean that those who make great contributions in life are those who are willing to go far beyond the normal call of what "ought to be done" and see rather what "should be done" if the godly causes in this world are to come to fruition.

SUNDAY EVENING, MARCH 30

Title: Forgiveness: The Goal of Church Discipline

Text: "Moreover if thy brother shall trespass ..." (**Matt. 18:15**).

Scripture Reading: Matthew 18:7–22

Introduction

Modern churches do not usually exercise church discipline as churches in the past have done. At least this is true in the formal sense of the term *church discipline.* However, modern Christians probably do exercise more informal discipline over one another than most of us realize, and this is the best kind of church discipline. Informal discipline may limit knowledge of the offense to the smallest number of persons possible, thereby minimizing the damage and the needless talk about the event. However, there may still be occasions in which church congregations must exercise discipline over their members.

I. A definition of forgiveness.

In biblical teaching, there are two emphases in the term *forgiveness*: (1) the removal of the barrier of sin and (2) the restoration of fellowship. The offense committed forms a barrier between a person and God and between two people, thereby alienating the two. Forgiveness is the gracious act that removes that barrier and restores the fellowship of the people involved.

In the Old Testament, sin is against God. Consequently, only God can forgive sin. Sin may be a transgression against God, disobedience to God's law, unbelief, rebellion, or something else. It is a barrier that stands in the way of fellowship between a person and God, and like a stain, it demands cleansing or removing. To forgive sin means (1) to send it away, (2) to lift it up as one would lift a burden, (3) to cover it, or (4) to blot it out.

In the New Testament, there are some distinctively new ideas about forgiveness. Jesus forgave sins "in his own name," thereby incurring the charge of blasphemy, since only God can forgive sin. Jesus taught that people cannot know the forgiveness of God unless they are willing to forgive others. Evidently, one who is not sensitive enough to understand the suffering in the conscience of the sinner is not able to accept God's forgiveness. Jesus taught that repentance precedes forgiveness, as in the case of the Pharisee and the publican. When asked how often a person must forgive, Jesus responded that a person must forgive seventy times seven times. One of the clearest insights in the New Testament regarding forgiveness is that it is a personal act, never a legal act.

II. Three New Testament passages dealing with church discipline and forgiveness.

A. *When the church is called on to settle personal disputes (Matt. 18:15–22).* When Jesus instructed his disciples about settling disputes between brothers, he first advised the offended party to take the initiative and go to the offender in a personal attempt to solve the problem. Jesus said, "If he listens to you, you have gained your brother." It should be noted that this method limits the knowledge and, consequently, the damage of the offense to the smallest number of persons. If the two people are reconciled at this point, there is no reason for anyone else to know about the problem.

If the first step fails, the Christian is to take two or more brothers with him and try again to talk to the offending brother. This method accomplishes three things: (1) it provides witnesses who will know exactly what was said and be able to overcome the subjective prejudice of the two members; (2) it will therefore offer a better opportunity for settling the original problem; and (3) it will still limit the knowledge of the problem to a small circle of people.

If both attempts fail, the offended one is to tell the problem to the church. There are several implications in this action. The action assumes that both people are members of the church and that their membership means something to them. It also implies that the church, like a family, is involved when two of its members are at odds with each other. It seems to imply that the congregation will care enough to want to settle the problem, thereby redeeming both persons involved and the fellowship of the congregation. It should be noted, however, that reporting personal difficulties to the church is a last resort; this is to be done only after all other attempts have failed.

When reconciliation is not achieved even in the context of a church hearing, Jesus advised that the church should regard the offender as an "outsider." This implies that in the teaching of Jesus there is no notion that the church would do any kind of punishing. The severest action is to regard the offender as outside the fellowship.

It is significant that Jesus, after stressing the importance of people's actions on earth and in the church, which has the power of binding and loosing in heaven, went on immediately to answer Peter's question about forgiveness. Peter asked, "Lord, how oft shall my brother sin against me, and I forgive him? till seven times?" Jesus responded, "I say not unto thee, until seven times: but until seventy times seven" (Matt. 18:21–22).

This brief paragraph establishes at least two major Christian emphases: (1) the whole point of personal and congregational efforts to deal with those guilty of offending is that they be forgiven, (2) and the church must never set a limit on how many times a person will be forgiven. He will be forgiven as often as he asks to be forgiven, even to the point of "seventy times seven" times.

B. *Church discipline in the case of immorality (1 Cor. 5:1–5)*. In this passage, Paul wrote to the Corinthian church about the case of serious immorality among them. He did not give details regarding the efforts that had been made in the past to correct the wrong of this man who was guilty of incest. The implication is that these efforts had been made and had failed. Paul recommended that this person be removed from the church.

Paul suggested that the church in assembly should take official action to exclude the man from formal membership in the body. He used language that is strange to us when he said, "You are to deliver this man to Satan." This should not be understood to imply that Satan is some kind of agent for God or that Christians in a sense use him as a sort of prosecuting attorney or prison warden. Instead, Paul alludes to the Christian conviction that within the fellowship of the church one enjoys the protection of God, the fellowship of the Holy Spirit, and the prayers and encouragement of fellow Christians. In this context, one can be secure from the destructive power of sin. However, if the Christian is separated from this setting, he will be overcome by sin. In other words, out in the realm of Satan he has no protection and no defense. But the purpose of this action, according to Paul, is that the man "may be saved in the day of the Lord Jesus."

It is important that in this instance of immorality, exclusion is the most serious act of the church, and the purpose of that act is that the offending man will eventually be brought to the awareness of his sin so that he can be saved or forgiven.

103

C. *Forgiveness must follow punishment (2 Cor. 2:5 – 11).* Paul writes here about some brother in the church in Corinth who committed a serious act against both Paul and the church. While no details are given, we would assume that he did something to undermine or attack Paul and in the process disrupted or divided the congregation. It would be unwise to speculate as to what his sin was or to give illustrations from modern times. However, in this instance, the church took some kind of formal or official action against this person. Paul referred to it as "punishment by the majority."

The most significant theme in this passage is that Paul advised that their punishment or censure was "enough." Then he said, "You should rather turn to forgive and comfort him, or he may be overwhelmed by excessive sorrow. So I beg you to reaffirm your love for him" (2 Cor. 2:6 – 8 RSV).

This entire passage deals almost exclusively with the Christian theme that the person guilty of offending the church should be forgiven and that the sole purpose for any action against him is that he be brought to forgiveness. Paul wisely enjoins the congregation to forgive him quickly lest he be driven into depression as a result of the action against him.

A great deal of injury is done to persons when they are left in their guilt and in punishment for a long period of time. When parents use discipline on their children, they are wise if they limit the punishment to a very short period of time and then fully restore the children to the family fellowship. Exclusion or rejection of a person from the family is a very severe punishment that usually results in the deterioration of the offender. The church family may be required to take action against its members on occasion, but it is "Christian action" only if its eventual purpose is to bring about the reconciliation of the person involved.

Conclusion

Just as Jesus Christ came to reconcile sinful people to God, so he left his church as a reconciling agent in the world. He has entrusted to us "the message of reconciliation" (2 Cor. 5:19).

The church is made up of those who have been forgiven by God. They have learned the meaning of forgiveness, and they forgive one another. The church as such is in the business of forgiving. All around the church there are individuals and families estranged from each other and desperately needing help in the achievement of forgiveness. The church knows best how to do this and should be diligent in the practice.

The passages we have studied clearly lay out a number of principles for Christians to follow.

To care for other persons and deal with their offenses is not necessarily meddling. It takes a lot of courage and concern for a Christian to go to another person who has offended him and attempt to settle that problem before it becomes serious. The passages indicate that if an individual or small group will go to the offending person at an early stage, they may save him and prevent him from going deeper into the wrong, thereby hurting himself and others. These passages suggest that knowledge of personal difficulties should be restricted to the smallest number of persons possible. Confession of sin is the honest acknowledgment of it to the person or persons against whom the act is done. Disclosure of such information beyond this circle is not confession but publicity.

These passages do indicate that Christians are responsible for their brothers and sisters and on occasion must do the very difficult task of going to an offender to try to solve a serious problem. It may seem unfair that the offended person must take the initiative, but in reality, that person is more able to take up the problem because of his or her sensitivity to the wrong. Also, it is possible that the offender is not aware that he or she has offended. The single most important emphasis of these passages is that the church may have to exercise discipline over its members, but when it does, it must do so with the goal of reconciling the person or persons involved.

"Be kind to one another, tenderhearted, forgiving one another, as God in Christ forgave you" (Eph. 4:32 RSV).

APRIL

■ **Sunday Mornings**

Continue with the theme "The Life and Works of the Lord Jesus."

■ **Sunday Evenings**

Improvement in the quality of our worship experiences is always needed. We must worship in spirit and in truth. The suggested theme for this month is "Making Our Worship More Meaningful."

■ **Wednesday Evenings**

Continue with the theme "The Bible Speaks to Our Condition." The theme verse for the month is "Thy word is a lamp unto my feet, and a light unto my path" (Ps. 119:105).

WEDNESDAY EVENING, APRIL 2

Title: The Bible Speaks to Our Condition
Scripture Reading: Acts 4

Introduction

The chapter that serves as a basis for our Bible study today will provide us with light for the road ahead. In the first verses, we find the apostles being obedient to the Great Commission in the manner in which our Lord intended that all of us should be obedient. In their going about from place to place, they were sharing their information and their experience of what Jesus Christ meant to them. They had not internationalized or professionalized the Great Commission. They simply went about talking to people about the Lord Jesus.

I. Filled with the Spirit (Acts 4:8).

To be filled with the Spirit means to be aware of his indwelling presence and to be committed fully to his guidance and leadership. It means to consciously be dependent on him for the wisdom, knowledge, guidance, and spiritual vitality that are necessary for the doing of God's work. All of us are commanded to "be filled with the Spirit" (Eph. 5:18). To neglect or to refuse to be filled with the Spirit is to be disobedient to the will of God for our lives.

II. The only way of salvation (Acts 4:12).

In dramatic words that bear memorization, the apostles declared that Jesus Christ is the only way to salvation. This salvation is more than a ticket to heaven: it provides forgiveness from the penalty of sin, which is death. It offers power for living a victorious life in the present. It promises deliverance from the very presence of evil in the future. This salvation can be experienced only through our Lord Jesus.

Peter's declaration here should challenge each of us to recognize the world's desperate need for Jesus Christ. By virtue of knowing Christ, we are under obligation to share him with all of those in our individual personal world.

III. The command to be silent (Acts 4:18–23).

In these words, we have a clear command from the religious and political authorities of that day to the apostles that they be silent rather than talkative concerning Jesus Christ. Our Lord had commanded them to be his witnesses, testifiers, testators.

Most of us are guilty of the terrible crime of being silent concerning the Lord even though we have received no commandment to be silent. Our command is to communicate with others about what Christ means to us.

How would we react if political authorities commanded us to say absolutely nothing about our Lord? Would we be intimidated, and would we be obedient to them? Or would we react as the apostles did and continue to speak boldly in the name of our Lord?

These early Christians had an inner compulsion to give their testimony. May God grant to each of us such an inner compulsion to oral confession of our experiences with Jesus Christ.

IV. The open door of prayer (Acts 4:24–31).

In times of difficulty and need, the early Christians entered the throne room of the Father God that they might obtain mercy and find grace for help in every time of need. It is interesting to note that in this experience of prayer they quoted to their own hearts the great promises of God's Word and claimed the promises of God as they presented their needs before their heavenly Father's throne of grace.

Instead of praying for release from the command to be witnesses, they prayed that God would grant them greater boldness to speak in the name of the Lord. Their prayer was heard, and God answered by granting their requests.

V. Great fellowship (Acts 4:32–37).

Their fellowship one with another and with God was unparalleled and is indescribable in human terminology. The Holy Spirit filled them with his presence and power. They were united in heart and soul and were overwhelmed with a spirit of generosity that caused them to share with and to meet the needs of others. They were unusually effective in communicating the message of God's grace as they had experienced it in Jesus Christ.

Conclusion

Let us pray that God will overwhelm us with the wonders of our great salvation. Let us pray for a new awareness of the presence of the Holy Spirit within our hearts, and may we be more responsive to him. Let us pray for an inner compulsion to share the good news of God's love with those about us. As we do so, others will come to know our Savior as we know him, and our joy will be like the joy of these early followers of our Lord.

SUNDAY MORNING, APRIL 6

Title: Jesus Did God's Will

Text: "Thy will be done" **(Matt. 26:42).**

Scripture Reading: Matthew 26:36–46

Hymns: "I am Resolved," Hartsough

"Make Me a Channel of Blessing," Smyth

"Wherever He Leads I'll Go," McKinney

Offertory Prayer: Our Father, we know there is much to be done in this world for you. We know that we can never do it all, yet we are grateful we can do some things. There are many places we cannot go individually, but we are grateful that through our gifts of money we can go other places to tell your message. Help us to see beyond the four walls of our own church building. May we see the world and all of its need. Help us to be always conscious of your all-inclusive love for people everywhere. Help us to remember the words of our Lord who said, "It is more blessed to give than to receive." Forgive us when we are more concerned with the act of getting than the act of giving. Help us to lay up treasures in heaven where moth and rust cannot corrupt. Take these gifts that we bring to you. We offer them with love and gratitude. We pray these things in Jesus' name and for his sake. Amen.

Introduction

Jesus' life was now in the shadow of the cross. The purpose for which he came was now squarely before him. He had a decision to make. Thus far Jesus had met every test and emerged victoriously. Satan had endeavored in vain to dissuade him from his task, yet the biggest test of all was immediately before him.

It is impossible for us, as human beings, to understand the great soul agony of Jesus that night in Gethsemane. He had no sin in him, but as he prayed in the garden, he felt the pressure of all the world's sin upon him. Because of his divine nature, he could foresee all of the things that awaited him on the cross. Yet because of his human nature, he sought an escape. Was there an escape? Was there any other way for God to redeem the world? If so, what was it? Jesus prayed, "If this cup may not pass from me, except I drink it, thy will be done." The divine plan for redeeming the world was formulated before the world was created. Peter speaks of our redemption and then refers to our Redeemer, "who was chosen before the creation of the world" (1 Peter 1:20 NIV). The implied answer to the

108

Gethsemane prayer was that Jesus must fulfill God's plan by going to the cross. There was no alternative.

I. God had a will for Jesus—and he has a will for every life.

As the Babe lay in Bethlehem, God had already mapped out his life. Jesus kept before himself constantly the Father's will. When his parents questioned him at the age of twelve about staying behind and talking with the religious leaders in the temple, his reply to them revealed his dedication to God's purpose for him. He said, "Didn't you know I had to be in my Father's house?" (Luke 2:49 NIV).

Likewise, God has a plan for each person's life. If not a single sparrow is forgotten by God, how much more does he know each of us by name and have a plan for our lives? John Wesley once said, "To find God's will is man's greatest discovery and to do God's will is man's greatest achievement." God even uses those outside his divine family to accomplish his redemptive purposes. When the Jewish nation was in Babylonian exile, God turned to a pagan ruler and laid upon his heart his purposes for his chosen people. As a result, Cyrus issued a decree that the Jews could return to their homeland. God thus used one who did not know him to accomplish his purpose. One great preacher preached a sermon titled "Every Life a Plan of God," based on the words of the Old Testament prophet Isaiah, "I will strengthen you, though you have not acknowledged me, so that from the rising of the sun to the place of its setting people may know there is none besides me. I am the LORD, and there is no other" (Isa. 45:5–6 NIV).

II. People can pervert the purposes of God.

Although God is sovereign, people have free will. It is possible, therefore, for people, finite though they are, to shake their fists in the face of Almighty God and say, "I will not do that which is your plan for me." History is filled with nations that have ignored the moral laws of God and plunged over the precipice into catastrophe. People with great potential for making major contributions to civilization have chosen to rebel against the purposes of God and have ended up on the rocky shores of frustration and misery. Could Jesus have rebelled against God at the last moment and refused to go to the cross? Another question is parallel to it. Could Jesus have yielded to Satan at the beginning of his ministry? The answer to both questions must be yes, for Jesus had a completely human nature as well as a completely divine one.

What about our temptations to pervert God's purposes for us? Are there safeguards we can set up to help us avoid the pitfalls of disobedience? One of the best ways to guarantee that we will fulfill God's purposes for us is to remain close to him in daily fellowship and thus find infinite resources available for the doing of his will. It isn't easy! Many things work to pull us away from dedicated devotion. The pressures of this world as well as our personal ambitions work to alienate us from a spiritual approach to life. When we allow these things to overcome us, the beautiful possibilities of life can become twisted, and defeat will be imminent.

III. How can we know God's will?

Although the first requirement for doing God's will is to want to do it, there is a great need for guidelines to help sincere Christians evaluate in day-to-day living the impressions they receive concerning God's will for their lives. There is an *intentional* will of God. He desires that all people be happy. Yet we are thrown into life situations that are influenced by the presence of sin in the world. These circumstances force us many times to make adjustments. We need to distinguish between God's *intentional purpose* and God's *circumstantial will* because of human conditions that are brought about by the sins of society. We cannot tell a woman whose son has been hit and killed by a drunken driver that this was the "will of God" and that she must accept it. Drunken driving has nothing to do with the will of God. This young man was caught in a circumstance beyond his control, and he suffered for it. We are guilty many times of glibly saying that this is "God's will" when we should examine the situation further. We receive many good things in life because good people before us have been dedicated in some field of research. Likewise, we will receive many evil things in life because evil people have lived and set into motion the law of sin and retribution for society. We are bound together in a bundle of life, and we cannot ignore the implications of living in tightly knit circumstances.

Are there not, however, aids for our own individual choices concerning God's will? To be sure, there are. Much has been written on the subject. Some have pointed out that conscience helps us. It does indeed, but it is never an infallible guide. We should listen to our consciences but be careful not to be deceived by an untrained conscience in the hands of a rationalizing sinner. Others have suggested a lowly signpost that we call common sense. Still others have suggested that we counsel with friends and heed closely their advice. We can use the mind and wisdom of others as we read it in great literature. We can listen to the voice of the church and its feelings about matters. The Quakers have spoken of the inner light, which is probably another way of saying "be led by the Holy Spirit." One of the most meaningful illustrations, however, is the one of the man who was bringing a ship into harbor. A passenger asked him how he was certain that he would bring it into port correctly. He pointed to three guiding lights and said to the passenger, "When I line this ship up according to these three lights, I know she is in perfect shape."

Conclusion

In seeking for a practical application, we should recognize that God's will should be considered in a twofold manner. First, we should ask ourselves what our long-range plan for life should be with reference to God's will. Every person should have ideals and plans for the future. People who have life goals are happy and are less liable to waste time in either immoral living or superficial living. We also need to ask ourselves each day what God's will is for each moment of our lives. Of course, the cumulative total of our actions day by day will result in our accomplishing or failing to realize God's will for our entire lives.

It is not easy to know God's will, because God's will is not a static thing. It is progressive and often flexible. We should meet each day with the determination that we will approach every event in the light of what we feel Jesus would have us do. We must not be conformed to the will of worldly people, but we should rather be transformed as our lives are hid with God in Christ. In this way, we can both find and do his good and perfect will.

SUNDAY EVENING, APRIL 6

Title: Why People Do Not Go to Church

Text: "Not forsaking the assembling of ourselves together, as the manner of some is" **(Heb. 10:25)**.

Scripture Reading: Hebrews 10:23–27

Introduction

Over the last decade, church attendance has been in steady decline. Vast numbers of people do not identify themselves with any church. Millions of people are growing up without what has been termed a "Christian memory," that is, they have no background in or basic knowledge of the Bible and the Christian faith. The secularizing trend in our society has tended to relegate religion to a private matter and to remove its vestiges from public life and institutions.

Religious freedom means not only the freedom to worship but also the freedom not to worship. In early American life, the church was the center of the social life as well as of the religious life in the community. The Lord's Day was observed as a holy day instead of a holiday. In colonial times, a person either went to church or had no place to go.

Today many other activities compete for our loyalty. Sunday is a work day. In many stores, it is the busiest day of the week. Some employees cannot come to church services because the public demands their services on Sunday. The boat, the lakeside cabin, the golf course, and sports events all beckon to the family. The church is more and more the loser to exciting substitutes.

A young preacher was having a hard time with his sermon. He had experienced many interruptions during the week, and he was not well prepared. He perspired as he tried to rise to the occasion. The scattered congregation was half asleep. It was with relief that he came to the close of the sermon and dismissed the people. Rushing to the door, he took his place to greet the worshipers as they left. A stranger started out. The minister gripped his hand and uttered the cliché, "Come back again." The stranger looked him in the eye and responded with the shattering question, "Why?" Are people staying away from church because they are not helped when they come? Empty seats are a liability any way you look at them. Empty seats are a warning. They say something to us.

The absence of some people may be a compliment. When someone says, "I quit the church because they welcome people of all races," this is a tribute to the church being the church. If people stay away because the preacher is a prophet and they only desire to hear pleasing platitudes and gushing flattery about their so-called goodness, the church is not to be condemned. If the presence and power of the Holy Spirit are so intense that people stay away because they are running from God and the claims of Christ, we are not responsible.

But some people stay away who desperately need to come. Their needs could be supplied if they regularly attend worship services.

I. Our own unworthy lives.

People are watching us. If our lives reflect that our faith means little to us, observers conclude that it will mean little to them. Some tell the truth when they say, "I'm better than some of those down at the church." Being good is not all of it, but not being good turns off many people who need the Lord.

In his early adult life, Mahatma Gandhi found himself in South Africa on a Sunday. Although he was not a Christian, he greatly admired Jesus, and he decided to go to church. He was turned away at the church door by a white-faced, black-hearted usher who mistook him for a black. He vowed never to enter a Christian church again. And Gandhi had a way of keeping his vows.

II. People do not know that we care.

How can people know that we care if we do not let them know? Some do not come to church because they have not been invited. If we do not care enough to invite them, we do not care very much.

Some come to church but do not return regularly because we do not let them know that we miss them when they are gone. How far we have drifted from the Great Shepherd who missed the one sheep and left the ninety-nine to bring him back.

III. The church service fell short of meeting their needs.

Perhaps visitors were not made to feel welcome and wanted. We may be too concerned with our own little circle of friends to widen the circle and include a stranger. Maybe the service was cold and formal. Or maybe the service was ill-prepared and disorganized. Could it be that visitors looked up to be fed and went away hungry? What a responsibility and privilege we have when people in need come to worship!

Conclusion

In the latter years of the nineteenth century, a man made a fortune in mining operations in Montana. He decided to spend some of his money building the "ideal community." He dedicated a thousand acres and laid out the town site. He paved the streets and laid the sewer and water lines. He developed parks and built schools, a theater, a dance hall, and several saloons. Businesses were established, and homes were built in neat lines.

The pet aversion of this man was the church. He had a reversionary clause written into every deed that if property were sold for religious purposes, it would revert to the original owner. Then he invited people to come. Soon between four and five thousand people arrived. There were no female schoolteachers, but immoral women were plentiful. High-minded parents would not come, for they did not want their children to grow up where there was no church. Within five years, the bottom dropped out and bankruptcy proceeded. The owner issued the following manifesto:

> God knows that there is no such person as God, and my motto has always been, "To hell with religion." But for some fool reason which no man can fathom, I have found from experience that we cannot do business in this country on any other basis than that silly bit of sentiment which we stamp on our coins, "In God We Trust," and "We are going to build a church."

Thus ended his ignoble experiment.

WEDNESDAY EVENING, APRIL 9

Title: The Bible Speaks to Our Condition

Scripture Reading: Acts 11

Introduction

The chapter from which we seek light for the road of life today marks a dramatic new beginning in the life and activity of the early disciples. This chapter reveals the result of what God was trying to communicate to Peter and through Peter to the church by way of Peter's experience with Cornelius the Gentile. The one great truth that comes through in Acts 11 is the all-inclusive nature of the love of God. Up to this point, the church had been primarily a Jewish institution. Henceforth it would include Gentiles as well.

I. The dissolving of racial and religious prejudice (Acts 11:1 – 18).

Up to this point in the history of the Christian movement, it had involved primarily Jews. Even the apostles were the children of the age in which they lived. The Jewish people had been very narrow, nationalistic, and exclusive. They refrained from contact with anyone other than Jews. They did not believe that Gentiles were included in the loving purpose of God. God tried repeatedly to convince Peter that Gentiles were also included in God's love (Acts 10:10 – 16). In addition to this threefold vision, Peter heard the voice of the Spirit of God commanding him to follow through and to go with the men who were at the gate inviting him to Cornelius's house (Acts 10:19). It was not accidental that Peter took six witnesses with him on this trip (11:12). Jewish law required that there be at least two witnesses. Peter took three pairs of witnesses with him so that these events could be firmly established in the minds of everyone when he came back to report to the church in Jerusalem.

The gift of the Holy Spirit to the house of Cornelius convinced Peter and the witnesses with him, as well as the church in Jerusalem, that God had granted to the Gentiles the gift of repentance and faith that brought life and immortality.

II. The purpose of God includes the Gentiles (Acts 11:19–24).

Following this experience in the household of Cornelius, some of the disciples went to Antioch and preached the Good News to non-Jews, and they believed and were converted. This concerned the church at Jerusalem to the extent that they sent Barnabas to investigate. Barnabas was a great and good man under the control of the Spirit of God. He evaluated what God was doing and did all that he could to encourage these Gentiles to trust and obey the Lord.

What happened in Antioch was a new departure in the redemptive program of God as far as the Jewish believers were concerned. This was to produce controversy and conflict that would lead to the great church conference later (Acts 15).

III. Christian conduct results from Christian teaching (Acts 11:25–26).

It is interesting to note that at the end of the year of teaching activity, the disciples of our Lord were called Christians. Today we instantaneously identify new believers as Christians by their profession of faith. It is questionable whether we should do this. To be Christian is to be Christlike. Conversion does not instantaneously produce Christian character and Christian conduct. We probably would be more correct if we identified new converts as believers, as disciples, as children of God. The term *Christian* should be a title bestowed on believers when others can see the beauty of Christ in them.

IV. The practice of generosity (Acts 11:27–30).

The early Christians possessed an attitude of compassionate concern toward others who were in need. Evidently they believed as our Lord taught that more happiness was to be experienced as a result of giving than could be experienced by getting. Not because of a command, but because of compassion, they shared with those in need.

Conclusion

In the light of this chapter, let us examine our hearts to see if racial or religious prejudice is hindering our religious testimony. Are we fully aware that everyone is included in the loving purpose of God? Do we possess in our own attitudes, actions, and ambitions a spirit that would cause others to call us Christian? Are we generous and gracious in ministering to the needs of others? May God the Father grant that we respond fully to the great truths revealed in this chapter from his Word.

SUNDAY MORNING, APRIL 13

Title: Jesus Died for Our Sins

Text: "God commendeth his love toward us, in that, while we were yet sinners, Christ died for us" **(Rom. 5:8)**.

Scripture Reading: Matthew 27:33–50

Hymns: "Glory to His Name," Hoffman

"Beneath the Cross of Jesus," Clephane

"Near the Cross," Crosby

Offertory Prayer: Our Father, we recognize you as the Eternal One. You have been our dwelling place in all generations. As we bring our offerings this morning, we pray for all who shall be supported by these gifts. Bless the work of this local church. Bless the causes we support in the larger ministries of God's kingdom. We thank you for your innumerable blessings. We bring these gifts with joy and thank you for the privilege of sharing in the witness of the gospel. We pray these things in Jesus' name and for his sake. Amen.

Introduction

When we come to deal with the crucifixion, we are at the heart of the gospel. The Old Testament symbolized the death of Christ in many ways. All of the predictions and types converged and found fulfillment on that day when Jesus hung for six hours on the cross. The events leading up to Christ's death are all filled with emotion, but it is when the Lamb of God becomes the substitute for humans that we stand speechless before the infinite grace of God.

It is the general consensus of scholarship that Jesus was crucified on the Passover. He had eaten the supper with his disciples the preceding night. Then they went to the garden to pray. Jesus was arrested, and before 9:00 a.m. the next day, he had been tried six times—three times before a Jewish group and three times before a Roman court. He refused to speak in his behalf. False witnesses were hired against him, and he was treated shamefully. Many illegal acts were performed in connection with his trials. They placed on him a crown of thorns and spat on him. At his crucifixion, they divided his garments and gambled for them. They put him on a cross and crucified him between two thieves. All of these events show the mockery and ridicule that accompanied his crucifixion.

Yet God was at work! That which the satanic forces did in an attempt to eliminate Jesus of Nazareth was the one act that God used to bring redemption to the world. No one has ever completely understood the cross and its meaning. No one illustration can gather up within it all of the truths contained in the redemptive message of Christ that was made reality through the atonement. If the cross were not too broad for human comprehension, it would be too narrow to meet human need. God's ways are above those of humanity. Yet when we come to the cross in faith saying, "I am a sinner, and I fling myself upon the mercy of

115

God as revealed in the death of his Son," a miracle happens in our lives. Paul called it being "saved," and Jesus spoke of it as being "born again." Many other metaphors and similes are used throughout the New Testament to describe the wonderful thing that happens when a sinful person comes face-to-face with self and with God in the saving work of Jesus Christ. Although we cannot explain the cross completely, we can analyze it prayerfully.

I. The Man of the cross.

Jesus was a man. He was more than man, but he was a man. He was the best man who ever lived. He was the only man who was conceived by the Holy Spirit and born of a virgin. Those who knew him in the flesh testified concerning his true nature. At Caesarea Philippi, Simon Peter called him "the Christ, the Son of the living God" (Matt. 16:16). John the Baptist testified, "Behold the Lamb of God, which taketh away the sin of the world" (John 1:29). After the resurrection, Thomas exclaimed, "My Lord and my God" (John 20:28). History is filled with the testimony of people who, though they lived after him, have felt the full impact of his mission to the world and have joined those who knew him in the flesh in proclaiming not merely his greatness as a man but his unique deity and his equality with the Father.

II. The Maker of the cross.

Who was responsible for Jesus' death? If we were to look at the matter from merely a human standpoint, we might say that the Roman soldiers who nailed him to the cross were actually the doers of the deed. They carried out the execution orders and did a job similar to the one they had done many times before in a routine manner. If we want to go back a little farther, we might say that Jesus' crucifixion was Pilate's fault, for he failed to set Jesus free when the evidence clearly indicated that there was no guilt. He took a bowl of water and washed his hands, declaring that he was innocent of the blood of "this just person." If we wish to go back still farther, we can blame the Jewish people, for in reality they were the ones who brought about the act. They handed Jesus over to Pilate because of envy. Jesus refused to accept their type of religion—a legalistic code of obedience to externals with little or no spirit and far less human compassion. Or we might blame Judas, for he identified Jesus in the garden so that the Roman soldiers might arrest him.

Yet all of these are superficial ways of placing the blame. The death of Jesus was more than the death of any other man. It was an event that had been in the mind of God from the creation of the world. All of God's dealings with humanity had pointed toward it. This was the Lord's doing! Christ had to die in order that God's redemptive program be consummated.

Scriptures show that the sinfulness of humanity made redemption a necessity. People are not convinced of their sinfulness through logic or proof. They must be convicted by the Holy Spirit through the written Word. Humans are sinners both by nature and by practice, and they can never be good enough to save themselves. Humanity's sin drove Jesus to the cross. Horatius Bonar says:

'Twas I that shed the sacred blood.
I nailed Him to the tree.
I crucified the Christ of God.
I joined the mockery.

Of all that shouting multitude
I feel that I am one.
And in that din of voices rude
I recognize my own.

III. The mercy of the cross.

It is on Calvary at the death of Jesus that we see the heart of God as at no other place in the Bible. Christ poured out his soul as an offering for our sin when he gave his life. His life was not taken away from him; he gave it. He made it very clear while in the days of his flesh that he laid down his life of his own free will. In the garden of Gethsemane, he said to Peter that he could pray to the Father and more than twelve legions of angels would come to his rescue. The reason he offered no resistance to his arrest and crucifixion was because of his great love for sinful humanity.

Lost people do not need justice; they need mercy. If God dealt with us on the basis of justice, all people would be lost. Our salvation is all of grace because God loves the undeserving. Grace has been defined as the free and undeserved mercy of God.

IV. The message of the cross.

A twofold call comes from Calvary. To the one who has never repented of sin and trusted in Jesus for salvation, the message is to receive Christ as personal Savior. When Jesus died on the cross, God put the sin of every individual on Jesus' back. He suffered all that the sinner deserves to suffer throughout eternity. Because he was God in the flesh, he had infinite ability to suffer everything that humans deserve to suffer. The cross of Jesus calls for repentance of sin and complete trust in Jesus as personal Savior. People begin life as Christians when they are born from above by accepting the justification that awaits them at Calvary. In justification people receive a new standing before God. People are justified on the basis of the one who has died in their place. Accompanying justification is regeneration. This is the change that takes place in the hearts of people when the death of Christ on the cross moves their hearts and the Holy Spirit makes them new persons in Jesus Christ.

For ones who have already been saved, the cross has a continuing message. We are to live constantly beneath its shadow and never forget that we are redeemed through the blood. The same blood that washed us from our sins signed us up to a lifelong commitment to the lordship of Christ. It is not enough to be saved from sin. We are saved for godly living and unselfish service. Every time we think of Calvary, we should remember afresh that it is through his mercy, not through works of our own, that we are children of God.

Conclusion

Do you know the peace that comes by surrendering your will completely to God? It comes, first of all, through the initial experience of becoming a Christian. This involves denying our own merit and accepting the merit that comes through the shed blood of the one who died on the cross and rose again. Being a Christian comes by a visit to "the old rugged cross" and finding there full pardon and complete forgiveness.

SUNDAY EVENING, APRIL 13

Title: Why People Do Go to Church

Text: "I was glad when they said unto me, Let us go into the house of the LORD" (**Ps. 122:1**).

Scripture Reading: Psalm 122

Introduction

Why do people attend church on Sunday morning? Not because of coercion. We live in a free country; attendance is optional. It is not for amusement. The world has the church beat by a mile when it comes to sheer entertainment.

In fact, some who attend church regularly find themselves wondering why some people come to church. Dr. Leslie Weatherhead, who had once had a distinguished ministry with the great City Temple of London, commented, "Now I am at the listening end of services. Sometimes I come away feeling frustrated and angry that a vital, glorious, joyous thing like the Christian religion should have been made so dull, so boring, so irrelevant, and so meaningless!"

Jesus attended the synagogue regularly. When he returned to Nazareth, where he was brought up, "as his custom was, he went into the synagogue on the sabbath day" (Luke 4:16). He had a habit of going to church. He did not wait to see if it was raining or if he had a headache before he decided whether he would attend. He certainly did not agree with everything the speaker was saying, and probably many services were boring; but he found his way to God's house. We are not following the example of our Lord if we do not have the custom of going regularly to God's house.

Some people are in church through unworthy motives. They go for respectability or status or to see the latest fashions or to salve their conscience because of their uncommitted lives. They go just out of habit.

But there are proper reasons for going to church.

I. To worship God.

In the heart of each of us is a need for God. In the soul is a capacity to worship God. God can be worshiped anywhere, but he can be best worshiped in his house. Someone said, "I can worship God in the out-of-doors, on the lake, or on the golf course." President Theodore Roosevelt's answer to this is a classic,

118

"You can, but you likely won't." Worship involves other people. Where even two or three are gathered in Christ's name, he promises to be in their midst. There is something about singing, praying, listening, and responding together that makes for a satisfying worship experience. Worship involves praise, the highest form of worship.

II. To experience forgiveness.

Worship also involves confession. The church is for sinners. In fact, you cannot be received into the church membership unless you confess that you are a sinner saved by grace. When we confess our sins, we experience the forgiveness of God. There we find the atmosphere that makes it possible to forgive ourselves and to forgive others.

III. To find Christian fellowship.

It is not the *job* of the church *to furnish* fellowship. It is the *mission* of the church *to be* a fellowship. We are made for each other. There is loneliness in isolation. We must bear one another's burdens and pray for one another. We love one another. A church that is a warm, dynamic fellowship is a going church.

IV. To be a part of God's great movement.

Jesus said, "Thou shalt worship the Lord thy God, and him only shalt thou serve" (Matt. 4:10). We enter to worship. We depart to serve. For a long time, we equated the work of the church with what happened inside its walls. Now we realize that "church" is not over when the congregation is dismissed.

In worship services, we witness "the church gathered." Our minds are instructed, our hearts are inspired, our souls are fed, and our wills are motivated. Then we go out into the world, still as the church, but now as "the church scattered."

Both roles of the church are vital. The church is not a fortress where we gather in isolation to enjoy God and each other. Neither is the church a scattered activist group without organization or roots or permanency. Such is a movement and not a church.

If this concept is true, then what happens inside the church building is important. What happens to us in the church will determine our effectiveness later when we become the church in the world.

Conclusion

A family in Ohio claims to have the smallest church in the world. A tiny church building has room for only two pews facing each other, with an altar in the midst. The message and the mission of the church are absent. It is not enough just to meet and talk and sing and listen and have fellowship. The church must make disciples and grow mature Christians and must change the world. True worship of God by the church is a vital and necessary part of that mission.

WEDNESDAY EVENING, APRIL 16

Title: The Bible Speaks to Our Condition
Scripture Reading: Acts 18

Introduction

In seeking light for the road of life today, it is always helpful if we can understand the controlling purpose of the Scripture writer. Acts 18 reveals one of the major purposes Luke had for writing the Acts of the Apostles. In this chapter, we have the dramatic point at which the official Jewish position toward the Christian movement is articulated. The Jews had repudiated Jesus Christ. They continued to reject the apostles' interpretation of Christ's life, death, resurrection, and continuing redemptive purpose. So Paul turned to the Gentiles with the gospel.

It has also been suggested that one of Luke's controlling purposes was to demonstrate that in every contact with Roman judicial authorities, Christianity had been revealed to be a religious movement rather than a subversive organization that threatened the Roman government. Gallio refused to indict Paul, for he found nothing for which he should condemn Paul.

I. A blessing in disguise (Acts 18:1–3, 18–19, 26–28).

We can well imagine the inconvenience and trouble to which the decree of the Roman emperor put Aquila and his wife, Priscilla, when they had to leave Rome. They could not know at that time that this decree would lead them into contact with Paul through their common trade. This contact with Paul was to lead to their conversion and to their use by God for the advancement of his redemptive purpose.

That which appeared to them as a calamity turned out eventually to be God's great and good blessing for them. God is at work in all things for good for those who love him. Have you experienced some failure, some tragedy, some great disappointment? Is it possible that God has something better in store for you? By faith, look for it. Let him bless you as he did Aquila and Priscilla. Not only did they experience conversion, but they became the companions of Paul, and they proved to be a great blessing to Apollos, who was one of the Lord's chosen servants.

II. The mission to the Gentiles begins (Acts 18:4–6).

When Ananias received the commission from God to go and minister to the new convert Saul, he was informed that Saul was a chosen vessel who would give testimony concerning Jesus Christ before the Gentiles (Acts 9:10–15). Many days and many events were to take place before Paul was actually to begin his evangelistic and missionary ministry to the Gentiles. This ministry was to begin when the Jewish rejection of the gospel brought about their self-exclusion and the opening of the door of opportunity to Gentiles.

God is eager to use any and all who will open their minds and hearts to him. Let us be cautious lest our unbelief and disobedience cause us to exclude ourselves from God's redemptive purpose.

III. The encouragement of God (Acts 18:9–10).

The apostle Paul ministered in the face of severe criticism and hostility. There was great opposition to him in the city of Corinth, as is revealed by his later arrest and presentation before the court of Gallio (18:12, 17). In the time of danger, God came to Paul and gave him an awareness of the divine presence with him at all times. God gave Paul a promise of protection. Jesus had given the same promise to his disciples when he voiced the command we know as the Great Commission (Matt. 28:19–20).

God will come and give to each of us encouragement as we need it. We can depend on the divine presence and divine provisions as we are obedient to his command.

IV. The need for spiritual strength (Acts 18:22–23).

In the last verses of this chapter, we have a compact account of Paul's journey from Corinth by way of Ephesus to Jerusalem and his return to Antioch and then the beginning of another missionary journey. It is declared that as he went from church to church that he had established on previous missionary journeys, he concentrated on strengthening the disciples.

God's children continue to need the strength that comes through devotional study of his Word. Let us let God speak to our condition through the pages of his Word.

We need the strength that comes through earnest, sincere prayer. Let us be certain that we listen as we pray.

We need the strength that comes through the testimony of others who have obeyed God and found him to be faithful to all of the promises he has made.

We need the strength that comes through an awareness of the abiding presence of the Holy Spirit within our hearts. The Holy Spirit can make us sufficient and adequate for any crisis, need, or opportunity that presents itself.

Conclusion

The Bible is not a mere record of what happened in the past. It is a record of what can happen in the present as we walk and talk with our Savior and as we minister in his name.

Let us look for the blessings that come to us in disguise. Let us be open to new ministries that the Lord might have for us. Let us always respond and trust in the encouragement that God sends to us.

SUNDAY MORNING, APRIL 20

Title: Jesus Arose with Power

Text: "That I may know him, and the power of his resurrection" (**Phil. 3:10**).

Scripture Reading: Matthew 28:1–10

Hymns: "Crown Him with Many Crowns," Bridges

"Christ Arose," Lowry

"He Lives," Ackley

Offertory Prayer: Our Father, we come on this Easter Sunday morning recognizing you as Lord of life. You are the Author and Finisher of our faith, and we are grateful because we know that your desire is to make life abundant for all people everywhere. We are grateful that even as the discouraged, disappointed, and seemingly defeated disciples were transformed by the risen Christ, so we today can participate in his triumph and find radiant hope as we walk with him in faith. We now bring our gifts to you. We are grateful that you have given us the ability to earn money. We count it a joy to invest in the work of your kingdom through the bringing of tithes and offerings. May we find deep satisfaction in obedience to your command of bringing the full tithe into the storehouse. Give us eager hands and willing hearts to do more than merely bring money. May we dedicate ourselves in personal service and never grow weary in well doing. We pray in Jesus' name and for his sake. Amen.

Introduction

Christianity is a supernatural religion, but it has its basis firmly rooted in history. The greatest miracle of all is the resurrection of Jesus Christ. Our faith depends on it. The issue is clearly drawn — either Jesus Christ arose from the dead or he did not. The Bible says he arose, and the history of Christianity proves that he arose. Eleven men were depressed and nearly defeated, but something completely transformed them and set them on fire with a zeal that could not be quenched. The personal experience of every born-again believer agrees with the biblical record. Jesus Christ is alive.

I. The fact of his death.

Skeptics have attempted to explain away the resurrection of Jesus by contending that he never actually died. The infamous "swoon theory" has, however, been repudiated even by some of the skeptics. It is ludicrous to think one could come from the grave weak and in need of medical treatment and tender care but at the same time inspire his followers so dynamically that he changed their sorrow into enthusiasm and elevated their reverence into worship. The biblical record makes it clear that Jesus died. The soldiers broke the legs of the two thieves who were crucified with Jesus, but when they came to Jesus, they found he was already dead and therefore did not break his legs. No external evidence indicates that the scriptural account is erroneous. Joseph of Arimathea begged for Jesus' body. He took it down from the cross, wrapped it in linen, and laid it in a sepulcher. Matthew tells how the Pharisees came to Pilate and asked him to be certain that the sepulchre "be made sure" to prevent Jesus' disciples from stealing his body. According to Matthew's account, this was done, and thus every bit of evidence points to the fact that Jesus died.

II. The events of the resurrection morning.

One of the strongest proofs that Jesus actually arose is that his followers were so slow to accept his resurrection as a fact. The four gospel writers tell the story—each from his own viewpoint. Although each gives his own interpretation of the facts as he was inspired by the Holy Spirit, there are no contradictions, and the stories blend into one beautiful account.

The first people to see Jesus alive after his resurrection were the women who came to the tomb early that morning. They wondered about moving the great stone in the door of the tomb but found when they arrived that it had been removed and the tomb was open. Mary Magdalene ran immediately to find Peter and John and tell them that someone had taken Jesus' body. While she was gone, the other women entered the open tomb and saw an angel who told them that Jesus had arisen. They departed quickly to tell the disciples. Meanwhile, Mary Magdalene found Peter and John. She told them what she had seen and then returned to the tomb. It seems Peter and John arrived before her. John ran faster than Peter and arrived first, but he only looked into the tomb and did not enter it. When Peter came, he at once entered the tomb, and then John followed him. They saw the linen cloths lying together and the napkin that had been around the head of Jesus rolled up in a place by itself. John immediately knew no grave robbers had been at the tomb. He was the first of the apostles to believe that Jesus had risen from the dead.

After Peter and John left, Mary Magdalene arrived a second time. It was then that she saw Jesus. This was the first postresurrection appearance of Jesus and is one of the most tenderly touching passages in the New Testament.

From then on events happened quickly. Jesus met the women as they were going to carry the apostles news of the resurrection. He next appeared to Simon Peter. His fourth appearance was to the two disciples journeying from Jerusalem to Emmaus. He then appeared to the disciples, minus Thomas, in the upper room and a week later to the disciples, including Thomas. Judas was, of course, absent, having killed himself after betraying Jesus.

Long before the modern skeptics with their fine-spun theories, there were those who supposed the whole story to be the wild imaginings of a group of excited and hysterical women. Subsequent events, however, proved undoubtedly that their enthusiastic testimony was true. After the first few fears of the disciples were dispelled, they became men of joy, boldness, and dynamic energy. They left those feelings of depression and self-pity that had characterized them during those hours between the burial of Jesus and the time when they were convinced beyond doubt of his resurrection. The events were proof in themselves. Jesus was alive.

III. The power that came.

There never has been in the history of the world a transformation so imme-diate, radical, and thorough as the resurrection of Jesus Christ. It turned eleven men who were utterly defeated into a bold, death-defying, completely committed band of witnesses. They became the nucleus of the greatest group of people the earth has ever seen—the true believers in Jesus Christ, his militant army that has marched forward through the centuries. This power cannot be explained on naturalistic or psychological grounds. These trembling followers were standing helpless before their hopeless inadequacy, and suddenly they flamed with assurance and became irresistible with their rocklike spirit. Those who think they can explain this transformation in terms of autosuggestion or deal with it on the basis of a nonsupernatural theology are simply ignoring the facts.

Is resurrection power available for us today? In many ways, our world is living under the same conditions as those discouraged, depressed, and defeated disciples were from burial day to resurrection day. It is true that we have not been with Jesus historically as they were in the days of his flesh. This does not mean, however, that we are, in any sense, limited. Actually, there is a sense in which even more power is available to us, for the greatest victories come through complete faith. Jesus recognized that Thomas believed because he saw, but he said, "Blessed are those who have not seen and yet have believed" (John 20:29 NIV). We are in that great group. We have seen and believed not with the eyes of flesh but with the eyes of faith.

Faith brings power. When we link our lives with a great ideal, there is no estimating the dynamic that is available. When that ideal is personified, as in Christianity, with a person who has unlimited compassion and unlimited resources, it is impossible to imagine the potential that may be realized. When Paul wrote to the Philippians (3:10 NIV) concerning the great desire of his life, he said, "I want to know Christ—yes, to know the power of his resurrection."

Conclusion

It was in the power of the risen Christ that the early Christians went forth to change the face of the world. Because of their fresh and vital experience with the resurrected Christ, they were able to work miracles in his name. In what sense is that power available to us today? Could it be that we are weak and anemic in our faith because we simply have not surrendered ourselves completely to the risen Christ? A minister in Birmingham, England, tells how one Saturday afternoon when he was making his final preparation for the Easter Sunday morning message the truth that Jesus is alive suddenly gripped him. He says that although he had believed this before, it gripped him in a new way. A new world opened to him, and his ministry underwent a change that was nothing short of miraculous. Do you need this change in your life? Perhaps we need the faith of the little schoolgirl years ago whose teacher asked the class to list the three greatest living people. The little girl wrote on her paper, "General MacArthur, President Eisenhower, and Jesus Christ." Her teacher corrected her by saying, "The first two are fine, but I asked you to list *living* people." The little girl replied, "Oh yes, ma'am, I understand. But Jesus Christ *is* living. He's alive. He rose from the dead." When this fact grips our hearts as it should, we can begin to live in the power of the risen Christ.

SUNDAY EVENING, APRIL 20

Title: The King Is Dead

Text: "In the year that King Uzziah died, I saw the Lord" **(Isa. 6:1 NIV)**.

Scripture Reading: Isaiah 6:1–13

Introduction

In 1952 the sad word went forth from London, "The king is dead." King George VI had died in his sleep at the age of fifty-six. He was a modest, retiring man, greatly respected and admired. His reign had carried him through the rigors of World War II, the election of a socialist government, and the dissolution of the worldwide colonial kingdom. His tired heart gave way. Britons flocked to churches to worship, to pray, and to seek comfort and hope.

In 1963 another shocking word encircled a disbelieving world: "The president is dead." John F. Kennedy, young, vibrant, and dynamic, was cut down by an assassin's bullet, and a nation was plunged into grief. People flocked to churches in the greatest numbers since the announcement of the close of World War II. Ministers changed their sermon texts and preached a gospel of healing and hope to the people of America.

About seven hundred years before Christ was born in Bethlehem, the sad announcement was made, "The king is dead." King Uzziah, the eleventh king of Judah, had died. Crowned at the age of sixteen, he had reigned fifty-two years. Despite his failings, he was the greatest king since David.

The heart of young Isaiah was broken. Uzziah was not only his king; he was also his friend. In his heartbreak, Isaiah made his way to the temple to worship and to seek comfort and renewed faith. The house of God is a good place to go when sorrow comes. Some Christians stay away from church for months after a loved one dies. Then they find that the first Sunday they return is a hard one. We should pray for strength and courage to be good stewards of our sorrow. Seeing us promptly back in God's house will impress others that we have inner resources that are adequate even in such a time of grief.

Isaiah learned that the king was dead but that God was not dead. Isaiah had lost his king but he discovered the King of Kings. He had a worship experience that radically changed his life.

I. Isaiah saw the Lord.

Isaiah saw God's nature and character. He saw God high and lifted up as Lord upon his throne. He saw God as the object of praise surrounded by heavenly courtiers. He saw him in all of his glory. He saw him in perfect holiness.

Only Isaiah saw the vision. If others were seated around him, they had no such experience. There is a sense in which corporate worship is still a very individual matter. One person is moved to tears while another in the same row is unmoved. One repents while another trusts in his own self-righteousness. One

125

responds to the claims of Christ and another vigorously resists the persuasion of the Holy Spirit.

II. Isaiah saw himself.

Isaiah did not see himself as a good person, deserving the commendation of God and the praise of people. He did not say to himself, "I must be a good person. I must be the best person here, for God has honored me alone with a vision of himself." Instead, he cried, "Woe to me! I am ruined! For I am a man of unclean lips" (6:5 NIV).

The closer we get to God, the more clearly we see our sins. The contrast between his holiness and our unholiness gives us a vivid awareness of our sinfulness. The times we feel we are good Christians is when we neglect to pray and worship and feel the presence of the Holy Spirit. When Peter was closest to Jesus, he said, "Depart from me; for I am a sinful man." When the vision of Christ the King was revealed to John on Patmos, he wrote, "I fell at his feet as dead." A lost sense of God brings a lost sense of sin.

III. Isaiah saw God's cleansing power.

When Isaiah confessed his sin, God was faithful and just to forgive his sin and to cleanse him of all his unrighteousness. The burning coal of purification and cleansing was applied to the member of his body that openly betrayed his inner sinfulness—his unclean lips. Isaiah experienced the sweet, clean feeling of forgiveness and peace. This is the blessing of confession in worship.

IV. Isaiah saw his work.

Isaiah heard the voice of the Lord saying, "Whom shall I send? And who will go for us?" (6:8 NIV). I can hear Isaiah asking, "Would God call a sinful man?" There is no other kind. Sometimes God calls the most sinful person to preach his Word. Yes, he calls sinners to go for him. He does not call sinless angels; he calls sinful people.

But God sends people only after they have been cleansed of their sins by his grace. The message of God must be spoken through clean lips. The work of God must be poured from clean vessels.

Conclusion

Isaiah did not say, "Where do you want me to go?" "What is in it for me?" "What are the calculated hazards involved?" "What is the salary?" "What are the retirement benefits?" Isaiah signed a blank check. He drove no bargain with God. He negotiated no compromise. God called. Isaiah answered. God commanded. Isaiah obeyed. Such an unconditional response comes only through the inspiration of the vision through worship.

The same thing can happen to us in this worship service today. The King is alive! He was dead, for he died for our sins on the cross. But he arose from the grave and lives today and is alive forevermore. Jesus is Lord. He requires unconditional surrender. He commissions us to look upon the fields ready to be harvested and to go into all the world as his witnesses. God help us to say, "Here am I. Send me!" (1:8 NIV).

WEDNESDAY EVENING, APRIL 23

Title: The Bible Speaks to Our Condition

Scripture Reading: Acts 25

Introduction

This chapter portrays the perplexity of the Roman officials as they sought to articulate an accurate and worthy charge to be brought against the apostle Paul when he stood before Caesar's judgment seat. Paul was no criminal. He had committed no crime against the nation of Israel or against the Roman Empire.

Some scholars have taken the position that one of Luke's controlling purposes as he wrote the book of Acts was to reveal that Christianity was not a subversive movement that threatened the Roman Empire. In every instance where there was a legal or judicial confrontation between the early Christians and the Roman officials, the decision of the court revealed that Christians were innocent of the charges brought against them. Christianity was not a threat to the Roman Empire as such; consequently, the Roman Empire had no reason to seek to eradicate Christianity from its borders.

I. Undeserved sufferings.

This chapter opens with Paul still in prison in Caesarea. He had remained in prison for the last two years. He was guilty of no crime except that of preaching the gospel of God's grace to Gentiles as well as Jews.

Paul was the object of the hatred and hostility of those who opposed his viewpoint and who would have brought Christianity to an end. Paul responded to the situation, in which he found himself positive and triumphant.

A. *Not all suffering is the result of sin committed by the sufferer.* We must repudiate the idea that all suffering is due to some failure or due to some error in the life of the one suffering.

B. *There are many causes for undeserved suffering.*
   1. We suffer because of the carelessness of others.
   2. We suffer because of the selfishness of others.
   3. We suffer because of the suffering of others.
   4. We suffer because of the activity of Satan.
   5. We suffer sometimes because of our own carelessness.
   6. Sometimes there is absolutely no earthly explanation for the suffering that we have to endure.

C. *We could find some comfort in the truth that no suffering comes to us outside of the permissive will of our loving God.*

127

II. Opportunity for unique witnessing.

As we search for some light from this chapter for the road of life today, we can be reminded that every situation provides some opportunity for a Christian witness. Paul had given his Christian testimony time and time again to Felix and Drusilla, his wife (Acts 24). In Acts 25, Paul had the privilege of giving his Christian testimony to Festus, the Roman procurator, and to King Agrippa and Bernice, and to the other Jewish and Roman officials who must have been present on this occasion.

This experience provided Paul with the opportunity to fulfill the intent the Lord had for him at the time of his conversion and call to a missionary ministry (Acts 9:15). Paul was experiencing what our Lord had foretold would happen to his faithful disciples (Matt. 10:18).

Conclusion

Today, like yesterday and tomorrow, will provide us with some unique opportunities to share with others the good news of God's love and grace as we have experienced it in Jesus Christ. May we seize our opportunities and use them for his glory as did the apostle Paul.

SUNDAY MORNING, APRIL 27

Title: What Will You Do with Jesus?

Text: "What shall I do then with Jesus which is called Christ?" **(Matt. 27:22)**.

Scripture Reading: Matthew 27:15–26

Hymns: "O Jesus, Thou Art Standing," How

          "How Sweet the Name of Jesus," Newton

          "Tell It to Jesus," Rankin

Offertory Prayer: Our Father, we recognize this is a day when, as never before, we are utterly dependent on you. The problems that face us in this world are too great to be solved by human ingenuity. As we approach you this morning, we recognize our inadequacy, but we also have confidence because of your resourcefulness. We are glad because we know that you do love us and that you do desire for us the best in life. Help us to realize, however, that we must respond with dedication if we are to realize the fruits of your love. As we come to make our offering this morning, may we realize that this is a needy world. Make us aware anew that only the gospel of Jesus Christ can bring permanent peace to troubled and rebellious hearts. Use these offerings to your glory and to the proclamation of the message that Jesus Christ died for our sins, was resurrected for our justification, and is coming again to receive the saved unto himself. We pray these things in Jesus' name. Amen.

Introduction

For a number of weeks, we have looked at the life of Jesus. We have endeavored to see his ministry in miniature. The major events that are representative of his work have been emphasized. Underlying all of these truths has been the fact that he came into the world on a redemptive mission — to seek and to save that which was lost. A study of the life of Jesus in history lays the foundation for a great question. This morning we consider the all-important matter of our own relationship to him. What have we done with him personally? Have we received him into our hearts as both Savior and Lord? Is he a part of our daily experiences in life?

Pilate faced the question of a decision for Jesus. He wanted to remain neutral, but he could not push aside a decision. So it is with us. To refuse to decide for Jesus is to reject him. The question Pilate asked is a comprehensive one. Some other questions arise from it.

I. Who Is Jesus?

If the Bible is so bold as to proclaim the necessity of our making a decision concerning Jesus, surely we have the right to ask questions about him and his nature. Was he just another teacher, preacher, or religious reformer? Or was he more? The verdict of history is that Jesus was far more than just an ordinary human being. When Ralph Waldo Emerson finished his work *Representative Men*, someone asked him why he did not include Jesus Christ. He replied that it would require too much strength of constitution to put Jesus Christ in the same category with ordinary human beings. All of us who know Jesus in personal forgiveness of sin recognize that though Jesus was a great teacher and preacher, he was far more. We should remember, of course, that Jesus can truly be understood only from within the context of a personal experience with him. It was when Thomas finally understood Jesus that he shouted, "My Lord and my God" (John 20:28).

The Man who dares to come and demand a decision from us is not merely a peasant from a small town in a captive province. He is the one who has proved to the world both in the days of his flesh and in subsequent history that he is worthy of complete allegiance and is alone the Lord of both death and life.

II. What can you do with Jesus?

There are only two possibilities open concerning Jesus. First, he may be accepted. You may receive him into your heart as Savior. You may recognize your own sinfulness and inadequacy to cope with the problems of life, death, and eternity. You may see that in him the Father's love is demonstrated. In Jesus our guilt may be removed. We may be justified by his grace. We may accept the atonement as the substitute for the penalty of our sins and become a redeemed creature and a member of God's family. This is what all wise people do when they hear the gospel preached in its fullness.

There is another alternative: mortals may reject the divine Christ. Regardless of our beliefs about predestination or God's foreknowledge, the fact remains that people have a free will. People can refuse God. Even though Christ died for all, all will not be saved. Only those who receive Christ as Savior will enter into the fullness of joy that God has provided for his redeemed people. You can receive Jesus, but you also can reject him.

There is no third alternative. Actually, there is no essential difference between rejecting Jesus outright and postponing the decision. Both are dangerous and both can be fatal to one's spiritual destiny. The gospel of Jesus Christ is a very dangerous thing. When it is preached to an individual, it has one of two effects. Either that person receives Christ as Savior or that person's refusal to accept Christ drives him or her farther away from the salvation God offers.

III. What does it really matter?

Is there any great issue at stake? After all, Jesus lived so many hundreds of years ago, does it really matter whether I make a decision concerning him or not?

The verdict of history proves that it does matter—it matters much. First, it matters in this life. Followers of Christ are the truly happy people. They are the ones who are making this world a better place in which to live. If there were no such thing as a life beyond, it would still be a wise course of action to be a Christian because of the joy that comes in this life to those who are surrendered to the Lord's will.

Second, it matters in death what we do with Jesus. Daniel Webster was once asked what was the greatest thought that had ever entered his mind. He answered with great emotion, "My personal responsibility to God." Death comes to all of us. It comes to the aged person as he walks falteringly. Often its trumpet sound is heard by one who is barely halfway in the journey of life. Many times its icy grip hushes the laughter of little children. Salvation through Jesus is more than merely "death insurance," but it is this—if one wishes to call it by that name. On his deathbed a great scientist was asked, "What are your speculations now?" He replied, "Speculations? I have none. I know whom I have believed." To be able to face death calmly and with assurance that all is well is a worthy goal. For one to have Jesus as personal Savior and the witness of the Spirit within produces a peace that the world cannot give and cannot take away.

The third reason why our decision concerning Jesus matters greatly is that we will spend eternity somewhere. The Bible does not hold out three possibilities—only two. There is a heaven prepared for those who love Jesus, and there is a hell for the devil and his servants. Eternity is forever. Throughout its endless ages, we will reap the result of our decision concerning the Savior. It matters greatly what we do with Jesus!

IV. Who will decide the question?

In the light of normal intelligence, to ask this question is but to answer it. There is nothing in the Bible nor in the processes of rational logic to give us any hope that someone else can answer the question for us. Some wives would answer for their husbands if they could, and vice versa. Some parents would answer for their children, and some children for their parents. Friends often plead with friends to receive Jesus, but this is as far as they can go. The question is an intensely personal one. Joshua spoke to an audience of perhaps two million Jews.

He recited the history of God's providential dealings with the nation, and then he pleaded, "Choose for yourselves this day whom you will serve" (Josh. 24:15 NIV). It is significant that he used the second person singular pronoun, which indicated that although he was addressing a multitude of people, the choice was a personal one. Each person must decide for himself or herself.

V. When should the question be decided?

A minister was pleading with his people to turn to God. A man asked the minister when he should do it. The minister replied, "On the last day before you die." "But I do not know the day I will die," said the man. The minister replied, "Then come to God today." The matter of life's uncertainty is, of course, a strong reason for coming to Jesus today. There are, however, other motivations. The longer we put off our decision for Christ, the harder it becomes. Just as Pharaoh's heart was hardened each time he rejected God's will in the days of Moses, so we jeopardize our ability to make a decision in the future when we turn down God in an earlier encounter.

The highest reason for coming to Christ *now* is that the sooner we become a Christian, the sooner we begin to enjoy the fruits of the Christian life. This is the motivation that a lost person can seldom understand. It is usually the crisis concerning our lostness and the punishment that awaits that leads us to Jesus as Savior, but it does not need to be this reason. Jesus offers an abundant life. We are not only saved from hell, but we are saved to a spiritual fellowship with our Lord that begins in this life and continues throughout eternity.

Whatever motivation moves us, we should act on it and decide today. It is the safe course to pursue and the one that will begin spiritual dividends that will last throughout eternity.

Conclusion

This series of messages has sought to bring us face-to-face with the living Lord. God revealed himself through Jesus in history, but his revelation is above history. Jesus is timeless because he is truly the "Man for all seasons." The same Jesus who nestled in his mother's arms as a babe and walked the dusty streets of Galilee and the rocky plateaus of Judah, who was nailed to the cross and arose from the tomb, is the Jesus who confronts us today and demands our allegiance. His voice is tender and winsome, but it is also stern and challenging. What have you done with him? What will you do with him? Your life's momentous issues will be decided by the answer you give to his call.

SUNDAY EVENING, APRIL 27

Title: The King in His Glory

Text: "As he was praying, the appearance of his face changed, and his clothes became as bright as a flash of lightning" (**Luke 9:29 NIV**).

Scripture Reading: Luke 9:28–37

Introduction

Many great spiritual experiences in the Bible took place on mountains. Most of them were viewed by very few witnesses. On Mount Moriah, Abraham offered up his son Isaac. On Mount Sinai, amid lightning and thunder, Moses received the Ten Commandments. On Mount Carmel, Elijah called down the fire of God and devastated the religion and priests of Baal. The wilderness temptations included one from a mountaintop. Christ died on Mount Calvary. On the Mount of Ascension a cloud received him out of the onlookers' sight.

It was probably on Mount Hermon where Jesus was transfigured. He had set himself apart for some very important reasons.

First, Jesus set out to seek the guidance of his heavenly Father. He was on the way to the cross, and he felt the need to pray. He never took a step without listening to the voice of God. When he had a problem, he did not proceed on human advice. He sought out a lonely place where he could have fellowship with God.

Second, Jesus needed strength. He was under tremendous pressure. Those who sought his life were closing in. He was misunderstood, even by his friends. He was lonely, for even his most devoted disciples rebuked him when he tried to inform them of his impending death. His human nature recoiled against the prospect of death. He sought the fellowship of God. He received the fellowship of heavenly visitors who understood his mission.

Moses represented the law. He was the lawgiver and could see the fulfillment of the law in Jesus. Elijah, the greatest of the prophets, represented the prophets. Some even mistook Jesus as Elijah arisen from the dead. The two conversed with Jesus about his "departure" (Luke 9:31 NIV). The word "departure" in the New Testament has the same meaning as the word "exodus" in the Old Testament. *Exodus* means "going out." The second book of the Bible is titled "Exodus," meaning the children of Israel going out from the bondage of Egypt into the Promised Land. What a description of the death of the believer! Death to the Christian is going out from the bondage of this life into the freedom of that glorious land our Savior is preparing for us.

As Jesus prayed, he was transfigured. A radiance shone from within. A cloud descended, and the voice of God spoke his pleasure in his Son. It was a high and holy hour.

The three disciples who accompanied Jesus were deeply impressed and moved. The spiritual ecstasy Peter experienced surpassed any other event in his life. The wonder and adoration of the moment were overwhelming. We can hear him saying, "Lord, it is good to be here. Let's stay here. This is as near heaven as I can stand. Let us build three tents, one for you, one for Moses, and one for Elijah. As far as John and James and I are concerned, we'll be happy to sleep on the ground."

God rebuked Peter, and Jesus led the three disciples down into the valley where a crisis awaited them. The nine remaining disciples had sought to heal a tragically ill boy and had not been successful. The enemies of Jesus were exultant. It was a crisis for the kingdom as well as a crisis for a father and his sick son. Our impotence is an embarrassment to Jesus. Our lack of faith reflects on him. With a word he healed the boy and gave his disciples a lesson on faith.

There are two vital lessons we learn from this experience of worship on the mount:

I. Communion with God transfigures.

Worship changes the worshiper. The disciples could see the difference in Jesus' countenance. Moses' face shone as he came down from Mount Sinai after a time with God. The face of the martyr Stephen shone as he looked up and saw Jesus standing at the right hand of God. Neither of these men was aware that his face shone. If it is a genuine radiance, we are the last to notice it.

Dr. George W. Truett, pastor of the First Baptist Church, Dallas, for most of the first half of the twentieth century, was a man of devout prayer and spirituality. A columnist for the *Dallas News* wrote an article about the great pastor just a few years before he died. Truett went one day from his study to an urgent appointment in downtown Dallas. As he walked down the busy street, his eyes straight ahead, his mind intent upon his mission, a man coming from the opposite direction got one glimpse of his face. That man's feet were bent on a mission of evil. He did not know the pastor; he had never seen him before. But there was something about his face, his eyes, and his bearing that prompted that man to turn aside from his sinful errand. And Dr. Truett never knew of it until he read it in the *Dallas News*.

II. Prayer equips for the valley.

Peter wanted to prolong the great moment on the mount, but there was a need down in the valley, and Jesus and the disciples could supply that need.

We cannot live all our life on the mountain. Neither must we live all our life in the valley. We must climb the mountain and experience the worship of God. Then we must take the mountaintop back into the valley to those who have not been up the mountain. We must witness the glory of God on the mountaintop so we may minister to the misery of man in the valley. We cannot live Sunday all seven days of the week. We must worship God and renew our bodies and minds and spirits. Then God gives us six week days back in the valley to take the spirit and inspiration and witness of the Lord's Day to the people. We must meet God in the secret place and in the church meeting place so that we may meet sinful and needy people in the marketplace. We take our needs to God so that we may be strengthened to meet the needs of other people.

Jesus said, "Thou shalt worship the Lord thy God, and him only shalt thou serve." We have not really worshiped unless our worship equips and motivates us to serve.

Conclusion

As a college student, I was privileged to attend a weekend retreat with students from all over the state. Friday night was a helpful service. Saturday the spirit rose higher and higher. On Saturday night, we were on the mountaintop. In a testimony service, students shared their dread of having to go back to their cold, secular campuses the next day.

Finally, a new Christian began to speak. "You think you've had a great experience! Think about me. A few weeks ago, I didn't know anything like this existed in this life or in a life to come. It is great! It is wonderful! And I can hardly wait for the retreat to end tomorrow so I can get back on our campus and share it with everybody I see." He had caught the vision. How we need the fire of God within us. How we long for the transfiguring experience of exalted worship that we may be equipped to minister to the multitudes who hurt in the valley.

WEDNESDAY EVENING, APRIL 30

Title: The Bible Speaks to Our Condition
Scripture Reading: Romans 4

Introduction

In our chapter for today, Paul is seeking to clarify the way of salvation as being by grace through faith rather than by obedience to the law. He has contended that the believer finds a condition of acceptance before God on the basis of faith rather than by the works of the law (Rom. 3:24, 28). Abraham, the father of the faithful, illustrates this thrilling truth.

I. Abraham received justification on the basis of his faith (Rom. 4:1–8).

The word *justification* is a legal term and refers to the activity of God. It is that act of God in which he declares a person acceptable in his sight. God justified Abraham on the basis of Abraham's faith.

II. Abraham received justification before he received circumcision (Rom. 4:9–12).

Circumcision was a sign or seal of the covenant relationship. Paul affirms that the covenant relationship was established prior to circumcision. Circumcision followed justification rather than justification following circumcision.

III. Abraham received the divine promise before the giving of the Law (4:13–15).

Abraham preceded Moses by four hundred years. There was no way by which he could have kept the law of Moses, yet he did receive the divine promise.

Israel had made the fatal mistake of substituting the law of Moses for the faith of Abraham as a way of finding favor in the presence of God. They substituted law for faith. We need to beware of the same peril.

IV. Abraham would encourage us to claim the promises of God (Rom. 4:16–25).

We receive justification from God through faith that it might be based on God's grace rather than on human achievement.

Abraham believed God and put confidence in God's promises. He was not weak in faith. He did not stagger back in unbelief when God came to him with some great promises. Abraham was persuaded that God was faithful, dependable, and trustworthy, and that he could depend on God to keep his promise.

At this point, Abraham would speak to us. He would encourage us to discover God's promises, claim God's promises, and march forward depending on God to keep his promises.

This passage was recorded in Scripture not in order that we might merely know about Abraham but that we might be encouraged to trust God as Abraham did. "Lord, increase our faith."

MAY

■ **Sunday Mornings**

The suggested theme for Sunday mornings in May is "The Needs of the Family."

■ **Sunday Evenings**

The suggested theme for the evening messages is "Teens: Problems and Potential." The young people in your congregation need specific guidelines and encouragement as well as warnings from the pulpit.

■ **Wednesday Evenings**

Continue the series of Bible studies with the theme "The Bible Speaks to Our Condition." The theme verse for the month is "These were more noble than those in Thessalonica, in that they received the word with all readiness of mind, and searched the scriptures daily, whether those things were so" (Acts 17:11).

SUNDAY MORNING, MAY 4

Title: Maintaining Communication Lines within the Home

Text: "A soft answer turneth away wrath: but grievous words stir up anger. The tongue of the wise useth knowledge aright: but the mouth of fools poureth out foolishness" **(Prov. 15:1–2)**.

Scripture Reading: 1 Peter 3:1–12

Hymns: "Love Divine," Wesley

"The Christian Home," Spitta

"Lead Me Gently Home, Father," Thompson

Offertory Prayer: Our heavenly Father, we thank you for your blessings on us through the home. May our tithes and offerings be used to bring about the conversion of boys and girls, men and women, who will be able to serve you better in their homes. Bless this act of worship as each of us brings of our material substance to express concern for the advancement of your kingdom through Jesus Christ our Lord. Amen.

Introduction

We live in a fantastic age of instant worldwide communication. We can converse with and instantaneously send communications to people on the other side

136

of the earth. We can even watch and listen by means of television or the Internet as people converse while living in a space station in outer space. We are able to do this because of the excellent communication facilities that modern technology has made available to us.

All of us are involved in the communication business in one way or another. People are communicators. This is a part of their uniqueness as the crown of God's creation made in the image of the Creator.

The Bible teaches us that God is a communicator (Heb. 1:1–2). The Bible is the record of God's self-revelation and his effort to communicate his goodwill to humans. God continues to seek to communicate with people through the pages of the Bible and through the experiences that his children have through faith and obedience.

The experience that we call prayer is actually an experience of communication with the Father God. Believers not only approach the throne of grace in prayer to present confessions, praises, and petitions, but if prayer is to be meaningful, they must listen. God is a communicator, and humans have a built-in receiving set.

Our Lord, following his victorious resurrection from the dead, charged his disciples to become communicators. The Great Commission is concerned with communication. There is no way by which we can think of continued existence except in terms of both giving and receiving communications from others. In no area of life is good communication more important than within the family circle.

I. A marriage is a result of a communication process.

It is often said that people get married because they fall in love with each other. The experience of falling in love is the end result of a process of communication. By the process of courtship, they sell each other on the idea that their greatest future happiness is to be found in a union of their two lives in marriage.

The communication that leads to marriage may take many different forms. The man and woman may dialogue often on a variety of subjects. They may communicate by email and text and chat on the phone. They may communicate with each other by exchanging gifts. Communication may take the form of a smile or a frown. Holding hands is a form of communication, as is a kiss.

Because the man communicates something that is very desirable to the woman, and because the woman communicates something that is very desirable to the man, they decide to enter marriage that they might live in communication with each other on a continuing and permanent basis.

Marriage is the result of love, but it is also the result of a process of favorable communication between a man and a woman.

II. The peril of poor communication in the home.

Many dangers imperil the lines of communication in the world. A power failure may occur or an accident may interrupt the lines of communication. Likewise, there are many hindrances to good communication within the home.

A successful marriage requires effective and benevolent communication between husband and wife and between parents and children. Communication is a primary problem in all types of family difficulties.

A. *Some marriages fail because the couple ceases to communicate with each other.* The wise man said, "Death and life are in the power of the tongue" (Prov. 18:21). Are you using types of communication in your home that will destroy the desire of others to be in communication with you?

B. *Some marriages fail because of destructive and inappropriate types of communication.* Examine the types of communication you use within the home.

1. Beware of the cutting criticism that creates hostility. The courtship process consisted of a man and a woman bestowing one compliment after another on each other. If marriage is to continue to be happy and satisfying, the expression of compliments and approvals must continue. If criticism is ever offered, it should be combined with compliments. An appropriate time and mood should be selected for the expression of any criticism.

2. Beware of emotional outbursts. Regretfully, much of the destructive communication in the home takes place on the level of an emotional outburst. We need to beware of dated emotion. An unpleasant experience in our early life can so injure us as to cause us to react in an unfavorable manner at any time when similar circumstances remind us of the pain we experienced at that time. We also need to beware of misplaced emotion in which we express anger toward one person when, in reality, we are upset about something else.

3. We need to beware of a dogmatic attitude that does not consider the opinions of others. One man said with sarcasm, "My wife has never made a mistake in our fifteen years of marriage." She was a dogmatic soul who could never admit being wrong.

4. Beware of insulting each other. An insult will always provoke an angry retaliation. Husbands and wives often insult each other. Parents who are guilty of insulting their children should not wonder why their children are angry.

5. Examine the tone of your communication. You may communicate more by the manner in which you speak than with the words you use. The wise man said, "A soft answer turneth away wrath" (Prov. 15:1). He also said, "A word fitly spoken is like apples of gold in pictures of silver" (Prov. 25:11).

III. Building good communication lines within the home.

When a husband and wife have broken the lines of communication between themselves, a third party may be needed to help reconstruct these lines. A couple went to their pastor with an apology: "Pastor, we need help. We don't want to get a divorce, but somehow our marriage has ceased to be beautiful and meaningful like it once was. Can you assist us?" The pastor congratulated the couple on their wisdom and listened to their problems. Then he suggested some guidelines for rebuilding the lines of communication that had been so meaningful to them in the past. His suggestions may prove helpful to you.

    A. *Ask the Lord for help.* Establish a time each day in which together, even if you pray silently, you lift your home, with its problems and potential, up before God's throne of grace.

    B. *Accept the fact of human frailty and imperfection.* Do not expect perfection from family members, and be certain to recognize your own imperfection and incompleteness.

    C. *Develop a concern for the feelings of others.* Both husband and wife have individual personal feelings that are of supreme importance to them. Children also have emotional needs. We must be concerned about the feelings of others.

    D. *Apologize for improper and hurtful words and actions.* Ask the Lord to help you say "I'm sorry" to the members of your own household when you mistreat them. This takes faith and courage and grace.

    E. *Practice the fine art of forgiveness.* You must forgive others if you want God to forgive you. Renounce the right to retaliate, and instead restore a warm feeling.

    F. *Recognize the importance of listening to others.* Listening takes time and concentration. Others need to know that you are listening.

    G. *Determine to become a giver, and recognize the good in others.*

        1. Give praise to others in the household.

        2. Express gratitude to others in the home.

        3. Express confidence in others in the home.

        4. Create a sense of high esteem in others. Do not cut others down. Build them up and encourage them.

Conclusion

Good communication is dialogue not monologue. Listen to those in your home as well as speaking to them.

God is seeking to communicate with you his love, his forgiveness, his hope, his help, and the happiness that can be yours.

Decide now to listen to the Lord, hear his words, and believe his promises. Confess your need for him. Invite him into your heart and into your home. Welcome him now.

SUNDAY EVENING, MAY 4

Title: Teens and Rebellion

Text: "As soon as ye hear the sound of the trumpet, then ye shall say, Absalom reigneth in Hebron" **(2 Sam. 15:10).**

Scripture Reading: 2 Samuel 15:1 – 14

Introduction

There is a long-haired youth in the Bible who reminds me of some modern teenagers. His name was Absalom. He had many fine qualities. Of all David's sons, he was the most promising. He was handsome and intelligent. He had leadership capabilities, a sense of humor, and a magnetic personality. He was adventuresome and ambitious, wholehearted, and daring. He had an unembarrassed confidence in his own ability. He lived magnificently in the king's palace. Common people loved him. Though he was an aristocrat, he was not aloof. He drove a chariot with fifty men running before him, and he had the fastest horses in the royal stables.

Absalom was a genius with the human touch. One day, in the foolishness of his youth, he revolted against his own father. He stole the hearts of the people. The new generation challenged the old. With his admirers and loyal friends and leaders about him, Absalom crowned himself king in Hebron.

I. Age of rebellion.

What happens when a person stomps his little foot and shakes his little fist toward heaven and says, "Leave me alone, God; I'm going to live my own life"? Absalom is what happens. Judas Iscariot is what happens. Adolf Hitler is what happens. Teenagers arrested for serious crimes in cities all across America are what happens!

The rebel spirit is as old as the garden of Eden. Adam and Eve were rebels when they chose to eat of the fruit of the Tree of the Knowledge of Good and Evil. The children of God rebelled against his ways and sought to build a tower to heaven. The prodigal son rebelled against his father and went away to the far country. Rebellion lies deep in the very nature of everyone who lives on this earth. The question is how to make this rebellion creative, for it can be either creative or destructive. We can gather up these tendencies and be carried to the heights, or these pent-up emotions can cast us down to the depths. Anyone can break an egg, but who can put Humpty Dumpty together again?

I wonder if our society is not aiding the rebel spirit. Absalom's society and home, his environment, added fuel to the flame of his rebel spirit. Too much leisure time, a father who lavished every luxury and comfort upon him, giving him expensive gifts, the finest clothing, and horses and chariots (today it would be automobiles), encouraged his rebellion. His father gave Absalom everything materially, but he neglected Absalom's moral and spiritual training. Some of us give our children everything except the one thing that really counts most, companionship. A society that distributes obscene literature and portrays filth and immorality on television and in the movies encourages a bad environment and insecurity and running with the wrong crowd and longing for love. These are all fuel that adds flames to the fire of a rebel spirit. What if this revolt is a symbol of deep hunger and thirst within for God and for a deeper meaning to life?

II. Avenues of rebellion.

Absalom revolted against authority and restraint. He was a victim of self-will.

140

"I will do what I want to do. I will do as I please. I will love my own life. No one can stop me. Leave me alone." This is rebellion against any demands, against any discipline, against the cross. A new resident of a town informed the visiting minister when he called that she and her family were looking for a good, "modern church that won't make any demands on us." This is a part of the spirit of our age.

Another avenue of rebellion is that of indulgence. "I will drown myself in drink, or drugs, or delinquency. I can forget myself for a little while in my escapades, my dreams, and delusions." The results of this type of rebellion are skid row and incarceration. Another road of rebellion is the way of the stoic. "I can be my own God. I can be the master of my soul." Then there are those who seek to escape from reality. They become the dropouts. They lose themselves through conformity. They pretend to be someone else. They wear a mask. To wear a disguise to a party may be innocent fun, but to compel oneself to wear it in broad daylight is another thing.

III. Answer to rebellion.

There is a thin line of difference between adventure and daring on the one hand and unfruitful rebellion on the other. Rebellion can be a noble thing. It is noble for youth to be adventurous and daring. Jesus revolted against tradition and custom in his day. He refused to treat people of other races with pride, hatred, and contempt. He ate with sinners and publicans. He refused to adopt outward customs that were meaningless. However, it is one thing to revolt against custom and tradition, and it is another to revolt against justice, righteousness, and temperance. Sometimes it is wise to rebel, and other times it is foolish. True rebellion is creative rather than destructive. If youth can choose the truth and move on to higher and nobler things, then to rebel is a wonderful thing. The youth who will accomplish the most in our world today are those who reach up to God for life, light, and leadership.

The love of David followed after Absalom. He felt that some day love would overtake his son. We hear the great cry of David in the room above the gate as the news comes that Absalom has been killed in battle. This love is perfect in purity, unflagging in purpose, and invincible in appeal. Hear the great king say, "O Absalom, my son, my son, would God I could have died for thee!" I wonder if Absalom really knew his father loved him like that. If Absalom could have heard it, he might have come home.

Conclusion

Today we should listen for the voice of God saying, "My child, I have died for you." The Absalom spirit of our hearts should hear it. There is an old story of a couple engaged to be married. Just before the wedding day, the bride jilted the groom and ran away with another man. It broke his heart so that he could never go with another woman. A few years later, she returned to the community, having been deserted and broken by her lover. Everyone expected her old fiancé to jeer and say, "Serves her right for what she did to me." However, to their amazement, he went to her and professed he still loved her and would forgive all. She could not believe him. So great was her shame and sorrow that she could not comprehend that such love was still possible. He tried again and again to convince her, but his words were impotent. One day she was driving through town in her buggy. Something frightened her horse, and it started to run away. Her life was in danger, and the former fiancé, seeing the situation, ran out and brought the horse under control. In so doing, he was severely injured, but as the woman took his head in her arms, he managed to say weakly, "Maggie, don't you believe me now? I do love you." In the same way, God spoke of his forgiving love, but sinful people did not believe it, and so, in the fullness of time, he came in human form. He flung himself into the midst of our runaway world and in so doing was badly mangled, even killed on a cross. But does not that very act say to us, "Won't you believe me now? I do love you."

This is the story of the gospel. This is the love of God that reaches out to draw those with the Absalom spirit to himself. The answer to rebellion is the cross.

WEDNESDAY EVENING, MAY 7

Title: The Bible Speaks to Our Condition

Scripture Reading: Romans 11

Introduction

Romans 9–11 is a passage that is difficult for the casual reader to understand. It demands a knowledge of the historical situation in which Paul wrote. Paul was writing to the Christian community in Rome, where a large Jewish community had been for about two hundred years. Some of these Jewish people had been converted to Christianity, but the overwhelming majority of the believers were Gentiles. As time went by, Gentiles greatly outnumbered Jewish converts. This gave rise to questions concerning the place that the Jewish people now occupied in the purpose of God.

Paul registers the great concern of his heart for the conversion of his kinsmen (Rom. 9:1–4; 10:1–3). He discusses how that the Jewish people, in trying to obtain righteousness by the law rather than through faith, have disqualified themselves to be the instrument of God for evangelizing the world.

This entire passage deals with God's mercy and the mystery of God's dealings with people. Daily we should study the Scriptures that we might better understand God's plans for our lives.

I. God's dealings with people are always based on his grace (Rom. 11:5–6).

In the book of Romans, Paul emphasizes that God in grace approaches people in their need. God does not deal with people on the basis of their merit or achievement.

II. People respond to God through faith (Rom. 11:20, 23).

Through faith we receive a "faith righteousness" rather than a "law righteousness." The Jewish people were seeking to pursue and obtain righteousness by keeping the law. Paul affirms repeatedly on the basis of the experience of Abraham (Rom. 4) and the teaching of the prophets that people obtain justification (a condition of acceptance before God) by faith rather than by keeping the law of Moses.

III. There is hope for Israel through faith in the Messiah (Rom. 11:12, 14–15).

The people of Israel had excluded themselves from the redemptive program of God because of their unbelief in the promises and provisions of God. This was their record through history. It came to a crowning climax in their rejection of Jesus Christ as the Messiah.

In the heart of God, there continues to be a hope for the redemption of Israel through faith in the Messiah. This chapter opens with the question, "Hath God cast away his people?" With a strong negative, the apostle declares that they continue to be in the scope of God's loving, redemptive concern.

The present-day church has not faced up to its responsibility and opportunity to evangelize those who make up modern-day Judaism. The Jews of today need to be pointed to the Messiah through whom they can experience justification and obtain righteousness by faith.

IV. Humility, rather than conceit, should characterize Christians (Rom. 11:18).

It is possible that some of the Gentile Christians in Rome were boastful and proud of their privileged position in the program of God. Paul rebuked this attitude of conceit and encouraged an attitude of humility and gratitude for the privilege of being in God's great redemptive program.

V. God's ways are above human understanding (Rom. 11:33–36).

Some things concerning the work of God are mysterious and impossible for human beings to understand. He is the Eternal One, and we are creatures of the day. He has all knowledge, and we see only little fractions of truth.

Instead of questioning the judgment of God, we should respond to our opportunities for worship and witness day by day in the confidence that the Lord will bring all things to a wonderful consummation.

Conclusion

God has been good to us. He wants to continue to be gracious to us. Let us go out into this day and every day as his messengers and servants, rejoicing in his goodness.

SUNDAY MORNING, MAY 11

Title: Christ in Your Home

Text: "And again he entered into Capernaum after some days; and it was noised that he was in the house" **(Mark 2:1).**

Scripture Reading: Mark 2:1–12

Hymns: "Have Faith in God," McKinney

"O Blessed Day of Motherhood," McGregor

"Faith of Our Mothers," Patten

Offertory Prayer: Our Father, on this special day, we pause to thank you for your wonderful gifts to us through our mothers. Help us to be mindful that every good and perfect gift is from you. You have been most generous toward us. Today, as we give our tithes and offerings, help us to be grateful for your great love toward us in the giving of your Son in our place on the cross. In Jesus' name. Amen.

Introduction

The Jesus of history wants to be the Christ of our present-day experience. If we would experience the benevolent and powerful presence of Jesus Christ, we must let the Christ who once lived, died on the cross, and conquered death to live again come to live where we live today.

We can let this living Christ speak to us from the mountainside as he did in the past. As Christ spoke to his disciples while on board ship in the midst of a storm, so we can let him speak to us in the storms that threaten us. As Christ's disciples listened to him in the temple, so we need to listen to him when we go to the place dedicated to prayer and worship. Christ will speak to us in dialogue as individuals as he did during his ministry if we will but put ourselves in the middle of these passages as recorded in the New Testament.

Today, on this day called Mother's Day, let us listen to Christ and look at him while visiting a home. It is possible that these words that were spoken and the event described took place in the home of Simon Peter (Mark 1:29–31). While there Christ ministered to Peter's mother-in-law. He brought healing to one who was sick and in pain. Christ specializes in bringing healing into the home. He is eager to bring relief from pain and suffering. Is there need for healing and health and relief in your home?

I. Invite Christ to come into your home.

We can be safe in assuming that our Lord entered the home of Simon Peter by invitation. He was welcome there.

The events surrounding the healing of the man who was paralyzed may have taken place while Jesus was in the home of Simon Peter. Wherever it was, we can be safe in assuming that Jesus was in the home by invitation.

A. *Ideally, the entire family should invite Jesus Christ into the home.*

144

B. *Many times Jesus enters the home because of the invitation of one individual.* It may be the wife or husband. In many instances, a child comes to have faith in Jesus Christ. By means of dwelling in one individual heart, Christ comes to live within a house; and by means of that individual's Christian testimony, a companion can experience conversion, a parent can receive the gift of faith, and children can come to know the Lord Jesus Christ.

C. *On this Mother's Day, every mother would be wise to extend a personal invitation to Jesus Christ to come and live within her heart and her home.*

II. Christ carries on a spiritual conversation in the home (Mark 2:2).

In the last phrase of verse 2, we read, "And he preached the word unto them." This phrase could leave a false impression. The word translated "preached" is not the word that refers to a proclamation or an official announcement. It is not the word that refers to evangelism and announcing the Good News. Rather, it is the word that means "to speak, talk, converse." It literally means that our Lord carried on a conversation with the people in the house concerning spiritual matters.

It is possible for the living Christ to so dwell within us that in our conversations we can discuss spiritual things and encourage each other's faith and experience the presence of the living Christ as we do so. We must not labor under the impression that the living Christ is limited to the place of public worship and to the altar dedicated to him.

We would be exceedingly wise in the home if we would give the Christ an opportunity to converse with us. Some suggestions are offered.

A. *We should engage in a sincere prayer of thanksgiving at the table before meals.*

B. *We should memorize verses of Scripture that contain great truths about God, and these should be repeated from time to time so that they can be written on the walls of our memory.*

C. *We can read selected passages from the Bible and discuss the meaning of these passages within the family circle.*

D. *We can sing a familiar hymn on appropriate occasions.*

E. *We can pray together in a family circle with hands joined from time to time.*

F. *We can read or tell a bedtime Bible story to children.*

G. *We can encourage private daily Bible study for each family member.* Christ will join in these times of conversation and dialogue if we will let him.

III. Christ will encourage hope while in the home.

Many people came to the home in Capernaum where Jesus was. It was impossible to conceal his presence there. If we let him live in our home today, his presence will affect us, and the results will become known to those about us. People will be drawn to the house in which Christ dwells as is described by the passage of Scripture we have read today.

A. *Some came to see Jesus out of mere curiosity.*

B. *Many sought to enter the house because they needed the help Jesus could give.* His very presence was a basis of hope. Some of them were hoping for a revolution against the tyranny of Rome. Others came because they felt a great need for a fresh and loving word from God.

C. *Four men came bringing a friend, hoping for the return of his health, happiness, usefulness, and productiveness.*

D. *The helpless one was brought on a pallet for the return of that which he had lost.* When Christ is permitted to dwell in a home, he imparts hope for something better in the hearts of all who live within that home.

IV. Christ announced forgiveness while he was in the home (Mark 2:5).

A. *Jesus met the man's spiritual need before giving attention to his physical need.*
1. The two needs may have been vitally related.
2. Jesus recognized the spiritual need of the man to be of primary importance.
3. In other instances, Jesus met the physical need as if it were of primary importance.

B. *Unforsaken and unforgiven sin always creates pain and sickness.* Sin is a cheater and a robber. Sin separates people from their highest and best self. It literally cripples them and trips them up from becoming what they are capable of being.

C. *Christ specializes in forgiving sin.*
1. Christ deals with us in mercy and love as well as in power.
2. When Christ forgives, he removes the pain created by our alienation from him.
3. When Christ forgives, he restores a warm relationship with the sinner.
   It could be that the greatest need in your home is the need for forgiveness. Do mother and father need to forgive each other for some act or attitude of unkindness? Do parents need to have a forgiving attitude toward children who have disappointed them and perhaps disobeyed them?
   Forgiveness that is full and free and forever can bring about health and happiness that nothing else can bring.

Conclusion

Christ revealed who he was in the home. He revealed that he was the Son of Man, the Promised One of God, the Lamb of God who came to take away our sins. He was and is the Lord over all. In this passage, he assumed the role of God in forgiving sin. He made illness and pain disappear.

Christ can make a great difference in your heart and home. He wants to communicate with you day by day. He wants to encourage hope and enable you to meet the crises and responsibilities of life with courage. He will deal with your sin problem. You must make him the Lord of all if you want to know life in its fullness.

Invite Jesus to make his home in your heart. He will bring heaven into your life in the here and now, and he will take you to heaven in the hereafter. But you must first invite him into your heart and into your home.

Sunday Evening, May 11

Title: Teens and War

Text: "Then Abner said to Joab, 'Let's have some of the young men get up and fight hand to hand in front of us' " (**2 Sam. 2:14 NIV**).

Scripture Reading: 2 Samuel 2:8–14

Introduction

War is hell! Visit the war cemeteries of the world and see for yourself. Gaze upon the white crosses at the Battlefield of Gettysburg and feel a great sigh of sadness. Go to the National Cemetery in Arlington, Virginia, and see there the casualties of war. Go to Flanders Field and see the poppies growing between row upon row of crosses. I visited Europe following World War II and saw the rubble and the destruction. I saw what the bombs did in Mannheim and Frankfurt, Germany, and I said, "War is hell."

In my text, we find these words, "Then Abner said to Joab, 'Let's have some of the young men get up and fight hand to hand in front of us.' " And Joab said, "All right, let them do it." The young men, who have little or nothing to do with the precipitating of war, have to bear the brunt of the fighting. There was a time when those who fought wars suffered the most, but we live in a day when the civil population, women and children, also suffer. War seems to have lost its power to protect the innocent. Now it often destroys the innocent.

Why do people fight wars? Listen to James 4:1: "Is it not your passions that are at war in your members?" (RSV). People refuse to reason things out and therefore end up fighting them out.

I. Three attitudes toward war.

A. *Holy war—the attitude that the war has been willed by God.* In the Old Testament, God sent his people out to fight battles and destroy their enemies. Many wars of history have been fought as holy wars. In the Crusades, the monks and the priests went up and down the land crying, "God wills it. Deliver Jerusalem from the pagans." Today certain sects of Muslims threaten *jihad,* or holy war, against Jews and Christians.

B. *The second attitude is that of a just war.* The idea is that war is evil but that it is a lesser evil. People have felt a compulsion to defend their nation against barbarians, to defend a Christian nation against pagans. All theologians have recognized war as evil, but sometimes the lesser evil. It is a lesser evil than a godless tyranny, a totalitarian state. As one man said, "I'd rather die on my feet than live on my knees." Having seen the evils of Hitler and the mass murder of six million Jews, I'm sure that some of us have felt that war, under certain circumstances, is justified.

C. *But the third attitude is that of rejection.* According to some historians, the early Christians were overwhelmingly pacifists. We find no writer who

147

condones war during the first few centuries after Christ lived. One has given four reasons why the early Christians were pacifists:

1. They expected the return of our Lord.
2. They felt no compulsion to fight.
3. They saw no difference in killing privately or corporately.
4. As followers of the Prince of Peace, they felt they should have no part in the bloody business of war. We see then a higher revelation of God in Christ. We find more of the will of God in Jesus Christ.

II. Today a major war would be great evil.

Today there is the possibility of complete annihilation. When the tumult subsides, our planet will be an irrevocable inferno of radioactive debris.

We have enough bombs in our stockpile of nuclear arms to overkill the world many times. Of course once is enough. Bacteriological and chemical warfare also pose a great danger. Someone asked Einstein about the weapons of World War III. He said, "I don't know, but I'll tell you the weapons for the one after that will be stones, arrows, and clubs." Yes, when the bombs of World War III hit, this beautiful earth will become a swirling hell of death.

III. Jesus throws a different light on the concept of war.

We need to sit at the feet of the Prince of Peace and learn of him. I do not believe that Jesus Christ would approve of warfare. You say, "Well, didn't he drive out the tax collectors from the temple and use force against them?" He took a whip of small cords and drove out the sheep and the oxen, but there is no evidence that he used such physical violence on any person. Jesus Christ is the God who overcomes evil with good, hatred by love, and the world by a cross. Jesus said, "My kingdom is not of this world, else would my servants fight" (Matt. 18:36).

A verse in the New Testament says, "And when they saw the ... soldiers, they stopped beating Paul" (Acts 18:32 RSV). Military power can be used to protect the innocent, but the time has come when the innocent suffer with the guilty. Sometimes women and children do the most suffering. To compare war to killing a mad dog is a false analogy. In war the mad dog is not the only one killed. Innocent people are slaughtered. Further, the prophets envisioned world peace. Isaiah and Micah saw people beating "their swords into plowshares and their spears into pruning hooks" (Isa. 2:4; Mic. 4:3). In Matthew 26:52, Jesus said, "All who draw the sword will die by the sword" (NIV). In the book of Acts, we find Christians defying government to do the will of God and saying, "We must obey God rather than men" (Acts 5:29 RSV). There is no clear teaching against war in the New Testament, but the whole direction of the New Testament is toward peace. Reconciliation is at the heart of the Christian message.

Conclusion

What shall we do? We must be more, as a church, than a feeble echo of the military. There is a place for those who work for peace. There is a place for reconciliation. We should increase the social and political contacts with all nations, because the more we come to know each other, the greater friendships are formed, and the greater opportunity we have for living together in peace. We must learn how to live together. Christian people should work together with Jesus Christ, our Lord, in bringing peace to this earth. Our lives have meaning and purpose and destiny, so we can have confidence and hope. We must have great faith in God and work with him to bring in his kingdom.

WEDNESDAY EVENING, MAY 14

Title: The Bible Speaks to Our Condition

Scripture Reading: 1 Corinthians 2

Introduction

In the chapter for devotional study today, we find worldly wisdom and the work of the Holy Spirit in sharp contrast. Reference to wisdom appears in six verses of the chapter, and the work of the Holy Spirit is referred to in seven verses. The word *wisdom* is used in a variety of different ways. It does not mean the same thing each time it occurs. In some instances, it refers to the strivings of humans as they approach life from a commonsense standpoint without any assistance from the Holy Spirit. In other instances, it refers to God's plan and purpose of salvation in and through Jesus Christ.

I. Christ at the very center (1 Cor. 2:2).

Paul was determined to exalt Jesus Christ at the expense of all other efforts and objectives. In a crucified and risen Savior, humanity had a revelation of God's love, power, and purpose. Christ crucified must be at the very center rather than on the circumference of our lives and ministries.

II. The wisdom of this age (1 Cor. 2:1, 4, 6, 13).

Do you live solely by the principles of common sense, or are you open to the possibility of walking by faith in the promises of God? The wisdom of this age is merely human interpretation of God and life unaided by the Holy Spirit. The minds of humans are subject to deception by others and even by self-deception. We must be open to God's revelation of himself through Jesus Christ as the Holy Spirit guides.

III. The work of the Holy Spirit.

The chapter of the Word of God that we should search diligently this day speaks most dramatically of the work the Holy Spirit wants to do in the heart of the individual Christian and in the life of the congregation.

A. *The Holy Spirit makes the giving of our Christian testimony effective (2:4–5).*

B. *The Holy Spirit reveals the rich spiritual gifts that God has bestowed upon us*

(2:9–13). Verse 9 is often used as a reference to what God has provided in heaven. In reality it is talking about what God has provided for us in the present. Rich relationships and inexhaustible resources are available right now to the child of God who by faith will follow our Lord in devoted service.

C. *The Holy Spirit makes it possible for us to understand the mind of Christ (2:16).* The natural man does not understand the things of God, because they can be grasped only by those who have been born of the Spirit and who are open to the guidance of the Holy Spirit (2:14).

If we would truly become Christlike in spirit and action, we must become like Christ in our thoughts.

Conclusion

As we give ourselves day by day to a reverent, responsive study of God's Holy Word, the Holy Spirit will guide us and teach us the things of God so that we can think the very thoughts of Christ (John 14:26; 16:13–15).

To neglect a daily reading of God's Holy Word is to deprive ourselves of the privilege of becoming better acquainted with our living and loving Lord.

SUNDAY MORNING, MAY 18

Title: The Value of a Good Name

Text: "A good name is rather to be chosen than great riches, and loving favour rather than silver and gold" **(Prov. 22:1).**

Scripture Reading: Exodus 20:7; 1 Timothy 6:1

Hymns: "O Worship the King," Grant

"Jesus Is All the World to Me," Thompson

"Take the Name of Jesus with You," Baxter

Offertory Prayer: Holy, heavenly Father, today we thank you for life. We thank you for opportunities and responsibilities. We praise you for your goodness to us in every area of life. We come during this hour of worship to offer ourselves for ministries of mercy that will bring glory to your name and will release your blessings into the lives of others. We bring our tithes and love offerings as an indication of our desire that all of life be dedicated to you. In Jesus' name. Amen.

Introduction

In modern times, a family name means little more than the name that designates us as individuals who live at a certain place at a certain time. Such has not always been the case. In biblical days, great stress was placed on the name of individuals and places. The name of a person provided insight into his character and life. Perhaps both our secular lives and our spiritual lives would be greatly enriched if greater emphasis were placed on the value and significance of a good name. People's names really stand for their person, character, reputation, and integrity.

Throughout Scripture people are warned against using the name of God carelessly. To use his name is to involve him in either their conversation or their activity. God does not want to be misrepresented by the careless use of his name. Likewise, a family should be vitally concerned about its good name. Rich indeed are the children who receive a good name from their parents. The value of one's name should be maintained at all times.

It would be helpful if we would recognize and respond properly to the names that have been bestowed on us as the children of God and as the servants of the Lord Jesus. In the New Testament, we find at least five names or titles that are applied to us that we should bear with gratitude, dignity, and honor.

I. We are called "believers" because of our faith.

It is by faith that we respond to the love of God as revealed in the person of Jesus Christ. Because of our faith, God justifies us—declares us righteous and gives us a position of acceptance in his presence. We do not find acceptance in the presence of God on the basis of our keeping the law or on the basis of our moral perfection. It is by faith that we please God, and it is by faith that we achieve significant goals in the Christian life.

If we are to wear this title of "believer" with honor, we must exercise faith and grow a great faith.

II. We are called "brothers" because of our love.

The new birth produces a spiritual infant who becomes a member of God's family. We become brothers and sisters of each other in God's family. As brothers and sisters, we should love each other sincerely and steadfastly. We should rejoice with those who rejoice and weep with those who weep. We should make a positive, creative contribution toward the welfare of others within the family. We are under obligation to be especially gracious and kind toward those who are of the household of faith (Gal. 6:9–10).

Let us respond to the brotherhood of faith with a persistent, unbreakable spirit of goodwill.

III. We are called "disciples" because of our learning and knowledge.

The disciples of our Lord were his followers. They listened to his teachings. They were enrolled in his school. They recognized their need for the new truths that he was seeking to communicate. To be a true disciple, we must sit at the feet of Jesus Christ and recognize him as heaven's infallible and authoritative teacher. We are not only to hear, but we are to heed his teachings and commandments. We can never become Christlike in conduct until we become Christlike in our thinking. We must let the mind of Jesus Christ become our mind.

To be a disciple is to accept a discipline. The words *disciple* and *discipline* have the same root meaning. To be a disciple, we must let the way of Christ become our way.

IV. We are called "saints" because of our holiness.

Some people think of saints as being unearthly heavenly creatures who have achieved a degree of perfection that has permitted them to enter heaven on the basis of their own merit. This is a nonbiblical concept. To be a saint is to be a dedicated one. It means to be set apart for the purposes of God. The New Testament uses the word *saint* to refer to all believers, to all converts, to all of the children of God. We are not our own; we have been bought with a price. We belong to God. We need to face up to the divine ownership and recognize our Savior's lordship. As saints, we have been called to be saintly both in spirit and in conduct.

V. We are called Christians because of our spirit and because of our works (Acts 11:26).

We should not use the term *Christian* as a synonym for a believer or for a disciple or even for a brother. Ideally we would bestow the title *Christian* upon only those who have let the mind of Christ so take possession of them that the Spirit of Christ permeates all they say and do.

To be genuinely Christian is to be Christlike in our attitudes, affections, ambitions, and actions.

Conclusion

The Bible bestows many good names upon us. With the help of the Holy Spirit and with the guidance that we can find in the Word of God, it is possible for us to wear each of these good names with honor and dignity. By so doing, we bring glory to the name of our God, and we obtain a good name for ourselves.

SUNDAY EVENING, MAY 18

Title: Teens and Drinking

Text: "Wine is a mocker, strong drink is raging: and whosoever is deceived thereby is not wise" (**Prov. 20:1**).

Scripture Reading: Proverbs 23:19–31

Introduction

One of the most serious problems facing American youth is drinking. We face a crisis. Alcohol is a dangerous enemy of youth, of the home, and of the nation. Even in Old Testament days, when people used and drank wine, it soon became a problem. Proverbs 23:29–35 (NIV) speaks of this:

> *Who has woe? Who has sorrow?*
> *Who has strife? Who has complaints?*
> *Who has needless bruises? Who has bloodshot eyes?*
> *Those who linger over wine,*
> *Who go to sample bowls of mixed wine.*

Do not gaze at wine when it is red,
  When it sparkles in the cup,
  When it goes down smoothly!
In the end it bites like a snake
  And poisons like a viper.
Your eyes will see strange sights,
  And your mind will imagine confusing things.
You will be like one sleeping on the high seas,
  Lying on top of the rigging.
"They hit me," you will say, "but I'm not hurt!
  They beat me, but I don't feel it!
When will I wake up
  So I can find another drink?"

I. Alcohol is a dangerous enemy of youth.

A. *The first reason that alcohol is an enemy is because it kills.* Not only does alcohol destroy the bodies of those who use it, but it also triggers tragedies that kill others. More than half of all fatal automobile accidents are due to alcohol. Put a drinking person behind the wheel of an automobile, and you have a potential killer on the highway.

B. *Alcohol is addictive.* Alcohol is a habit-forming, addiction-producing drug. There are millions of alcoholics in the United States and millions more family members affected by alcoholism. More than two-thirds of all alcoholics began drinking while in high school. So it is about as safe for youth to play Russian roulette as it is for them to drink.

C. *Drinking causes juvenile delinquency.* Alcoholism is one of the most devastating factors contributing to juvenile delinquency. One newspaper carried this report: "A fifteen-year-old girl was arrested for drunkenness. Her mother finally came to get her at the juvenile court and looked startled and said, 'I'm amazed. Why, I thought I had taught her to drink like a lady.' "

D. *Drinking causes law enforcement problems.* DD (drunk and disorderly), DWI (driving while intoxicated), and DUI (driving under the influence) are the most common items on police blotters.

E. *Alcoholism is often behind other problems.* It contributes to poverty, broken homes, crime, unemployment, immorality, misery, tragedy, and death. We can say, then, that alcohol is at the root of most, and the ally of all, the evils that infest our society.

  Drinking impairs reason, will, self-control, judgment, physical skill, and endurance. It removes inhibitions and weakens social controls, which in translation means that when you drink, you lose control of your thinking and your standard of values. I have never been amused at the antics of one who is under the influence of drink. It is always sad to me. I feel like saying with Shakespeare, "Oh, God, that men should put an enemy in their mouths to steal away their brain, that we should for pleasure and applause transform ourselves into beasts."

II. Why do people drink?

There must be some value in it! Surely, so many millions of people cannot be wrong!

A. *Many professing Christians in America have ties to the world.* They live in an affluent society, like leisure time, and want to enjoy all the good things of life. Thus, with leisure on their hands and the desire to keep up with the Joneses, the average American has begun to drink to add pleasure to life. It has become a part of the social pattern.

B. *There are three reasons why people drink:*
   1. They desire to be sociable.
   2. They like the taste of alcohol.
   3. Alcohol makes them feel good. As one person said, "I take it to relax, to get along with people, and to calm my nerves."

   Alcohol gives temporary relief from worry, abolishes mental tension, disfigures difficulties, relieves a feeling of inferiority, and makes a weak person feel strong, an ignorant person feel smart, a poor person feel rich, and an oppressed person feel free. People drink for immediate thrills and excitement, to have a big time! People drink to escape the pressures of something in their experience, in themselves, or in their surroundings. They use alcohol to escape pain, failure, boredom, frustration, fear, or guilt. In every congregation, there are varied reactions to drink. Some are struggling with problems, some enjoy drinking socially, some feel it necessary to drink for business or health reasons, but some are violently opposed to drink. Now, I do not want to preach at or condemn anyone. I want you to reason together with me about some reasons why it is smarter not to drink.

III. What shall we do?

To drink or not to drink is the question. In light of the facts, each person must decide for himself or herself. I think we should have a compassionate understanding for those who feel that it is right for them to drink. I fear that sometimes the nagging, self-righteous, condemnatory attitude of good people makes drinking problems worse in some people. Abstinence does not make you a fine Christian! I have known many church people who would not touch a drop but were hateful, mean, cruel, self-righteous, and critical.

A. *What is the Christian view of alcohol?* The teaching of Christ emphasizes the sacredness of human personality. Anything that blights and destroys human personality is opposed to the gospel of Christ. I wish you could sit where I sit and see what drink does to people's lives, homes, and children! I believe Christians should regard total abstinence as an essential part of our witness to the faith. When we remember the compassionate Great Physician, Jesus Christ, and his love for people, we know that he would not condone what liquor is doing to the people of this nation. I believe that Jesus Christ would take his stand against it.

B. *You and I should accept responsibility for living up to our highest and best.* We should face reality. There is something noble about self-control.

C. *The use of alcohol violates the Christian principle that we each are our brother's keeper.* We are stewards of our influence. One who uses alcohol may, by example, lay a stumbling block in the path of a brother or sister and thus contribute to the destruction of another person. The influence of personal example is a sacred trust. For a Christian, the use of alcohol is a fundamental moral question that must be answered in the light of the gospel of Jesus Christ. Habakkuk 2:15 says, "Woe to him who gives drink to his neighbors, pouring it from the wineskin till they are drunk" (NIV).

D. *Remember that your body is a temple for the dwelling place of the Holy Spirit.* The Bible says that if anyone destroys God's temple, God will destroy him, for God's temple is holy, and you are that temple. It is a frightening thing to be a temple of God. We are to live so that we will not desecrate our bodies. No greater sorrow can come than the realization that one has destroyed the temple of his life. "If your hand or your foot causes you to stumble, cut it off and throw it away" (Matt. 18:8 NIV). There is nothing about a hand or a foot in itself that requires it to be cut off, but if gangrene is present, the entire body is in danger, and amputation saves life. If alcohol affects your body, your life, your integrity; if it endangers your home, then throw it away!

Conclusion

Are you one who has tried and failed to stop drinking or one whose heart has been broken by some problem related to drink? Remember the power of Jesus Christ to forgive, to redeem, and to restore. There is always hope as long as we have faith in God.

WEDNESDAY EVENING, MAY 21

Title: The Bible Speaks to Our Condition

Scripture Reading: 1 Corinthians 9

Introduction

Paul's epistle to the Corinthians deals with problems that perplex the fellowship of the church. By its very nature, the epistle is instructive and corrective in nature. Evidently this church had written to Paul concerning certain questions and problems that distressed them. Paul seeks to answer these questions one by one as he writes this epistle.

I. Paul's reply to criticism (1 Cor. 9:1–17).

As we read between the lines and examine the questions Paul raises and answers, we discover that he had experienced severe criticism from someone in Corinth.

Kindly, logically, and firmly he replies to this criticism of his apostleship and his authority as an authentic teacher and servant of God. He defends his right to participate in many privileges he had voluntarily denied himself for the sake of the gospel. Paul was determined to keep personal privileges and rights from hindering the advance of the gospel (9:12). Paul had denied himself financial support from those to whom he ministered lest this become a hindrance to the gospel (9:13–15).

II. For the advance of the gospel (I Cor. 9:19–23).

Paul's consuming ambition was to proclaim the good news of God's love to as many people as he possibly could. He adapted both his conduct and his presentation of the Good News to various classes and conditions so as to effectively communicate to them the truth of God's love, be they Jews, Gentile converts to Judaism, or pagans.

Great changes would take place in our lives and in the lives of those about us if we had this compassion that caused us to always think in terms of helping others come to know the Lord Jesus.

III. Voluntary self-discipline is essential (I Cor. 9:24–27).

The apostle was familiar with the great athletic events of his day. He uses athletic terminology to describe the voluntary self-discipline that is essential if the servants of Christ are to be effective. We should run like members of a track team so as to win the approval of our Lord. Instead of acting like a boxer who swings wild haymakers, we should fight to win in the battle with evil. Paul declares that we must keep under rigid discipline lest the evil within and about us cause us to be disqualified to participate in the great race.

In verse 27, the apostle is not thinking in terms of losing his salvation but in terms of losing the privilege of being an effective servant for the Lord. He is determined that he will not disqualify himself as an effective communicator of the good news of God's love.

Conclusion

Criticism is bound to come. We must not let it discourage and defeat us.

We must adapt the Good News to meet the unique needs of each individual to whom we communicate. Personal, voluntary self-discipline will always be essential for the person who wants to be a genuine follower of the Lord Jesus Christ.

SUNDAY MORNING, MAY 25

Title: A Proper Love for Self

Text: "Love your neighbor as yourself" (**Matt. 22:39 NIV**).

Scripture Reading: Matthew 22:35–39

Hymns: "Love Divine, All Loves Excelling," Wesley

"O Love of God Most Full," Clute

"More Love to Thee," Prentiss

Offertory Prayer: Gracious God, help us always to be conscious that we are but stewards of your grace. Help us to be good managers of that which you have entrusted to our care. Help us this day to bring a tithe and an offering that would indicate the sincerity of our love and a deep concern that all of the world might hear the gospel of your redeeming love through the missionary outreach of the church. In the name of our Lord we pray. Amen.

Introduction

If we were to condense into capsule form the total duty of man to God and the total duty of man to man, we would find such in the two commandments found in Matthew 22:37–39: "Love the Lord your God with all your heart and with all your soul and with all your mind" and "Love your neighbor as yourself" (NIV). These commandments are invitations that enlarge, increase, and enrich life rather than being rules that restrict and impoverish life.

One of the greatest truths to be found in these commandments may be missed by the casual reader. The second commandment reveals that the measure of our love for self is the measure of love that we are to express toward our neighbor. It follows that if we do not have a proper love for self, we will have no authentic guideline for loving others as we do ourselves. If we have a low view of self, we will have a low view of others. If we hate ourselves, we cannot love others. And we cannot really love God until our hate is dissipated.

Unless we can come to a proper evaluation of self, it will be impossible to truly love God and others. The best way to come to this estimation of self is through a discovery of the extent to which God loves us. Do you find it difficult to love God? Do you find it impossible at times to love others? If you answered in the affirmative, could it be because you have a very low view of yourself?

I. What are the symptoms that indicate the lack of a proper love for self?

A. *Do you have a habitual tendency to belittle yourself?* This can be a form of self-destruction that indicates a lack of a proper love for self.

B. *Do you refuse to believe in your own ability to achieve meaningful goals in life?* If you cut yourself down, it may indicate that you have a lack of respect for yourself.

C. *Do you hesitate to attempt that which is new or difficult?* If so, is it because of laziness or is it due to a lack of confidence in yourself, which in turn is a result of your low self-esteem?

D. *Do you reject your real self by attempting to escape through artificial means?* Some resort to the use of drugs because they have a very low estimate of themselves. Alcohol is often used by those seeking to escape from a concept of reality in which they consider themselves to be less than they ought to be.

E. *Do you reveal an improper love for yourself by a continuing flight from one place to another and from one situation to another?*

F. *Suicide may be the ultimate in self-hate.* One who commits suicide often is one who has had very low self-esteem and has felt unworthy to exist.

II. What are the factors that contribute to this lack of a proper love for self?

A. *Some experience an absence of love in early youth.* It is highly important that children experience the genuine, steadfast love of parents. Children who are raised without parents often come to believe that they were rejected because they were unlovely. To feel unloved does something to a child's sense of self-esteem. This deficiency of affection can lead to mental illness and to various kinds of abnormal and destructive activity.

B. *Some are overwhelmed by negative and insulting criticism during their formative years.* Parents and teachers need to be very cautious lest they resort to cutting criticism in their efforts to provide guidance for children. They should major on constructive criticism that contains stimulating compliments.

C. *Some have a low opinion of themselves because of uncomplimentary comparisons with others.* This comes about as a result of an individual's failure to recognize oneself as a unique creation of individual worth.

People must accept themselves as they are and appreciate their strengths without letting their weaknesses destroy their sense of self-confidence and personal worth.

D. *Some belittle themselves and even hate themselves because of unresolved guilt.* To deal with this problem properly, we need to recognize the sinfulness of sin and acknowledge our personal responsibility for our sin.

We can resolve the guilt that destroys by confessing our sin to God and accepting his forgiveness. God is the God of forgiveness. When God forgives, he holds the sin against us no longer, and he restores a warm relationship.

Perhaps the best way to solve the problem of unresolved guilt is to accept God's forgiveness and then forgive ourselves. If God forgives us, then we should forgive ourselves also.

E. *We must not forget that Satan is an accuser.* The basic meaning of the name Satan is "to accuse." The Bible teaches us that the devil is a liar, a deceiver, and a falsifier. He is in the business of trying to destroy us. Often he destroys us by calling our attention to our own faults, flaws, and failures. If he can destroy self-confidence and self-respect, he will make midgets out of those whom God wants to be giants.

III. Suggested steps for developing a proper love for self.

If we would love our neighbor as God commands us to, we must have a proper love for self. There is no better place for the individual to develop this proper love for self than within the home. The following suggestions are offered for consideration within the home.

A. *Recognize God's love for you and find full forgiveness in his offer of salvation through faith in Jesus Christ (John 3:16).*

B. *Fully forgive yourself.* Praise God for his mercy and grace and respond to the truth that when God forgives, God forgets. Accept the truth that Jesus Christ died for your sins. Quit looking back to the failures of the past. Look forward and encourage others to look forward.

C. *Evaluate yourself properly.* Jesus encouraged his disciples to overcome the agony of anxiety by coming to a proper evaluation of their personal worth in the sight of God (Matt. 6:25–26).

D. *Decide to accept the uniqueness of your own person (Matt. 6:27).* You are the only person in existence that is exactly like yourself. Accept yourself. Be at peace with yourself. Do not fret because you are not like someone else.

E. *Decide to discipline yourself (Matt. 7:13–14).* In these words, our Lord is describing the narrow, disciplined life that leads one to life on its highest plane and to its richest quality. This kind of life comes to those who discipline themselves.

F. *Dedicate yourself to the highest and to the best (Matt. 6:33).* Many of us live on a low level because we never dedicate ourselves to the highest. Jesus would invite and encourage us to dedicate ourselves to the doing of God's will in life.

Those who live day by day to fulfill the will of God for their personal lives and who give themselves in ministries to others will come to have an attitude of appreciation for self as well as for the Lord and for others.

Conclusion

If we are to be able to love others as self, we must first of all love ourselves properly. We come to a proper evaluation of self as we recognize ourselves to be the objects of God's supreme concern.

God loves you. God *really* loves you. He gave his Son on the cross to reveal the extent of his love for you. Since God loves you so much, you should recognize your own personal worth. As you recognize your worth, you will find yourself recognizing the worth of others also.

SUNDAY EVENING, MAY 25

Title: Teens and Doubt

Text: "When John, who was in prison, heard about the deeds of the Messiah, he sent his disciples to ask him, 'Are you the one who is to come, or should we expect someone else?'" **(Matt. 11:2–3 NIV).**

Scripture Reading: Matthew 11:1–11

Introduction

A figure clothed in camel's hair looks through the bars of the window of his cell. John the Baptist is in the desert prison of Machaerus. As he stands there, tall and strong, the wavy locks of his hair lie about his broad shoulders. His dark eyes flash with the spirit of a man who has known the freedom of the outdoors. His firm, drawn lips speak for the fearless heart of a man who was sure of his mission and would never compromise with evil. His hands grasp the prison bars, and he asks: "Why should my life's work be suddenly stopped at the end of six months of calling people to repent? Why am I in prison when I have work to do for God?"

John walks back and forth in his cell, and questions keep coming: "When will my disciples return with a message from Christ? I must be sure." Early that morning, John had sent his disciples to Jesus to ask, "Are you the one who is to come, or should we expect someone else?"

I. The struggle with doubt.

A. *If you have doubted, you are in good company.* The great Christians of all the ages have had their doubts too. John the Baptist doubted. Thomas doubted. The psalmist doubted.

We live in an age of skepticism. There are many honest doubters. If you have doubts, I wish to speak to you today. Most of us have known the agony of doubt. Thomas à Kempis said, "I have never known anyone so religious that he had not felt at some time a withdrawing of grace, a decreasing zeal."

A great preacher entitled a sermon "The Importance of Doubting Our Doubts." He said that the capacity to doubt is one of humanity's noblest powers. It has fostered much of the progress in today's world. Honest doubt ministers spiritual growth. It helps us outgrow our old concepts. Sometimes it is pulling down the old house of faith in order that we might build a bigger and stronger house.

B. *We need not be ashamed of our doubt any more than we need be ashamed of growing pains of adolescence.* There is faith in honest doubt—that is the essential message of the book of Job—the moving story of a righteous man who suffered cruel calamities.

C. *The message of the Bible is "Don't be ashamed of your doubt; welcome it."* You not only have the capacity to doubt, but you have the duty to doubt if you would grow into an understanding of God that will meet the needs of your life and the life of the world. Do not repress your doubts. Throw them out into the open and face them.

In the Bible, the great believers were the great doubters. The agony of doubt is no time to throw away the Bible or turn our backs on the church. Stay close to God and the resources of the Christian faith. Doubts may be the means of a deeper dedication, a greater understanding, a stronger devotion.

II. The source of doubt.

A. *As John the Baptist walked back and forth in his cell, he remembered so vividly why he was in prison.* Herod Antipas was living in adultery with his brother's wife, and John felt called of God to go to the palace and proclaim a message of condemnation. Standing before them, he pointed the finger of God in their faces. He denounced their sin. It was a sin against love, home, and society. It was a sin against the Almighty. He called for them to repent.

Now John was a prisoner because of his message. Why did Jesus not come and free him? Why did he not come to answer his questions? How long must John wait? In his perplexity, he was asking, "Why were those who lived in wickedness and mocked at God allowed to openly jeer at his prophecies of their destruction?"

Have you ever questioned God?

B. *What is the source of doubt?*

1. Disappointment with our lot in life may cause doubt. You may have wanted one thing and have had to settle for another. Maybe you have asked, "Where am I getting in my life? I try so hard yet seem to get no results." Now you have begun to doubt the meaning and purpose of life.

2. Disillusionment also causes doubt. Like John, you may have been disillusioned with the way of Christ. You wanted him to come in judgment, in wrath, in condemnation. You wanted him to send fire from heaven. One thing is certain: the person who waits for savage wrath will always be disappointed in Jesus. The one who waits for things to happen in dramatic and cataclysmic ways will usually be disillusioned. It is only as we wait for God to work in love that we see him accomplishing his purpose and plan.

3. Discouragement is another source of doubt. Do you feel discouraged with the way things are going? Sometimes we put too much confidence in our feelings, and our assurance fluctuates. Sometimes we feel good, and sometimes we feel bad. Feelings are unreliable like the weather. One man said, "Sometimes I'm up, sometimes I'm down, but I'm leaning on the Lord."

III. The solution to doubt.

A. *Evening has come at Machaerus.* The soldiers enter John's cell. They taunt him as they bring him his evening meal of pork and wine. Jestingly they set it before him. He looks at them and asks, "Why do you jest with one who has set himself under vow to God? Have you no respect for a prophet?"

Not far away, in the city of Jerusalem, in the palace of Herod, the royal feast has begun. At midnight the feast reaches its climax. The guests call for a dance from Salome. The demand grows. "Give us Salome," they shout. Herod demands that she dance, and as Salome moves about the floor, she charms the revelers. "Dance, Salome, dance!"

Salome dances, and Herod is enthralled. Foolhardily, he promises her whatever she would ask. Salome hesitates. Again he promises her whatever she would ask, and pledges it with an oath. She whispers to her mother. Her mother whispers to her. In frenzied curiosity, the revelers await her request. Then she speaks, and her voice carries throughout the room, "I want the head of John the Baptist on a silver platter!" Silence falls like death on the banquet hall. Herod is horrified.

B. *Now, what will happen to John?* We see him waiting in the desert prison. We wonder if he will die before the answer comes to his doubts. In the middle of the night, John's disciples hurriedly return to Machaerus bearing a strange message.

John's disciples enter his cell. "What did he say?" John demands. "Is he the Messiah? Deliver me from these doubts, these fears!" The disciples reply, "We arrived early in the morning with your message. He heard us gladly. Then he asked us to stay with him that day. We heard him speak. We saw him heal the sick, feed the hungry, and cleanse the lepers. At the close of the day, he called us and said, 'Go, tell John of the things you have seen and heard.'"

"What did he mean, John?"

John replied, "He is the Messiah."

"How do you know?"

"His works tell us who he is. The things you saw him do tell us that he is the Son of God."

Jesus' words tell us, too. No one has ever spoken like Jesus. His life tells us who he is. No one has ever lived like he lived. No one has ever demonstrated such love. John's doubts were resolved as he waited for the Lord to reveal himself.

C. *Doubts are always resolved as we wait on Christ to reveal God's glory.* God always comes. Victory is assured to those who wait. The Lord God breaks through to reveal himself to people in need. People are always leaving the theater before the show is over. But in leaving the theater, they never see the end of the play. John did, and so do some of us. We will emerge victorious only as we wait upon God to show himself.

Conclusion

Do you have doubts? Keep doing your very best right where you are. Keep faithful. Keep trusting. Keep following. Keep serving. God will reveal himself.

George Matheson, a young Scottish preacher, was once so beset with doubts that he wanted to give up the ministry. His friends counseled him to go on living up to the best that was in him, just as if he still believed. Matheson held on and became one of Scotland's greatest preachers. Believing when we can't see is what makes faith, faith! Faith is the way to victory over sin, suffering, sorrow, and skepticism. "This is the victory that overcomes the world, even our faith."

WEDNESDAY EVENING, MAY 28

Title: The Bible Speaks to Our Condition

Scripture Reading: 1 Corinthians 16

Introduction

Note the sharp contrast between what Paul has been discussing in this epistle and what he now begins to discuss in chapter 16. First Corinthians 15 is the classic chapter in the New Testament having to do with the resurrection of Christ and the resurrection of the saints. Immediately following this tremendous passage, Paul makes a very practical suggestion.

I. Now concerning the collection (1 Cor. 16:1–4).

This passage contains one of Paul's four different references to a generous offering for the poor saints in Jerusalem (see also Rom. 15:25–29; 2 Cor. 8:9; Gal. 2:10). These followers of our Lord were encouraged to contribute on a regular, systematic, individual, proportionate basis.

Would God speak to us on the basis of this passage and tell us that we should bring our generous offerings to the church on every Lord's Day on a voluntary basis and in proportion to our income? It is interesting to note that nowhere in the Scriptures is a portion less than the tithe mentioned.

II. Concern for Christian friends (1 Cor. 16:10–12).

Paul was vitally concerned about the welfare of Timothy and Apollos, his colaborers and fellow missionaries. He encourages the church at Corinth to extend to them Christian hospitality and every possible assistance.

Our Lord would have us to cooperate and participate with those who are advancing his work.

III. Practical suggestions (1 Cor. 16:13–14).

Five imperatives are given, and Godlike love is to characterize all we do.

The badge of Christian discipleship is love, understood as a persistent, unbreakable spirit of goodwill.

IV. Christian greetings (1 Cor. 16:19–24).

Paul closes his epistle with Christian greetings to friends in Corinth. His prayer for them is that they might experience the grace of the Lord Jesus and be assured of his continuing love.

Conclusion

Commendation, complaints, correction, counsel, and comfort come to us through Paul's epistle to the Corinthians. Let us listen as our Lord speaks to us as we study this wonderful book.

JUNE

■ **Sunday Mornings**

The Sunday morning theme for June is "Faith for Frightening Times."

■ **Sunday Evenings**

Continue with the theme "Teens: Problems and Potential."

■ **Wednesday Evenings**

Continue to encourage the reading of a chapter a day from the Word of God with the theme "The Bible Speaks to Our Condition."

The theme verse for June is "This book of the law shall not depart out of thy mouth, but thou shalt meditate therein day and night, that thou mayest observe to do according to all that is written therein: for then thou shalt make thy way prosperous, and then thou shalt have good success" (Josh. 1:8).

SUNDAY MORNING, JUNE 1

Title: The Authority for Faith: The Bible

Text: "From a child thou hast known the holy Scriptures, which are able to make thee wise unto salvation through faith which is in Christ Jesus. All Scripture is given by inspiration of God, and is profitable for doctrine, for reproof, for correction, for instruction in righteousness: That the man of God may be perfect, thoroughly furnished unto all good works" **(2 Tim. 3:15–17)**.

Scripture Reading: 2 Timothy 3

Hymns: "Break Thou the Bread of Life," Lathbury

"Holy Bible, Book Divine," Burton

"Wonderful Words of Life," Bliss

Offertory Prayer: Our Father, we thank you for all the blessings of life. We thank you for faith, which is your gift to us. We know that we have faith because you have approached us, not because we have found you. Father, sometimes we are frightened by life. The times in which we live are difficult times. The demands of faith sometimes seem more than we can meet. But then we realize that your grace is sufficient for every need. And then we remember that faith in you can overcome all obstacles. So, Father, take the things that we give to you this morning to use for your glory. Give us a greater faith so that we will be able to live courageously in these frightening times. In Jesus' name we pray. Amen.

Introduction

In our frightening times, we have a need for intelligent faith that can face the realities of life and still be anchored to the reality of God and his love and care for us.

What is the authority for this faith? It is the Bible, the revealed Word of God to us. Only through the Bible can we know of God's character and work. Only in the Bible can we read of God's acts among us.

The editor of a well-known London newspaper once sent a letter of inquiry to one hundred important men—peers, members of Parliament, university professors, authors, merchants—a varied list. He asked: "Suppose you were sent to prison for three years and could take only three books with you. Which three would you choose? Please state them in order of their importance."

Out of the replies, ninety-eight put the Bible first on their list! Few of these men were keen about religion, many were not even churchgoers, others were agnostics or atheists. Yet they knew that no other could give them cheer and comfort and help in dark and difficult days (Robert G. Lee, *The Bible and Prayer* [Nashville: Broadman, 1950], 8–9).

Why was this? The Bible is not just any book—it is the book of life, eternal, unchanging, ever-dependable. Because of this very fact, the Bible is our authority for faith. We know that faith can be true, because we know the Bible is true. Listen to Bernard Ramm: "The Bible is not the authority for the Christian because it was written by religious geniuses. Nor is it the Christian's authority because it has been pragmatically verified through the centuries, nor because it inspires great religious experience. The Bible is binding upon the Christian because it is part of the organism of divine revelation. It is a divine revelation in written form in various literary genres.... The Bible is authoritative because it is the Word of God (that is, it is part of the organism of revelation) and for no other reason" (*The Pattern of Religious Authority* [Grand Rapids: Eerdmans, 1957], 38).

This is our authority for faith: the Bible. We can know God and have faith in God through the revelation of himself given in the Bible.

I. The Bible is the authority for faith because of its inspiration.

The word *inspiration* means "God-breathed." Second Timothy 3:16 says, "All scripture is given by inspiration of God...." All the Scriptures were written by men who were inspired, or breathed into, by God. Of course, Paul was writing about the Old Testament Scriptures at this point. At the time of this writing, the New Testament had not been completely written and collected. But if what Paul claimed for the Old Testament was true, it is surely true for the New Testament Scriptures too.

We must confess that we do not know exactly how God went about inspiring the men who wrote the Scriptures. We know that they recorded the acts of God. And we know, too, that they used their own personalities and vocabularies in doing it.

God acted among us. That we know. The Holy Spirit then inspired someone to record these acts of God. The Holy Spirit also illumines these records. God still speaks to us from out of the pages of the Bible. So it seems to be a process of revelation, inspiration, and illumination.

We must also consider that Scripture forever stands as authority. Repeated attacks have been made on the Bible, but it still stands, and God still speaks through it. Only inspiration can account for this.

II. The Bible is the authority for faith because of its importance.

Second Timothy 3:16 asserts that Scripture is profitable. This ought to mean something to this materialistic culture of ours. The Word of God has profit for us; it is useful; it is important to our lives. Notice how.

A. *It is important for the teaching of doctrine.* The Bible must be the source of our doctrine. All the doctrine or teaching to which we subscribe must be tested against God's Word as revealed in the Bible. What we believe and how we live are tied closely together.

We cannot expect to find all the answers clearly outlined for us. If the explicit answer for every social question of every age were contained in the Bible, it would soon be outdated. In the Bible, we find the principles that guide all who believe in God no matter what century it is. The particular problems might change; the principles of God do not change.

B. *It is important for conviction.* "Reproof" here does not mean faultfinding so much as it means conviction. In the Bible, we find the conviction of our sins.

C. *It is important for correction.* The Bible must correct our understanding and our obedience. The *Amplified New Testament* translates it as: "For correction of errors and discipline in obedience." The real meaning of this is that all theories, all theologies, and all ethical teachings are to be tested by the teaching of the Bible.

D. *It is important for instruction in righteousness.* This could be understood as "training in good living." There is no other place to learn the meaning of righteousness than from him who is righteous—God as revealed in Jesus Christ.

III. The Bible is the authority for faith because of its intent.

A. *It has the intent of salvation (v. 15).* Through the Bible we can come to salvation. A colporteur, or seller of Christian books, was caught one night by brigands in a forest in Sicily. He was held up at the point of a revolver. He was ordered to light a fire and burn his books. He lit the fire and then asked if he might read a little from each book before he dropped it into the flames. He read the Twenty-Third Psalm from one; the story of the Good Samaritan from another; then the Sermon on the Mount from another; and finally 1 Corinthians 13 from yet another. At the end of each reading, the brigand said, "That's a good book; we won't burn that one; give it to me." In the end, not a book was burned. The brigand left the colporteur and went off into the darkness with the books. Years later that same man turned up again. This time he was a Christian minister, and it was to the reading of the books that he attributed the change (William Barclay, *The Letters to Timothy, Titus, and Philemon,* Daily Study Bible [Philadelphia: Westminster, 1960], 231).

B. *It has the intent of equipping for service (v. 17).* Salvation is only the beginning of the Christian life. The Lord intends for the Christian to serve him. The Scriptures will completely equip a person for service.

Conclusion

In these frightening times, we can have faith in God. The authority for faith is the Bible. It leads us to God.

SUNDAY EVENING, JUNE 1

Title: Teens and Fleshly Lust
Text: "Flee also youthful lusts" **(2 Tim. 2:22)**.
Scripture Reading: Matthew 5:28; 2 Timothy 2:22; 1 Peter 2:11; 1 John 2:16

Introduction

The other day I read what someone had written about youth: "There is little doubt that the present generation of young men and women is in serious moral difficulty. Compared with the generations preceding, they have shunned discipline and a willingness to excel in their studies. Many give little or no thought to the serious issues of life. Common modesty and decency in manners and dress apparently are things of the past. The fact that evil is called good while good is called evil seems to be of small concern to them. Student groups indulge in wild orgies and self-gratification...." Do you know when those words were written? They were written by Aristophanes more than four hundred years before Christ. This simply says that teenagers through all ages have struggled with the problem of fleshly lust.

I. The struggle with the problem.

A. *Consider certain Scriptures.* Peter said, "Abstain from sinful desires" (1 Peter 2:11 NIV). In 2 Timothy 2:22, Paul said, "Flee the evil desires of youth" (NIV). And in Romans 13:14 we read, "Do not think about how to gratify the desires of the flesh" (NIV). Jesus told men not to look at women to lust after them.

B. *There has been a revolutionary change in the public attitude toward sex.* The way people talk openly about sex today is shocking. You find sex talk and innuendo in literature, drama, theater, the movies, and television. The trend in modern dress is another illustration of the revolution, as is the number of teenage pregnancies.

C. *Another evidence of the revolutionary thinking is the breakdown in the sacredness of the marriage relationship.* It used to be that only movie actors had several marriages. Now more than half of all marriages end in divorce. Divorce is common even among clergy.

D. *The problem of fleshly lust is real.* Jesus spoke of lust in a look. He warned about looking upon a woman with lust. John warned about the "lust of the eye." The Bible speaks of "evil imaginations" from which come all kinds of crimes. Anything that incites evil thoughts, whether it is a picture, a movie, or a book, is dangerous.

II. Wrong view of the problem.

A. *It is wrong to think that premarital sex helps build a relationship.* The Bible teaches us that "whoso commiteth adultery ... lacketh understanding" (Prov. 6:32). The sordid story of Tamar and Amnon in the Old Testament illustrates this principle. Amnon seduced young Tamar and thought he had gotten away with it. Many modern novels might end there, but not the Bible. It tells the story of the next day. It says very bluntly, "The hatred with which he hated her was greater than the love wherewith he had loved her" (2 Sam. 13:15). It is an old story, as old as human nature, that such an experience breeds, sooner or later, a terrible self-hatred and a hatred of others.

B. *It is wrong to think that the physical side of life has nothing to do with the rest of the personality.* The Bible does not separate the physical from the spiritual. The word for soul in the Old Testament is *nephesh*, meaning a union of body and spirit. This teaching saved Christianity from two early evils:
   1. That the body is bad, so try to get rid of it with its desires and demands.
   2. That the things of the body are indifferent, that they have nothing to do with the spirit. The thought that you can be cultured with the mind and yet in things of the body be utterly debased and immoral is wrong.

C. *It is wrong to think that the suppression of this natural desire is psychologically dangerous and can do emotional and even mental harm to the persons involved.* Paul knew that this was a problem that all people face and urged that Christians keep their lives honorable and clean. This was important, for the world of Paul's day was rife with immorality. Lust was given almost unbridled expression. It made it all the more imperative that Christians should show that they were different from the pagans, that they were followers of Christ. So the apostle Paul, writing to the Christians in Thessalonica, laid stress on the necessity that they remember and obey the will of God, "even your sanctification, that ye should abstain from fornication" (1 Thess. 4:3). One eminent psychiatrist says that the basic findings about sex in psychoanalysis agrees with the fundamental Christian view!

D. *It is wrong to think that love covers all things.* It is wrong to think that if two people love each other, having sex is all right. These concepts are utterly wrong, unchristian, and tremendously dangerous to the moral well-being and salvation of humankind.

II. What is the Christian view?

A. *Recognize God as Creator.* In Genesis 1, we read, "In the beginning God created ... male and female created he them," and God saw everything that he made and "behold, it was good." Thus we believe that the physical side of life is good, not bad. There is nothing dirty or ugly or sinful about the physical side of life in itself. Humanity misuses, abuses, and perverts that which God meant for good. To the Corinthians, Paul said, "Know ye not that your body is the temple of the Holy Ghost? ... therefore glorify God in your body" (1 Cor. 6:19–20). Recognize the sacredness of life.

B. *Wholesome discipline of the body.* J. Wallace Hamilton, in *Ride the Wild Horses,* uses an interesting analogy in comparing basic human instincts to a wild stallion that must be broken. He says that some use the theory of self-assertion, letting the wild horse run and giving free rein to natural instincts. Others go to the opposite extreme, with self-rejection. Instead of eliminating the rider and throwing the reins over the horse's head for him to run free, they eliminate the horse. This is like trying to get rid of your headache by cutting off your head. The Bible teaches that there is power in the discipline of the body. Like a river without banks, the wrong expression of this natural desire can get out of bounds, creating a swamp that becomes a breeding place for disease and misery. Kept within the confining banks of God's laws and love, it can be a mighty force for individual happiness as well as for the well-being of society and the strengthening of family life.

The temptations of our day can be overwhelming, but with God's help, there is no temptation that you cannot handle. Many young people have found themselves in the situation in which Joseph found himself as depicted in Genesis 39. The Bible is very plain in describing the bedroom scene. Joseph was handsome, and after a time his master's wife cast her gaze upon Joseph and said, "Lie with me." You remember the outcome? Joseph didn't answer, "I'm afraid I might get caught." His whole refusal was rooted in his faith. "How then can I do this great wickedness, and sin against God?" (Gen. 39:9). This is the secret, and this can be your success. Remember, you are not your own—you belong to God.

Conclusion

But what if you do sin? You need to come back to God. Adultery, fornication, and perversion can be forgiven. To the woman caught in adultery, Jesus said, "Neither do I condemn thee: go, and sin no more" (John 8:11). We are not told what happened, but I have the feeling that she went away determined to live up to her highest and best from that hour. As she came face to face with the living Christ, she found a new way for her life. You, too, can climb from the low road to the high road.

WEDNESDAY EVENING, JUNE 4

Title: The Bible Speaks to Our Condition

Scripture Reading: 2 Corinthians 7

Introduction

When God commissioned Joshua to lead the children of Israel into the Promised Land, he insisted that Joshua follow divine instructions, "This book of the law shall not depart out of thy mouth; but thou shalt meditate therein day and night, that thou mayest observe to do according to all that is written therein: for then thou shalt make thy way prosperous, and then thou shalt have good success" (Josh. 1:8). Although the thought is repeated on many occasions, this is the only time the word "success" appears in the King James Version of the Bible. It is interesting to note that success is promised to those who daily give heed to the Word of God.

Let us let God speak to us from 2 Corinthians 7.

I. The promises of God (2 Cor. 7:1).

Paul has just completed a challenge to the Corinthian Christians to separate themselves from evil and to dedicate themselves to a faithful relationship with God. He bases this appeal on the precious promises of God (2 Cor. 6:17–18). This promise is a condensation of the many exceeding great and precious promises of God.

We should give careful attention to the Word of God that we might discover God's great promises for the encouragement of our faith, the deepening of our love, and the enrichment of our service and ministry.

II. The joy of restored fellowship (2 Cor. 7:2–4).

When we read 1 and 2 Corinthians, we are impressed with the corrective nature of these two epistles. There were some strained relationships between the apostle and some of the leaders in the Corinthian church. The Corinthian believers were immature and continued to harbor many of the attitudes and ambitions associated with their preconversion life. Some of them resented Paul's authority. They were upset because of his rebukes and his efforts to lead them to conform in both thought and conduct to the mind of Jesus Christ. Some of them had attacked his apostleship and his authority.

In verses 2–4, Paul expresses joy over a great improvement in the Corinthians' fellowship. He does this because finally they have reacted positively to his rebuke and correction. Restoration of fellowship always produces joy.

III. The comfort of God (2 Cor. 7:6–16).

    A. *The coming of Titus (7:6, 13).* Titus had been to Corinth and had learned of the change in the Corinthians' attitude toward Paul and the Lord's will. He brought news of this to Paul, and Paul was comforted and strengthened in the midst of his tribulations.

170

B. *Comfort from the church (7:7–13).* Paul was greatly encouraged because of the response of the church to his message, which had taken the form of a rebuke and a correction. He felt that he had been vindicated.

Paul had suffered greatly as a result of the Corinthians' misunderstanding of him. It was exceedingly difficult for Paul to truly be God's servant and their minister. This should comfort us when life proves to be difficult and painful. The good news from the church was really God's comfort to the heart of the apostle.

C. *The comfort of accepting correction (7:8–12).* Paul had strongly rebuked the Corinthians. His rebuke had produced sorrow and remorse that led to repentance rather than to despair and hostility. Their sorrow had been a godly kind of sorrow that led to repentance, cleansing, and health. The Corinthian Christians experienced the comfort and the joy of being cleansed, corrected, and placed in harmony with God and with his servant, the apostle Paul.

Conclusion

Sorrow and remorse that leads to despair and destruction should be avoided at all costs. But when God's Word rebukes us, let us respond properly in order that we might experience joy and peace.

SUNDAY MORNING, JUNE 8

Title: The Basis for Faith: God

Text: "Tell ye, and bring them near; yea, let them take counsel together: who hath declared this from ancient time? who hath told it from that time? have not I the LORD? and there is no God else beside me; a just God and a Saviour; there is none beside me. Look unto me, and be ye saved, all the ends of the earth: for I am God, and there is none else" **(Isa. 45:21–22).**

Scripture Reading: Isaiah 45:20–25

Hymns: "Immortal, Invisible," Smith

            "A Mighty Fortress Is Our God," Luther

            "To God Be the Glory," Crosby

Offertory Prayer: Our Father, we come to you this day with a full realization and full recognition of what you are and what we are. We acknowledge that you are our Creator and the giver of all good gifts. We understand that we are creatures: sinful, rebellious, disobedient, but seeking you. Forgive us of our sins, Father. Help us to be strong in the face of the adversities and the disappointments we face each day. Help us to know your grace, your strength, and your guidance in every moment of life. Grant us the awareness of the power and presence of your Holy Spirit. We come at this time to return to you a portion of what you have given us. Help us to give from love and as a response to your grace. You have not withheld any good gift from us. Help us not to withhold our time, talents, or treasure from you. But, rather, may we give with the liberality of love that you have shown us. In Jesus' name we pray. Amen.

Introduction

In his book *The New Shape of American Religion,* Martin E. Marty accuses the American people of having a "faith in faith." He indicates that in the revival of interest in religion many people have not put their faith in God but in faith itself. But is this the proper basis for faith? If you are to have faith, shouldn't it be based on something more objective, something more real than just the act of faith? The basis for faith is God.

In these frightening times, we can have faith because this faith is based on God. Isaiah the prophet expressed the reason that faith must be based on God and on nothing else: there *is* nothing or no one else.

The Bible does not argue for the existence of God. To the biblical writers, the existence of God was a self-evident fact. The Hebrews of the Old Testament were concerned with the character and activity of God. They knew the character and activity of God by what he had done among them.

The opening words of the Bible are "In the beginning God...." This sets the stage for all else that follows. Because God is from the beginning, is the Creator and Sustainer of the world, and is the Savior of the world, we can have faith in him. Rather than trying to prove God, the Bible records his acts. It declares God's majesty and power. His presence and will are made known. The Bible is the authority for our faith, and God is the basis for our faith.

I. God is the basis for faith because of reality.

Do we know that God exists? We certainly do. We have not seen him, but we have felt his presence. We have not touched him, but he has touched our lives. We have not heard his voice speak audibly, but we have heard the still small voice speak to the depths of our souls. God cannot be measured by the mathematician, analyzed by the chemist, or conjured by the philosopher, but any person who reaches out in faith can know that God is. This is the reality of God.

How do we know there is a God? Surely the Bible tells us; surely creation shouts it to the universe; but we can know decisively because we have known him. God is personal, loving, and seeking. This is the reality of our lives, and this is the basis for our faith.

II. God is the basis for faith because of revelation.

What do we know about God? Revelation includes not only how we know God but also what we know about God. Everything we know about God has been revealed to us by God himself. He has made himself known to us through the testimony of his creation, through the words of Scripture, and through our experiences with him. The final and complete revelation of God is in Jesus Christ. What do we know about God?

A. *The natural attributes of God.*
   1. God is all present: the omnipresence of God. God is present everywhere. But more important to faith is the biblical emphasis that God is present at particular places. After Jacob's dream at Bethel, he said, "Surely the LORD is in this place; and I knew it not" (Gen. 28:16).
   2. God is all knowing: the omniscience of God. God knows everything. But God also knows everyone. God's knowledge is particular, personal, and redemptive.
   3. God is all powerful: the omnipotence of God. God can do anything that power can do. Personally, it is important to know that God has the power to save. God's greatest demonstration of power was Jesus' crucifixion and resurrection.

B. *The moral attributes of God.*
   1. God is righteous, and he requires righteousness of us. But God gives the righteousness that he requires. All that is right and good is found in God.
   2. God is holy. Holiness basically means to be "separate." God is separate and distinct from humans. There is mystery about God that we will never comprehend.
   3. God is love. The basic characteristic of God is love. God has shown his love to us in many and varied ways.

III. God is the basis for faith because of relationships.

How are we related to God? J. S. Whale has said, "The fundamental question is this: How do we pass from abstract argument about God to living awareness of God?" (*Christian Doctrine* [London: Fontana, 1957], 29).

Our relationship with God is one of faith. This is the faith with an adequate basis: faith rested securely in God.

God loves us and seeks us. From the time God walked through the garden of Eden shouting, "Adam ... where art thou?" (Gen. 3:9), to the cross where Jesus said, "Father, forgive them; for they know not what they do" (Luke 23:34), to the last chapter of Revelation where these words are found: "The Spirit and the bride say, Come. And let him that heareth say, Come.... And let him that is athirst come. And whosoever freely" (Rev. 22:17), the Bible is the story of God's search for humanity. Even in the midst of our sin and rebellion against God, he loves us and seeks us. We can be related to God through faith and commitment.

A seminary student affected by skepticism talked with an older, wiser minister one day. He expressed his doubts about God and the Bible. To explain what he considered the contradictions of the Bible, he mentioned the reference that "God is love" and that "God is a consuming fire." How were they to be reconciled? The preacher stopped in the lovely garden path where they were walking and pointed to a beautiful blooming flower. They agreed that it owed its beauty to the sun. Then they noticed a flower that had been pulled and was wilting and curled. That, too, was due to the sun. Then the minister stated that the same sun could feed and nourish or wither and kill depending on the relationship to it. And it is that way with God. When we are rightly related to God, we have his strength, love, and salvation. When we are not rightly related to him, we know his judgment. By faith we can know God.

Conclusion

God is the basis for our faith. Were there no God, we would have no faith. But there is a God, and we can know him through faith. This carries us through frightening times.

SUNDAY EVENING, JUNE 8

Title: Teens and Marriage

Text: "What therefore God hath joined together, let not man put asunder" **(Matt. 19:6)**.

Scripture Reading: Matthew 19:1–12

Introduction

The marriage picture is not a clear one. When a child registered for school, the secretary asked him if he had any brothers or sisters. "No," he said, "I don't have any brothers or sisters, but I have three mamas by my first papa, and two papas by my second mama." That was not an unusual scenario for the secretary, and she was quite accustomed to registering entire households of children where none of them had the same last name because they all had different fathers. Furthermore, she sometimes registered children who had two parents of the same gender. Ours is a kind of sad, mixed-up world.

The breakdown of the home has become the number one problem in our nation. I do not fear that my country will fall from without, but I do fear disintegration from within. As the psalmist asked, "If the foundations be destroyed, what can the righteous do?" Teenage marriages are adding to the problem (Ps. 11:3). More than one out of every two teenage marriages ends in divorce. Many married teenagers don't receive high school diplomas, and some of the hardships they face start them on a life of crime. Teenagers need to give serious consideration to marriage, for anything so important, anything that is to last for a lifetime, demands thoughtful and prayerful consideration.

I. Stoplights on the road to marriage.

A. *If you are marrying a man to reform him, stop right now!* If he drinks, gambles, uses pornography, or is dishonest, unfaithful, or deceitful before marriage, he will likely continue on in sin after marriage. Know that a man is the right kind of person before you marry him. This rule holds true for women as well as men.

B. *If you have the feeling that "if this marriage doesn't work, we can always get a divorce," please stop right now!* Don't get married. Jesus said that marriage is forever. Psychologists say that it is harder for a child to lose a parent by divorce than it is by death. In some cases, the emotional trauma of divorce affects children even after they are well into adulthood. Don't hurt one of these little ones.

C. *Another stoplight is, do you have the counsel and consent of your parents?* In years past, it was customary for a man to ask a girl's father for permission to marry his daughter. This custom may no longer be followed, but it is always proper to seek parental approval. Isaac's father helped him find a wife. He did a good job, for he found for him Rebekah, and they loved each other. Samson fell in love with a Philistine girl. His parents pleaded with him not to marry her, but they finally gave in, and Samson married her, only to bring heartache, misery, and tragedy into his life. It is wise to seek the counsel and the consent of parents before marriage.

D. *Have you sought God's will?* Have you prayed about this? If it lies beyond prayer, then stop; do not proceed. John the Baptist told Herod, who had taken his brother's wife, "It is not lawful for you to have her." What about the will of God? Have you prayed until God has given you a green light?

II. Caution lights on the road to marriage.

Give serious consideration before you proceed. Here are some danger signs:

A. *The first danger signal is that of a mixed marriage, in which a person of one faith marries a person of another.*

B. *A second danger sign is marriage with an unbeliever.* Second Corinthians 6:14 gives a warning about this matter. "Be not unequally yoked together with unbelievers."

C. *Consider before you marry.* "Is this real love, or is it infatuation?" A great marriage counselor and pastor has said, "Most young people think they are in love at least four or five times before they find the real thing."

It is possible, perhaps, to love as sincerely at thirteen as at twenty-five, but not with the same discernment. Wait until you are old enough to love intelligently, maturely, and permanently. Youth has its infatuations, its transient flames, its momentary crushes. But these are but rungs in the ladder by which we climb upward toward the emotional and spiritual maturity necessary to build a home.

Relationships of young men and women today are undoubtedly the freest of any period in history. A wise young person does not allow every passing fancy, every infatuation, to become too highly emotional or physical.

D. *Another caution light is, "Are you willing to assume the responsibilities that marriage demands?"* There are floors to be vacuumed, beds to be made, children to be cared for, endless meals to be prepared, and money to earn. Are you ready for some trials? Some hard work? Are you ready, young man, to provide for a family? The Bible says, "If any [man] provide not for his own ... he is worse than an infidel" (1 Tim. 5:8).

III. Green lights on the road to marriage.

How can you know you are ready for marriage?

A. *Marriage counselors have suggested the following questions:* Are you from similar backgrounds? Are you mentally and socially congenial? Do you share a common faith? Are you mutually proud of each other? Do you get along with the families involved? Do you come from happy homes yourselves? Do you share a common vocational interest? Do you measure up in the matter of Christian character—not given to drinking, lying, cheating, profanity, gambling, etc.? Have you completed your education? If your answer to these questions is yes, you may have a green light.

B. *But here are some questions to ask.*

1. Can you sincerely respect this prospective partner? Do you respect this person socially? Intellectually? Physically? This includes pride of vocation.
2. Is he or she emotionally mature? What kind of a disposition does he have? Does he sulk? Does he pout? Is she neurotic? Can you get along with each other? A reasonable congeniality is essential to a happy marriage. If you cannot get along before marriage, do not think it will be easier after you get married.

    Are you old enough to get married? It is best to wait until one is in his or her twenties and has established a career before marrying, but the emotional age is most important. Mature people are responsible, flexible, and unselfish. Most quarrels over money, in-laws, recreation, or religion that wreck marriages stem from immaturity.

    Some adjustments have to be made, but probably spiritual adjustments, in the wake of great personal loss, are the greatest. One young couple earnestly prayed for a child. In due time, when a beautiful baby girl was born, their joy was boundless. But the passing hours revealed that the infant's heart was impaired, and the fragile thread of life would soon break. It was a tragic, bitter adjustment for two young people to make. They met their disappointment with Christian grace. Can you adjust to making decisions independent of family and friends? Are you willing to cut loose from Mom's apron strings and Dad's wallet?
3. You have a green light if these things are right and if this partner is a growing Christian. Being a church member is not enough, but to seriously follow Jesus Christ gives strength to a marriage like nothing else will.

Conclusion

I have known brides and grooms who thought it did not matter whether their mate was a Christian, but when they had children, their anxiety increased. They wanted their little ones to be brought up where there is hope and faith and love.

Most men feel somewhat like Lord Byron did when he said, "Much as I hate bigotry, I think it is a thousand times more pardonable in a woman than irreligion." But, in the marriage relationship, at least, this is also true of men. Many women suffer insecurity and loneliness because the one who walks by their side does not know God.

If you are not a Christian, you are not ready for marriage. You are not ready for parenthood. You are not ready for your life's vocation. You are not ready for tragedy and sorrow. You are not ready for life. You are not ready for death. You are not ready for the judgment of God. Will you give your life to our Lord? Will you trust him?

WEDNESDAY EVENING, JUNE 11

Title: The Bible Speaks to Our Condition

Scripture Reading: Galatians 1

Introduction

Paul writes to the churches in Galatia that he might give them the message of the Lord. As we read this chapter today, let us let God speak to our hearts.

Paul begins this epistle with a doxology of joy and praise for what God had done for him and for the Galatians in the person of Jesus Christ. He has recognized and responded to the truth that the death of Jesus Christ was intended to deliver us from the penalty of our sins as well as from the power of evil in this present world (1:4). The death of Jesus Christ and his redemptive purpose was in line with the will of our Father God.

I. The danger of departing from the gospel (Gal. 1:6–9).

Paul was greatly disturbed because the believers in Galatia had departed from the gospel of grace. They had listened to false teachers who had added to and thus perverted the gospel. Paul warned them against the great danger of adding to the gospel the requirement that one must also keep the law in order to secure a position of acceptance before God.

We need to recognize and respond to the fact that we are saved, not because we are good, but because God is a God of grace. Our position of acceptance before the Father God is not determined by our merit or obedience. We find acceptance before him in the basis of our faith in Jesus Christ who died for our sins. We must beware lest we depart from this pure gospel of grace.

II. Seeking to please Christ (Gal. 1:10).

Paul's supreme desire was to please Jesus Christ at all times. This desire took precedence over his desire to have the approval of people.

Because it is basic to our human nature to desire human approval, we must beware lest this desire take precedence over our need to please Jesus Christ.

III. The need for personal experience with God (Gal. 1:11–17).

In reply to the charge of some that Paul had received his authority from the apostles in Jerusalem, Paul affirmed that his message was a direct revelation from Jesus Christ. The truth that he preached was based on personal experience with Jesus Christ. His message and his authority were by divine authority based on personal experience with God.

Conclusion

How deep is your personal experience with God? Have you let the truth of God's Word become the authoritative guideline for your thoughts and your ambitions?

It is wonderful to have a good pastor who can give you guidance. It is very profitable to have parents who set before you the right example. Each person needs a faith that is personal and genuine, growing out of a personal experience with Jesus Christ. Such can be possible if we will let God speak to us day by day through his Word.

SUNDAY MORNING, JUNE 15

Title: An Example of Faith

Text: "So Jesus came again into Cana of Galilee, where he made the water wine. And there was a certain nobleman, whose son was sick at Capernaum. When he heard that Jesus was come out of Judea into Galilee, he went unto him, and he sought him that he would come down, and heal his son: for he was at the point of death. Then said Jesus unto him, Except ye see signs and wonders, ye will not believe. The nobleman saith unto him, Sir, come down ere my child die. Jesus saith unto him, Go thy way; thy son liveth. And the man believed the word that Jesus had spoken unto him, and he went his way. And as he was now going down, his servants met him, and told him, saying, Thy son liveth. Then enquired he of them the hour when he began to amend. And they said unto him, Yesterday at the seventh hour the fever left him. So the father knew that it was at the same hour, in the which Jesus said unto him, Thy son liveth: and himself believed, and his whole house" (**John 4:46–53**).

Scripture Reading: John 4:46–53

Hymns: "Faith of Our Fathers," Faber

"Have Faith in God," McKinney

"Faith Is the Victory," Yates

Offertory Prayer: Our Father, on this day when we think particularly of fathers and their influence on our lives, we are grateful that we can call you "Father." We are grateful that you are indeed our Father through faith. As a father you are interested in our best development, our proper growth, and our abiding relationship with you. Help us to achieve these things by your grace. We are thankful for all the blessings you have bestowed upon us. Make us aware of their source, and make us responsive to your Spirit. We come now to show tangible proof of our gratitude, our love, and our faith. Please accept these gifts and bless them to your use. And bless each one who gives. This we pray in the name of Jesus, your Son and our Savior. Amen.

Introduction

I am convinced that the greatest legacy that my father left was a legacy of faith. He was not a minister; he was a deacon who took his Christian faith very seriously. He did not leave vast land holdings; he did not leave huge insurance policies; he did not leave large blocks of stocks. But he did leave a legacy of faith that would always challenge and inspire each of his children. A father's faith lives forever in the minds and lives of his children.

There are times when a father's faith makes requests of the Lord in the interest of his family. This was the case of the unnamed nobleman in John 4. He had evidently heard of the miracles that Jesus had performed at other places. Then when he learned that Jesus was only twenty or twenty-five miles from his home, he rushed to him to ask him to heal his sick son. At the outset, his faith was only that Jesus could work a miracle and save his son's life. But under the skillful hand of Jesus, his faith developed more completely.

When we seek faith for frightening times, we need an example of faith. We need to know that in his own experience at least one other person has expressed faith. And on Father's Day, there is no better place to turn for an example of faith than to a father's faith. Faith is the greatest legacy a father can leave his family.

I. A father approaches the Lord in faith.

A. *By faith the father approached God for help.* At the beginning, the nobleman's faith was not spiritually motivated. He was making a desperate plea for help. From the agony of his heart, he asked Jesus to go to Capernaum to heal his son. The significant thing is that "he besought him"—he approached Jesus.

Our approach to Christ for help may not always be properly motivated, but God can take an imperfect approach and turn it into a perfect blessing.

B. *The approach of faith believes God's power.* This man did not know all about Jesus, but he did have confidence in his power.

Belief in the power of God may be the greatest ally we have in life. Moses believed the power of God in the face of seemingly unconquerable obstacles, and through God's power he led the children of Israel out of Egypt.

C. *The approach of faith accepts God's opportunities.* After hearing the nobleman's plea, Jesus said to him, "Go thy way; thy son liveth" (v. 50). Jesus knew that the man wanted a miracle, the healing of his son, but he gave him an opportunity to act in faith.

Repeatedly God has given us opportunities to act in faith. We must accept the opportunities that God has given us and exercise faith.

II. The father's faith grows.

A. *Faith begins at the miracle level (v. 48).* At first this father only wanted a miracle. He would believe if Jesus would heal his son.

Jesus chided those who would not believe without a sign. This is the lowest level of faith. This is the faith that must have proof through a visible sign or miracle. The faith that demands a guarantee is really no faith.

B. *Faith advances to the "believe at his word" level (v. 50).* The faith that can accept Jesus at his word is a higher level of faith.

This does not always involve a full understanding of what has happened or will happen. Likely the father thought that Jesus knew by some intuitive knowledge that the son was better.

We can accept Jesus' promises and simply take him at his word because he is trustworthy. Calvin Coolidge's father told of a characteristic his son had upon becoming the president of the United States. His father said that often when he had to go to town, he would leave certain instructions with Calvin about things that ought to be done before he returned. And, he said, he never at any time when he returned looked to see if these things had been done. He knew without looking that they would be done because he knew that he could rely absolutely on his son Calvin to do them. Jesus is that trustworthy and more.

C. *Faith reaches its height in simple belief in Jesus (v. 53).* When we believe Jesus, we have reached the pinnacle of faith. Isn't it strange that the height of faith is where faith should really start?

Faith reaches its climactic moment when we trust Jesus completely as Lord and Savior.

III. The father's faith enjoys victory.

A. *The victory of faith is in the act of God's promise.* Faith reached its victory when Jesus did what he said he would do: he healed the boy. Jesus was faithful to his word. At the same hour that Jesus said the boy was healed, the boy began to improve.

In 1941, when General Douglas MacArthur left the Philippine Islands after the fall of Corregidor to the Japanese, he made the promise, "I shall return." When he waded ashore with the attacking troops in 1944 as the battle to regain the Philippine Islands reached the invasion stage, he proclaimed, "I have returned." He had brought fulfillment to his promise. And so does God fulfill the promises he has made.

B. *The victory of faith is the realization of spiritual gifts.* Jesus had to convince the troubled nobleman that the most valuable thing he had to give was not physical healing but spiritual strength that comes from God. This is the best gift that he could give to any of his children.

C. *The victory of faith is as a guide to God.* Verse 53 indicates that not only did this nobleman believe Jesus but so also did his whole house. Because of a father's faith, a whole family came to have faith in God through Jesus Christ.

No matter what else a father may provide, he has not really supported his family until he has served as a guide to God for them.

In the Hebrew tradition, a father served as a representative of God in leading the family in worship. Much of Hebrew worship is centered in family worship in the home. A modern father may not understand his role as a representative of God, but he can surely be a guide to God. Through his faith, through his participation in worship, and through the sharing of his faith in God, a father can guide his family to God.

Conclusion

A father's faith serves as a stirring example of faith for frightening times. This father was frightened because his son, perhaps his only son, was at the point of death. In faith he turned to Jesus.

SUNDAY EVENING, JUNE 15

Title: Teens and Jesus

Text: "Jesus increased in wisdom and stature, and in favour with God and man" **(Luke 2:52).**

Scripture Reading: Luke 2:52; 4:16; Mark 6:3

Introduction

Jesus Christ, who walked in the flesh through Galilee nearly two thousand years ago, is accessible to us today. There are many ways of realizing the reality of Jesus. Some make their vital contact through worship, others through prayer, and others through fellowship. Some minister to others. Another way to understand Jesus is to study his earthly life. With John Ruskin, we can be present as if in body at each recorded event in the life of the Redeemer. Let us look at Jesus today and look and look and look until he becomes gloriously real to us. Look at Jesus as a teenager. There are some things we know about his early years.

I. Think of Jesus' life in the home.

I'm thinking of the boy who came to his pastor and said, "Was Jesus ever a little boy like me?" There was a time when Jesus was a boy. The book of Hebrews says he learned obedience as a son. The childhood of Jesus was probably a time of great happiness as he grew up wondering at the beauty of his Father's world, loving all and beloved of all, playing among the wood shavings, roaming the hills, carrying wood, drawing water, rejoicing in childhood games and pranks, getting his feet wet, misplacing Joseph's tools, attending the village school, reciting his first verses of Hebrew Scripture, picking flowers in the woods, watching the glories of the sunset, and being startled at the mystery of the dawn. He was a happy, normal boy. He learned respect for his parents during those years. Joseph must have been a wonderful father. Barclay tells us that Jesus called God "Father," but in Gethsemane, in the midst of great struggle, he called him Abba. *Abba* is the word by which a little Jewish boy calls his father in the home circle. It would be translated "Daddy." That is the name Jesus gave to God. And we are told in Romans 8 and Galatians 4 that we can call God Abba.

Jesus got his idea of fatherhood from Joseph. Joseph was honored when Jesus taught his followers to pray, "Our Father, which art in heaven. . . ." He could never have been taught that God is like a father unless Joseph had been a wonderful father. Jesus also learned the importance of worship in the home. The New Testament speaks of this: "As was his custom, he went into the synagogue on the sabbath day." Worship is a habit, but it must be more than a habit.

We know also that Jesus had four brothers and two sisters. They would not always agree. Tempers would flare. There would be misunderstandings and arguments. You may have problems at home — Jesus did! His parents were concerned when he came up missing on their return trip from Jerusalem. Most scholars speculate that Joseph must have died when Jesus was about thirteen, leaving him to be a big brother. He learned responsibility by caring for a widowed mother and younger children. The home life of Jesus should challenge us to make our homes centers of faith, love, and prayer.

II. Think of Jesus' education in the school.

The Bible says that Jesus grew "in wisdom and stature, and in favour with God and man." His mental development is stressed. This literally means he became full of wisdom. At age fifteen, he started studies at the village school in Nazareth. A village teacher in Nazareth taught the boy who was going to have more impact on history than any other person ever had. We will never know the teacher's name, but he taught the boy who was the Son of God. In those days, of course, people did not have any books. Everything had to be handwritten on scrolls, which were very expensive. Nobody could possess one for his own. Therefore, if a boy was going to learn anything, he had to learn it by heart.

The foundation stone of all Jewish education was the Old Testament. From early childhood, Jesus, like all Jewish children, would be brought up in the atmosphere of Genesis, Deuteronomy, Psalms, Isaiah, and Jeremiah. He must have spent long hours of his growing youth poring over the sacred page.

Jesus grew up in Nazareth, a little village of prosperous plainsmen and sheep raisers, a crossroads of that ancient world. Since roads that led to Egypt, Damascus, Syria, and the Far East all ran through Nazareth, caravans and merchants came through this little village. Roman soldiers were there. He knew about riots in the streets and the clashing of swords. He was educated in a town where his eyes and ears were open to the farthest corners of the world. He lived in a time of tumult and strife.

In John 7:15, we find that the people marveled at Jesus' teaching, saying, "How did this man get such learning without having been taught?" They meant that he had never studied in their schools, yet he possessed that which their schools could not give him. The essence of distilled wisdom was evident in his simple stories. Jesus Christ encourages inquiry. He was always questioning his disciples, trying to bring them to the light. We grow through intellectual struggle. Such learning was a part of the early years of Christ.

III. Think of Jesus' work in the carpenter's shop.

In Mark 6:3, we hear people ask, "Is not this the carpenter, the son of Mary?" In the carpenter's shop, we see Jesus earning his living by exhausting labor and carrying with him a burden that lines the face and weighs on the heart—the burden of responsibility for the welfare of other people. The Greek word for carpenter is *tekton*. This word pictures more than a simple carpenter. It actually has in it the idea of "craftsman," the "master of the tools." He was a builder. We see him making tables, chests, and yokes, and fitting door frames in houses. We see him planing wood, melting glue, hammering nails. He was a craftsman. One legend tells us that Jesus made the best ox yokes in the whole of Galilee and that people beat a path to his door to buy the yokes he made. In those days, they had trade signs, and it has been suggested that over Jesus' carpenter shop there was a sentence, "My yokes fit well." Jesus was a working man familiar with labor problems. Jesus puts glory in our common life by making the humblest task meaningful and significant. Devoted skill and labor went into those Nazareth yokes, plows, tables, and chests. They were rendered as an offering to God. Toil has been hallowed forever because of Jesus. There is no division of the sacred and the secular; all work is sacred if performed unto the Lord. I believe Jesus can be identified with progress and improvement in our cities, parks, streets, slums, schools, hospitals, and colleges.

Do you suppose Jesus ever felt restricted by his circumstance—having to earn bread for a widowed mother and her children? Do you suppose he ever asked, "Why do I have to stay in this carpenter shop when I long to preach and to teach and to minister?" I have wondered at times why certain things have happened in my life. God helps people find fulfillment in their work even when they have to wait for the fulfilling of his will.

IV. Think of Jesus' sense of mission.

Remember when Jesus was twelve years old and lost to Mary and Joseph until they finally found him in the temple. He said, "Didn't you know I had to be in my Father's house?" (Luke 2:49 NIV). Here we see the dawning of a higher allegiance. There was a gradual unfolding of God's will, but even in those early years, Jesus felt God had something for him. There is an old legend that one night Jesus was tired after a long day's work, and he arose and stretched himself, and as he did, the shadow of his arms and body formed a cross on the wall, and he whispered, "The cross!" Even as a teenager, Jesus had an amazing awareness of God, of God's plan, and of God's will.

Conclusion

A sense of mission often comes early. God speaks to the hearts of youth.

"Remember now thy Creator, in the days of thy youth." Jesus Christ, through a larger goal, found the key to a larger life.

Relate your life to the world in which you live. The happiest people are those who find ways to serve. Life takes on meaning as you respond to the voice of God. Jesus Christ set his face to do the will of his Father. What is your goal for life?

WEDNESDAY EVENING, JUNE 18

Title: The Bible Speaks to Our Condition

Scripture Reading: Ephesians 2

Introduction

Today's chapter for careful study and prayerful meditation emphasizes God's wonderful grace toward sinners. God's grace has been defined as "what people need but don't deserve." *Grace* is probably the greatest word in the New Testament. It is a word that contains God's love, mercy, kindness, forgiveness, and generosity—all in motion toward the undeserving sinner.

I. The believer is resurrected from the dead (Eph. 2:1–5).

While we look forward to the resurrection from the grave, we can presently rejoice in a resurrection from spiritual death because of God's grace. In the conversion experience, God gave life to us who were dead in trespasses and sins. We did not possess the divine life that comes to us in the miracle of the new birth. We can rejoice in that we have been raised from the dead.

II. The display of the riches of God's grace (Eph. 2:6–10).

Each convert is an exhibition of the miracle of God's grace. Paul declares that in the future ages the exceeding riches of God's grace through Jesus Christ will be demonstrated and disclosed in heavenly places. We can be sure that when God puts something on exhibit it will be glorious. We can rejoice in anticipation of what is in store for us through faith in Jesus Christ.

This chapter contains one of the great passages of the New Testament on the grace of God as being the source and the basis for our salvation (Eph. 2:8–9). Our salvation from the penalty of sin is not due to human merit or achievement. We are saved by the pure grace of God plus nothing. We receive this salvation through the channel of faith, and even our faith is the gift of God.

III. God's poems (Eph. 2:10).

The word *workmanship* comes from the Greek word *poiema*, meaning "that which has been made—a work" or "a poetical work" or "a poem." Hence it is clear that we are God's poems. The word implies artisanship and craftmanship. Paul is declaring that we are God's harmonious, beautiful, lovely creations through faith in Christ Jesus.

IV. The past contrasted with the present (Eph. 2:11–22).

Paul is writing to Gentile converts who previously were without Christ and were alien from the commonwealth of Israel. They were strangers from the covenants of promise, having no hope and without God in the world. In the present, in Christ Jesus they are now "insiders" as far as God's great redemptive activity is concerned. It is the plan and purpose of God that Jews and Gentiles combine to form "one body" (2:16).

Gentile believers are no longer strangers and foreigners but are fellow citizens with the saints and are members of the very household of God (2:19). Gentile believers can rejoice in the privilege of being a part of God's chosen people through whom he will bless the world if they will be faithful to his purpose for them.

Conclusion

God, by means of his Spirit, is eager to dwell in the midst of us and, not only bless us, but through us bless the world. We must beware lest we like national Israel of old distrust our Lord and follow a pathway of disobedience rather than obedience. We have been saved by the grace of God to serve that through us others might experience salvation.

SUNDAY MORNING, JUNE 22

Title: The Object of Faith: Jesus Christ

Text: "Let this mind be in you, which was also in Christ Jesus: who, being in the form of God, thought it not robbery to be equal with God: But made himself of no reputation, and took upon him the form of a servant, and was made in the likeness of men: and being found in fashion as a man, he humbled himself, and became obedient unto death, even the death of the cross. Wherefore God also hath highly exalted him, and given him a name which is above every name: that at the name of Jesus every knee should bow, of things in heaven, and things in earth, and things under the earth; and that every tongue should confess that Jesus Christ is Lord, to the glory of God the Father" (**Phil. 2:5–11**).

Scripture Reading: Philippians 2

Hymns: "Jesus, the Very Thought of Thee," Bernard of Clairvaux

"All Hail the Power of Jesus' Name," Perronet

"Blessed Redeemer," Christiansen

Offertory Prayer: Our Father, we come to you today thankful for the bountifulness of your mercy, grateful for your love and grace, and aware of our sins and failure. We ask that your love would be made known to us, that your grace would be realized by us, and that your forgiveness would be received by us. When we think of Jesus Christ, your Son, we are all but overcome by your goodness. We praise you for Jesus Christ. And we open ourselves to him that we might know him personally, that we might be filled with his love, and that we might follow him in all of life. We pray that you would accept our gifts and bless them to your service. In Jesus' name. Amen.

Introduction

I once knew a prison chaplain who did not surrender to the ministry until rather late in life. He was already married and operated a laundry business. When the Lord called him to the ministry, he sold his business and moved to another city to begin his Bible college studies.

He had a Jewish friend in his home city who was a laundry supply salesman. When the friend heard of his impending move, he visited with him and asked if he could be of any help. Since he had just sold his business, he had no financial needs at the time. So he told his friend, "I need a new Bible. My Bible is worn out. If you want to, you can buy me a new Bible." And he did. And throughout this man's ministry he has supplied him with Bibles.

The Jewish friend asked the minister, "Tell me one thing. Why did you do this? Why did you leave an established business and submit yourself and your family to long years of schooling? Why did you leave your friends and home to move to a place where you knew no one?" This was his answer: "It was all because of a man. I met a man named Jesus who saved my soul and my life. I owe everything to him. When he called me to serve him, there was nothing else I could do."

Jesus Christ is the object of our faith. The Bible is the authority for our faith. We have a basis for faith because God is and draws us into a relationship with him. He can give validity to faith for frightening times.

Nowhere in the Bible is the object of our faith presented more clearly than in Philippians 2:5–11. These verses come about as close as any in the Bible to a systematic statement about the person of Jesus Christ. And it is interesting to note that they were not written as a theological statement but as an illustration. They are found in the midst of an exhortation to unity. The apostle is calling for the Philippians to have the same attitude as did Jesus Christ.

Why discuss the person of Christ? There is no part of our faith more practical than that which expresses what we believe about Jesus. Christ is central to our faith. What we believe about the person of Christ will determine what we believe about the nature of salvation and the cause for conduct. Faith for these frightening times must be centered in Jesus Christ. He is the object of our faith.

I. Christ is the object of our faith because of his preexistence (Phil. 2:5–6).

Preexistence means that Christ existed before he was born on this earth. He existed as God before he existed as man. He had a home in heaven before he had a home in Bethlehem. We cannot explain exactly how this happened; it is a mystery of faith.

  A. *The fact of Christ's preexistence.* In verse 6, "being" can be translated "existing." Throughout all eternity, Jesus had existed.

  The butterfly can perhaps serve as an illustration of this. The butterfly first existed as a caterpillar. Then it spun a cocoon and after a while emerged from this as a beautiful butterfly. It had first existed as a caterpillar, then existed as a butterfly. Yet it was the same being in both states. So it is with Jesus. He first existed as God. Then he existed as man. He was the same being in both forms of existence.

B. *The manner of Christ's preexistence.*
  1. He existed in the form of God.
  2. He existed on an equality with God. Jesus shared in the glories and prerogatives of deity. These he put aside when he came to earth.

C. *The attitude that possessed Christ's mind.* Jesus was willing to renounce his rights, privileges, and claims as God on behalf of sinful humanity. He did not count this as something to be selfishly grasped to himself.

D. *Stanley Jones once told of a little boy who stood before a picture of his absent father.* He then turned to his mother and said wistfully, "I wish Father would step out of the picture." And that is what God did at Bethlehem. God stepped out of the picture into the human scene when Jesus Christ was born.

II. Christ is the object of our faith because of his incarnation (Phil. 2:7–8).

Incarnation means "the state of being clothed with flesh." When we speak of the incarnation of Christ, we are talking about the clothing of God in human flesh when God became a man in Jesus.

A. *The reality of the incarnation.* When the Scripture says that Jesus "made himself of no reputation," it means that he emptied himself of the visible glories and prerogatives of deity, the outward manifestations of deity.

  In relation to God, he became a servant. Traditionally Christians have interpreted the "Suffering Servant" passages of Isaiah as referring to Jesus.

  Jesus became a man. Being "in the likeness of man" was more than just an appearance; he was a real man. It was as man that the New Testament believers first encountered Christ. They did not immediately know that he was God. Look at Hebrews 2:17–18 and 4:14–16. This was a real man who was also God.

B. *The aim of the incarnation.*
  1. Identification. In the incarnation, God identified himself with humanity. He could sympathize with humans because he knew what they felt. For the gulf to be bridged between God and humanity, God would have to become a man—man could never become God.
  2. Redemption. Jesus Christ was obedient—even to death on a cross. The extent of God's love can be seen in the extent of Christ's obedience. Only by his death on the cross could there be atonement for our sin.

  If one were to jump in the water to rescue another when nothing was wrong, it would be an act of folly. But if one were drowning and another jumped in, swam to him, and rescued him, it would be an act of love. This Christ did for us on the cross.

III. Christ is the object of our faith because of his exultation (Phil. 2:9 – 11).

A. *Christ is exalted because of his redemptive deed.* "Wherefore" (v. 9) refers to what immediately preceded: the redemptive deed of Christ on the cross.

B. *The exaltation of Christ is absolute.* The exaltation of Christ is unqualified. It is universal. Even if all people do not recognize Jesus as Lord now, at some time they will.

Jesus Christ is to be the absolute Lord of every area of life. There is no part of the life or will that can be reserved from him. The demand of Jesus is for this absolute lordship to be now. The reason that we are to make Jesus the absolute Lord of our lives is because he is the incarnate God and he does redeem us from our sin.

Conclusion

Christianity's greatest need is a rediscovery of Christianity as a vital relationship to a living Christ. Christ is the object of our faith. Through faith in him, we can have eternal life. This relationship with God through Christ gives us faith for frightening times.

SUNDAY EVENING, JUNE 22

Title: Teens and the Will of God

Text: "And I said, 'What shall I do, Lord?'" (**Acts 22:10**).

Scripture Reading: Acts 22:1 – 14

Introduction

I will never forget the night I bowed my head before God and said, "Lord, your will be done in my life." I cannot describe the joy that flooded my soul. I think this is the most thrilling experience of life. When we submit our lives to Christ, it is, in the phraseology of Sir Winston Churchill, "our finest hour."

Paul tells that one day he was walking down the Damascus Road, and suddenly a great light shown round about him, and he fell to the ground. He heard the voice of God asking, "Why persecutest thou me?" A little later he surrendered and cried out, "What wilt thou have me to do, Lord?" Paul had been rebelling against God, but now he yielded his life to God's will. This was his concept of salvation. As we follow Paul on his great missionary journeys, we notice that it was always "the will of God be done." One time Paul wanted to go to Bithynia. The Spirit of God said, "No, go to Troas." He went on in the face of hardship, danger, beatings, stonings, and imprisonments. The great apostle went on preaching the gospel from city to city.

Paul was greatly successful in his missionary endeavors. What was the secret of his success? He lived at the center of God's will. In the place of God's will, there is guidance, joy, and power. Living there enables you to be silent when criticized, humble when praised, and patient when ignored. Paul's concept of God's will involves three things:

I. God's will involves a plan for every life.

A. *Paul cried out, "What shall I do, Lord?"* Paul felt that God had something for him to do. He describes how Ananias came and placed his hands on his head and said, "The God of our fathers hath chosen thee, that thou shouldest know his will." In spite of his past life, God had a place in his will for Paul.

You recall that Horace Bushnell, the famous preacher of the last century, had a great sermon entitled "Every Man's Life a Plan of God." As an artist has a plan in his mind for the portrait he is to paint before he takes up the brush, as a potter has a plan in his heart before he takes up the clay, as the sculptor has a plan before he takes up his tools, so God had a plan in his heart for your life and mine before we were ever born.

God has a place for every life.

Dr. Marshall Craig, pastor of the Gaston Avenue Baptist Church in Dallas for many years, told of speaking in a series of services at a university chapel. He gave the invitation, pleading with young men and women to lay their lives, their all, on the altar. They began to come. The president of the student body, some of the football players, campus leaders—many came, sincerely giving themselves to Christ. Then he saw a strange thing. At the rear of the auditorium he saw a boy start down the aisle toward the front crawling on his hands and knees.

Dr. Craig turned to the university president, who said, "It is all right, sir. The boy is one of our students who is disabled, and the only way he can get around is on his hands and knees."

Dr. Craig waited at the altar for him. He leaned down, and the young man looked up at the great preacher and said, "Sir, you said God had a place for every man. I know God has a place for these athletes, these campus leaders. But tell me, sir, does God have a place for a wreck like me?"

Dr. Craig spoke through tears to say, "Son, God has been waiting for a wreck like you."

Whoever you are, whatever you have been, God has a place for you, a plan for your life. As every instrument has a place in the orchestra, as every star has a place in the heavens, as every flower has a place in the flower garden, so every person has a place in the great plan of God.

B. *It is wrong to think that God has a will for the missionary, the preacher, the educational director, the music director, and so on, but has no plan for the butcher, the baker, and the candlestick maker, this "vulgar group."* God has a plan for every life.

Do you want to have the greatest thrill of your life? Do you want to experience the highest joy? Do you want to live at your highest and best? Do you want to be successful in your work? Then find God's will, fit into it, and fulfill it.

II. God's will involves service.

Paul cried, "What wilt thou have me to *do*?" Ananias gave him the instructions from God: "Thou shalt be his witness."

A. *What are you going to do with your life?*
  1. You can waste it in dissipation and indulgence, in eating, drinking, and being merry.
  2. You can spend your life in self-pleasing. You can say, "Leave me alone, God. I'll run my life. Hands off!" You can do this and be a good citizen and a good neighbor, but there will still be something lacking.
  3. You can dedicate your life to the service of humanity. Any concept of salvation that minimizes service is wrong. Salvation and works are so vitally related that they cannot be separated. "Faith without works is dead." Paul interpreted the will of God in the realm of service.
B. *What is God's will for us?* It is clear that we are to love God and to love people. We are to minister to the needy, the suffering, the poor, the diseased. We are to reconcile people to God and to their fellow humans. We are to be instruments of healing and blessing and life to the world.

We can know God's will for our lives. We can find God's will through reason, through the counsel of friends, through conscience, by reading the biographies of great people, by the study of our talents and our abilities, through prayer and communion with God. Most of all, we know his will by what the Quakers call "inner light," the impulse of the heart.

The will of God, if it means anything, involves a life of service.

Here is our missionary impulse, our evangelistic motive. It is God's will that if we have the gospel, if we know the Good News, then we must share it with the people of the earth who do not have it. Too many of us have taken a seat on the sidelines. We have become spectators, sitting in the box seats of comfort and complacency. God calls us to come down out of the gallery and fight the good fight of faith, run the race set before us, serve him with all our hearts.

C. *God may be calling you.* It may be to preach or to be a missionary or a nurse. It may be to do some special, definite Christian work. It may be to sing in the choir or to visit the sick and the needy. We know for certain that God's will is that everyone who names his name be a faithful witness, serve him, and bring other people to him wherever we are, whatever we do.

III. God's will involves pleasing God.

A. *"What shall I do, Lord?" Paul asked.* He was really saying, "Tell me what you want me to do, Lord, and I will get busy doing it." Pleasing the Lord was Paul's deepest desire. He said, "This one thing I do, forgetting those things which are behind, and reaching forth unto those things which are before, I press toward the mark for the prize of the high calling of God in Christ Jesus" (Phil. 3:14).

Every step Paul took was taken in the will of God. From the very first day when he was stricken down on the Damascus Road by a light from heaven, by the outpouring of the Spirit of God, until forty years later when he was killed for his faith, he was always seeking to do God's will.

190

A little while before his death in Rome, Paul said, "I am now ready to be offered, and the time of my departure is at hand. I have fought a good fight, I have finished my course, I have kept the faith." Paul kept his face turned toward God's will.

B. *What is the direction of your life?* God's will is never revealed to us all at once, but one step at a time. If you follow the light you have today, more will be given you tomorrow. "In all thy ways acknowledge him, and he shall direct thy paths" (Prov. 3:6).

Conclusion

Are you ready and willing to yield your life, whatever it costs? The highest, the holiest, the happiest calling in all the world is the call to do God's will. He calls you to accept Christ as your personal Savior. Will you turn to him? Will you do God's will?

WEDNESDAY EVENING, JUNE 25

Title: The Bible Speaks to Our Condition

Scripture Reading: Philippians 3

Introduction

God will speak words of guidance to us through his Word as he did to Joshua in ancient days if we will meditate on his teachings and open our heart so as to receive his counsel.

Paul's note of joy with which this chapter begins is all the more significant when we remember that this epistle was written from a prison cell. Paul was waiting to be tried before the judgment seat of Caesar. The outcome of that judicial experience was unknown at the moment. Despite the discomfort of imprisonment and the humiliation that must have been associated with it, the apostle Paul was able to rejoice in the Lord and to encourage others to rejoice in him. Today let us rejoice in the Lord.

I. A warning against false teaching (Phil. 3:2–9, 17–19).

It is interesting to note the corrective nature of many sections of Paul's epistles. It is also interesting to note how much space he gave to warning his beloved friends against the peril of being misled by false teachers.

Paul was vitally concerned that the disciples of our Lord in Philippi not be misled by those who were insisting that a person found a position of acceptance before God on the basis of obedience to the law of Moses.

Paul affirmed that he had repudiated all claims of righteousness on the basis of the law in order that he might have the righteousness that comes through faith in Jesus Christ alone. As he compared the two forms of righteousness, he declared that the righteousness that comes by keeping the law is of no more value than garbage as compared with the righteousness that comes through faith in Jesus Christ.

Are you solidly resting in the grace of God through faith in Christ Jesus, or are you trying to earn a position of favor in the presence of God because of your own achievement? May God grant to each of us the faith that will enable us to respond to and rejoice in the righteousness that comes through faith plus no human merit at all.

II. Experiential knowledge of Christ Jesus (Phil. 3:10–12).

The apostle Paul had been a disciple of Jesus Christ for many years. He had an outstanding reputation as a missionary, evangelist, and theologian. Still he had a deep desire to enter into a richer experiential knowledge of Jesus Christ.

You can get fully acquainted with some people in a short time. Once you come to know them, you have no desire for a deeper experiential acquaintance with them. Such is not the case with Jesus Christ. The more we get to know him, the more we want to know him. We want to have a deeper experience with Jesus Christ.

This knowledge of Christ comes through a devotional and responsive study of his Word. It comes through transforming prayer experiences and implicit trust in his promises. It comes as we give full obedience to his commands. May it be that each of us will have a growing knowledge of our Lord Jesus.

III. The power of a compelling purpose (Phil. 3:13–14).

Most of us drift aimlessly through life. We never clearly define our goals and objectives. Consequently, we waste our energy because of the absence of clear priorities for the use of it.

Paul's compelling motive was to fully experience and achieve that for which the Lord had called him. Like an athlete running in a race to win a prize, Paul was pressing toward the mark in order that he might fully achieve God's high call for his life.

God has a high call for each of us. We would be exceedingly wise if we were to lift our eyes to discover his high call and then without reservation give ourselves continually to that quest.

Conclusion

Today's chapter closes with a reminder that believers are citizens of heaven and that their habits and ambitions should conform to their heavenly citizenship (3:20). Paul looked forward to the time when at the consummation of the ages our frail bodies will be transformed into the likeness of the body of the glorified Christ (3:21).

SUNDAY MORNING, JUNE 29

Title: The Outreach of Faith: The Christian Life

Text: "For we are the circumcision, which worship God in the spirit, and rejoice in Christ Jesus, and have no confidence in the flesh" **(Phil. 3:3)**.

Scripture Reading: Philippians 3

Hymns: "When We Walk with the Lord," Sammis

"More Like the Master," Gabriel

"Take My Life and Let It Be," Havergal

Offertory Prayer: Father, thank you for the blessings of life you have so richly given us this past week. We praise the name of Jesus Christ for the salvation we have through him. We commit ourselves more completely to you and to your will. We pray that you will show us the paths that we should take, the decisions that we should make, and the stubborn areas of our wills that we should break. As we consider the life that you have called us to have, the Christian life, we ask for your strength to live it. Help us to be both witnesses and ministers. Fill us with your Spirit that we can live for you. Take now the gifts that we bring. These gifts are material expressions of the life that we have already given to you. Use these gifts for your glory. And use our lives in your will. In Jesus' name and for his sake we pray. Amen.

Introduction

John A. Mackay, former president of Princeton Theological Seminary, in his book about South America titled *That Other America,* tells of an interesting interview with a full-blooded Peruvian Indian. This man had a Ph.D. degree from a leading university in the United States and was an authority in pre-Incan civilization. He knew both personally and academically what had happened to the culture of his people. The question Mackay asked him was this: "Can religion change a person?"

This is a tremendously important question. We operate on the assumption that religion can change a person. We gather at least once a week for worship, and we spend vast sums of money on places of worship. We send people all around the world to try to win people to Christ. Yet sometimes this haunting question lurks in the background. The problem is that we have seen too many people whom religion has evidently not changed.

This is not the type of question that can be answered with a glib word. It is a question that can best be answered by illustration. True, you can point out those who were supposedly failures of faith. But on the other hand, you can point out others who are veritable walking trophies of grace. Yes, religion can change a person. A vital faith in Jesus Christ is the greatest force in the world.

This response to God through Christ in faith we call the Christian life. Christian life is not only begun by faith, it is lived by faith. Faith for frightening times has an outreach: the Christian life.

Philippians 3:3 gives what one New Testament scholar has called "one of the clearest, most concise statements describing a Christian found in the Bible." Paul identified the true believers in God to the Philippian Christians. Their marks are spiritual rather than physical. This one verse gives us three insights into why the Christian life is the outreach of faith.

I. The Christian life is the outreach of faith since it is a life of response to God.

Notice that Paul identified the true people of God as those who "worship God in the spirit." Jesus taught us that God is Spirit and that those who worship God must worship him both in spirit and in truth (John 4:24).

A. *Worshiping God in spirit frees worship.* God is not bound nor contained. Worship can be conducted any place where a person meets God.

Worshiping God in spirit also frees the form of worship. A true worship experience does not have to follow set patterns. Jesus promised: "For where two or three are gathered together in my name, there am I in the midst of them" (Matt. 18:20). We can worship God by the leading of the Spirit of God.

B. *Worshiping God in spirit defines worship.* What is worship but response to God? We meet God face-to-face in worship. In a church service, in a moment of prayer, while reading the Bible, we meet God. And when we meet God, we are to respond in repentance and faith. True worship is not just keeping the forms of worship but is responding to God.

From true worship will flow the results of the Christian life: mission, witness, Bible study, ministry. But it all comes about in response to God, and we do not respond to God if we do not worship God.

II. The Christian life is the outreach of faith since it is a life of commitment to Jesus Christ.

A. *Commitment to Christ is the means of salvation and the essence of the Christian life.* People cannot enter the Christian life until they have met Christ and have committed their lives to him in faith. This removes all source of pride. If salvation were attained by our goodness or by our efforts, we could have room for pride. But Scripture plainly teaches that salvation is the gift of God's grace. And since it is by God's grace, there is no place for pride. Our rejoicing can be in nothing else but Jesus and his salvation.

B. *Commitment to Christ is the means of Christian growth.* The Christian life is to be a life of growth in grace, and the way we grow is through commitment to Christ.

Nathaniel Hawthorne's legend of the Great Stone Face reminds us of this. The boy Ernest would look longingly at the great stone face on the side of the mountain. It was a strong, kind, honorable face that thrilled the heart of this boy. There was a legend that some day a man would appear who would look like the Great Stone Face. Through all his childhood, and even after he became a man, Ernest kept looking at the great face and for the man who was like it. One day, when the people were discussing the legend, someone suddenly cried out, "Behold, behold, Ernest is himself the likeness of the Great Stone Face." By committing our lives to Jesus and looking to him, we can grow to be like him.

III. The Christian life is the outreach of faith since it is a life of continual faith in God.

The response of faith in God must be continual. Paul designated the ones of the true covenant as those who "have no confidence in the flesh." This means that our confidence or faith cannot be on outward privileges, such as who we are, what we have done, or where we came from, but only in God.

The Christian life is wholly a life of faith. It is not just the faith of a moment but the faith of a lifetime that matters. Remember the battle cry of Martin Luther? "The just shall live by faith," he proclaimed. In Romans 1:17 where these words are found, the full quotation is: "For therein is the righteousness of God revealed from faith to faith: as it is written, The just shall live by faith." "From faith to faith"—we are to live from one level of faith to another.

Faith is a growth process. The faith one has when accepting Christ as Savior should not be the faith that is held after years as a Christian. Faith should grow, mature, and strengthen.

If the Christian life is a life of continuous faith, then some things will have to be removed. First Peter 2:1–3 lists some things that must be removed from our lives. One can hardly grow in faith while burdened with these elements that should be stripped away.

In humility we approach God and ask for the renewal of strength, the forgiveness of sin, the cleansing of life, and the firming up of faith. Our confidence must be in God alone.

Conclusion

These are frightening times, but God has not called us to fear but to have faith. The faith that we have in God is sufficient for us to meet any problem in the time in which we live. The outreach of faith is the Christian life. In faith we live, witness, and minister for God.

SUNDAY EVENING, JUNE 29

Title: Teens and Prayer

Text: "But thou, when thou prayest, enter into thy closet, and when thou hast shut thy door, pray to thy Father which is in secret; and thy Father which seeth in secret shall reward thee openly" (**Matt. 6:6**).

Scripture Reading: Matthew 6:1–15

Introduction

In the words of our text, our Lord assumed that his disciples would pray. It was natural for him to assume that the children of God would desire communion and fellowship with God. The need for guidance as well as the need for forgiveness leads one to desire the help of God.

I. Prayer is a privilege.

Some people think of prayer as a duty, and it is. Some people think of prayer as a stewardship, and it is. Some people think of prayer as a necessity, and it is.

But prayer is also a priceless privilege. By means of prayer, we talk to the eternal, loving Father. Prayer is more than a monologue; it is also listening for the still small voice of the God who loves us with a perfect love and with perfect wisdom.

II. Prayer is a private affair.

"Enter into thy closet, and when thou hast shut thy door...."

Jesus did insist that the conversation of a child with the Father and the Father with the child be a private and confidential conversation. Perhaps he was insisting in these words that we go apart to a secret place where we can shut out all distractions and interruptions.

Jesus is not forbidding public prayer or united prayer with these words. He is simply declaring that we have the privilege of a private audience with our Father God. The inexperienced teenager can enjoy this privilege as well as the seasoned pastor, evangelist, or missionary.

III. Prayer is a personal experience.

"Pray to the Father." We are not to approach God as one of a vast multitude who clamors for his attention. God is personal. He inclines his ear to each of us as if we were the only person in existence.

We have a parent-child relationship with God. Here Jesus does not suggest that we approach God as an almighty and eternal God or as the high and holy King of the universe. As needy children, we are to approach our Father God in prayer on a very personal basis.

IV. Prayer can be a most productive experience.

"Thy Father which seeth in secret shall reward thee."

Indeed, prayer can be a most profitable experience. When we pray with a reverent, trusting, submissive attitude, God reveals himself to us as the loving Father who is always present with purposes of grace, mercy, and guidance. This is perhaps the greatest reward that comes to the one praying following the initial plea for pardon from sin and acceptance into the family of God.

In the prayer experience, God lets us see ourselves. We see our need for forgiveness and cleansing. We see our need for guidance, to find our place in the plan and purpose of God.

In the prayer experience, our Father also opens our eyes to see the needs of others. He speaks to us and gives us instructions concerning the work he wants us to do.

Conclusion

Prayer is a privilege. It is a private and personal experience with God and can be a most productive experience. It should be a personal experience in the life of each teenager as well as each adult.

We should not be content with the great prayer experiences of our past. We should not look forward wistfully to a mountaintop experience at an undetermined date in the future. Instead, we should find a quiet place and have dialogue with the heavenly Father day by day.

JULY

■ **Sunday Mornings**

People have always had a problem with sin. The theme for a series of topical sermons on this timeless problem is "The Sins That Damage and Destroy." This series is introduced with a consideration of humankind's plight as sinners.

■ **Sunday Evenings**

The suggested theme for the evening messages is "The God with Whom We Have to Do." The messages are doctrinal in nature and practical in objective.

■ **Wednesday Evenings**

Continue with the theme "The Bible Speaks to Our Condition." The theme verse for July is "Study to shew thyself approved unto God, a workman that needeth not to be ashamed, rightly dividing the word of truth" (2 Tim. 2:15).

WEDNESDAY EVENING, JULY 2

Title: The Bible Speaks to Our Condition

Scripture Reading: 1 Thessalonians 2

Introduction

The words of our chapter for today are addressed to beloved friends in the city of Thessalonica where Paul had had a very brief but significant missionary ministry (Acts 17:1–10).

I. Boldness after suffering (1 Thess. 2:1–2).

Paul had suffered great pain for the sake of the gospel in Philippi. This did not dissuade him or intimidate him from continuing to preach the gospel when he arrived in Thessalonica. His example should challenge us to be faithful to our Lord in the face of possible misunderstanding and hardship, and in some instances, persecution.

II. Trustees of the Gospel (1 Thess. 2:4).

Paul felt that he had been entrusted by the Lord with the Good News for the benefit of both Jews and Gentiles. The only manner in which he could be faithful to his trusteeship was by communicating the Good News.

Each follower of Christ is a trustee of the gospel. We prove to be worthy trustees as we try to give the Good News to as many as we possibly can.

III. The worthy walk of children (I Thess. 2:12).

Paul urges the Thessalonian disciples to walk worthy of their new relationship to God as Father and child. He describes the manner of his walk and work among them as an example for them to follow. He speaks of loving them as a mother cherishes her children and as a father loves and comforts his children.

If we wear the name of the Lord, we should remember that there are responsibilities that go along with this privilege.

IV. The power of the Word of God (I Thess. 2:13–14).

These people in Thessalonica had received the Word of God and had permitted the Word to produce a powerful effect in their lives (1:9–10). When the authoritative Word of God is received into the heart, it produces a dynamic transformation. It changes our thoughts, affects our emotions, and changes our choices.

As we prayerfully and responsively read a chapter a day, let us accept it as the truth of God for our lives.

V. The hindrances of Satan (I Thess. 2:18).

Satan stood in the pathway of Paul to hinder him all of the way. Satan had tried to hinder our Lord as he faced his redemptive mission.

Satan will attempt to hinder each of us each day. He will hinder us from the experience of worship if we permit him to do so. He will attempt to hinder us from giving a witness and will try to hamper our work for God.

Our only hope of overcoming Satan's hindrances is through the strength and power that come through prayer and faith in our Lord (Eph. 6:10–18).

VI. The joy of the faithful witness (I Thess. 2:19–20).

Paul looked forward to the time of the second coming of the Lord Jesus Christ. Each convert was a source of joy and happiness to his heart.

Each of us should face the question, "Have I been instrumental in helping someone come to know Jesus Christ?"

Conclusion

Did you let God speak to your heart as you read through this chapter? Perhaps his message will come through more clearly and more authoritatively if you will read it again.

SUNDAY MORNING, JULY 6

Title: Humankind's Plight as Sinners

Text: "If we say that we have no sin, we deceive ourselves, and the truth is not in us" (**1 John 1:8**).

Scripture Reading: Romans 1:18–25

Hymns: "Christ Receiveth Sinful Men," Neumeister

"Amazing Grace," Newton

"Love Lifted Me," Rowe

Offertory Prayer: Dear Father, in our unworthiness you redeemed us. In our disobedience and faithlessness, you have forgiven. Now, dear Lord, take the fruit of our labors and bless it to higher use. Cleanse the stain of sin that so often mars our gifts, and grant your Spirit to reign in us, through Jesus Christ our Lord. Amen.

Introduction

The age-old problem so often wrestled with in people's minds and reflected on at length in the Scriptures is the raising of lowly humans into fellowship with the divine. How are the "sons of men" to become the "sons of God"? This is a greater problem than the divine relationship to "lower" life, because the matter of human will is involved. The higher the ambition God held for humans, the greater became the problem introduced by free will. In order to form character in people, God had to take terrible risks. He had to leave people the choice of good or evil. That was both humanity's great opportunity and humanity's occasion for falling.

The Bible attributes people's sins to their willful abuse of their God-given freedom of choosing the basic course and character of their lives. Paul, in writing to the Roman Christians, outlined the truth concerning humanity's plight as sinners (Rom. 1:18–25).

I. The seriousness of sin.

A. *Sin involves the total being of people.*
  1. Not just the flesh or material part.
  2. Not only a mental condition.
  3. Sin is in the heart of people, at the very center of selfhood.
B. *The New Testament's appraisal of sin in people.*
  1. Sin in the "flesh" describes living apart from God (Rom. 8:4–5, 13; 2 Cor. 1:17; 10:2).
  2. Sin in "your bodies" means sin in your personal being (Rom. 6:12–13; 12:1).
  3. Sin in the "soul" is also referring to oneself or person. The soul or person sinning "shall die" is a warning to the total person. (Use Acts 2:41 or 3:23.)

     Sin is serious, for it involves the total person. People do not have in themselves the strength to solve their problems. Their whole beings are adversely affected. Sin has invaded their thinking, their will, their sense of values, their natural responses, and their relationships.

II. Slavery to sin.

A. *In people's expressions of self-will, they lose their freedom.*
  1. From trusting God to self-trust.

199

2. From obeying God to self-assertion.
3. From serving God to slavery of sin.

B. *In sinning, people bring community to be under dominion of sin (Rom. 6:6; 7:24).*

C. *Sin snatches and exercises lordship over people (Rom. 6:14; 7:17; Gal. 3:22).* Living is described as serving either "good" or "evil." People's acts have repercussions beyond the sensations that they momentarily feel. Their acts are testimonies for God or for Satan. The constant plea of the New Testament is for people to "serve God" and thus find the liberation for which people were created. When sin is served, humanity's true destiny is denied, their created role is forfeited, and they fall under the bondage of sin and death.

III. The surrender to sin.

Humanity's surrender of "sonship" to God brings into light their personal responsibility for guilt.

A. *The Bible holds people guilty for their own sin.*
1. Sin is not the responsibility of past generations (Deut. 24:16; Ezek. 18:2–4).
2. People are responsible for the actions of the group of which they are a part.

B. *People are guilty for the environment they help create.*
1. We speak of *my* country, *my* city, *my* home.
2. No person lives to self; living is influencing.
3. People face their sin alone.

Conclusion

Humanity's problem is sin. People may have many problems in life, such as problems in finiteness, fate, and function. They are plagued with involvement in the material aspect of their lives and by their ignorance. When all is said, humanity's plight, however, is one of sin. The Bible holds people guilty for their sin. People and people alone stand responsible and in total solitude to face their sin. To meet this condition, there came the Good News. When people are willing to admit that sin is their own and their's alone, the Savior will bear it. "Christ Jesus came into the world to save sinners" (1 Tim. 1:15).

SUNDAY EVENING, JULY 6

Title: In the Beginning God

Text: "In the beginning God created the heaven and the earth" **(Gen. 1:1)**.

Scripture Reading: Genesis 1:1–2:3

Introduction

The Bible begins with "In the beginning God" (Gen. 1:1). John begins his gospel with "In the beginning was the Word, and the Word was with God, and the Word was God. The same was in the beginning with God" (1:1–2). Someone has said, "The Bible begins and ends with God." The Bible does not seek to define God, nor does it present an array of arguments to prove that God exists. It simply announces that there is a God. The words "In the beginning" in Genesis 1:1 are out of regular Hebrew order. The words stand first in the sentence when normally they would come at the end. This arrangement in the sentence emphasizes the absolute fact of creation, that nothing existed before God.

People's concepts of God vary. Some think of him as only a concept of the mind. Some think of him only in anthropomorphic terms. Some think of him as a long-whiskered, white-headed, doting grandfather. Some think of him as a remote deity who is too far away to be interested in human affairs. Some think of him as a celestial computer who has all the facts. Some think of him as a tranquilizer who is to be used in an hour of tension, turmoil, anxiety, or death. Some think of him as an opiate, a narcotic. Apart from the biblical revelation, people are sure to get a distorted concept of God.

Let us consider what the Bible has to teach concerning God.

I. God is a person.

A. *God is a real person.* He is not a mere idea or concept; he is a reality. He exists and is self-existent. He lives. He is a person who possesses qualities attributed to personality—intelligence, self-determination, and moral consciousness.

B. *God is a spiritual person.* Jesus said, "God is a Spirit; and they that worship him must worship him in spirit and in truth" (John 4:24). What is the meaning of this verse? It evidently means that the essence of his being is spirit rather than matter. God does not have a body; he is not material. He is not limited as is matter. The Bible does speak of God as having hands, feet, arms, mouth, eyes, and wings. These are anthropomorphic terms to enable us to understand God. To make our understanding of God still clearer, we have the incarnation of God in Jesus (John 1:14; 14:9). He is a spiritual person.

C. *God is a triune person.* The word *trinity* is not found in the Bible. Tertullian of the second century used it to express the truth taught about God as a triune person. The Trinity of God was revealed to humanity by God. God has revealed himself to humanity as God the Father, God the Son, and God the Holy Spirit. All three manifestations of God are found at the baptism of Jesus.

II. God is absolute.

A. *God is self-existent.* When we speak of God as absolute, we mean that he is not dependent on anything outside of himself. He is not dependent on the world; the world is dependent on God. God can exist without the world, but the world cannot exist without God. He has the source of his being in himself.

B. *God is one.* There is one absolute, self-existent being, and that one is God. God is indivisible. This fundamental truth is taught in both the Old and New Testaments. The fact that God reveals himself as Father, Son, and Holy Spirit must not be construed to teach tritheism, or the doctrine of three gods. The fact that God is one (monotheism) excludes polytheism and idolatry. There is only one true God. In the New Testament, the one true God is revealed to humanity by Jesus Christ.

C. *God is omnipresent.* God is not limited by space and time. He is present everywhere in space and time. God is accessible to all at all times and in all places (Ps. 139:7 – 12).

D. *God is omniscient.* By omniscience we mean that God is all-knowing, has all knowledge. Since God is omniscient, he knows everything simultaneously. God even knows beforehand.

E. *God is omnipotent.* He is all-powerful. God has power to do anything that is not inconsistent with his nature, character, and purpose (Gen. 17:1; 18:14). The only limitations on God's power are self-imposed (Gen. 18:25).

III. God is moral.

Moral consciousness is an essential element in personality, and God is a moral person. Consider four moral attributes of God.

A. *God is holy.* The word *holy* means to separate, to set apart, to cut off. God is holy in the sense that he is separated or distinguished from the finite and created. He transcends finite things. His ways and thoughts are not man's but are higher than those of man (Isa. 55:8 – 9). Isaiah saw the character of God as holy (Isa. 6:1 – 4). God's character is holy, and man's character is imperfect. His goodness is more than that of man. Everything about God is excellent. His character is perfect. He is holy.

B. *God is righteous.* God's character is upright. In him is no evil. The apostle John expressed the righteousness of God when he said, "God is light" (1 John 1:5). In God there is no darkness. He is free from anything evil. Dr. W. T. Conner said, "He is not only free from evil, he is opposed to the evil. All the energy of his being is set against sin. He put himself against sin and for the right" (*Revelation and God* [Nashville: Broadman, 1936], 247).

C. *God is love.* The apostle John said, "God is love" (1 John 4:8). The love of God is difficult to define. Dr. E. Y. Mullins defined love "as the self-imparting quality in the divine nature that leads God to seek the highest good and the most complete possession of his creatures. Love in its highest form is a relation between intelligent, moral, and free beings. God's love seeks to awaken a responsive love of man to God. In its final form, love between God and man will mean their complete and unrestrained self-giving to each other and the complete possession of each by the other" (E. Y. Mullins, *The Christian Religion in Its Doctrinal Expression* [Nashville: Broadman, 1917], 236).

Dr. W. T. Conner describes the qualities of God's love as intelligent, benevolent, righteous, self-giving, and demanding humanity's love. Love belongs to the very nature of God.

D. *God is truth personified.* He is the source and ground of all truth. He is the basis of all human knowledge. If we reject God, we lose all criteria of truth (Isa. 38:18). All facets of truth are grounded in God.

IV. God is at work.

A. *God was at work when he created the world.* The Bible points out that the origin of the world is the creative work of God (Gen. 1:1; Col. 1:16; Heb. 11:3). The how and when of creation are not as important as the fact that God did it in his own way.

B. *God is at work preserving the world.* God not only made all things, but he upholds all things and controls all things (Col. 1:16–17; Heb. 1:3).

C. *God is at work seeking to save sinners.* "For the Son of man is come to seek and to save that which was lost" (Luke 19:10). "For by grace are ye saved through faith; and that not of yourselves: it is the gift of God: not of works, lest any man should boast" (Eph. 2:8–9). "Therefore if any man be in Christ, he is a new creature: old things are passed away; behold, all things are become new" (2 Cor. 5:17).

Conclusion

"In the beginning God" (Gen. 1:1) and throughout all time and eternity God! Believe in him today!

WEDNESDAY EVENING, JULY 9

Title: The Bible Speaks to Our Condition

Scripture Reading: 1 Timothy 1

Introduction

A careful study of God's Word with a heart open to receive God's instructions can guide us toward the abundant life.

Paul's epistle to Timothy is addressed to him as one who is very dear to Paul. He considers Timothy to be his own son in the faith and in the ministry. He greets him and wishes for him three great blessings from God the Father and from the Lord Jesus Christ—grace, mercy, and peace. There could be no greater blessings from God than these. These blessings are offered to each of us through faith in and faithfulness to the Lord Jesus Christ.

I. A warning concerning false teachings (1 Tim. 1:3–11).

The apostle Paul charges Timothy to correct and bring back some of those who have been diverted from the way of truth into falsehood by false teachings. He emphasizes the importance of being correct in our beliefs. He warns us against becoming involved in needless inquiries and unprofitable controversies. Even the law of God can be studied with unworthy motives, and it can be interpreted in such a way as to confuse and mislead.

203

Each of us needs to accept responsibility for the correctness of our beliefs, for our actions are the results of what we deeply believe.

II. Gratitude for the faith of Christ (I Tim. 1:12).

While we should be grateful for the faith we have in Christ, Paul was rejoicing because of the faith Christ had put in him.

How many of us are aware of the faith Christ has in us? He has entrusted into our care and custody and use the precious gospel. He has given to us the story of his love as expressed in his death, resurrection, and living presence. He depends on us to share this Good News with a needy world. He has put great confidence in us. We should not disappoint him.

III. An example of the scope of God's grace (I Tim. 1:13–17).

Paul considers himself an example of the extent to which God's grace goes in its effort to rescue a sinner from the waste and ruin of sin. He had been a blasphemer and a persecutor and had given his consent to the death of Stephen. Even a sinner of this extent is still an object of God's love. God deals with sinners on the basis of his own wonderful grace.

The example of Paul's being saved should encourage us to believe that any sinner in our community can be touched and redeemed by the grace of our great and good God. Paul is an illustration of the extent of that grace. While we have not sinned as Paul did, each of us is also an illustration of the extent of God's grace.

IV. The weapons of our spiritual warfare (I Tim. 1:18–20).

Paul's son in the faith, Timothy, was facing some difficulties as he sought to be a true servant of the Lord Jesus. The apostle Paul urges upon him that he live by the principle of faith, and, at the same time, that he guard the purity of his own conscience. He gives illustrations of people who forsook the way of faith and did not listen to the voice of their own conscience. They brought about the destruction of their own testimony and their usefulness to the Lord.

Conclusion

If Timothy needed to be encouraged to walk by faith and to live by the dictates of a pure, clean conscience, it follows that each of us should approach life with all of its perplexities and its uncertainties with faith in God for divine leadership and for a determination never to violate our conscience as it is illuminated by the indwelling Spirit.

SUNDAY MORNING, JULY 13

Title: The Sin of Pride

Text: "When pride cometh, then cometh shame: but with the lowly is wisdom" (**Prov. 11:2**).

Scripture Reading: Daniel 5:17–22

Hymns: "Though Your Sins Be as Scarlet," Crosby

"I Lay My Sins on Jesus," Bonar

"I Am Resolved," Hartsough

Offertory Prayer: Our God and Father, giver of all perfect gifts and supplier of our every need, grant us the wisdom to be humble. When we bring our offerings, let us recognize your offer. When we bless your name, help us to receive your benediction. For the manifold riches provided in Christ Jesus, we thank you. For an opportunity to share in proclaiming his name, we are grateful. In his name we pray. Amen.

Introduction

Pride is the first sin of which we have any knowledge. Through pride the angels fell. So it was with our first parents, for in the garden the tempter whispered, "Ye shall be as gods" (Gen. 3:5). The danger of this sin and its destructive results are echoed through the biblical writers.

"The fear of the LORD is to hate evil: pride, and arrogancy." (Prov. 8:13)

"Therefore pride compasseth them about as a chain; violence covereth them as a garment." (Ps. 73:6)

"Out of the heart of men, proceed evil thoughts ... an evil eye, blasphemy, pride, foolishness: All these evil things come from within, and defile the man." (Mark 7:21–23)

"For all that is in the world, the lust of the flesh, and the lust of the eyes, and the pride of life, is not of the Father, but is of the world." (1 John 2:16)

It is our task to search into the subtlety of damaging sins, to expose the manner in which they beset us, and to make ineffective their attack on character's bastion. The essence of sin is selfishness. Pride is the inordinate assertion of self.

Our text is the natural development of pride in our lives. How conscious we are that (1) "When pride cometh," (2) "then cometh shame," (3) "but with the lowly is wisdom." In the example of Belshazzar (Dan. 5), we can identify our struggle with pride.

I. When pride cometh.

A. *The Latins saw pride as "aiming at that above."*
   1. This type of pride is not mere desire to improve; it is the drive to rule or ruin.
   2. We may excel without excessive pride. The learned person is wise, recognizes his or her wisdom, and is extremely humbled by it.
      The morally clean young woman refuses bad company and in deep gratitude thanks God for his cleansing.

205

3. When the charge of "pride" is made, both the accuser and the accused are judged.
4. Scripture says: "God resisteth the proud, but giveth grace unto the humble" (James 4:6) and "Wherefore come out from among them, and be ye separate" (2 Cor. 6:17).

B. *Pride holds in itself the element of falsehood.*
   1. It claims merit not possessed.
   2. It hates those who estimate us at true worth.
   3. Our false estimate of ourselves is the mark of pride. "[Love] suffereth long, and is kind; [love] envieth not; [love] vaunteth not itself, is not puffed up" (1 Cor. 13:4).

II. Then cometh shame.

There are many kinds of pride: that within which desperately drives its victims to take every advantage; that without which manifests itself in appearance and possessions.

A. *Speech betrays pride.*
   1. Discussion topics are centered on self.
   2. People labor to convince others of their superiority but transparent vanity makes them a laughingstock.
   3. Boastfulness leads to exaggeration and on to falsehood. Many find it hard to speak the truth about self. They exaggerate everything that happens to them. What they have or do is better; and when something bad happens, of course their situation is more tragic. Soon others say, "You can't believe a word he [or she] says."

B. *Sources of shameful pride.*
   1. In the gifts of nature. "Be not wise in thine own eyes." (Prov. 3:7).
   "And he [the Lord] said to me, My grace is sufficient for thee: for my strength is made perfect in weakness" (2 Cor. 12:9).
   "Favor is deceitful, and beauty is vain" (Prov. 31:30).
   2. In the gifts of fortune. "Bless the LORD, O my soul: and forget not all his benefits" (Ps. 103:2).
   "Thou art waxen fat, thou art grown thick, thou art covered with fatness; then he forsook God which made him" (Deut. 32:15).
   "Beware of covetousness: for a man's life consisteth not in the abundance of the things which he possesseth" (Luke 12:15).
   3. In the spiritual gifts. "Do ye look on things after the outward appearance?" (2 Cor. 10:7).
   "But he that glorieth, let him glory in the Lord" (2 Cor. 10:17).
   "I tell you, this man [a publican] went down to his house justified rather than the other; for every one that exalteth himself shall be abased; and he that humbleth himself shall be exalted" (Luke 18:14).
   "For by grace are ye saved through faith; and that not of yourselves" (Eph. 2:8).

III. With the lowly is wisdom.

Pride, even in the spiritual realm, renders progress impossible. When our lives are full of the sense of personal merit, there is no room for love. Throughout the biblical account and especially in the life of Jesus, we are reminded that true greatness consists of service.

A. *God removed pride from his kings.*

1. Saul said at the time of his selection, "Am I not a Benjamite, from the smallest tribe of Israel, and is not my clan the least of all the clans of the tribe of Benjamin? Why do you say such a thing to me?" (1 Sam. 9:21 NIV).

2. The Lord said to Samuel in the selecting of David, "Look not on his countenance, or on the height of his stature; ... for the Lord seeth not as man seeth; for man looketh on the outward appearance, but the Lord looketh on the heart" (1 Sam. 16:7).

3. Solomon prayed when selected, "O Lord my God, thou hast made thy servant king ... and I am but a little child: I know not how to go out or come in" (1 Kings 3:7).

B. *The role of Savior was one of humility.* "He is despised and rejected of men ... he was despised, and we esteemed him not" (Isa. 53:3).

"He hath no form nor comeliness; and when we shall see him, there is no beauty that we should desire him" (Isa. 53:2).

"Take my yoke upon you, and learn of me; for I am meek and lowly in heart" (Matt. 11:29).

"For ye know the grace of our Lord Jesus Christ, that, though he was rich, yet for your sakes he became poor" (2 Cor. 8:9).

Conclusion

The sin of pride has its cure in the encounter with Christ. One cannot kneel with the animals in Bethlehem or sit with the publicans in Jerusalem or dine with the fishermen of Galilee and retain pride. Certainly it is difficult to stand beside a cross and glory in anything within ourselves. God forbid that we should glory save in that cross.

SUNDAY EVENING, JULY 13

Title: How to Have the Guidance of God

Text: "And he said, 'O Lord God of my master Abraham, I pray thee, send me good speed this day, and shew kindness unto my master Abraham. Behold, I stand here by the well of water; and the daughters of the men of the city come out to draw water: And let it come to pass, that the damsel to whom I shall say, Let down thy pitcher, I pray thee, that I may drink; and she shall say, Drink, and I will give thy camels drink also; let the same be she that thou hast appointed for thy servant Isaac; and thereby shall I know that thou hast shewed kindness unto my master'" **(Gen. 24:12 – 14).**

Scripture Reading: Genesis 24:1 – 33, 57 – 67

Introduction

Sarah, Abraham's wife, lived to be 127 years old. To Isaac the death of his mother, Sarah, was a very great personal loss. Although he was a grown man at the time of her death, he had always lived at home, had been the recipient of his mother's love and devotion, and was the subject of her constant hope and prayer.

Abraham, Isaac's father, made plans with his chief servant to secure a wife for his lonesome son. The faithful servant made the journey requested by Abraham and brought Rebekah to Isaac without Isaac's approval or disapproval. The selection of Rebekah for Isaac was the custom of that day, but it also reveals the meekness and acquiescence of Isaac. Abraham and his servant did a good job in selecting Rebekah for Isaac. The Bible portrays her as a kind, gracious, beautiful, and charming woman.

The story as told in Genesis 24 reveals to us how we can have the guidance of God in daily matters. Let us delineate these important and instructive guidelines based on the story.

I. To have the guidance of God, we must realize that we have been sent on a mission.

"But thou shalt go unto my country, and to my kindred, and take a wife unto my son Isaac" (Gen. 24:4). The thought of a bride for Isaac originated in the mind and heart of Abraham as the outcome of his love for his son. Abraham chose his eldest servant for the task of selecting a bride for Isaac, and the servant set out to accomplish the task his master had given him.

All of us have tasks to perform in life. In fact, God has a purpose for every life. To put it more succinctly, God has a purpose for you. If we are to perform his will, we must know what it is and have the guidance of God in doing it.

II. To have the guidance of God, we must be "in the way" (Gen. 24:27).

Being "in the way" means having our feet in the path God approves, doing what God wants us to do. Being "in the way" means being involved in the task set out for us.

Jesus enunciated this great principle when he said, "If any man will do his will, he shall know of the doctrine, whether it be of God, or whether I speak of myself" (John 7:17).

III. To have the guidance of God, we must ask for it.

It is clearly evident that Abraham's servant asked for and got the guidance of God in finding Isaac a bride. His task was more than that of obeying his master Abraham; the task of finding a wife for Isaac became his evident delight. What a grand privilege it was to secure a bride for Isaac, his master's son. He gave himself to the task when he asked God to guide him. The Bible teaches, "Ask, and it shall be given you; seek, and ye shall find; knock, and it shall be opened unto you" (Matt. 7:7). "If ye abide in me, and my words abide in you, ye shall ask what ye will, and it shall be done unto you" (John 15:7).

God's guidance is yours for the asking. God's will and the accomplishment of his will come through the privilege of prayer.

IV. To have the guidance of God, we must expect it.

Abraham's servant prayed earnestly that God would guide him. He said, "And let it come to pass, that the damsel to whom I shall say, Let down thy pitcher, I pray thee, that I may drink; and she shall say, Drink, and I will give thy camels drink also: let the same be she that thou hast appointed for thy servant Isaac; and thereby shall I know that thou hast shewed kindness unto my master" (Gen. 24:14).

The servant had prayed thus, and now he expected an answer to his prayer. He was prepared to accept God's answer and to accept whomever God appointed. He prayed, expected, and answered and left it all in God's hands.

We will have the guidance of God when we pray and expect an answer to our praying. We must not say, "O, Lord, guide me," when all the time we mean, "Let me guide Thee."

V. To have the guidance of God, we must look for it in other persons.

"And they called Rebekah, and said unto her, Wilt thou go with this man? And she said, I will go" (Gen. 24:58). The trusted servant could see the guidance of God in Rebekah's answer, in Rebekah's actions. He understood that God had been at work in her life too. Often when God speaks to us, he speaks to others about us. He also speaks to us through others. Sometimes we can see his guidance for our lives in the lives of others.

VI. To have the guidance of God, we must proclaim God's purpose (Gen. 24:34–56).

The servant's one purpose was to announce his master's purpose—the will of Abraham. The servant not only proclaimed it; he went on to proclaim the resources of Abraham (v. 35) and the glory of the son (v. 36).

Christians are instruments in the hands of the Holy Spirit to proclaim the greatness of the Father and the glory of Christ, the Son. When we proclaim his will, he gives us guidance all the way.

VII. To have the guidance of God, we must accept it when given.

What did the servant do when it became evident that Rebekah was to become Isaac's bride? He immediately talked with her family, secured permission to take her to Isaac, and proceeded to bring her to him. There he introduced them to each other. The Bible says, "Isaac ... took Rebekah, and she became his wife" (Gen. 24:67).

WEDNESDAY EVENING, JULY 16

Title: The Bible Speaks to Our Condition

Scripture Reading: 2 Timothy 2

Introduction

In our chapter for today, the apostle Paul is expressing a fatherly concern for his son in the ministry. The content of this chapter is filled with practical suggestions for one who faces great difficulty in rendering a significant ministry to people for the Lord. Each of us can read this chapter and make personal applications.

I. Paul encourages a willingness to suffer (2 Tim. 2:1–14).

Paul encourages Timothy to find strength in the grace that is in Christ Jesus. He points out that achieving success always involves self-discipline and the overcoming of difficulties. He uses a number of illustrations to strengthen his suggestion.

    A. *The example of a good soldier (2:3–4).*
    B. *The example of an athlete (2:5).*
    C. *The example of a hardworking farmer (2:6).*
    D. *We are to remember the example of Christ (2:8).*
    E. *Paul reminds Timothy of the suffering involved in Paul's own imprisonment.* Paul endured suffering in order that others might experience salvation. We should be willing to suffer for the same purpose.

II. Paul warns against foolish disputes (2 Tim. 2:14–19, 23–26).

Paul points out that there are always many controversies raging. To participate in these controversies can color people's personalities and affect their ministries. He encourages Timothy to avoid a reputation for being a disputer in foolish controversies. In contrast he encourages him to be a diligent student so that he can rightly divide the "word of truth" and present it to his hearers in a spirit of gentleness and meekness.

III. Paul issues a challenge to disciplined living (2 Tim. 2:20–22).

Paul points out in specific terms that one must exercise a voluntary discipline if he wants to become a chosen vessel in the hands of the Lord accepted for every good work. There must be great negatives in the life of the Christian as well as a positive seeking of that which is good.

Conclusion

Each of us can profit from Paul's suggestions to Timothy. The Holy Spirit will speak to us if we read this chapter with an open, responsive heart.

If we seek and follow the guidance of God, it will lead to victory. God never commands without providing what we need to get the job done and guiding us in the way. His grace is sufficient for his will for our lives. Receive his guidance now!

SUNDAY MORNING, JULY 20

Title: The Sin of Greed

Text: "He that is greedy of gain troubleth his own house; but he that hateth gifts shall live" **(Prov. 15:27)**.

Scripture Reading: 1 Timothy 6:6–10

Hymns: "Give of Your Best to the Master," Grose

"I Surrender All," Van Deventer

"Take My Life, and Let It Be," Havergal

Offertory Prayer: We tremble in your presence, dear Father, for we have not come to master our possessions. The things of the world are too much with us, and too often they influence our thinking. Receive this gift that we bring. It represents a freedom that we find in you. Father, we are free only as we commit to you our concerns and our possessions. Accept our offering, and accept all that we are for your own use. Amen.

Introduction

In the history of humankind, the sin of greed has played a conspicuous and evil role. A high percentage of wrongs and heinous crimes are due to the inordinate greed of gain. "So are the ways of every one that is greedy of gain" (Prov. 1:19). Greed corrodes the hearts of people, spoiling family happiness, and setting people in conflict. Jesus pointed out the terrible dangers of greed as he related the story of "the soils." "These are they which are sown among thorns; such as hear the word, and the cares of this world, and the deceitfulness of riches, and the lusts of other things entering in, choke the word, and it becometh unfruitful" (Mark 4:18–19). Surely much of the value of loving God with the whole heart is that it leaves no place for greed to take root. The combination of our texts from Proverbs and from 1 Timothy teach us of (1) gain in contentment, (2) trouble in one's own house, and (3) living beyond bribes.

I. Gain in contentment.

Paul encourages young Timothy by writing that "godliness with contentment is great gain." What a need there is for this teaching today when people are ever conscious of stock holdings, real estate holdings, and position holdings! When we consider inflation, deflation, and rate of growth, what is the market value of contentment? Over against this contentment, Paul lists "the love of money" as "the root of all evil." After all allowances have been made in translation, and it has been noted that the text reads "love of money" not "money," that correctly it is "a root" not "the root," Paul is possibly saying that every kind of evil at one time or another springs from this root. Certainly the words refer to the widespread evil that money promotes.

A. *Wealth in satisfaction.*

211

1. My father often said, "There are two ways to be wealthy: earn a sufficient amount or learn to be satisfied with less."
2. Often what we give in life is more significant and adds to happiness more than what we get.

B. *Health is related to contentment.*
1. Was John pronouncing our doom as paupers when he wrote, "I wish above all things that thou mayest prosper and be in health, even as thy soul prospereth" (3 John 2)?
2. Paul noted that those not spiritually in accord "are weak and sickly among you, and many sleep" (1 Cor. 11:30).

II. Trouble in one's own house.

A. *Inhumanity springs from a person's desire to possess that belonging to another.*
1. Lust of one country for soil of another has often let loose war and pillage on the innocent.
2. In every age, the powerful, under the sway of greed, plunder and oppress the weak.
3. In our contemporary society, some employees cheat employers. And sometimes employers take advantage of employees.
4. Love of money has begotten the courage of the highjacker, sharpened the ingenuity of the thief, and put a knife in the hand of the murderer. For thirty pieces of silver, Judas sold his Lord.

B. *A person's inner being is destroyed by greed.*
1. Greed causes some to commit sordid sins daily.
   a. A merchant to adulterate his goods.
   b. A clerk to put his hand in the till.
   c. A salesperson to lie for a sale.
2. The unpardonable sin of the twentieth century is poverty.
   a. People make haste to be rich; if they succeed, everything is forgiven.
   b. Gates of highest society swing open to the person with money, and he is not asked how he came by it.
   c. Poor people who commit a crime go to jail while rich criminals buy their way to freedom.

C. *One offspring of greed is gambling.* The desire to get rich quick is at the bottom of gambling. People want to get rich without investing time and effort.

III. Living beyond bribes.

"He that despises bribes shall live," said the sage of Israel. When money is used properly and creatively, it results in blessedness. Strong convictions can arm us against greed.

A. *Know there are better things than money.*
1. The blessings of good health.
2. A keen intelligence.
3. A sympathetic heart.

4. A clear conscience.
B. *Know that money is not an end in itself, only a means.*
  1. What would you do with great wealth?
  2. What are you doing with what you have?
C. *Know that wealth cannot be kept forever.*
  1. Money is a trust, as we see in the parable of the talents.
  2. "Lay not up for yourselves treasures upon earth, where moth and rust doth corrupt, and where thieves break through and steal" (Matt. 6:19).

Conclusion

In the life of Jesus, we see two basic concerns relative to the material: (1) that people be free from the tyranny of things and (2) that they be concerned over the needs of their fellow humans. Our true attitude toward God is reflected in our attitude toward others. We are to "seek ... first the kingdom of God, and his righteousness; and all these things shall be added unto [us]" (Matt. 6:33). If we master things, we will not be mastered by greed. The key, Jesus said, is, "Do not be anxious about your life, what you shall eat or what you shall drink, nor about your body, what you shall put on" (Matt. 6:25 RSV). The alternate to worrying over things and falling victim to greed is to trust in God. Jesus challenges us never to use our possessions to divide persons when we may use them to unite (Luke 16:19–31).

SUNDAY EVENING, JULY 20

Title: Walking with God
Text: "Enoch walked with God: and he was not; for God took him" **(Gen. 5:24).**
Scripture Reading: Genesis 5:21–24

Introduction

The Bible says, "Enoch walked with God." Who was Enoch? The Bible tells us that he was the son of Jared (Gen. 5:18), the father of Methuselah (Gen. 5:21–22), and the seventh in descent from Adam in the line of Seth (Jude 14). The Bible says he lived 365 years. The brief record of his life is written in the words, "Enoch walked with God: and he was not; for God took him" (Gen. 5:24).

The words "walked with God" denote a devout life lived in close communion with God. The words "and he was not" are explained by Hebrews 11:5, "By faith Enoch was translated that he should not see death; and was not found, because God had translated him: for before his translation he had this testimony, that he pleased God." The words "lived," "begat," and "died" in Genesis reveal how brief and uniform are our lives.

Enoch was a man who walked with God. Using the story of Enoch's life, I want to share with you some pertinent points concerning walking with God.

I. The companion of walking with God.

A. *The companion for life's walk is a divine companion.* Paul said: "What agreement hath the temple of God with idols? for ye are the temple of the living God; as God hath said, I will dwell in them, and walk in them; and I will be their God, and they shall be my people" (2 Cor. 6:16). The agnostic and the skeptic ask, "Where is God?" The Christian, like Enoch, is quietly walking with this divine companion.

B. *The companion for life's walk is a close companion.* The Bible says, "A friend loveth at all times" (Prov. 17:17), and God is a companion who is near at all times. He makes his abode in the Christian and walks with him or her always.

C. *The companion for life's walk is a faithful companion.* We can trust him, for he is faithful and just. He does not desert us before our foes. He wants to be with us and is preparing a place for us where we will live with him forever.

II. The demands of walking with God.

A. *Walking with God demands entire surrender.* The name Enoch means "dedicated, one yielded up to God, to be conformed to God's mind and will." Walking with God demands surrender to God's will. Paul indicated this surrender when he wrote, "I consider everything a loss because of the surpassing worth of knowing Christ Jesus my Lord.... I consider them garbage, that I may gain Christ and be found in him, not having a righteousness of my own that comes from the law, but that which is through faith in Christ—the righteousness that comes from God on the basis of faith" (Phil. 3:9 NIV).

B. *Walking with God demands unbroken fellowship.* As Enoch walked with God, he had fellowship with God. The two were in perfect agreement. Amos said, "Can two walk together, except they be agreed?" (Amos 3:3). Enoch had good company for the road of life. Walking with God makes the trip of life enjoyable.

C. *Walking with God demands continual progress.* Our knowledge of God must continually be growing, because the chariot wheels of life never stand still. Each day is a new journey, for we have not passed this way before. We journey toward a new country, the upward way, the Promised Land.

D. *Walking with God demands complete separation.* Walking with God prohibits indulgence in the sinful pleasures of the world. God is light, and those who walk with him do not walk in darkness. Paul said: "Set your affections on things above, not on things on earth" (Col. 3:2). The book of Leviticus says, "Sanctify yourselves therefore, and be ye holy; for I am the LORD your God" (Lev. 20:7).

E. *Walking with God demands suffering.* Those who walk with God suffer the criticism and hatred of the world (John 15:18). They suffer as good soldiers of Jesus Christ (2 Tim. 2:3).

III. The manner of walking with God.

A. *Walking with God means walking by faith.* We receive Christ through faith. Paul said, "Ye are all the children of God by faith in Christ Jesus" (Gal. 3:26), and "For by grace are ye saved through faith; and that not of yourselves, it is the gift of God: not of works, lest any man should boast" (Eph. 2:8–9). We walk by faith in happiness, sorrow, turmoil, and death. Without faith it is impossible to please God (Heb. 11:6).

B. *Walking with God means not walking in a hypocritical way.* We do not walk with faces disfigured but transfigured, not conformed to the rites of humanity but transformed by the power of God. We do not walk with a pious face but with a pious life. We do not walk with ears opened to idle tales or gossip, but to the voice of God.

C. *Walking with God means walking in truth.* Jesus said: "I am the way, the truth, and the life" (John 14:6). John the apostle said, "For I rejoiced greatly, when the brethren came and testified of the truth that is in thee, even as thou walkest in the truth" (3 John 3).

D. *Walking with God means a spiritual walk.* Paul said, "Walk by the Spirit, and you will not gratify the desires of the flesh.... Since we live by the Spirit, let us keep in step with the Spirit" (Gal. 5:16, 25 NIV).

IV. The privileges of walking with God.

A. *Walking with God assures us of the forgiveness of our sins.* John the apostle said, "If we confess our sins, he is faithful and just to forgive us our sins, and to cleanse us from all unrighteousness" (1 John 1:9). The greatest of all feelings is the joy of walking with God on the highway of life and knowing that you are forgiven and cleansed (Isa. 35:8–9).

B. *Walking with God assures us of strength day by day.* The Lord has promised to be with us always (Matt. 28:20). Paul said, "The Lord stood with me, and strengthened me; that by me the preaching might be fully known, and that all the Gentiles might hear: and I was delivered out of the mouth of the lion. And the Lord shall deliver me from every evil work, and will preserve me unto his heavenly kingdom, to whom be glory for ever and ever. Amen" (2 Tim. 4:17–18). As we walk with him, he does give us strength when it is needed!

C. *Walking with God assures us of comfort for life's sorrows.* Enoch did not die, but I am sure he had sorrows along life's journey. Who doesn't? Many passages of God's Word assure us of comfort for life's sorrows. God is with us, and he speaks to us (Ps. 23; John 14:1–6).

D. *Walking with God assures us of happiness for life's journey.* Walking with God is happiness, true happiness. Paul knew about that joy even in prison and wrote to the Philippians urging them to "Rejoice in the Lord alway: and again I say, Rejoice" (Phil. 4:4).

Conclusion

Begin today your walk with the Lord Jesus Christ, and he will go with you each step of the way.

WEDNESDAY EVENING, JULY 23

Title: The Bible Speaks to Our Condition

Scripture Reading: Hebrews 1

Introduction

In these Wednesday evening Bible studies, we have been emphasizing that the Bible speaks to our condition. The opening verses of the chapter for this day provide us with a dramatic statement of the truth that God has been seeking to communicate his love and purpose to people through the ages.

The writer of the book of Hebrews illustrates how God's final and supreme word comes to us in and through Jesus Christ. He addresses himself to Hebrew Christians who are recent converts from Judaism. In Judaism they had thought of the prophets and the angels as mediums through whom the message of God was communicated to people (Heb. 1:1, 4). The writer demonstrates through this book that Christ is superior to the prophets, the angels, the Mosaic law, and the Levitical priesthood. He encourages new converts to look to and listen to Jesus Christ as God's authentic and supreme messenger to the hearts of people.

I. Christ is superior to the prophets (Heb. 1:1–3).

  A. *Christ is the exact image of God (1:3).* The original glory of God belongs to him.

  B. *Christ is the appointed heir of all things (1:2).* Christ is the goal toward which everything moves.

  C. *Christ is the creative instrument by which God created the world (1:2).*

  D. *Christ is the sustainer of the universe (1:3).*

  E. *Christ is our Redeemer, "having himself purged our sins" (1:3).*

  F. *Christ is our Priest-King (1:3).*

II. Christ is superior to the angels (Heb. 1:4–14).

In the Old Testament, God often communicated with people by means of angelic messengers. The writer of Hebrews emphasizes that Christ is superior to the angelic messengers in the following manner:

  A. *The angels are described as the servants of God (1:7) as well as the servants of the heirs of salvation (1:4).* The Christ is described and declared to be the very Son of God.

  B. *The Christ is superior to the angels in that he is the object of angelic worship (1:6).*

  C. *The Christ is superior to the angels in that upon him has been bestowed kingly sovereignty in the kingdom of God (1:8).*

D. *The Christ is superior to the angels in that he is the Anointed One of God, selected and equipped to be our Redeemer (1:9).*

E. *The Christ is superior to the angels in the same manner in which the Creator is superior to his creation (1:10).*

F. *The Christ is superior to the angels in that he is eternal and superior to all created things and beings (1:11–13).*

Conclusion

While the angels were mediums of communication, the Christ is the actual communication of God to the hearts and lives of people. Let us listen to the message of the prophets, the priests, and the psalmists. Let us learn from the patriarchs and from all persons with whom God has dealt. Let us bow in worship before the Christ as Redeemer and Savior. Let us make him the Lord of our lives this day.

SUNDAY MORNING, JULY 27

Title: The Sin of Sensuality

Text: "For to be carnally minded is death; but to be spiritually minded is life and peace" **(Rom. 8:6)**.

Scripture Reading: Romans 1:18–32

Hymns: "Whiter Than Snow," Nicholson

"Grace Greater Than Our Sin," Johnston

"Though Your Sins Be as Scarlet," Crosby

Offertory Prayer: In lovingkindness you have come, O Lord, to redeem us from ourselves. We are tempted daily to keep ourselves from you and spend ourselves in lesser causes. Our dissipation of life is ever a shame to us. Our waste of things leaves us ever in want. Today we come to invest in your kingdom. Use, we pray, this gift and our love that your purposes may be accomplished. Amen.

Introduction

Sensuality, or licentiousness, is sin against the seventh commandment—"Thou shalt not commit adultery" (Ex. 20:14). It is difficult to speak on this subject—so much so that I would find it embarrassing if I were to read our Scripture lesson in Romans from the Greek using a less staid translation than that of King James' time. On such subjects, I often feel the less said, the better. Silence is sometimes more eloquent than speech. Certainly the reticence in which this sin is shrouded is the severest of all condemnation. I feel as Paul that sins of this kind are so loathsome that "it is a shame even to speak of those things" (Eph. 5:12).

Of necessity, the Bible is not silent on our subject. From Sinai to Calvary, we hear the thunder against unchastity and impurity. Not only in the Word is God's judgment against sensuality heard, but "the wrath of God is revealed from heaven"

217

(Rom. 1:18). "Therefore thou art inexcusable, O man" (Rom. 2:1). The sin of sensuality is a threat to the highest earthly relationship. In our social order, it is essential to guard that relationship, the family, upon which all others are built. The very unity of humankind grows out of the unity of husband and wife. It is our purpose to examine the strata of society and see in each case the damaging sin of sensuality.

I. The individual's problem of carnality.

    A. *The contribution of the book of Proverbs:*
        1. Is intended as a handbook for life's journey.
        2. Treats no other sin with such amplitude and repetition.
        3. Depicts lasciviousness as the way of death.
    B. *Contemporary conditions.*
        1. Abundance of facts known to all presses pastors to speak firmly and fearlessly.
        2. If we play ignorant, we give temptation a cruel advantage, for the force of temptation often lies in surprise.
        3. Even in our schools, attempts are made to corrupt minds.
        4. Young men face assault on their virtue from most unlikely quarters.
        5. Young women are warned that their ruin may come by the very persons from whom they should receive protection.
        6. There is a danger of kindling by my words the very fire we wish to quench, but there is an instinct in healthy minds that tells them what is said on this subject proceeds from moral earnestness.
    C. *Our basic problem is in "thoughts."*
        1. "Whosoever looketh upon a woman to lust after her hath committed adultery already in his heart" (Matt. 5:28).
        2. How dangerous it is when licentious thoughts form a part of the pleasure of existence.
        3. The life of dreams is invaded by the habit.
        4. Our defense against the tyranny of foul imagination is preoccupation with healthy subjects.

II. Unchastity and the family.

    A. *The sacredness of motherhood and childhood is pointed out in the divine institution of marriage.*
        1. Character may be judged by one's attitude toward God's institutions.
        2. One is reminded of Joseph's great respect for chastity: "How then can I do this great wickedness, and sin against God?" (Gen. 39:9).
    B. *Appetites are not given to us merely for indulgence; we can learn from restraint.*
        1. A person matures by mastering impulses.
        2. If the rule of chastity seems harsh, remember it guards the most perfect flower of human happiness.

III. Unrestraint in society.

    A. *The sin of sensuality involves another soul.*

1. Libertinism is a foolish argument that carnality is native to humanity.
2. Society is a union of families. Any sin that blights the marriage relation and destroys the family is an enemy of society.
3. The adulterer is an enemy of the state.

B. *"Righteousness exalteth a nation: but sin is a reproach to any people" (Prov. 14:34).*
C. *"Let us walk honestly, as in the day; not in rioting and drunkenness, not in chambering and wantonness, not in strife and envying" (Rom. 13:13).*

Conclusion

A message on sensuality is difficult to bring in a society where profligacy reigns. It may seem as trifling as a snowflake in the gutter. We must be reminded that enough snowflakes can beautify the winter world about us. God's Word speaks often and sure, and he does have concern for our conduct. In spite of changes in customs and differing styles, the apostle's words ring true to our better selves, "Know ye not that ye are the temple of God, and that the spirit of God dwelleth in you? If any man defile the temple of God, him shall God destroy" (1 Cor. 3:16–17).

SUNDAY EVENING, JULY 27

Title: How Does God Speak Today?

Text: "God, who at sundry times and in divers manners spake in time past unto the fathers by the prophets, hath in these last days spoken unto us by his Son, whom he hath appointed heir of all things, by whom also he made the worlds" **(Heb. 1:1–2)**.

Scripture Reading: Psalm 19:1–14; Hebrews 1:1–2

Introduction

The question most often asked of ministers by sinners is "How can I get forgiveness for my sins?" The question most often asked by Christians is "How can I know God's will for my life?" or "How does God speak today?"

God is continually speaking his will to people. Of course, some people doubt that God speaks at all to people today. Joan of Arc was one of the most spectacular military leaders France ever had. As a simple peasant girl, she started her career by getting a French army commander to arrange an interview for her with King Charles VII. When she told him voices were bidding her to become the leader of her nation's armies, the king impatiently replied that if God had any word for France, it should come to him as ruler. Joan of Arc assured him that voices did come but that he did not hear them because of his failure to pray and listen.

How does God speak today? In many ways. Let us note a few.

I. God speaks through history.

My history professor in college said, "History is 'his story,'" speaking of

Jesus Christ. A noted historian said, "History is a voice forever sounding across the centuries the laws of right and wrong." Thomas Arnold reviewed the downfall of the great world empires of the past and summed up what had happened by saying, "Down they come, one after another, and all for the lack of righteousness."

God controls the universe by physical and moral laws. Ruthless leaders who seek to rule by military force may find success for a brief time but will in the end perish. Unjust, greedy, selfish men who exploit others for gain may appear successful for a brief spell, but they too will soon perish. God has a universal law: "Be not deceived, God is not mocked: for whatsoever a man soweth, that shall he also reap" (Gal. 6:7). Surely God speaks to us through history, for no nation or individual can permanently endure who defies God and his laws.

II. God speaks through nature.

The writer of Psalm 19 said, "The heavens declare the glory of God; and the firmament sheweth his handiwork" (v. 1). The writer of Romans said, "For the wrath of God is revealed from heaven against all ungodliness and unrighteousness of men, who hold the truth in unrighteousness; because that which may be known of God is manifest in them; for God hath shewed it unto them. For the invisible things of him from the creation of the world are clearly seen, being understood by the things that are made, even his eternal power and Godhead; so that they are without excuse" (Rom. 1:18–20).

I remember hearing of a Frenchman who had incurred the displeasure of Napoleon and was cast into a dungeon. Forsaken by his family and friends, forgotten by everyone in the outside world, he wrote on the wall of his cell, "Nobody cares." One day a green shoot came through a crack in the floor. Each day the Frenchman shared his water with the little green plant. The plant grew and grew toward the small window in the cell, and one day the Frenchman found on the plant a beautiful blue flower. As he looked at the beautiful blue flower, he scratched away the words "Nobody cares" and wrote, "God cares." God had spoken through nature, through a plant with a blue flower.

III. God speaks through conscience.

The inner voice, the conscience, speaks according to a person's standard of right and wrong. If the voice of the conscience is ignored, the individual is left without a guide. If the voice of conscience is ignored, a Christian will be unable to tell the difference between right and wrong. Let each one of us read God's Word, pray, worship, witness, and work that our conscience might guide us aright!

IV. God speaks through human instrumentality.

There is no way in which God speaks to us more convincingly than through the lives of others. How often have we heard others say, "I am a Christian because I saw Christ in you"? No wonder the Bible says, "He that winneth souls is wise"

(Prov. 11:30). When we witness, God speaks through us to others. Paul said, "Ye are our epistle written in our hearts, known and read of all men" (2 Cor. 3:2).

Yes, God speaks through you. You are his human instrument.

V. God speaks through the Bible.

The Bible is the written record of the revelation of God to man. The Bible is God's Word for today, this generation, and for all time. The Bible testifies, "All scripture is given by inspiration of God, and is profitable for doctrine, for reproof, for correction, for instruction in righteousness: that the man of God may be perfect, thoroughly furnished unto all good works" (2 Tim. 3:15–17).

A young man who had lost his arm in battle was frightened, depressed, and disturbed as he began his voyage home. He wondered if he could face his family, face the world, make a living, and be a real man without his right arm. On the verge of panic, he opened his Bible and his eyes fell on the words, "If God be for us, who can be against us?" (Rom. 8:31). As he read, he became aware that God had spoken. He had the divine answer, the answer from heaven. He came home to meet life victoriously and successfully. God had spoken to him through his Word.

VI. God speaks through prayer.

I once asked my pastor's wife, Mrs. J. D. Grey, concerning her favorite verse in the Bible. Her answer was, "Call upon me, and I will answer thee, and shew thee great and mighty things, which thou knowest not" (Jer. 33:3). Surely this verse contains one of the greatest invitations in the Bible. Jesus said, "Ask, and it shall be given you; seek, and ye shall find; knock, and it shall be opened unto you" (Matt. 7:7). Let the person who desires to hear God speak go to him in prayer.

Prayer is the means by which God reveals himself to the individual soul. Spend much time in prayer if you desire to hear God's voice.

VII. God speaks through his Son Jesus Christ.

The Bible teaches that "God, who at sundry times and in divers manners spoke in time past unto the fathers by the prophets, hath in these last days spoken to us by his Son" (Heb. 1:1–2). Jesus Christ is the apex of God's revelation to man. Jesus Christ is the final revelation of God to man and is the only adequate revelation of God to man.

A. *God speaks through his Son's character.*

B. *God speaks through his Son's sacrifice.*

C. *God speaks through his Son's love.*

Conclusion

Has God been speaking to you? He speaks through history, nature, conscience, human instrumentality, the Bible, prayer, and Jesus Christ his Son. Surrender to him and follow his voice as he speaks!

WEDNESDAY EVENING, JULY 30

Title: The Bible Speaks to Our Condition

Scripture Reading: Hebrews 8

Introduction

The chapter for today's prayerful meditation and study comes from a section of the book of Hebrews that deals with Christ as the High Priest of the new covenant. Emphasis is placed on the fact that he is the mediator of a covenant that is superior to the old covenant.

The book of Hebrews may appear deep and difficult to the casual reader who has no knowledge of the Old Testament background that provides the framework for the writer's message to the Hebrew Christians. An effort is being put forth to reveal that God's final revelation of himself and God's complete provisions for his children are to be found in Jesus Christ rather than in the worship rituals and the sacrifices of the Levitical priesthood. A knowledge of the Old Testament is essential for a full understanding of this New Testament book.

This particular section of the book of Hebrews emphasizes the high priestly ministry of Jesus Christ. A priest was a mediator, or go-between, a bridge-builder between humans and God.

The writer declares that Christ is a merciful and faithful high priest (Heb. 2:17–18) as well as a sinless yet compassionate one (4:4–16). Christ is our living and eternal High Priest who makes intercession for us (7:22–28).

I. Christ is the mediator of a better covenant (Heb. 8:1–6).

The scriptural writer is comparing the Levitical priesthood and the old tabernacle with the present priesthood of Christ in the new tabernacle, which is heaven itself (cf. Heb. 9:11–12). Instead of ministering in a tabernacle built by the priest according to the instructions of Moses, Christ Jesus has entered into heaven itself, which is indeed the Holy of Holies. He goes not with the blood of animal sacrifices, but with his own precious blood as a sacrifice of atonement for the sins of believers. His priestly ministry on our behalf is superior to the priestly ministry known under the old covenant in the old tabernacle.

II. The nature of the new covenant (Heb. 8:7–13).

The writer speaks of a new covenant that supersedes the old covenant between God and Israel. The new covenant is said to be better than the old covenant because it is established on better promises. Notice these:

"I will make a new covenant with the house of Israel and with the house of Judah" (8:8).

"I will put my laws into their mind, and write them in their hearts." (8:10)

"I will be to them a God, and they shall be to me a people." (8:10)

"I will be merciful to their unrighteousness." (8:12)

"Their sins and their iniquities will I remember no more." (8:12)

The giving of this new covenant had been predicted by the prophets (Isa. 59:21; Jer. 31:31–34; Ezek. 36:25–26).

The people of God had repeatedly broken and violated the old covenant. It had proved to be ineffective. The new covenant would be both new and different in a number of respects.

A. *It would be better in quality in that it is based on better promises to God's people.*
B. *It would be new in scope in that it would unite the house of Israel and the house of Judah, which had been separated for hundreds of years.*
C. *It would be new in its universality.* "For all shall know me, from the least to the greatest."
D. *It would be new in its inwardness.* "I will put my laws into their mind, and write them in their hearts."
E. *It would be new in that it would effect forgiveness (8:12).*

Conclusion

In Jesus Christ, God has offered and initiated a new covenant relationship with those who are willing to trust Jesus Christ as Lord and Savior. This new covenant will be inward, personal, and spiritual. It provides an inward cleansing through the blood of Jesus Christ that soothes the conscience. It offers a high moral standard to challenge the will of God's children. And it offers a divine fellowship with God that can satisfy the deepest spiritual hunger.

AUGUST

■ Sunday Mornings

Continue and conclude the series "The Sins That Damage and Destroy." Be certain to focus attention on the Savior who can deliver us from the sins that damage and destroy.

On the last Sunday of the month, begin the series "Our Lord Speaks through Parables." These messages will speak words of warning as well as words of inspiration to God's people.

■ Sunday Evenings

Begin the series "The Great Christian Virtues." Make certain that each message praises the God of glory who revealed himself in Jesus Christ and who works by means of the Holy Spirit to make these virtues real in our lives. Only the Holy Spirit can produce the fruit of the Spirit.

■ Wednesday Evenings

Continue with the theme "The Bible Speaks to Our Condition." The theme verse for August is "For the word of God is quick, and powerful, and sharper than any two-edged sword, piercing even to the dividing asunder of soul and spirit, and of the joints and marrow, and is a discerner of the thoughts and intents of the heart" (Heb. 4:12).

SUNDAY MORNING, AUGUST 3

Title: The Sin of Envy

Text: "Resentment kills a fool, and envy slays the simple" (**Job 5:2 NIV**).

Scripture Reading: Genesis 4:1–10

Hymns: "Ye Must Be Born Again," Sleeper

"Depth of Mercy," Wesley

"God Calling Yet! Shall I Not Hear?" Borthwick

Offertory Prayer: Dear Father, our help in all ages and our strength in all circumstances, help us in this day of rapid change. We are so prone to lose sight of the harbor lights, and our vision ever falls short of your possibilities. Take this token of our love, we pray, and break it as the five loaves to meet many needs. In Jesus' name we pray. Amen.

Introduction

Can one be of such sweet disposition as to say anything good about envy?

224

Many of those most skillful with pen have aptly described its blight. To William Shakespeare it was "green sickness," to John Churton Collins it was "the sincerest form of flattery," and to Ambrose Bierce it was "emulation adapted to the meanest capacity." Biblical writers have shown equal distaste for the sin of envy. "A sound heart is the life of the flesh: but envy the rottenness of the bones" (Prov. 14:30). "Wrath is cruel, and anger is outrageous; but who is able to stand before envy?" (Prov. 27:4). "Just as they did not think it worthwhile to retain the knowledge of God, so God gave them over to a depraved mind, so that they do what ought not to be done. They have become filled with every kind of wickedness.... They are full of envy" (Rom. 1:28–29 NIV). Envy is a damaging sin whose impact reaches beyond the realm of social distaste. No wonder many early writers called it a "deadly sin." Envy is no less a deadly tool of Satan in our more sophisticated contemporary times.

I. A sin that brings grief when others prosper.

    A. *Judas Iscariot's problem was not his poor lot in life—it was that others had a better lot.*

    B. *Selfishness is the poisonous ingredient in envy.*

        1. We hurt when another rises or rejoice in his fall.

        2. It is sadly true that many find secret satisfaction in the misfortune of friends.

    C. *Envy and emulation are both excited by another's good.*

        1. Envy produces a sense of depression.

        2. Emulation gives a feeling of admiration.

        3. Emulation may desire to excel but not for the sake of putting another down.

        4. The difference essentially is that envy is ill-humored while emulation is good-humored.

II. A sin that steals love from character.

    A. *Some crimes are authored by envy.*

        1. Murder of Abel. Cain could not tolerate Abel's acceptable offering when his own was rejected.

        2. The early church's persecutions and martyrdoms came as a result of envy.

    B. *The worst sins of the tongue are products of envy.*

        1. Disparaging remarks about others.

        2. Spirit of gossip: "He is a wonderful person *but....*"

            Why should humiliation of another afford us gratification?

    C. *Fear reigns in our hearts lest another attain honor we cannot reach.*

        1. Sickness comes because others are happy.

        2. Envy is its own punishment.

        3. Listen closely to political speeches and hear how often envy speaks.

        4. Envy often destroys relationships: family, race.

III. A sin that attracts the strong.

A. *Many "isms" today use people's proneness to envy for their propaganda.*
   1. Honorable institutions, even the church, can fall under the spell of envy.
   2. Removing envy solves most class problems.

B. *World leaders have been affected by envy.*
   1. Alexander the Great permitted no praise for his generals because it detracted from him.
   2. Attitude of Nero.
   3. Envy often occurs with limited knowledge. If we knew all about the wealthy man or the talented woman, we might covet that person's position less.

IV. A sin that has a remedy.

A. *Count your blessings.*
   1. The envious are always comparing their lot with the more fortunate. Try contrasting with the less fortunate.
   2. A visit to a children's home or nursing home will help you to recognize how blessed you are.

B. *Learn to love excellence for its own sake.*
   1. It is not so important who plays lovely music as long as the right note is sounded.
   2. I have a sign above my desk that reads, "What wonderful things are wrought for God when we work without concern for who gets the credit."

Conclusion

God has put a "For Rent" sign on the universe. It is yours for the appreciation of it. The bird sings as sweetly for the pauper as for the prince. Water quenches the thirst of the vagabond as readily as for the tycoon. If we keep our hearts right, the world is ours. I never owned a foot of land but found much delight in hiking through the woods. The owner of the property I hiked on approached me once, saying, "It pleases me to see you so enjoy my woodland. How I wish I could enjoy it as you do." I was glad that he owned the land but also grateful for the capacity to appreciate what God had given to me.

John the Baptist set the stage for all to conquer envy. Upon seeing his followers turn from him to Jesus, he said, "He must increase, but I must decrease" (John 3:30).

SUNDAY EVENING, AUGUST 3

Title: Salvation and Its Fruit

Text: "The fruit of the Spirit is love, joy, peace, longsuffering, gentleness, goodness, faith, meekness, temperance: against such there is no law" (**Gal. 5:22–23**).

Scripture Reading: Hebrews 2:1–4, 9–12

Introduction

For generations people have so concerned themselves with the question "Who is God?" that they have forgotten another important question: "Who am I?" Some answer the question quickly: "I" am merely the train of thoughts and feelings and emotions that, like an Aeolian harp, played on by the wind of sensation, react to my environment. But my conviction goes beyond that. I am a person, separated from all other persons and remaining always the same being whatever changes may take place around me. I am a self conscious of self.

Within this self there occur some very positive notions. I find myself saying, "I ought to do certain things," or "I ought not to do other things." The mystery of this authoritative utterance of the self within me demands my attention. What is the "I ought" that I feel?

Paul says that it is "the law [of God] written in their hearts" (Rom. 2:15). John suggests that it is "the true Light, which lighteth every man that cometh into the world" (John 1:9). Whatever the feeling that requires response, it is in this that I differ from other animals. It is in this that I find my relationship to my Creator. So it is that out of inner struggle, out of the warfare within the soul, there comes peace.

Humanity's cumulative acts of bad choices and good choices through the years have come to complicate our "soul struggle." It has become such a mess that two thousand years ago a man complained, "For the good that I would I do not: but the evil which I would not, that I do" (Rom. 7:19). But now "in these last days," the God who "in the past ... spoke to our ancestors through the prophets at many times and in various ways" has "spoken to us by his Son" (Heb. 1:1–2 NIV). Now his Son's message is, "Come unto me, all ye that labour and are heavy laden, and I will give you rest" (Matt. 11:28). This is our salvation. This we cannot miss.

I. No escape...

"... if we ignore so great a salvation ... which was first announced by the Lord" (Heb. 2:3 NIV).

A. *Salvation for each individual.*
   1. We may "come boldly unto the throne of grace" (Heb. 4:16).
   2. We may "reason together" with the Lord concerning sin and its removal (Isa. 1:18).
   3. We may be saved "by grace through faith" (Eph. 2:8).
   4. We may find a creative force in grace. "I laboured more abundantly than they all" (1 Cor. 15:10).

B. *Salvation from God.*
   1. "Election"—the purpose and initiative of God in salvation.
   2. "Calling"—shows God's choice of humanity prior to humanity's choosing God.
   3. The seeking God. "The Son of Man came to seek and to save the lost" (Luke 19:10 NIV). "We love because he first loved us" (1 John 4:19 NIV).

227

II. No glory...

... if we refuse suffering, for "[Jesus] suffered death, so that by the grace of God he might taste death for everyone" (Heb. 2:9 NIV).

A. *Dying to live.* "Unless a kernel of wheat falls to the ground and dies, it remains only a single seed. If it dies, it produces many seeds" (John 12:24 NIV).

B. *Dying to self.* Paul often set before the people the fact of Christ's dying as a challenge for self-denial. "While we were yet sinners, Christ died for us" (Rom. 5:8). "Christ Jesus who died—more than that, who was raised to life—is at the right hand of God and is also interceding for us" (Rom. 8:34 NIV). "Whether we live therefore, or die, we are the Lord's" (Rom. 14:8).

C. *Our glory.*
  1. "Christ in you, the hope of glory" (Col. 1:27).
  2. "We beheld his glory" (John 1:14).
  3. "All have sinned, and come short of the glory of God" (Rom. 3:23).
  4. "As Christ was raised up from the dead by the glory of the father, even so we also should walk in newness of life" (Rom. 6:4).
  5. "Whatsoever ye do, do all to the glory of God" (1 Cor. 10:31).
  6. "I ask you ... not to be discouraged because of my sufferings for you, which are your glory" (Eph. 3:13 NIV).
  7. "At the name of Jesus every knee should bow ... and every tongue acknowledge that Jesus Christ is Lord, to the glory of God the Father" (Phil. 2:10–11 NIV).

III. No fellowship ...

... if we resist his "bringing many sons unto glory" (Heb. 2:10).

The great apostle prayed that the Ephesians would be strengthened to understand "with all the saints" the love of Christ and in so doing be filled with the fullness of God (Eph. 3:18). The Bible is the record of God in Christ saving humanity by creating a new fellowship of people who will serve under the lordship of Christ. It is in this fellowship of believers that the message of reconciliation takes meaning and is passed to successive generations.

A. *Fellowship in the preaching of the gospel.* Witness—"For we preach not ourselves, but Christ Jesus the Lord; and ourselves your servants for Jesus' sake" (2 Cor. 4:5).

B. *Fellowship in the matter of giving and receiving (Phil. 4:15).*

C. *Fellowship in the sharing of the Lord's Supper (Acts 2:42).* Paul's emphasis as he writes to the Corinthians is on the oneness of Christ's body that is proclaimed in the Lord's Supper. The Supper is to proclaim the body of Christ, not the broken body. Breaking bread suggests that many partake of one loaf, not that one loaf is broken into many pieces. It is fellowship in Christ, not credential for partaking, that is Paul's concern.

Conclusion

Salvation is a gift of God. Humans do not earn, merit, or deserve it. It is a relationship with Christ offering redemption from bondage, forgiveness for guilt, reconciliation for estrangement, and a renewal for the marred image of God. This glorious salvation and the fruit it bears in our lives will demand our interest for the next seven Sundays. Do you know the fruit of the Spirit?

WEDNESDAY EVENING, AUGUST 6

Title: The Bible Speaks to Our Condition

Scripture Reading: James 2

Introduction

The theme of the book of James is the practice of pure religion. Chapter 2 deals with the practice of pure religion in our relationship to others.

I. The practice of pure religion does not express itself in snobbery (James 2:1–13).

A. *The command against snobbery (2:1).*

B. *An illustration of the snobbery that is forbidden (2:2–3).*

C. *The application and warning against snobbery (2:4–13).*

　　1. Snobbery shows a divided allegiance to the Lord (2:4).

　　2. Snobbery reveals evil motives in the heart (2:4).

　　3. Snobbery dishonors the poor (2:5–7).

　　4. Snobbery violates the royal law of love (2:8–13).

II. The practice of pure religion issues in loving obedience (James 2:14–26).

The world about us issues the command, "Show me your faith." Even our Father God says to us, "Show me your faith."

All scriptural writers are in agreement that salvation is by God's grace through faith rather than by human achievement. All biblical writers are in agreement that good works are the fruit of a genuine salvation experience.

This chapter, which emphasizes the place of works in the life of the believer, does not conflict with other passages of Scripture. It contrasts a genuine faith with a spurious faith. It declares that genuine faith is a living experience that produces gracious, loving works in the life of the believer.

A. *A genuine faith is more than a mere "profession" of faith (2:14–17).* Faith that has nothing but words to prove its existence is dead faith. Genuine faith will have works as well as words to prove its existence.

B. *Genuine faith is more than an acceptance of a creed (2:18–20).* James points out that even the demons give mental assent to the existence of God. One must do more than believe about God to have a genuine faith in God (Heb. 11:6).

C. *Illustrations of genuine faith and pure religion (2:21–26).*

　　1. Abraham was willing to sacrifice his son Isaac (2:21–24).

　　2. Rahab risked possible execution in order to help the spies (2:25–26).

Conclusion

Let each of us examine the faith we claim. Is it genuine? Does it express itself by a genuine practice of the royal law of love toward the poor and the unfortunate as well as the rich and the privileged?

Is our faith an inward experience that produces obedience to God and loving service to others? If it is, let us rejoice. If it is not, then we need to seek Jesus Christ as our own Lord and Savior that ours might be a genuine experience with God.

SUNDAY MORNING, AUGUST 10

Title: The Sin of Appetite

Text: "Many live as enemies of the cross of Christ. Their destiny is destruction, their god is their stomach, and their glory is in their shame. Their mind is set on earthly things" **(Phil. 3:18–19 NIV)**.

Scripture Reading: Proverbs 13:18–25

Hymns: "God of Grace and God of Glory," Fosdick

         "A Charge to Keep I Have," Wesley

         "Rise Up, O Men of God," Merrill

Offertory Prayer: Dear Father, forgive our foolish ways. We set our hearts on things that perish and waste our strength in grieving over their loss. In poor judgment and excessive appetites, we prostitute your precious gifts. Forgive us for what we are. As we invest ourselves in your will, we recognize what we may become in you. Father, accept our humble gifts and ourselves. Transform us by your power to make us usable, through Jesus Christ our Lord. Amen.

Introduction

Because of appetite's necessary role in the economy of life, we are reluctant to think of its function as sin. Of course, it is not its use but its abuse wherein sin lies. People experience appetite in three distinct ways: hunger, thirst, and sex. Since the matter of sexual appetite was considered in the message on sensuality a couple of weeks ago, today we will give attention to hunger and thirst.

Biblical writers were alert to the sin of appetite and frequently pointed to it as the basis of other evils. Job, in castigating the hypocrites and their "tabernacles of bribery," wrote, "They conceive mischief, and bring forth vanity, and their belly [appetite] prepareth deceit" (Job 15:35). Proverbs, in similar fashion, when pointing out the way of transgressors, testifies, "The righteous eateth to the satisfying of his soul: but the belly [appetite] of the wicked shall want" (Prov. 13:25). The New Testament is equally sharp in its scorn of the gluttonous. In counseling young Titus, Paul acknowledged his familiarity with the uncouth citizens of Crete. He quoted a Cretan prophet as saying, "Cretans are always liars, evil brutes, lazy gluttons" (Titus 1:12 NIV). This proclivity toward food and drink caused Paul to press Titus to "rebuke them sharply" (Titus 1:13). Paul also made a connection between "those who cause divisions" (Rom. 16:17 NIV) and those having predilection to excesses. "For such people are not serving our Lord Christ, but their own appetites" (Rom. 16:18 NIV). He warns the Philippians, "Many live as enemies of the cross of Christ. Their destiny is destruction, their god is their stomach, and their glory is in their shame" (Phil. 3:18–19 NIV). The extreme interest shown appetite today would convince us that little heed is given to biblical exhortation; therefore, words on the sin of appetite are most needful and appropriate.

I. Consider eating and drinking.

A. *Time and energy of much of the population is used to provide food.*
1. Hunger is called the mainspring of the human machine.
2. We are fortunate that the means of supplying appetite of thirst is less costly than food.

B. *We should be thankful that the satisfying of appetite is pleasurable.*

II. The sin of gluttony.

A. *Special message to fat clergymen.* The libidinous attitude toward eating and drinking often brings ineffectiveness and even death to many of the clergy.

B. *Sickening experience of seeing starving people eat.* When a supply of food is attained after long intervals of famine, they stuff themselves to the point of discomfort.

C. *Ancient Rome held carnivals of gluttony.*

D. *Even today children — and often adults — need assistance in gauging proper food intake.*

III. The sin of drunkenness.

A. *Many who can control the appetite of hunger fail with appetite of thirst.*

B. *Alcohol use is on the rise, especially among young people.*
1. Every act of drunkenness is sin.
2. Rational thinking surrenders to drink.
3. Drunkenness promotes other sins: immorality, anger, loss of self-control.
4. It is not surprising that Paul advises against keeping company with a drunkard (1 Cor. 5:11).
5. When listing those who are eliminated from the "kingdom of God," drunkards follow thieves and the covetous (1 Cor. 6:10).

C. *A drunkard's home is a proverb for misery.*

Conclusion

How often we see the image of God dragged through the mire of sin because of appetite's abuse. What a shame it is when the pleasures of controlled eating and drinking are dashed with the insatiability of gluttony and drunkenness. Paul reminds us, "The earth is the Lord's and the fulness thereof.... Whether therefore ye eat, or drink, or whatsoever ye do, do all to the glory of God" (1 Cor. 10: 26, 31).

SUNDAY EVENING, AUGUST 10

Title: Love: Complete Living

Text: "Over all these virtues put on love, which binds them altogether in perfect unity" **(Col. 3:14 NIV).**

Scripture Reading: 1 John 4:16–21

Introduction

Where does one start when preaching on love? Just to read the marvelous Scriptures on love would fill the hour. But I am restricting myself to the consideration of love as a fruit of salvation or as a trait of Christian character. Much of my interest will be in the life that emerges when under the mastery of love. To the student of Greek, I might say that *agape*, not *philia, eros*, nor *storge*, is my chief interest. It is the attitude that a person comes to have toward others after establishing a living relationship with Christ. Love is a fruit of salvation when it is growing and ever mellowing to accommodate others' needs. Life is full and complete when living the "Christ way" becomes natural, the warp and woof of daily decision making.

I. Christian life is to walk in love.

A. *Each Christian life is a spring.* "Jesus stood and cried, saying, If any man thirst, let him come unto me, and drink. He that believeth on me, as the scripture hath said, out of his belly [inner life] shall flow rivers of living water" (John 7:37–38). "But whosoever drinketh of the water that I shall give him shall never thirst; but the water that I shall give him shall be in him a well of water springing up into everlasting life" (John 4:14).

B. *Love is like a coat to put on.* "And above all these things put on [be clothed in] charity" (Col. 3:14). Love conditions for the day-to-day disposition in the same way that Paul called for the "whole armor" to meet temptation.

C. *The love of Christ identifies our walk.* "Walk in love, as Christ also hath loved us" (Eph. 5:2).

"He that loveth his brother abideth in the light, and there is none occasion of stumbling in him" (1 John 2:10).

II. The Christian purpose is to serve in love.

A. *All of our equipment is made effective in love.* Paul wrote in 1 Corinthians 13: "If I speak in the tongues of men or of angels, but do not have love, I am only a resounding gong or a clanging cymbal. If I have the gift of prophecy ... and if I have a faith that can move mountains, but do not have love,

I am nothing. If I give all I possess to the poor and give over my body to hardship that I may boast, but do not have love, I gain nothing" (1 Cor. 13:1–3 NIV).

B. *Love is not to be directed only to the lovable.* "I say unto you, Love your enemies, bless them that curse you, do good to them that hate you.... That ye may be the children of your Father which is in heaven" (Matt. 5:44–45).

C. *"Do everything in love" (1 Cor. 16:14 NIV).*

III. Christian strength is unity in love.

A. *Love is to be the distinguishing mark of the Christian.* "By this shall all men know that ye are my disciples, if ye have love one to another" (John 13:35). It is not subscribing to a doctrinal position, attending church, or even being baptized that proves that we are Christian; it is a zeal for the welfare of people, a trust in people, and a love for people.

1. "He that loveth his brother abideth in the light" (1 John 2:10). It is he, not the cynic, who really sees into people's character.
2. In the long run, the person who loves and trusts is right because love and trust create what they believe.
3. No person can go on betraying a trust that is constantly renewed.

B. *Christians are "knit together in love" (Col. 2:2).*

1. Love is the solution to race problems.
2. If your love is not expanding, you are not growing as a Christian.

C. *The span of Christian love.* "And the Lord make you to increase and abound in love one toward another, and toward all men, even as we do toward you" (1 Thess. 3:12).

IV. Christian love is a fruit of the Spirit.

A. *As the disciples found the teaching of Jesus difficult and said, "This is a hard teaching. Who can accept it?" (John 6:60 NIV), we find teaching on Christian love hard.*

1. Love is not human achievement; it is a fruit of the Spirit.
2. Love is possible only in Christ.

B. *When a person is born again, Christian love begins to flow.*

Conclusion

"So Christ himself gave the apostles, the prophets, the evangelists, the pastors and teachers, to equip his people for works of service, so that the body of Christ may be built up until we all reach unity in the faith and in the knowledge of the Son of God and become mature, attaining to the whole measure of the fullness of Christ.

"Then we will no longer be infants, tossed back and forth by the waves, and blown here and there by every wind of teaching and by the cunning and craftiness of people in their deceitful scheming. Instead, speaking the truth in love, we will grow to become in every respect the mature body of him who is the head, that is, Christ. From him the whole body, joined and held together by every supporting ligament, grows and builds itself up in love, as each part does its work" (Eph. 4:11–16 NIV).

WEDNESDAY EVENING, AUGUST 13

Title: The Bible Speaks to Our Condition

Scripture Reading: 1 Peter 4

Introduction

The apostle Peter writes out of personal experience to assist Jewish believers who had been scattered abroad as they faced the possibility and the agonizing problem of undeserved suffering because of their faith.

I. The example of the sufferings of Christ (1 Peter 4:1–2, 12–15, 19).

To encourage those who are experiencing the agony of undeserved suffering, Peter points out how that Christ suffered in the flesh that he might be our Redeemer and Savior.

He tries to give them some assistance so that they might avoid suffering the due results of illegal or immoral activities. He points out that there is a difference between suffering for righteousness' sake and suffering for evil (1 Peter 3:13–17).

II. Guidelines for living on the edge of eternity (1 Peter 4:7).

Peter could have been referring to the end of the age, which will be consummated by the second coming of Jesus Christ. He could have been thinking about the possibility of their annihilation as a group by persecution and martyrdom. He provides some guidelines for proper conduct for believers as they live on the very edge of eternity.

A. *He encourages them to determine to be at their very best, "Be ye therefore sober" (4:7).*
B. *He encourages them to maintain constant communication with God (4:7).*
C. *The practice of genuine love toward each other is always important (4:8).*
D. *Love will render practical assistance to those in need (4:9).* There were no motels in those days, so it was absolutely essential that Christians provide hospitality to each other as they traveled or as they fled from persecution.
E. *Each one is to make responsible use of the spiritual gifts that have been bestowed upon him (4:10–11).*
  1. The ministry of words (4:11).
  2. The ministry of works (4:11).

Conclusion

This chapter comes to a conclusion with a challenge to the effect that the followers of Christ face the future with faith and with a determination to do God's will in all circumstances and at all times.

Do we have the kind of relationship with Jesus Christ that would stabilize and sustain us in the midst of terrible, undeserved suffering? Surely it would not be selfish for us to pray for deliverance from such, but we need to examine the nature of our faith to make sure that it is genuine, because suffering could be our lot in the future.

The practice of the guidelines that Peter suggested would be helpful toward building the kind of faith that would be needed in the midst of suffering that one did not merit.

SUNDAY MORNING, AUGUST 17

Title: The Sin of Anger

Text: "Be not hasty in thy spirit to be angry: for anger resteth in the bosom of fools" **(Eccl. 7:9)**.

Scripture Reading: Matthew 5:21–24

Hymns: "O Brother Man," Whittier

          "I Am Praying for You," Cluff

          "I Heard the Voice of Jesus Say," Bonar

Offertory Prayer: Dear Father, forgive me when I speak hasty words to my brothers and sisters. I consider so little when others seem wrong, and I judge so quickly when I don't understand. The gift I bring today does not equal the wrong of which I am conscious. I do not have enough to pay my debt of injustices toward others. Receive this offering, I pray, as a token of my love and acknowledgment of your goodness. Make it a blessing to others, and strengthen me in giving, I pray. In Jesus' name. Amen.

Introduction

It seems strange that at a time when we are afraid of being emotional we have turned out to be overly so. Emotionalism is rampant, and most of it is self-disruptive. A generation afraid of emotion ends up subscribing to the thing it fears. We have tried to suppress emotions that are an essential part of us and find only that our attempts at elimination end in complexes. We cannot set our emotions aside; we can only direct them to higher purposes.

We consider anger for our message today. Anger is basically an instinct of self-protection. We can describe it as a sudden heating of the blood and flushing of the face accompanied by forceful speech and swift action. Anger is not unlike some sort of military equipment that nature has provided to repel wrong. Paul's direction to "be ye angry and sin not" (Eph. 4:26) implies that there is an anger that is not sin. Perhaps our capacity to love the good determines our capacity to hate the evil. Of this we can be sure: it is our virtue, not our pride, that is to be lashed into a rage. There is a difference. One is connected with higher ends, thus constructive; the other is concerned with a wounded self, thus destructive. We face this message with the full awareness that anger can be righteous or unrighteous. The excellence of character depends on a sensitivity of honor latent beneath the outward aspect of civility. We know that to be completely blind to insult and injury is evidence of an inferior being. Jesus was observed as he "looked around at them in anger and deeply distressed at their stubborn hearts" (Mark 3:5 NIV).

I. Anger has a direction of flow.

A. *It may be directed in any number of directions for any number of reasons.*
1. Anger may be directed against what seems to be injustice.
2. For example, righteous anger would be provoked if a person were slain in the street before witnesses who would not help.
3. Toleration of evil is more truthfully called treason or dishonor.
4. Pride and selfishness turn to anger when not appeased.

B. *Sin in anger is seen when directed toward:*
1. Trivial differences.
2. Personal inconveniences.
3. Others asserting their rights.
4. Overconsideration of our own merits.

II. Anger has a depth of flow.

A. *The expression may be out of proportion with the cause.*
1. Husband's outbreak of anger over burned toast.
2. Cain's slaying of brother when his offering was not accepted.
3. Action of Joseph's brothers when he received a new cloak.

B. *Excessive anger destroys.*
1. It causes ulcers.
2. Ill will poisons.
3. Excessive anger turns to hatred.

III. Anger has a channel of flow.

A. *Profane language comes from anger in the wrong channel.*
1. We are disgusted to hear a maddened brain vent anger with profanity.
2. Could Simon Peter have cursed and denied his Lord apart from anger and fear?

B. *Violent acts induced by anger.*
1. "He that hateth his brother is in darkness ... because that darkness hath blinded his eyes" (1 John 2:11).
2. Inflicting a blow in frenzy.
3. Danger in surrendering to a passion.

IV. Anger has a tempo of flow.

A. *Temper is the chronic disposition to anger.*
1. The closing days of King Saul.
2. Who can justify acrimony?

3. Even David with his asperity listened to the calm reasoning of Abigail.
B. *Temper springs more quickly in familiar territory.*
  1. Anger is the sin of the home.
  2. Anger in the church. Much of the temper habit begins within the circle that favorably reacts to it. One's temper may rise, but the expression of it is usually by habit. The paroxysm is a much-practiced expression of temper.

Conclusion

Expression of anger is a triumph of the lower nature over the better life. It is righteous if it occurs because of what is done to others and is not an expression of a grudge on account of what happens to oneself. We have to be very careful, for the mind plays tricks on itself; it has been known to clothe its personal resentments in garments of righteous and religious indignation so they will pass inspection with our religious self. Many times what one says is a fight for principle is actually a fight for personal pique and pride.

SUNDAY EVENING, AUGUST 17

Title: Joy: Radiant Living

Text: "These things have I spoken unto you, that my joy might remain in you, and that your joy might be full" **(John 15:11)**.

Scripture Reading: Luke 15:3–7

Introduction

The common denominator of the Christian church is joy. This is not surprising to the faithful Bible reader, for in the New Testament we encounter more than 130 times the mention of joy or rejoicing. The early church did not characterize itself so much in organizational structure or doctrinal exactness as it did in an atmosphere of joy. It is a tragic commentary on the contemporary church that, in a world that is far less antagonistic toward our faith, we should see less evidence of joy in our fellowship. This fact probably accounts for the growing indifference toward church affiliation. Who wants to heap additional discord on the burden he or she is already bearing? Until "rejoicing in the Lord" again becomes an essential part of our religious exercises, we are not going to be very attractive to saints or sinners. I can think of a dozen places to go to commiserate and each with greater comfort than a church pew. It is interesting how Jesus Christ can be proclaimed in such gloom each week when in God's introduction of him it was with such joy (Luke 1:58; 2:10).

Today let us look at joy in the New Testament. Truly this was the tie that bound the early Christians into a distinct lifestyle, the dynamic that gave power to their witness. Joy was the force that made possible the fact that "they were all with one accord in one place" (Acts 2:1). Christian joy is seen to be the means by which people are introduced, reconciled, and given to the service of God.

237

I. The means of introduction.

A. *The coming of a Savior.*
   1. Joy in angels' message (Luke 2:10).
   2. Joy in wise men (Matt. 2:10).
B. *The teachings of Jesus.*
   1. Rejoice even in persecution (Matt. 5:12).
   2. Rejoice when the lost is found (Luke 15:9, 32).
C. *Believing in Jesus.*
   1. Look at the faith and baptism of the Ethiopian eunuch (Acts 8:39).
   2. Zacchaeus invited Jesus to his home (Luke 19:6).

II. The means of reconciliation.

A. *The fulfilling of joy in unity.*
   "Make my joy complete by being like-minded, having the same love, being one in spirit and of one mind.... Have the same mindset as Christ Jesus" (Phil. 2:2, 5 NIV). "I rejoiced greatly in the Lord that at last you renewed your concern for me" (Phil. 4:10 NIV).
B. *In conditioning for the "kingdom."* Paul's concern for the Colossians would cause him to pray for them that they "might walk worthy of the Lord" and "be fruitful in every good work," and "increasing in the knowledge of God," "strengthened with all might ... with joyfulness" (Col. 1:10–11). Paul warns the Romans, "Let not then your good be evil spoken of: for the kingdom of God is not meat and drink; but righteousness, and peace, and joy" (Rom. 14:16–17). "Let us therefore follow after the things which make for peace, and things wherewith one may edify another" (Rom. 14:19). Paul seems to be pointing out that when joy reigns, people are not offended, and reconciliation can be more easily effected.
C. *Jesus describes a generation of those refusing reconciliation as children arguing over games.*
   "To what, then, can I compare the people of this generation? What are they like? They are like children sitting in the marketplace and calling out to each other:

> " 'We played the pipe for you,
>   And you did not dance;
> We sang a dirge,
>   And you did not cry.'

"For John the Baptist came neither eating bread nor drinking wine, and you say, 'He has a demon.' The Son of Man came eating and drinking, and you say, 'Here is a glutton and a drunkard, a friend of tax collectors and sinners.' But wisdom is proved right by all her children." (Luke 7:31–35 NIV)

III. The means of service.

A. *Joy supersedes laws.*
   1. Stooped woman healed. "And when he [Jesus] had said these things, all his adversaries were ashamed; and all the people rejoiced" (Luke 13:17).

2. Man with withered hand. "Wherefore it is lawful to do well on the sabbath days" (Matt. 12:12).

B. *Joy accompanies progress.*

1. The disciples rejoiced when evil spirits submitted to them (Luke 10:17).
2. Paul was comforted by the progress of the Thessalonians: "How can we thank God enough for you in return for all the joy we have in the presence of our God because of you?" (1 Thess. 3:9 NIV).
3. Joy was even a purpose for Paul to live. "I know that I will remain, and I will continue with all of you for your progress and joy in the faith" (Phil. 1:25 NIV).
4. "No greater joy can I have than this, to hear that my children follow the truth" (3 John 4 RSV).

C. *Joy is the mission.*

1. "Jesus ... who for the joy that was set before him endured the cross, despising the same, and is set down at the right hand of the throne of God" (Heb. 12:2).
2. "My brethren, count it all joy when ye fall into divers temptations" (James 1:2).
3. "I trust to come unto you, and speak face to face, that our joy may be full" (2 John 12).
4. "But none of these things move me, neither count I my life dear unto myself, so that I might finish my course with joy" (Acts 20:24).

Conclusion

To the Christian, joy is an inner condition that comes through and flavors the atmosphere of life. It does not come, nor is it cultivated, by favorable winds. Paul demands, "Rejoice in the Lord always" (Phil. 4:4 NIV). Joy can be had even in tribulation and suffering. Such joy is possible, for it comes with Christ. If we must suffer for our relationship with Christ, we are still sustained by his Spirit.

Jesus comforted his disciples as he approached the cross, "And ye now therefore have sorrow: but I will see you again, and your heart shall rejoice, and your *joy* no man taketh from you" (John 16:22).

"Now unto him that is able to keep you from falling, and to present you faultless before the presence of his glory with exceeding joy, to the only wise God our Saviour, be glory and majesty, dominion and power, both now and ever. Amen" (Jude 24–25).

WEDNESDAY EVENING, AUGUST 20

Title: The Bible Speaks to Our Condition

Scripture Reading: 1 John 3

Introduction

John wrote this first epistle with many purposes in mind. One of his primary motives was to provide assurance of salvation to those who had put their faith and trust in Jesus Christ as Lord and Savior (1 John 5:13).

The chapter through which we would let God speak to our hearts today is one of the great chapters of the New Testament. It speaks concerning the fact, the nature, the obligations, and the basis for our assurance of divine sonship.

I. The unbelievable privilege of divine sonship (1 John 3:1–2).

John, the apostle of love, stood in amazement at the privilege of being a child of God through faith in Christ Jesus. He also recognized that his present experience of this wonderful truth was only partial. He looked forward to the final revelation of Jesus Christ at the end of the ages for the full revelation of what God has provided for those who love him.

II. The nature of our divine sonship (1 John 3:3–10).

A. *Our sonship is spiritual rather than natural (3:9).* We become the children of God by spiritual birth. We are the creatures of God by physical birth and the children of God by spiritual birth. We become children of God through faith in Christ Jesus (Gal. 3:26).

B. *The new birth results in righteousness (3:3–9).* John was dealing with a serious error that threatened the very existence of early Christianity. According to gnostic beliefs, one entered into a relationship with God through knowledge rather than through faith and commitment. Christianity insisted that God was a moral God who required moral conduct on the part of his children. John warned the followers of Christ against the erroneous beliefs of the Gnostics who taught that humanity's conduct did not in any manner affect their relationship with God or their service to God.

C. *The new birth produces obedience (3:22–24).* To really know God through faith in Jesus Christ is to experience a divine change within the heart that causes children of God to want to give themselves to God in loving obedience at all times.

III. The obligations of divine sonship (1 John 3:11–24).

There are certain obligations that go along with the privilege of being children of God. Toward God these obligations are faith and obedience. Toward our fellow Christians our obligations could be listed as follows:

A. *To love (3:11–16).* This love is a persistent unbreakable spirit of goodwill toward the objects of our love.

B. *A spirit of generosity toward the need of others (3:17–19).* Love that does not find expression in practical deeds of kindness is not genuine love.

IV. The basis of our assurance of divine sonship.

In this chapter, there are at least three bases for our assurance of divine sonship.

A. *The testimony of Scripture (3:1–2).*

B. *Our love for the brethren (3:14).* This is a subjective measurement by which we can examine our own hearts. If we find love for the people of God in our hearts, then this is an additional basis for our believing that we are indeed the children of God.

C. *The witness of the indwelling Spirit (3:24).*

Conclusion

We should rejoice in the glad consciousness of being children of God. We should respond with full commitment to the development of and the expression of the new life that has come to us through faith in Christ Jesus.

As we live a life of faith and faithfulness, love and generosity, others will become convinced that we are indeed the children of our heavenly Father.

SUNDAY MORNING, AUGUST 24

Title: The Sin of Laziness

Text: "The way of the slothful man is as an hedge of thorns: but the way of the righteous is made plain" **(Prov. 15:19).**

Scripture Reading: Hebrews 6:7–12

Hymns: "O Master Workman of the Race," Stocking

"To the Work," Crosby

"Ready," Palmer

Offertory Prayer: Dear Father, we see the work of your hands in all the world about us. How we rejoice and praise you that we may be a part of your creation. Now, dear Lord, continue in us your creation. Remake our hearts, cleanse our hands, and mold our minds. In our giving today, we give ourselves. Use us, we pray, for your purposes, and keep us to yourself, through Jesus Christ. Amen.

Introduction

I have never been of the persuasion that as a hard-and-fast rule "history repeats itself." In a most striking manner, however, we often see repetitions. Today we see in many of our contemporaries a repetition of the spirit prevalent during the close of the eighteenth and beginning of the nineteenth century. This spirit was manifested in an outbreak of literature throughout Europe that was filled with disgust with the world, life, and everything in it. Perhaps if Goethe and Lord Byron had known honest labor, they could have worked out some of their hypochondria instead of reflecting it through their writing. Indeed, the sin of laziness is a damaging sin and deserves our attention.

I. Human character is conditioned in work.

A. *Work is not a curse placed on Adam.* "And the LORD God took the man, and put him into the garden of Eden to dress it and keep it" (Gen. 2:15). This was before Adam's disobedience and prior to the curse pronounced in Genesis 3:17.

241

B. *God commands that we work.* "Six days shalt thou labour, and do all thy work" (Ex. 20:9). This commandment was given along with "Remember the Sabbath day, to keep it holy." The will of God for man is that he should work. Work and worship complement each other. He who never works is never fit for worship. If people never pause to worship, they are not capable of work. God's commandment is clear in declaring that people fulfill their right relationship to God as they become workers and worshipers.

C. *Jesus points to God's nature as a worker.*

1. After healing on the Sabbath, Jesus said, "My father is always at his work to this very day, and I too am working" (John 5:17 NIV).
2. Upon being questioned about a blind man, Jesus said, "I must work the works of him that sent me, while it is day" (John 9:4).
3. Jesus identified himself by working. "The works that I do in my Father's name, they bear witness of me" (John 10:25).
4. Jesus was worthy of trust because of work. "Do not believe me unless I do the works of my Father" (John 10:37 NIV).

II. The church's purpose realized in serving.

A. *Sloth is the church's greatest enemy.*

1. Some ministers are beset by procrastination and laxness.
2. In laggardness, a spiritual numbness steals over people.

B. *If not nurtured, faith becomes ingrown concern, limited to anxiety about its own welfare.*

C. *Worship is neglected when people become lethargic.*

1. The spirit of gratitude dies.
2. The challenge of outreach disappears.

D. *The spirit of missions involves an attitude of willingness to work.*

III. Human destiny is related to serving.

A. *Parable of talents.* The fearful servant said to his master, "I was afraid and went out and hid your gold in the ground." The master replied, "You wicked, lazy servant! ... You should have put my money on deposit with the bankers, so that when I returned I would have received it back with interest. So take the bag of gold from him and give it to the one who has ten bags. For whoever has will be given more, and they will have an abundance. Whoever does not have, even what they have will be taken from them" (Matt. 25:25–29 NIV).

B. *God's promises realized in serving.* "We do not want you to become lazy, but to imitate those who through faith and patience inherit what has been promised" (Heb. 6:12 NIV). "If any man will do his will, he shall know of the doctrine" (John 7:17).

C. *Entering the kingdom is service.*

1. "Verily I say unto you, Inasmuch as ye did it not to one of the least of these ... and these shall go away into everlasting punishment" (Matt. 25:45–46).

2. "Who then is a faithful and wise servant, whom his lord hath made ruler over his household, to give them meat in due season? Blessed is that servant, whom his lord when he cometh shall find so doing" (Matt. 24:45–46).

3. Parable of the laborers. "For the kingdom of heaven is like unto a man that is an householder, which went out early in the morning to hire labourers" (Matt. 20:1).

Conclusion

The thought that an ideal world is one without labor is not biblical. Labor is a necessary part of our world and a necessary condition for happiness. There is a period in youth when there comes recoil from the conventional and contempt for patterns. When this tendency is coupled with the energy lost in growing, indolence comes easily. Sometimes it takes less effort to criticize; so the world has never been short on young critics. One recognizes that young eyes see with greater clearness and many times can discern the noble and the base. Great good can come from noble discontent, but merely to criticize and do nothing (not work) wrecks character. It sours the temper and produces a spirit of discontent toward both people and God.

SUNDAY EVENING, AUGUST 24

Title: Peace: Superlative Living

Text: "And the peace of God, which passeth all understanding, shall keep your hearts and minds through Christ Jesus" **(Phil. 4:7)**.

Scripture Reading: Psalm 4

Introduction

When Jesus said, "Peace I leave with you, my peace I give unto you: not as the world giveth, give I unto you" (John 14:27), he was not speaking of the absence of war. As a matter of fact, he had spoken earlier that his disciples would face terrible circumstances because of him. "Brother will betray brother to death, and a father his child; children will rebel against their parents and have them put to death. You will be hated by everyone because of me, but the one who stands firm to the end will be saved" (Matt. 10:21–22 NIV). In the Bible, peace is not used primarily to describe circumstances but to indicate the perfection of relationships. Jesus could leave his disciples in a world antagonistic to them, yet in a relationship to himself that was "[his] peace." This right relationship, so described as "peace," may exist between human and human, country and country, country and God, or human and God.

Our chief concern is to study peace, the fruit of the Spirit, and see it as the foundation of superlative living. How do we attain this peace? From what source does peace come to us? When does it bring us to know superlative living? "They must turn from evil and do good; they must seek peace and pursue it" (1 Peter 3:11 NIV).

I. The attainment of peace.

A. *As a result of goodwill.*
1. The Hebrews greet with "Peace" [Shalom]. It is a wish or desire for the welfare of the one greeted. To say "Shalom" is in a sense uttering a prayer on the other's behalf.
2. God, in conveying his promise to Abram, concluded that the height of his blessing would bring him "to thy fathers in peace" (Gen. 15:15).

B. *As the obtaining of tranquility.*
1. When Judah and his brothers were deeply worried at finding money in their grain sacks, Joseph said, "Peace be to you, fear not" (Gen. 43:23).
2. When Jethro taught Moses how to organize his judges, he assured Moses, "If thou shalt do this thing, and God command thee so, then thou shalt be able to endure, and all this people shall also go to their place in peace" (Ex. 18:23).
3. Among the rewards promised by God to a faithful people, there was this one: "I will give peace in the land, and ye shall lie down, and none shall make you afraid" (Lev. 26:6).

C. *As the blessing of friendship.*
1. God offered special friendship to the young man Phinehas for his courage in slaying the arrogant Israelite and the Midianite woman. God stopped the plague and ordered Moses to give his message: "Behold, I give unto him [Phinehas] my covenant of peace" (Num. 25:12).
2. The unfriendly act of the Ammonite and the Moabite disqualified for ten generations their relationship with the Israelites. God ordered, "Thou shalt not seek their peace" (Deut. 23:6).
3. In spite of the trickery of the Gibeonites, Joshua stood by his "peace made with them," which was an agreement to let them live (Josh. 9:15).

II. The source of peace.

A. *Beyond human intrigue—from God.*
1. "The peace of God, which transcends all understanding, will guard your hearts and your minds in Christ Jesus" (Phil. 4:7 NIV).
2. The Danites requesting Micah to seek counsel of God receive the assurance, "Go in peace ... the LORD is your way" (Judg. 18:6).
3. Solomon required the death of Joab even while he held the horns of the altar. This brought "upon his throne ... peace for ever from the LORD" (1 Kings 2:33).

B. *Beyond human merit—gift of Christ.*
1. In introducing the Comforter and as a farewell gesture, Jesus said, "My peace I give unto you" (John 14:27).
2. Jesus also said, "These things I have spoken unto you, that in me ye might have peace" (John 16:33).

3. After his resurrection, Jesus said, "Peace be unto you" to his disciples in the closed room (John 20:19). He also gave this blessing when he sent out his disciples (v. 21) and when Thomas was with them (v. 26).

C. *Beyond reason with belief and trust.*

1. "[God] will render to every man according to his deeds: ... glory, honour, and peace, to every man that worketh good" (Rom. 2:6, 10).
2. "Now the God of hope fill you with all joy and peace in believing" (Rom. 15:13).
3. "By faith" Rahab is described as receiving the spies "with peace" (Heb. 11:31).
4. In the breaking down of the "middle wall of partition," Jesus "is our peace, who hath made both one" (Eph. 2:14).

III. The consummation of peace.

A. *In the establishing of brotherhood.*

1. "There is neither Jew nor Greek, there is neither bond nor free, there is neither male nor female: for ye are all one in Christ Jesus" (Gal. 3:28).
2. "Follow peace with all men, and holiness, without which no man shall see the Lord" (Heb. 12:14).
3. "Be diligent that ye may be found of him in peace" (2 Peter 3:14).

B. *In reconciliation with God.*

1. "For it pleased the Father that in [Jesus] should all fulness dwell; and, having made peace through the blood of his cross, by him to reconcile all things unto himself" (Col. 1:19–20).
2. "Therefore being justified by faith, we have peace with God through our Lord Jesus Christ" (Rom. 5:1).

Conclusion

The Christian life at its highest tide is described as peace. No question need continue in our minds as to our acquiring this peace. God is truly "the God of peace," and to know him is to have peace. In the same urgency that we seek the Father's face in prayer, we are to seek his peace. Paul offers the suggestion that in revealing to others our willingness to accept less than our due and in the practice of serenity and thanksgiving, a marvelous thing will happen. The peace of God will mount a guard for patrolling the perimeters of our hearts and minds (Phil. 4:5–7). This is indeed peace that passes all human understanding: it is of the Lord.

WEDNESDAY EVENING, AUGUST 27

Title: The Bible Speaks to Our Condition

Scripture Reading: Revelation 2

Introduction

To read this chapter is to experience the cutting edge of the living Word of

God. "For the word of God is alive and active. Sharper than any double-edged sword, it penetrates even to dividing soul and spirit, joints and marrow; it judges the thoughts and attitudes of the heart" (Heb. 4:12 NIV).

Revelation 2 contains four of the letters the living Lord dictated to be sent to churches in Asia Minor. Through these last written communications from our Lord to individual churches, we can learn much today. In each of these epistles, our Lord first of all identifies himself. He does so by using one of the descriptive phrases applied to him in Revelation 1.

I. The Christ: "I know thy works" (Rev. 2:1, 9, 13, 19).

The Christ with whom we have to do is the Christ who has complete knowledge concerning both our visible actions and our invisible attitudes. He knows all about us. Nothing is concealed from his piercing, penetrating eye. This thought can be shocking, but it can also be comforting, challenging, and stimulating.

II. The Christ offers commendation.

In each of these four verses, our Lord speaks words of commendation to the churches. He sees that which is good about them and calls attention to it. It can be comforting to know that our Lord will always look for that which is best in us first. He is more eager to commend than to rebuke.

III. The living Christ offers some complaints.

Our Lord offers complaints against each of these four churches with the exception of Smyrna. He charges the church at Ephesus with having lost their first love (2:4). The church at Pergamos was tolerant toward false doctrine, inappropriate worship activities, and immorality (2:14–15). Thyatira was also tolerant toward false teachings and immorality (2:20–21).

Our loving Lord speaks words of complaint to these churches upon whom he is depending to spread the good news of God's love and to demonstrate a new quality of life.

IV. The living Christ offers counsel to his churches.

Christ urged the church at Ephesus to remember their beginnings and repent (2:5). He encouraged the church at Smyrna to be faithful to the point of death (v. 10). He commanded the church at Pergamos to repent (v. 16). He had given the church at Thyatira an opportunity to repent, and they were responding negatively, so judgment was already on its way (vv. 21–23). Jesus encouraged those who had been faithful to "hold fast till I come" (v. 25).

Conclusion

Without exception, each of these letters to the churches of Asia Minor closes with the refrain, "He that hath an ear, let him hear what the Spirit saith unto the churches" (1:7, 11, 17, 29; 3:6, 13, 22). Our Lord wants us to read his book with hearing ears. He is insistent that we listen for the voice of the Spirit that dwells

246

within. It would appear that we must look upon prayer as a dialogue rather than a monologue and let God speak to our condition day by day and week by week.

God promised Joshua that if he would listen and heed and obey, then he would walk the highway to success and prosperity. It follows that if we would give proper attention to the instructions of our Lord and daily do his will, then his blessings will be upon us and in turn we will be a blessing to others. Let us let God's Word serve as a surgical knife to cut out of our minds and hearts and lives those attitudes and ambitions that are displeasing to our Lord. Let us listen to his counsel in order that we might hear his words of commendation.

SUNDAY MORNING, AUGUST 31

Title: The Vitality of the Kingdom

Text: "If anyone has ears to hear, let them hear" (**Mark 4:23 NIV**).

Scripture Reading: Matthew 13:1–8, 18–23; Mark 4:26–29

Hymns: "Praise Him, Praise Him," Crosby

"I'll Go Where You Want Me to Go," Brown

"Bringing in the Sheaves," Shaw

Offertory Prayer: Holy Father, today we thank you for all those you used in bringing to us the knowledge of Jesus Christ, our Savior. Today we offer ourselves as communicators of the old, old story that others might come to experience your love and mercy. Accept and bless these tithes and offerings in such a manner as to tell the gospel of Jesus and your love. Amen.

Introduction

"Jesus came into Galilee, preaching the gospel of the kingdom of God, and saying, The time is fulfilled, and the kingdom of God is at hand: repent ye, and believe the gospel" (Mark 1:14–15). In the parallel passage in Matthew, "kingdom of heaven" is used for "kingdom of God." The terms seem to be synonymous. Perhaps "heaven" was used for God by some because of the Jewish reverential fear lest by the very pronunciation of the name of God one might profane it. Even today we hear men pray, "May heaven grant...." What they really mean is "May God who is in heaven grant...."

The word *kingdom* as used by Jesus is not to denote a national, political, or geographical entity. It is better translated "rule" or "reign." In reality all that Jesus teaches is helpful in understanding the kingdom of God—that is, the reign of God and especially the principles and methods by which he deals with people. In a special way, he uses stories to illustrate truth. The word translated "parable" means "to throw alongside." These stories thrown alongside spiritual truth are called parables. Many of the more than fifty parables of Jesus begin: "The kingdom of heaven is like..." (NIV), which means that the story he is about to tell will illustrate one or more of the principles by which God deals with people.

247

Matthew 13, Mark 4, and Luke 8 record the first great group of parables Jesus spoke to the multitudes from a boat in the Sea of Galilee. How many parables Jesus spoke on that day we cannot know. (See Mark 4:33.) We are grateful for those the evangelists have recorded, and we shall use them in this series of messages. Eight of these parables fall into four sets of twin parables. The first set consists of the parable of the sower (Matt. 13:3–8, 18–23; Mark 4:3–9, 13–20; Luke 8:5–8, 11–18) and the parable of the seed growing itself (Mark 4:26–29). These parables emphasize the vitality of the kingdom.

I. The parable of the sower.

A sower sows his seed by hand. Whether the seed will germinate and grow depends on the kind of ground on which it falls. The sower is primarily Jesus but also anyone who preaches the Word. "The seed is the word of God" (Luke 8:11). The people who hear the gospel are as varied as are the soils of Palestine.

A. *Some seeds fell by the wayside (Matt. 13:4, 19).* These seeds fell on the road, or path. The birds ate some of them. The wind blew others away. The seeds had no chance to take root. This kind of soil represents the gospel-hardened person who has failed to respond for so long that he or she has lost the power to respond. An arm that is bound to one's body for weeks will become so weak that it cannot be used. The muscles will have atrophied. There is also an atrophy of soul to the one who repeatedly fails to respond to the gospel. Unless God sends some tragedy to plow a furrow of mercy down this person's hard heart, there is little hope for this person to respond to the gospel. Sometimes God does exactly that.

A young Christian mother had just given birth to her first child. The attending physician thought that all was well with both mother and child. Then there was a sudden, unexpected reversal of the mother's condition. She died within a couple of days. It seemed a case of unrelieved tragedy. What could the preacher say at the funeral service to justify the ways of God to people in such tragedy? A few weeks after that the father of the deceased mother came to the pastor's office. He said, "I have been a hard-hearted, stubborn sinner. God took my daughter to wake me up. I want you to know that I have become a Christian, but it took my daughter's death to do it." Who can rightly read God's providences? It may well be when the Christian husband, the Christian wife, and the Christian father meet in heaven, never more to part, that all will join in giving praise to God who can bring good out of evil. There is profit in tragedy that causes one to meet life earnestly.

B. *Some seed fell on the stony places (Matt. 13:5–6, 20–21).* The picture is that of a very thin layer of soil over a rocky ledge. The seed germinated quickly because it was near the surface, but having no root, it quickly withered in the hot sun. This soil represents the shallow person who upon sudden impulse decides to be a Christian but has not counted the cost. This person has no intention of loyalty to Jesus Christ in times of persecution. Quickly

248

come, quickly go! Jesus bids those who would be his disciples to count the cost and be willing to pay it. (See Matt. 10:32–42; Luke 9:57–62.)

C. *Some seed fell among thorns (Matt. 13:7, 22).* This seems to be ground that was already latent with thorn seeds. As the good seed grew, the thorns also grew and choked out the good seed. This represents the person of divided loyalties. "The cares of this world," and "the deceitfulness of riches" must be weeded out if the gospel seed is to bear fruit. This person would like to put Christ first but is not willing to do so. Jesus said, "No man can serve two masters: for either he will hate the one, and love the other; or else he will hold to the one, and despise the other. Ye cannot serve God and mammon" (Matt. 6:24). One who makes earthly treasures the end of life is foolish. Jesus himself says so: "So is he that layeth up treasure for himself, and is not rich toward God" (Luke 12:21).

D. *Some seed fell on good ground (Matt. 13:8, 23).* The good seed fell into the good ground that had been prepared for it. It germinated, grew, and brought forth good fruit. This is the purpose both of seed and of soil. God has made us in his own image. He has made us spiritual beings with the capacity for fellowship with him. He has done everything necessary to breach the barrier caused by our sins. He convicts of sin and invites to salvation. When one accepts the grace of God offered in Jesus Christ and is saved, it is as good seed sown in good ground.

Every saved person is not equally fruitful, but a saved soul "beareth fruit, and bringeth forth, some an hundredfold, some sixty, some thirty" (Matt. 13:23).

II. The parable of the seed growing of itself (Mark 4:26–29).

A. *The wonderful correspondence of seed and soil illustrates that the gospel and sinful people are made for each other.* The eye is made for seeing; God has also made the light by which one sees. The ear is made for hearing; the sound waves are adapted for one's hearing. The seed and the soil are made for each other. The gospel is adapted for the needs of sinful humanity.

B. *There is tremendous vitality in the seed.* It germinates and pushes itself through the soil with mysterious force. The seed grows though we "knoweth not how" (Mark 4:27). God's saving power is very mysterious.

C. *The plant grows in orderly fashion "first the blade, then the ear, after that the full corn in the ear" (Mark 4:28).* Paul said, "I have planted, Apollos watered; but God gave the increase" (1 Cor. 3:6). When the gospel is planted faithfully, God will give the harvest.

Conclusion

No earthly story can completely illustrate spiritual truth. The soils of life do not in every way parallel the soils of nature. There is little hope that the rocky soil can become good soil. The soils of Palestine do not have free will. They are not responsive to the Spirit of God. However, the hearts of people who are represented by these soils can change. Rocky soil of the heart can become good soil. A hardened heart can be convicted. A life choked with care can repent. The shallow, impulsive follower can consider and come to a deeper loyalty. In fact, that is what these parables are about. Hearing is urgent, important business. We are responsible for how we hear and heed the gospel. "If anyone has ears to hear, let them hear" (Mark 4:23 NIV). "Therefore consider carefully how you listen. Whoever has will be given more; whoever does not have, even what they think they have will be taken from them" (Luke 8:18 NIV).

SUNDAY EVENING, AUGUST 31

Title: Patience: Reconciled Living

Text: "Better is the end of a thing than the beginning thereof: and the patient in spirit is better than the proud in spirit" **(Eccl. 7:8)**.

Scripture Reading: Romans 5:3–6

Introduction

The idea of *patience* in the New Testament usually regards an attitude toward people, not things or events. James was very concerned about our patience with each other. He saw the need so greatly that he said to "count it all joy when ye fall into divers temptations; knowing this, that the trying of your faith worketh patience. But let patience have her perfect work, that ye may be perfect and entire, wanting nothing" (James 1:2–4). The concept of patience is also found in the description of God's attitude toward humans: the "riches of his goodness and forbearance and longsuffering" (Rom. 2:4) that Paul wrote of are to be copied by the believer. To Timothy he wrote, "I was shown mercy so that in me, the worst of sinners, Christ Jesus might display his immense patience as an example for those who would believe in him and receive eternal life" (1 Tim. 1:16 NIV).

Reconciled living is reflecting the forgiving, forbearing, patient attitude that God has shown toward us to those with whom we have associations. It is living in a security that rests on the acceptance of "Vengeance is mine; I will repay, saith the Lord" (Rom. 12:19).

I. The discipline of patience.

    A. *It is to control anger.*

        1. "The discretion of a man deferreth his anger; and it is his glory to pass over a transgression" (Prov. 19:11).

        2. An old saying goes, "The only value of anger is to put the curve in a cat's back."

        3. Patience is a requirement for bishops: "But [be] patient, not a brawler" (1 Tim. 3:3).

    B. *It is a teacher of humility.*

        1. When the severest tests came and the disciples were most tempted to

250

strike back, Jesus said, "Not a hair of your head will perish. Stand firm, and you will win life" (Luke 21:18–19 NIV).

2. Paul said, "We put no stumbling block in anyone's path, so that our ministry will not be discredited. Rather, as servants of God we commend ourselves in every way: in great endurance; in troubles, hardships and distresses; in beatings, imprisonments and riots; in hard work, sleepless nights and hunger" (2 Cor. 6:3–5 NIV).

3. "For ye have need of patience, that, after ye have done the will of God, ye might receive the promise" (Heb. 10:36).

C. *It is the meeting place for minds.*

1. "Don't grumble against one another....As an example of patience in the face of suffering, take the prophets who spoke in the name of the Lord" (James 5:9–10 NIV).

2. Even the church at Ephesus, who had left their first love, had a chance in that they had "persevered and ... endured hardships" (Rev. 2:3 NIV).

II. The creativity in patience.

A. *Forgiveness is possible.*

1. Forgiveness that is not creative is license.

2. The God who made a covenant with Moses on Sinai is described as "merciful and gracious, longsuffering, and abundant in goodness and truth" (Ex. 34:6).

3. God's patience is pictured as "patient with you, not wanting anyone to perish, but everyone to come to repentance" (2 Peter 3:9).

B. *Wisdom is born.*

1. Man is small; he is in a hurry. God is great; he has the ages, so he can be patient.

2. Of Bezaleel, Moses said that God had prepared him for intricate work with gold and silver: "He hath filled him with the spirit of God, in wisdom" (Ex. 35:31).

3. "With the ancient is wisdom; and in length of days understanding" (Job 12:12).

4. "Whoever is patient has great understanding, but one who is quick-tempered displays folly" (Prov. 14:29 NIV).

C. *True leadership emerges.*

1. "A hot-tempered person stirs up conflict, but the one who is patient calms a quarrel" (Prov. 15:18 NIV).

2. "Better a patient person than a warrior, one with self-control than one who takes a city" (Prov. 16:32 NIV).

3. Elihu said, "Age should speak; advanced years should teach wisdom" (Job 32:7 NIV).

III. Our godlikeness in patience.

A. *The expression "sons of God" implies that godlikeness is desired.*
1. "Let us run with perseverance the race marked out for us, fixing our eyes on Jesus, the pioneer and perfecter of faith" (Heb. 12:1 NIV).
2. "You have heard of Job's perseverance and have seen what the Lord finally brought about. The Lord is full of compassion and mercy" (James 5:11 NIV).

B. *". . . the longsuffering of our Lord is salvation" (2 Peter 3:15).*
1. Persistence is needed in soul-winning.
2. Love until love works patience.

C. *Be reconciled to God in Christ.*
1. "Once you were alienated from God and were enemies in your minds because of your evil behavior. But now he has reconciled you by Christ's physical body through death to present you holy in his sight" (Col. 1:21 NIV).
2. Even the two natures within us are brought together in Christ, "that he might reconcile both unto God in one body by the cross, having slain the enmity thereby" (Eph. 2:16).
3. "All things are of God, who hath reconciled us to himself by Jesus Christ, and hath given to us the ministry of reconciliation; to wit, that God was in Christ, reconciling the world unto himself" (2 Cor. 5:18–19).
4. "Now then we are ambassadors for Christ, as though God did beseech you by us: we pray you in Christ's stead, be ye reconciled to God" (2 Cor. 5:20).

Conclusion

Living described as patient—or as I have chosen to call it, "reconciled"—does not imply a negative reaction to happenings. It is not a grim wait until everything works out satisfactorily. It is positive. It is a trust that keeps hope alive as one labors under a difficult situation. It is faith in people, in what they can become when rightly related to God. Of all the fruits of salvation, patience is the greatest virtue. In it one shares so closely with the God we have known, the God who keeps loving people in spite of their sin, who ever probes the consciences of people even as their hearts are hardened, who with outstretched arms beckons when people continue to reject him.

Waiting with God, waiting with an expecting faith, waiting when others give up, waiting in joy, knowing that dawn comes and that the darkest hour precedes its light—that is patience; that is a reconciled life.

SEPTEMBER

■ **Sunday Mornings**

Continue the series "Our Lord Speaks through Parables."

■ **Sunday Evenings**

Continue the series "The Great Christian Virtues."

■ **Wednesday Evenings**

If the program of reading a chapter a day has been followed, the New Testament will be completed during the month of September. Continuing with the theme "The Bible Speaks to Our Condition," certain great chapters from the New Testament are selected for use for the Wednesday evening services. The theme verse for the month is "You make known to me the path of life; you will fill me with joy in your presence, with eternal pleasures at your right hand" (Ps. 16:11 NIV).

WEDNESDAY EVENING, SEPTEMBER 3

Title: The Bible Speaks to Our Condition

Scripture Reading: Revelation 9

Introduction

The book of Revelation has been neglected, misunderstood, pitifully mistreated, and grossly perverted. It stands uniquely alone in the New Testament.

It is a book of prophecy that utilizes apocalyptic literature as its medium of communicating the message of God to the hearts of people. This book cannot be properly understood or interpreted without a knowledge of the historical situation out of which it comes.

The chapter for study today is but a fragment of a larger section of the book that proclaims the judgments of God on the Roman Empire (Rev. 8, 9). Following the opening of the seventh seal, seven angels with seven trumpets proclaim the judgment of God (8:1–2). Judgment is proclaimed on the land (8:6–7), on the sea (8:8–9), on the fresh water (8:10–11), and on the heavenly bodies (8:12).

I. The terrible locust plague (Rev. 9:1–12).

As we read of this terrible plague, let us remember that the author is using symbolic language to communicate a great truth.

II. The army from the east (Rev. 9:13–19).

The sixth angel sounds a trumpet, and John sees a vision of a horrible army from the East invading the land. This may be a reference to invasion by the Parthians who inflicted great damage on the Roman Empire.

It is interesting to note in this series of visions that there are fifteen cases of destruction or judgment upon the people, and in twelve of these instances the extent of suffering is limited to "one-third." This is indicative of the fact that while the judgment and the suffering were to be severe, it was a limited judgment on those who rebelled against God.

III. The refusal to repent (Rev. 9:20–21).

The last two verses of this chapter reveal the purpose behind the judgments that are to befall the Roman Empire. In spite of all of the judgments of God, people refuse to forsake their idol worship and turn to the true and living God.

Conclusion

Repentance involves a basic change of mind toward God, toward sin, toward self, toward others, and toward things. Genuine repentance is accepting God's viewpoint concerning all things and then building one's life on that basis.

Let us be open and obedient at all times to God's way so that judgment will not come on us.

SUNDAY MORNING, SEPTEMBER 7

Title: The Enemy of the Kingdom

Text: "An enemy hath done this" (**Matt. 13:28**).

Scripture Reading: Matthew 13:24–30, 36–43, 47–50

Hymns: "Breathe on Me," Hatch

"Nothing Between," Tindley

"Yield Not to Temptation," Palmer

Offertory Prayer: Heavenly Father, today our hearts thank you for the abundance of your grace toward us. We praise you with our lips. We glorify you with our lives. We proclaim your salvation to people throughout the world. As an indication of our desire that others might know of your grace, we bring our tithes and offerings for the advancement of the work of your kingdom. Bless these offerings to that purpose. In Jesus' name. Amen.

Introduction

The kingdom of God (that is, the reign or rule of God) is illustrated by the following story. A man sowed good wheat seed in his field, but while he and other good men were sleeping, an enemy came and sowed tares. The tares were a kind of darnel that looked like wheat, but the grains were black and poisonous. These tares were not discovered until the grain began to form. The servants were surprised. They asked the householder, "Did you not sow good seed?" "Yes." "Then how do you account for these tares?" The householder replied, "An enemy has done this."

What could be done about it? The servants suggested that they pull out the tares. The householder knew that this was impractical. The tares looked so much like wheat that mistakes would be made and wheat would be uprooted also. Again the roots would be so intertwined that in pulling up the tares much wheat would be uprooted. The householder had a better plan. "Let both grow until the harvest: and in the time of harvest I will say to the reapers, Gather ye together first the tares, and bind them in bundles to burn them: but gather the wheat into my barn" (v. 30).

In Matthew 13:36–43, we find our Lord's own interpretation of this parable. The one sowing the good seed is the Son of Man, Jesus. The field in which he sows is the world. He sows good seed, which are sons of the kingdom, or saved persons. He expects them to be seed for the gospel, which will multiply many other saved people. The devil is the one sowing the tares, which are the sons of the evil one, or unsaved people.

I. The perplexing problem of evil in the world.

Now if this is God's world and he sows good seed, why should there be sons of the evil one? Why should there be lying, stealing, cheating, murder, war, and other forms of evil in God's world? "Master, didst thou not sow good seed?"

A. *Jesus recognizes sin as a reality.* It is a fact; tares, noxious weeds, are in with the wheat. They are fit only for destruction. Hear Dr. George A. Buttrick:

> *To regard evil as illusory solves no problems. A God who, eager to create children of His love, confronts them with a good and evil choice and so fills His universe with danger, is a God who by that act fills our minds with dismaying questions. But a God who suffers His children to live under illusions is not a winsome substitute! A world of real good and real evil does at least provide the setting for heroic character, but a world in which every one is victimized by false impressions is a mad world in very truth. Jesus says of the choking weeds of life, "I do not account for them, but they are the work of an 'enemy.'"* (The Parables of Jesus *[New York: Harper and Row, 1928], 66*)

B. *Jesus recognizes sin as the work of an enemy.* God with great courage of love has made people "in his own image," which among other things carries the power of moral choice. One may accept the grace of God and become a son of the kingdom or one may reject the grace of God and become a son of the devil. This power of choice that places humanity above the animal creation is both a precious and perilous possession. Character would be impossible without moral choice. Yet the same moral choice that opens heaven can be used to open hell. "Sin is enmity against God."

II. What are God's servants to do?

Some are willing to rush out and try forcibly to pull up the tares. History is filled with examples of those who in the name of Christ have been willing to root out the evil with the sword, but Jesus says otherwise. Wheat and tares look so much alike that no mortal can possibly draw the dividing line. "Man looketh on the outward appearance, but the LORD looketh on the heart" (1 Sam. 16:7). We have no doubt but that God and God alone can indicate at this very moment the lost or the unsaved condition of every person living on earth. He alone knows all of the facts including the motives that give moral quality to the actions. Our responsibility as servants of God is not to persecute others. "Judge not, that ye be not judged" (Matt. 7:1). Certainly, in trying to gather up tares, we would gather wheat with the tares and leave tares with the wheat.

The servants of Christ are to speak "the truth in love" (Eph. 4:15). "But ye shall receive power, after that the Holy Ghost is come upon you: and ye shall be witnesses unto me both in Jerusalem, and in all Judea, and in Samaria, and unto the uttermost part of the earth" (Acts 1:8). The weapon for that witness is not the sword of temporal power but rather "the sword of the Spirit, which is the word of God" (Eph. 6:17). In the natural world, there was no way by which tares could become wheat. In the spiritual world, however, sons of the devil can become sons of God through faith in Jesus Christ.

III. God's judgment is certain.

At the time of harvest, the tares and the wheat will be harvested with no difficulty in separation. The wheat without exception will be in the barn. The tares without exception will be destroyed by burning. The Son of Man himself will through his messengers do the harvesting. Not one saved will be among the unsaved; not one unsaved will be among the saved. The saved will shine forth as the sun in the kingdom of their Father. The unsaved will know anguish.

The parable of the net spoken later that same day emphasizes the same truth. It presents the familiar New Testament image of fishermen casting a net. The net drew in every kind of fish. The fishermen divided the good fish from the bad. They kept the good and cast the bad away. So at the end of the age, all will be judged. The angels as God's messengers will effect the separation as easily as fishermen sort fish.

The wheat is gathered into the barn (v. 30); the good fish are gathered into vessels (v. 48); then shall the righteous shine forth like the sun (v. 43). The wheat, the fish, the saved are valuable to their owners. These and countless other figures of speech in Scripture enhance the joy of salvation both to the believer and to the Lord. Their variety would warn against an insistence on too literal an interpretation.

The tares are bound in bundles for burning (v. 30); the bad fish are cast away (v. 48); the wicked are cast into the furnace of fire where there shall be wailing and gnashing of teeth (vv. 42, 49). These and other images are used of the sad fate of the wicked. Their variety should warn against acceptance with crude literalism, but the awful spiritual truth depicted by them must be accepted with all seriousness.

Conclusion

God will be the final Judge. He will not make any mistakes. There will be no idle arguments about the hypocrisies of others. "So then every one of us shall give account of himself to God" (Rom. 14:12). But God as Judge does not desire to pronounce the sentence of death. He is "not willing that any should perish, but that all should come to repentance" (2 Peter 3:9). In love he approaches sinful people with the offer of forgiveness and salvation.

In the spiritual realm, tares can become wheat; bad fish can become good fish; wicked people can become righteous. If God seems to delay his judgment, Paul suggests that mercy may be the reason: "When you, a mere human being, pass judgment on them and yet do the same things, do you think you will escape God's judgment? Or do you show contempt for the riches of his kindness, forbearance and patience, not realizing that God's kindness is intended to lead you to repentance? But because of your stubbornness and your unrepentant heart, you are storing up wrath against yourself for the day of God's wrath, when his righteous judgment will be revealed" (Rom. 2:3–5 NIV). "Now then we are ambassadors for Christ, as though God did beseech you by us: we pray you in Christ's stead, be ye reconciled to God" (2 Cor. 5:20). "Behold, now is the accepted time; behold, now is the day of salvation" (2 Cor. 6:2).

SUNDAY EVENING, SEPTEMBER 7

Title: Kindness: Sensitive Living

Text: "As God's chosen people, holy and dearly loved, clothe yourselves with compassion, kindness, humility, gentleness and patience" **(Col. 3:12 NIV)**.

Scripture Reading: Ephesians 4:25–32

Introduction

An anonymous writer has pointed out, "The ministry of kindness is a ministry that may be achieved by all people, rich and poor, learned and illiterate. Brilliance of mind and capacity for deep thinking have rendered great service to humanity, but by themselves they are impotent to dry a tear or mend a broken heart." Kindness made its most noticeable impact in the coming of Christ and in the lives of his early followers. One of today's greatest losses is that the Christian church has devoted more time in creating and preserving dogma than in practicing kindness.

Kindness is of God. This evening we will trace the evidence of God's kindness throughout the biblical record and relate it to what the Christian life is to be. As we discover the kindness of God in action, drawing people to himself in sacrificial love, we understand the challenge to us for sensitive living. Blessed are we when we get a grasp on Paul's depth of experience with his Lord. "Let love be without dissimulation. Abhor that which is evil; cleave to that which is good. Be kindly affectioned one to another with brotherly love" (Rom. 12:9–10).

Sensitive living for the Christian is practicing "do[ing] to others what you

257

would have them do to you" (Matt. 7:12 NIV), and then going a step further. It also means acting toward others in the same spirit that God has acted toward us.

I. Kindness of God in the Old Testament.

A. *He is deserving of our thanks.*

1. God answered the prayer of the fearful: "He showed me the wonders of his love when I was in a city under siege" (Ps. 31:21 NIV).
2. The redeemed of the Lord should say so, "for he is good: for his mercy [kindness] endureth for ever" (Ps. 107:1).
3. When Jeremiah was in prison, the Lord said to him, "Call to me and I will answer you and tell you great and unsearchable things you do not know" (Jer. 33:3 NIV). "Praise the LORD of hosts: for the LORD is good: for his mercy [kindness] endureth for ever" (v. 11).

B. *God's kindness has an affect on our relationships.*

1. In fellowship with each other. Jonathan said to David, "Show me unfailing kindness like the LORD's kindness as long as I live, so that I may not be killed" (1 Sam. 20:14 NIV). Naomi said to her daughters-in-law: "Go, return each to her mother's house: the LORD deal kindly with you, as ye have dealt with the dead, and with me" (Ruth 1:8). David said to the men of Jabesh-gilead: "May the LORD now show you kindness and faithfulness, and I too will show you the same favor because you have [buried King Saul]" (2 Sam. 2:6 NIV).
2. In association with God. Zion and the Lord: "For a small moment have I forsaken thee; but with great mercies will I gather thee. In a little wrath I hid my face from thee for a moment; but with everlasting kindness will I have mercy on thee" (Isa. 54:7–8). Zion to avert destruction: "And rend your heart, and not your garments, and turn unto the LORD your God; for he is gracious and merciful, slow to anger, and of great kindness" (Joel 2:13).

C. *God's kindness is to be seen around us.*

1. In the material world. "Truth shall spring out of the earth ... the LORD shall give that which is good; and our land shall yield her increase" (Ps. 85:11–12).
2. In God's hand in victory. "They shall abundantly utter the memory of thy great goodness, and shall sing of thy righteousness. The LORD is gracious, and full of compassion; slow to anger, and of great mercy" (Ps. 145:7–8).
3. In God's concern for the poor and to those of faith. "I am poor and needy; may the Lord think of me. You are my help and my deliverer; you are my God, do not delay" (Ps. 40:17 NIV). "O taste and see that the LORD is good: blessed is the man that trusteth in him" (Ps. 34:8).

II. Kindness of God in the New Testament.

A. *It is directed toward all.* "God raised us up with Christ and seated us with

258

him in the heavenly realms in Christ Jesus, in order that in the coming ages he might show the incomparable riches of his grace, expressed in his kindness to us in Christ Jesus" (Eph. 2:6–7 NIV). "Love your enemies, do good to them, and lend to them without expecting to get anything back. Then your reward will be great, and you will be children of the Most High, because he is kind to the ungrateful and wicked" (Luke 6:35 NIV).

B. *It is for man's salvation.* "Or despisest thou the riches of his goodness and forbearance and longsuffering; not knowing that the goodness of God leadeth thee to repentance?" (Rom. 2:4). "When the kindness and love of God our Savior appeared, he saved us, not because of righteous things we had done, but because of his mercy. He saved us through the washing of rebirth and renewal by the Holy Spirit" (Titus 3:4–5 NIV).

III. Kindness of God in Christian experience.

A. *It is a "fruit of the Spirit," an essential part of mature Christian living.*

1. Peter points out that by means of "precious promises" we might be partakers of the divine nature.

    By giving all diligence, he directs that we add to faith "virtue; and to virtue knowledge; and to knowledge temperance; and to temperance patience; and to patience godliness; and to godliness brotherly kindness" (2 Peter 1:5–7).

2. Paul held kindness among the things that "approve" the minister of God. He lists the order as "purity, understanding, patience and kindness; in the Holy Spirit and in sincere love" (2 Cor. 6:6 NIV).

B. *It is a pattern for growth.*

1. In prayer give attention to others. "And forgive us our debts, as we forgive our debtors" (Matt. 6:12).

    "For if ye forgive men their trespasses, your heavenly Father will also forgive you" (Matt. 6:14).

2. Bitterness, wrath, anger, clamor, and evil speaking are to be put away. These are replaced by kindness, tenderheartedness, and forgiveness (Eph. 4:31–32).

3. In Paul's exhortation of love as the height of Christian graces, he writes, "Love suffereth long, and is kind" (1 Cor. 13:4).

Conclusion

In Matthew 11, we find a series of colorful accounts of our Lord's activities. In that one chapter, we see Jesus commanding the Twelve, preaching in the cities, encountering John's disciples, evaluating John's ministry, denouncing the present generation, upbraiding the cities, praying to the Father, and inviting all who labor and are heavy laden to come to him. In this invitation, we catch a hurried view of the secret of sensitive living. Jesus is saying, "Take my yoke upon you, and learn of me; for I am meek and lowly in heart: and ye shall find rest unto your souls. For my yoke is easy [kind]" (Matt. 11:29–30). The marvelous message is that when Christ enters the hearts of people and conditions those hearts to a sensitive response to his will, he also monitors the load to be pulled, the yoke to be worn. "My yoke is properly fitted," says Jesus. We can come to him in perfect trust. If, in his love, our hearts are rendered sensitive, in his kindness our yokes are lovingly fitted.

WEDNESDAY EVENING, SEPTEMBER 10

Title: The Bible Speaks to Our Condition

Scripture Reading: Revelation 16

Introduction

The chapter for today's meditation from this strange and mysterious book at the end of the New Testament gives us a dramatic picture of the pouring out of God's wrath on the enemies of his people. Seven angels go forth with seven bowls filled with God's wrath. The inspired writer uses apocalyptic literature to express the message, and we must seek the truth behind the symbolic language.

The historic situation into which the book of Revelation was written probably requires that we interpret this chapter as being a prophecy of the wrath of God that was going to fall on the Roman Empire. It would have brought encouragement and hope to those who were distressed and in despair. This chapter reveals that God is the eternal foe of those who seek to destroy his people and his work in the world.

By all means, we should see this chapter as speaking of the final demonstration of God's wrath on those who reject him and blaspheme him as we come to the end of the age. Man in his unbelief and in his revolt against God will try to throw off the authority and the power of God.

I. The second coming of Christ (Rev. 16:15).

In the midst of this chapter that proclaims the wrath of God on the wicked, we find a clear promise of our Lord's personal return. He describes the manner of his coming as being sudden and unexpected.

II. A beatitude (Rev. 16:15).

In the midst of this chapter describing the judgment of God on the wicked, our Lord announces a beatitude on his disciples who are alert and watchful and responsive to his leadership. One of Jesus' primary purposes for this entire book was to assure his disciples of his abiding presence with them in all circumstances and to assure them of his ultimate victory over all adverse circumstances. They are encouraged to always be alert and responsive to their opportunities and responsibilities.

III. An encouragement to purity and fidelity (Rev. 16:15).

Another of the primary purposes of Revelation is to encourage the disciples of the Lord to be faithful, even to the point of death. Martyrdom was a real possibility for each one who was loyal to the Lord in those days. Faithfulness is required if we are to please the Lord and give an effective witness to our contemporaries.

Conclusion

Out of this very strange chapter that deals with both the past and the future, there comes a promise and words of encouragement for those of us who live today. Let us live in a constant expectancy of our Lord's return. Let us be faithful to him. Let us be ready at any time for his triumphant and victorious return.

SUNDAY MORNING, SEPTEMBER 14

Title: The Growth of the Kingdom

Text: "The kingdom of heaven is like to a grain of mustard seed" (**Matt. 13:31**).

Scripture Reading: Matthew 13:31–33

Hymns: "Praise to the Lord, the Almighty," Neander

"Take Time to Be Holy," Longstaff

"Brethren, We Have Met to Worship," Atkins

Offertory Prayer: Our heavenly Father, as we approach the harvest season of the year when people will be reaping the harvest from the fields, we remind ourselves of your bountiful goodness toward us. We thank you for every gift of your mercy. As we bring tithes and offerings of the fruits of our labor, we thank you for the opportunity to work and the power to get wealth. Help us never to forget that you are the giver of every good and perfect gift. Help us to give unto you even as you have given unto us, through Jesus Christ our Lord. Amen.

Introduction

Jesus was sure about God. Jesus never doubted God nor his ability to accomplish his purpose. "Have faith in God," he pleaded (Mark 11:22). "Ye believe in God, believe also in me" (John 14:1). You do not need to be afraid of the future; it is in God's competent hands.

Jesus had complete confidence in the success of his mission. Even as he faced death, it was in terms of victory. He faced the anguish and sorrow of the cross, but never for a moment did the cross represent defeat. Always his death was associated with victory and the accomplishment of the Father's will. He said, "I, if I be lifted up from the earth, will draw all men unto me" (John 12:32). In the upper room, Jesus was confident of the future: "In my Father's house are many mansions: if it were not so, I would have told you. I go to prepare a place for you. And if I go and prepare a place for you, I will come again, and receive you unto myself; that where I am, there ye may be also" (John 14:2–3). Jesus' disciples were not to despair nor faint at tribulation. "In the world ye shall have tribulation; but be of good cheer; I have overcome the world" (John 16:33).

On the cross, Jesus was sure of his saving mission. He assured the repentant robber of salvation (Luke 23:43–44). "It is finished," was a cry of victory. It seems to me that his cry "My God, my God, why hast thou forsaken me?" was also an affirmation of victory. He was beginning to quote Psalm 22 and applied it to himself. "Why" is "for that purpose," and the psalm answered the question. The Messiah suffered in order to be the Savior. "Father, into thy hands I commend my Spirit" was an affirmation of faith.

After the resurrection, Jesus had complete confidence in the worldwide nature of the kingdom of God. The commissions (see Matt. 28:18–20; Luke 24:44–49; Acts 1:8) all assume a worldwide conquest. Jesus would be with his followers during the gospel age in the person of the Holy Spirit. He would return at the end of the age in power and great glory. (See Matt. 25:31–46.)

Who of Jesus' contemporaries could have foreseen that Jesus would be the King of an eternal kingdom? He was of humble birth, the son of a carpenter (as the people thought) and of a humble Jewish maiden. He was a teacher who so enraged the religious authorities as to lead to his condemnation and death on a shameful cross. His followers were few and from the common people. Surely at his death his followers would disperse and his name vanish.

However, to the surprise of everyone except Jesus himself, his name did not vanish. Rather, "God also hath highly exalted him, and given him a name which is above every name: that at the name of Jesus every knee should bow, of things in heaven, and things in earth, and things under the earth; and that every tongue should confess that Jesus Christ is Lord, to the glory of God the Father" (Phil. 2:9–11).

I. The parable of the mustard seed (Matt. 13:31–32).

The unexpected growth of the kingdom of heaven from such humble beginnings to such importance is like the growth of a grain of mustard seed (which was the smallest of the seeds in common use) to become the largest of the garden herbs, growing to about ten feet in height, becoming a tree—in size rather than in nature—so large that even the birds found shelter in its branches. The mustard seed was proverbial in Jesus' day for something small and relatively insignificant. The emphasis of the parable is on the fact that a seed so small could grow into a bush so large. Thus did Jesus predict the expansive growth of the kingdom of heaven.

II. The parable of the leaven (Matt. 13:33).

The method by which the kingdom of heaven grows was illustrated by our Lord in his parable of the leaven. Often as a boy, Jesus had seen his mother take three measures of meal, probably wheat flour. This was the large quantity needed to bake enough bread to last a large family for several days. The leaven or yeast carefully saved from the last baking was placed in the dough. Immediately, quietly, continuously the leaven worked, changing particle after particle of the dough until the whole had been conquered by the yeast.

A. *Leaven works silently, inwardly.* The kingdom of heaven is the reign of God in the hearts of people. It comes as people yield their hearts to God. Jesus is the King of the kingdom of heaven. God, the Holy Spirit, is in charge of the present gospel mission of leading men and women, boys and girls to the acceptance of Jesus Christ as Lord and Savior. The Holy Spirit bears witness to the truth as it is revealed in Jesus Christ. (See John 14:16–17, 26; 15:26.) The Holy Spirit convicts of sin and invites to the acceptance of Jesus Christ. (See John 16:7–14.) The Spirit of God works quietly, powerfully, inwardly. Often great sources of power work quietly. Who hears light or electricity or atomic power? The solar system does not chatter in its course. Love does not make a big noise. God is at work.

B. *Leaven works continuously.* Whether the baker thinks about it or not, the leaven is continuously at its task. "Behold, he that keepeth Israel shall neither slumber nor sleep" (Ps. 121:4). The divine Potter has his hands in the clay of our humanity, seeking to make a vessel of honor. He uses the truth as his weapon. His providences—which may seem to us both good and ill—are to accomplish his purpose.

C. *Leaven works by contact.* One particle becomes leavened. This particle leavens the next, and so particle by particle the leaven relentlessly conquers the dough. It is an apt illustration of the way by which the kingdom of heaven expands. One life is changed by the Spirit of God. He who was dead in trespasses and sins has been made alive in Christ Jesus. A part of his new life in Christ is the compassionate desire that others might be Christian. He expresses that desire as he bears witness of his faith to someone in whom he is concerned. God uses the witness to help another to come to the truth. Note how the kingdom of heaven began to spread. John the Baptist pointed out Jesus to his disciples. John and Andrew spent the day with Jesus. They were convinced. "The first thing Andrew did was to find his brother Simon and tell him, 'We have found the Messiah' (that is, the Christ)" (John 1:41 NIV). John probably won his brother James. "Jesus ... finding Philip ... said to him, 'Follow me' " (John 1:43 NIV). "Philip found Nathanael and told him, 'We have found the one Moses wrote about in the Law, and about whom the prophets also wrote—Jesus of Nazareth, the son of Joseph" (John 1:45 NIV). And so the kingdom grows. God's method of winning the multitudes seems to be to win them one by one.

D. *The leaven works victoriously.* It has vitality and power to conquer the dough. We have already learned that a story from nature cannot always parallel spiritual truth, because nature lacks the quality of free will that humans have. To interpret "till the whole was leavened" to teach that all people will be saved would be too rigorous an interpretation. The parable of the tares and the parable of the dragnet as well as other explicit teachings of Jesus teach otherwise. The meal of our human life has the power to resist the leaven. It is true, however, that the leaven of the gospel will affect every particle in the meal. No person can escape a confrontation with the gospel.

Conclusion

The triumph of Christ's kingdom is assured. "For he must reign until he has put all his enemies under his feet" (1 Cor. 15:25 NIV). "The kingdoms of this world are become the kingdoms of our Lord, and of his Christ; and he shall reign for ever and ever" (Rev. 11:15). At the end Satan and those who follow him are cast into the bottomless pit. Jesus and those who follow him live and reign. The purpose of this gospel age is not to determine whether Christ or Satan will be victorious: that issue is already settled. The purpose is to determine who will be with Christ in victory and who will be with Satan in defeat.

The parable of the mustard seed assures us that the triumph of Christ will be greater than any of his contemporaries could have imagined. The parable of the leaven assures us that God is working quietly, effectively, continuously to add members to Christ's kingdom. Wonder of wonders, he can use us to help him in this significant work. Let us be willing witnesses for Christ.

SUNDAY EVENING, SEPTEMBER 14

Title: Faithfulness: Immutable Living

Text: "Moreover it is required in stewards, that a man be found faithful" (**1 Cor. 4:2**).

Scripture Reading: Luke 12:42–48

Introduction

The difference between the Christian person and the irreligious person is not that one has faith while the other has none, but rather it is that their faiths rest in different things. For the irreligious, seeing is believing. He has seen humanity's weakness and treads on it; he has seen the efficacy of material force and relies on it; he has seen the power of finances and makes use of it. There is another who believes in goodness of others and works for it; he trusts in the efficacy of sacrifice and suffers for it; he hopes for the vindication of righteousness and waits for it. With him all life is guided by a confidence in things hoped for, and each act is a testing of things not seen. Thus, the basic difference between people is not to be sought in their theological opinions but in the object of their practical trust.

When Paul came to write of faith as he listed the fruit of the Spirit, he was writing of ethical virtues. His interest was not so much in our relationship to God as it was in our affiliation with our fellow humans. Paul's concern was faithfulness, the character trait that may be described as reliability or loyalty. Paul described the Christian in whom there is no swerving in fidelity to Christ. This quality of reliability and trustworthiness is unchanging, invariable, and thus worthy of the name of "immutable living." Our message traces the biblical account of faithfulness in God, our Savior, the Word itself, and the Christian life.

I. A faithful God.

A. *Viewpoint of the Old Testament writers.*
   1. "Know therefore that the LORD your God is God; he is the faithful God, keeping his covenant of love to a thousand generations of those who love him and keep his commandments" (Deut. 7:9 NIV).
   2. The psalmist observes, "All your commands are trustworthy" (Ps. 119:86 NIV), and "The statutes you have laid down are righteous; they are fully trustworthy" (Ps. 119:138 NIV).
   3. Isaiah, in outlining the mission of Jehovah's servant, asserts, "Kings will see you and stand up, princes will see and bow down, because of the LORD, who is faithful" (Isa. 49:7 NIV).
B. *Testimonies from the New Testament.*
   1. When observing the withered fig tree, Jesus directed his disciples, "Have faith in God" (Mark 11:22).
   2. Paul affirms, "Faithful is he that calleth you, who also will do it" (1 Thess. 5:24). In his second epistle to the same Christians, he writes, "The Lord is faithful, who shall stablish you, and keep you from evil" (2 Thess. 3:3).
   3. In a most practical way, Paul points out that "God is faithful, who will not suffer you to be tempted above that ye are able" (1 Cor. 10:13).
   4. John declares that "God is light" (1 John 1:5). "If we confess our sins, he is faithful and just to forgive us our sins, and to cleanse us from all unrighteousness" (v. 9).

II. Jesus is a faithful Savior.

A. *An example to be followed.*
   1. We cannot believe that we have faith in Jesus if we continue to show partiality to persons (James 2:1). Jesus is the example of humility in that he showed no partiality.
   2. "Christ also suffered for us, leaving us an example, that ye should follow his steps" (1 Peter 2:21).
B. *A witness for pointing to God.*
   1. When compared with Moses, Jesus was as a son, Moses as a servant. "Christ Jesus; who was faithful to him that appointed him" (Heb. 3:1–2).
   2. "But I have greater witness than that of John: for the works which the Father hath given me to finish, the same works that I do, bear witness of me, that the Father hath sent me" (John 5:36).
   3. John introduced the Revelation as from "Jesus Christ, who is the faithful witness" (Rev. 1:5).

III. The Scriptures are the faithful Word.

Biblical writers affirm that the truth they reveal is completely trustworthy. Paul labored at one point to show that a particular idea was his and was not equal with those received of the Lord. "That which I speak, I speak it not after the Lord" (2 Cor. 11:17). The special occasions where there is notice of the "faithful word" are worthy of our attention.

A. *To be a good bishop, one must, among other qualities, be one "holding fast the faithful word" (Titus 1:9).*

B. *To Timothy, Paul punctuates the fact that "Jesus came into the world to save sinners" by saying, "This is a faithful saying and worthy of all acceptation" (1 Tim. 1:15).*

C. *John closes Revelation with caution for those who may "add unto these things" or "take away from the words" (Rev. 22:18–19).*

IV. The Christian life is a life of faithfulness.

A. *Loyalty to Christ.*

1. We have identity with Christ in his death and life. "I am crucified with Christ: nevertheless I live; yet not I, but Christ liveth in me: and the life which I now live in the flesh I live by the faith of the Son of God, who loved me, and gave himself for me" (Gal. 2:20).
2. Stephen, "full of faith and power," did many miracles. At Stephen's death, Luke recorded, "While they were stoning him, Stephen prayed, 'Lord Jesus, receive my spirit'" (Acts 7:59 NIV).
3. The responsibility of the ministry must be placed in loyal hands. "And the things that thou hast heard of me among many witnesses, the same commit thou to faithful men, who shall be able to teach others also" (2 Tim. 2:2).

B. *Faith, the foundation of life.*

1. Paul asserted that he was not ashamed of the gospel of Christ: "For therein is the righteousness of God revealed from faith to faith.... The just shall live by faith" (Rom. 1:17).
2. Jesus asked the fearful disciples in the storm on the lake, "Why are you so afraid? Do you still have no faith?" (Mark 4:40 NIV).
3. Just before speaking a parable "to some who were confident of their own righteousness," Jesus asked, "When the Son of Man comes, will he find faith on the earth?" (Luke 18:8–9 NIV).

Conclusion

In a world that changes daily, among a people whose chief fad is change, "let us hold unswervingly to the hope we profess, for he who promised is faithful" (Heb. 10:23 NIV).

Christian faith has learned to trust in the love of God. That love often makes stern demands; what it bids will seem impossible; it may seem outrageous; we see no evidence of forces working toward the goal to which it points. If we really trust

God, he will strengthen us to live by confidence in what we hope for and in the perpetual testing of forces we cannot see. In faithfulness we can come to know the sustaining strength of "such a great cloud of witnesses" (Heb. 12:1 NIV) that encompasses us.

WEDNESDAY EVENING, SEPTEMBER 17

Title: The Bible Speaks to Our Condition

Scripture Reading: Matthew 4

Introduction

Temptation is a universal experience. We read in the Bible that God tested Abraham. We also read, "Let no man say when he is tempted, I am tempted of God: for God cannot be tempted with evil, neither tempteth he any man" (James 1:13). These two references must be studied in their context. God tested Abraham to bring out the good. God never tests a person to bring out evil. Satan is responsible for that kind of temptation. Occasionally people are responsible for their own temptations when they deliberately expose themselves to that which is dangerous.

The act of being tempted should not be considered as sinful in itself. We read concerning our Lord that he was "in all points tempted like as we are, yet without sin" (Heb. 4:15). Our Lord conquered temptation and will show us the way to victory.

I. Victory over temptation (Matt. 4:1–11).

Satan tempted our Lord in the area of his natural appetites (vv. 3–4), the methods that he would use in his ministry (vv. 5–7), and the nature and purpose of his mission (vv. 8–11). Our Lord overcame the temptation of Satan on the basis of his pure manhood and on the basis of his absolute trust and recognition of the authority of God's Word.

Apart from a diligent study and a reliance on the great truths of God's Word, there is no way for us to have victory over temptation. Our Lord set for us an example that will point us toward victory over every temptation toward evil.

II. The call to repentance (Matt. 4:17).

The word translated "repent" literally means "to change the mind, to change the attitude, to change one's scale of values." It is a call to accept the mind of God rather than the mind of the natural man. Positively, repentance is a call to a proper attitude toward God, toward self, toward sin, toward others, and toward things. It is an invitation to a high, holy, happy way of life.

III. The call to service (Matt. 4:18–22).

Our Lord approached people on the basis of their native endowments, their natural dispositions, and the context in which they were living. He spoke to fishermen in terms of becoming fishers of men. He spoke to farmers in terms of sowing seed.

Jesus speaks to each of us in the context of where life finds us. He calls us to high, wonderful service to others in the world in which we live. To truly follow him involves a forsaking of the nets that would hinder us from being fully committed to him.

Conclusion

Our Lord went about teaching, preaching, healing, and ministering to those in need. If we would be his true followers, we would find ourselves following his example and ministering as he sought to minister.

SUNDAY MORNING, SEPTEMBER 21

Title: The Value of the Kingdom

Text: "The kingdom of heaven is like unto treasure" (**Matt. 13:44**).

Scripture Reading: Matthew 13:44–46

Hymns: "Holy, Holy, Holy," Heber

"Though Your Sins Be as Scarlet," Crosby

"Serve the Lord with Gladness," McKinney

Offertory Prayer: Holy and loving Father, we approach your throne of grace with our best. We would not come before you with that which is cheap and shoddy. Out of genuine love and deep gratitude we offer to you the fruit of our labor as an expression of the worship of our hearts. Accept these tithes and offerings as we seek to give ourselves completely unto you. In Jesus' name. Amen.

Introduction

These messages focus on the parables about the kingdom of God that were spoken in one day by Jesus as he preached from a boat. Four sets of twin parables are among those spoken.

The twin parables of the sower and of the seed growing of itself emphasize the vitality of the kingdom.

The twin parables of the tares and of the dragnet emphasize the enemy of the kingdom.

The twin parables of the mustard seed and of the leaven illustrate the growth of the kingdom.

The twin parables of the hidden treasure and of the pearl of great price emphasize the value of the kingdom, which is the theme of this message.

Like twins these parables are alike. They both emphasize the same great truth that the kingdom of God is more important than anything else in the world; that is, to be right with God, to possess the forgiving grace of God through Jesus Christ, is worth more than everything else.

Like twins there are some differences. The parables show that people come to Christian experience by diverse routes.

I. The parable of the hidden treasure (Matt. 13:44).

In Jesus' day, the finding of buried treasure was not an uncommon occurrence. The ground was the security vault of a people besieged by conquering armies. Even the man with one talent in the parable of the talents hid his money in the earth. He did not steal it; he did not waste it; he meant to preserve the precious talent by hiding it in the earth. A man plowing someone's field, apparently with no thought of finding treasure, drove his plowshare deep. The tip struck a strange object. He investigated, and there before his eyes was a treasure more valuable than he had ever imagined. He recognized its value and wanted to possess it at all costs. He covered it to keep others from finding and stealing it. Then he joyfully and quickly sold all that he had in order to buy that field and in accord with the law of his land claim the treasure as his possession.

II. The merchant seeking fine pearls (Matt. 13:45–46).

Pearls were valued in the New Testament world much as diamonds are today. The merchant went from place to place buying and selling pearls. He was always looking for pearls of more beautiful color, perfect size, and symmetry of form. One day he discovered a pearl more wonderful than he had imagined. He immediately appraised it as of more value than all of his possessions. He had to have it. Quickly he sold his possessions in order to buy that pearl.

III. Experiences by which people come to find the true treasure are in many ways alike.

A. *The surpassing value of the kingdom.* The man in the field realized that he had struck it rich. The connoisseur of pearls knew he had found the ultimate in value. "He that cometh to God must believe that he is, and that he is a rewarder of them that diligently seek him" (Heb. 11:6). What is the treasure? What is the pearl? Is it not to know God as revealed in Jesus Christ? It is to discover that he has forgiven our sins not in part but completely and that he has adopted us as children into the divine family. It is to be right with God. It is to enter the kingdom of God by being born again (John 3:3).

B. *Those who enter the kingdom of God must come by repentance and faith.* They part with all else to gain it.

   1. In the nature of the case, there can be no compromise here. For God to compromise on the terms of salvation and allow a person to be saved who refuses to renounce sin is a moral impossibility. "Unless you repent, you too will all perish" (Luke 13:3 NIV). The gospel that is to be preached among all nations is the message of "repentance and remission of sins" (Luke 24:47). Paul sums up the whole gospel for both Jews and Greeks as "repentance toward God, and faith toward our Lord Jesus Christ" (Acts 20:21).

2. The heart of the Christian experience is that one personally forsakes all in order to give his all in believing faith to the Lord Jesus Christ. Entry into the kingdom of God is not by outward ceremony nor by church membership. Judas was a member of the church but apparently not of the kingdom of God. Simon Magus was duly baptized, but he was headed for perdition. The robber on the cross was never baptized, but Jesus affirmed his salvation.

C. *With joy, both men parted with all else to possess the treasure.* The normal expression of Christianity is joy. The angels sang in heavenly chorus to announce the Savior's birth. "Jesus came into Galilee, preaching the gospel of the kingdom of God" (Mark 1:14). The gospel means good news. Those who have found Jesus do not emphasize how much they have given up but rather how much they have found. Suppose a man contemplating marriage begins to weigh the issue in this way: think of how much I will have to give up — *I will have to share my income; I will not be able to date other girls; I will have to stay home with my wife and not be out with the men as much as I would like. This marriage would surely cramp my freedom.* What do we know about this man? We know that he does not know what love is. The man truly in love thinks his intended bride is the most wonderful person in the world, and he counts himself to be truly blessed to be able to endow her with all of his worldly goods and to spend his time with her.

True Christians do not think about what they have given up for Christ. They rejoice in the true riches they have found in Christ.

For example, hear Paul exult in Philippians 3:7–11:

> But what things were gain to me, those I counted loss for Christ. Yea doubtless, and I count all things but loss for the excellency of the knowledge of Christ Jesus my Lord: for whom I have suffered the loss of all things, and do count them but dung, that I may win Christ, and be found in him, not having mine own righteousness, which is of the law, but that which is through the faith of Christ, the righteousness which is of God by faith: that I may know him, and the power of his resurrection, and the fellowship of his sufferings, being made conformable unto his death; if by any means I might attain unto the resurrection of the dead.

We "buy" what Jesus gives by being willing to "sell" all lesser values. We gain life by losing it. "Come, all you who are thirsty, come to the waters; and you who have no money, come, buy and eat! Come, buy wine and milk without money and without cost" (Isa. 55:1 NIV).

IV. Twins, even identical twins, have some differences, and so do these parables.

The ways by which people come to find the treasure are varied. The man in the field plowing had no thought of finding buried treasure. He was doing his daily tasks. Perhaps his very eagerness to do his work well by plowing deep helped him find the treasure. The merchant on the other hand was seeking. He had gone from place to place seeking the best. The man in the field was probably a poor man. The merchant was probably rich, although this is only a conjecture. In any case, the providence of God led both to the treasure in his own way.

Conclusion

Every individual's experience in coming to Christ is in some way different from that of others, just as he or she is different from all others. The apostle Paul was blinded by the light from heaven and heard Jesus' voice. It would be wrong to insist that others must do so to enter the kingdom. Some know exactly the time and place when they found Jesus precious to their souls. As one said to me, "Of course I know when I was saved; I was there." Others of us are not so sure about the time and place when we first loved Jesus. Some crossed over without any great emotional upheaval; it was the reasonable thing to do. Others prayed and agonized until relief came. To insist that one cannot be saved unless he or she sees the light, has a time and place experience, and experiences great emotion is to apply false tests. The true test is this: Is Jesus valued above all? Is life gladly yielded to him? The important question is not so much "When was I saved?" but rather "Am I saved?" "Is Jesus precious to me now?" The promise is "that whosoever believeth in him shall not perish, but have everlasting life" (John 3:16).

SUNDAY EVENING, SEPTEMBER 21

Title: Meekness: Self-Controlled Living

Text: "In your hearts revere Christ as Lord. Always be prepared to give an answer to everyone who asks you to give the reason for the hope that you have. But do this with gentleness and respect" **(1 Peter 3:15 NIV).**

Scripture Reading: Ephesians 4:1 – 7

Introduction

In dealing with an age-worn problem, that of evildoers prospering in a world where the righteous suffer, the psalmist concludes, "But the meek shall inherit the earth; and shall delight themselves in the abundance of peace" (Ps. 37:11). His argument is that judgment is often hasty, that one discovers the justice of the moral order when taking a longer view. Violence has never, and can never, inherit the earth. History bears testimony that meekness will prevail.

I have described this meekness as self-controlled living. I do not equate meekness with humility, nor is there an element of weakness in it. The Bible points to one: "The man Moses was very meek, above all the men which were upon the face of the earth" (Num. 12:3). This quality being described in Moses certainly was not weakness nor mere humility. His character trait described as meekness was his faith in God's purpose for his people and trust in his fellow Israelites that they would turn to God. Meek people see themselves as God's tools to be used in causes beyond themselves, and they see their contemporaries as possible instruments of God. They will not fret at personal inconveniences or rejections. In an attitude of self-effacement, they direct their energies toward the higher goal, God's will. Controlling self is the greatest task of kingdom service; it demands of us meekness. Let us consider the message of the Hebrews as they speak of the meek before God. Let us review meekness in the life of Christians and listen to the words of Jesus on meekness.

I. Standing of the meek before God.

A. *Seven times the psalmist points to the meek:*
1. 22:26: They shall eat and be satisfied; they shall praise the Lord; their heart shall live forever.
2. 25:9: God will guide in judgment; he will teach them his way.
3. 37:11: They shall inherit the earth; they shall delight themselves in peace.
4. 45:4: In majesty they shall ride prosperously.
5. 76:9: God arose to judgment to save them.
6. 147:6: The Lord lifted them up; he cast the wicked down.
7. 149:4: God will beautify them with salvation.

B. *Meekness, a basis of special relationship.*
1. By seeking the Lord, "perhaps you will be sheltered on the day of the LORD's anger" (Zeph. 2:3 NIV).
2. God will not turn away punishment for those who "turn aside the way of the meek" (Amos 2:7).
3. Among the glories for Jerusalem, "the meek also shall increase their joy in the LORD" (Isa. 29:19).

C. *Special message for the meek.*
1. "The Spirit of the Lord GOD is upon me; because the LORD hath anointed me to preach good tidings unto the meek" (Isa. 61:1).
2. The Spirit of the Lord shall be upon the rod out of the stem of Jesse. "With righteousness shall he judge the poor, and reprove with equity for the meek of the earth" (Isa. 11:4).

II. Meekness in the Christian life.

Dr. William Barclay has beautiful insight into meekness in the Christian life as he shows the association of other words used with meekness in the New Testament (William Barclay, *Flesh and Spirit* [Nashville: Abingdon, 1962], 115–18). He divides the words as those "keeping company" and those "contrasting."

A. *The companion words of meekness.*
1. Meekness and *love.* To face a problem in the church, Paul proposed to go to the Corinthians. He posed the question, "Shall I come unto you with a rod, or in love, and in the spirit of meekness?" (1 Cor. 4:21).
2. Meekness and *gentleness.* As an encouragement to godliness, Paul exhorted his readers "to slander no one, to be peaceable and considerate, and always to be gentle toward everyone" (Titus 3:2 NIV).
3. Meekness and *lowliness.* "Walk worthy of the vocation wherewith ye are called, with all lowliness and meekness" (Eph. 4:1–2).

B. *Words contrasted with meekness.*
   1. Chastening rod or meekness (1 Cor. 4:21).
   2. Brawling or meekness (Titus 3:2).
C. *Meekness is essential for Christian life.*
   1. Spirit in which one learns. "Wherefore lay apart all filthiness and super-fluity of naughtiness, and receive with meekness the engrafted word, which is able to save your souls" (James 1:21).
   2. Spirit in which discipline is exercised. "Brethren, if a man be overtaken in a fault, ye which are spiritual, restore such an one in the spirit of meekness" (Gal. 6:1).
   3. Spirit in which opposition is to be met. "Opponents must be gently instructed, in the hope that God will grant them repentance leading them to a knowledge of the truth" (2 Tim. 2:25 NIV).
   4. Spirit of Christian witness. "In your hearts revere Christ as Lord. Always be prepared to give an answer to everyone who asks you to give the reason for the hope that you have. But do this with gentleness and respect" (1 Peter 3:15 NIV).
   5. Spirit to prevail in whole life. "[Your beauty] should be that of your inner self, the unfading beauty of a gentle and quiet spirit, which is of great worth in God's sight" (1 Peter 3:4 NIV).

III. Jesus and meekness.

A. *Pronouncement of teaching.* "Blessed are the meek: for they shall inherit the earth" (Matt. 5:5). "Your king comes to you, gentle and riding on a donkey" (Matt. 21:5 NIV).
B. *Explanation of himself.* When inviting others to take his yoke and learn of him, Jesus said, "I am meek and lowly in heart" (Matt. 11:29).
C. *Paul's description of Christ.* "Now I Paul myself beseech you by the meekness and gentleness of Christ" (2 Cor. 10:1).

Conclusion

The more attention we give to the fruit of the Spirit, the more conscious we become that their attainment comes with the help of God. That is strikingly true in the matter of self-control. We can control self only when God's control is effective. Changing circumstances and personalities are too much for us. We can be meek only as the passions of our lives are subject to our Master's Spirit. We can know the Christian virtues only by committing ourselves to Christ.

WEDNESDAY EVENING, SEPTEMBER 24

Title: The Bible Speaks to Our Condition

Scripture Reading: Matthew 5

Introduction

The great New Testament chapter we examine today is the first portion of the Sermon on the Mount. Actually, it is the beginning of the lecture of heaven's infallible Teacher. Our Lord was not preaching as such; rather, he was teaching (Matt. 5:2; 7:29). In this great chapter, our Lord describes the ideal citizen of the kingdom of God with respect to inner spiritual attitude, influence, and superlative conduct.

I. The inner spiritual attitude of the ideal citizen of the kingdom of God (Matt. 5:1 – 12).

In these beatitudes, our Lord is giving a portrait of the inner spiritual attitude of an ideal citizen of the kingdom of God. There is a progression from one beatitude to the other. The great Christian life grows out of an awareness of spiritual poverty that leads to genuine grief because of sin and the lack of that which would be commendable in the sight of God. These attitudes lead to a spirit of meekness, open-heartedness, a spirit of being teachable and open to God's will. The meek person is one who hungers and thirsts with a deep intensity to be right with God and to be right with one's fellow humans. This ideal citizen is merciful in relationships toward others and has an undivided loyalty of heart to the Savior. This person becomes a peacemaker, aiding others in entering into a peaceful relationship with God and in a condition of peace one with another.

Often the influence of this kind of person on those who oppose the gospel will provoke persecution. Our Lord congratulates those who experience this persecution for righteousness and assures them that great is their reward in heaven.

II. The influence of the ideal citizen of the kingdom of God (Matt. 5:13 – 16).

Jesus declares that ideal citizens of the kingdom of God will serve as salt that purifies and preserves from decay and deterioration. They will also serve as light that illuminates and purifies and makes life possible.

Each of us should examine the quality of our commitment to Christ to see if we are serving as the salt of the earth and the light of the world.

III. The superior conduct of the ideal citizen of the kingdom of God.

The ideal citizen of the kingdom of God will seek to fulfill the law by living a life in both mind and spirit that exceeds the legal requirements of the law of the Old Testament. A number of illustrations are used to show the inward nature of the righteousness of the ideal citizen of the kingdom of God as compared with those who sought righteousness by keeping the law of Moses.

A. *The actions flowing from the righteous character of the ideal Christian are such as make for universal peace (5:21 – 26).* The true follower of Christ will refrain from disagreeable attitudes that create discord among fellow Christians.

B. *The new person in Christ will seek to be characterized by a perfect purity of mind and spirit (5:27 – 32).* He or she will seek to avoid the thoughts that endanger the sacred relationship of husband and wife and will banish lust from mind and heart.

C. *The speech of the Christian, which is an index to character, will be absolutely truthful (5:33–37).* The follower of Jesus Christ will make no provisions for dishonesty and untruthfulness in speech.

D. *The ideal citizen of the kingdom is the one who repudiates the right to retaliate (5:39–42).* This person refuses to live by the law of the jungle and instead chooses to live by the law of love.

E. *The ideal citizen will practice universal love toward all people and thus give evidence of a relationship to the heavenly Father (5:43–48).*

Conclusion

Our Lord is speaking to us through this chapter in his Word. May he bless us and help us as we seek to listen to and follow him.

SUNDAY MORNING, SEPTEMBER 28

Title: The Relevance of the Kingdom

Text: "Jesus said unto them, Have ye understood all these things?" (**Matt. 13:51**).

Scripture Reading: Matthew 13:51–52; 9:14–17

Hymns: "Love Divine, All Loves Excelling," Wesley

"May God Depend on You?" Martin

"O Jesus, I Have Promised," Bode

Offertory Prayer: Holy Father, today we thank you for all of your precious promises to us. We enjoy your gracious provisions for us. We thank you for enough and to spare of the physical necessities of life. Today we bring our gifts and offerings and, as an expression of our worship, we ask for your blessings on them for the preaching of the gospel to the relief of suffering and to the bringing of your ministries of grace to this community and to the world. In Jesus' name. Amen.

Introduction

In these five messages, we have used the parables recorded or spoken on one day by Jesus as he sat in a boat by the seaside. The parables have all related to the kingdom of God. To the final parable spoken that day, the parable of the householder, we add three similar parables spoken earlier—namely, the parable of the children of the bridechamber, the new patch on an old garment, and the new wine in old wineskins.

I. The parable of the householder (Matt. 13:51–52).

After speaking the parables publicly, Jesus explained them to his disciples privately in the house. Happily, some of these explanations have been recorded. The disciples affirmed that they understood what Jesus had been teaching.

A scribe was one who copied the Scriptures and was therefore familiar with the text. It was a natural step that a scribe should become an interpreter and teacher. A "scribe which is instructed unto the kingdom of heaven" would be a scribe or teacher who had become a disciple of Jesus. He now had more to teach than Moses and the Old Testament Scriptures. He had the new insights Jesus had added. He was "like unto a man that is a householder, which bringeth forth out of his treasure things new and old."

The work of a householder is illustrated in the parable of the tares. He had the responsibility for the operation of a farm. Old methods that had value would be retained, but he had to accept profitable new methods. The scribe of Moses who now became a scribe of the kingdom of God would find much in Moses to retain, but he would also adopt the fuller revelation in Jesus Christ.

The disciples of the law continually questioned the disciples of Jesus and Jesus himself. "Why do the disciples transgress the tradition of the elders? for they wash not their hands when they eat bread" (Matt. 15:2). Repeatedly they accused Jesus of not keeping the Sabbath. It was probably at this feast—held on a Jewish fast day on which John's disciples and the Pharisees were fasting—that Matthew gave a feast to introduce Jesus to his friends. John's disciples came to Jesus saying, "How is it that we and the Pharisees fast often, but your disciples do not fast?" (Matt. 9:14 NIV). Really the question is "Why do Christians not observe the requirements and traditions of Judaism?"

II. Jesus replied in parables to this challenge (Matt. 9:15–17).

A. *Parable of the children of the bridechamber (Matt. 9:15).* "Children of the bride-chamber" refers to a wedding party. A wedding is a time of joy. Fasting is a sign of sorrow. It would be most inappropriate for the wedding party to fast while the bridegroom was with them.

1. The kingdom of God is joyful like a wedding. The gospel is good news. Jesus said, "These things have I spoken unto you, that my joy might remain in you, and that your joy might be full" (John 15:11), and "Whosoever drinketh of the water that I shall give him shall never thirst; but the water that I shall give him shall be in him a well of water springing up into everlasting life" (John 4:14). He also said, "I say unto you, there is joy in the presence of the angels of God over one sinner that repenteth" (Luke 15:10). The author of Hebrews said it was joy that motivated Jesus to go to the cross. "Looking unto Jesus the author and finisher of our faith; who for the joy that was set before him endured the cross, despising the shame, and is set down at the right hand of the throne of God" (Heb. 12:2).

2. Fasting is a sign of sadness. Jesus foretold his death by indicating that the day would come when the bridegroom would be taken away. Fasting would then be appropriate.

   Under the Mosaic law, only the Day of Atonement was designated as a fast day. The Pharisees had multiplied the fast days. In the parable, the Pharisee congratulates himself by saying, "I fast twice in the week" (Luke 18:12).

276

B. *Twin parables illustrate the relation of the new to the old.*

    1. The parable of the new patch on an old garment (Matt. 8:1). Most clothes in Jesus' day were made of wool. Wool when first wet shrinks tremendously. It would be most foolish to sew a piece of wool cloth that had not been shrunk on an old garment that was fully shrunk. The patch would shrink, and the tear in the garment would be worse than before. Christianity is not a patch on Judaism; it is not a sect of Judaism. This was the issue in the Jerusalem conference. "Some of the believers who belonged to the party of the Pharisees ... said, 'The Gentiles must be circumcised and required to keep the law of Moses'" (Acts 15:5 NIV). Paul and the apostles recognized that this was contrary to the gospel, which teaches that all people, whether Jew or Gentile, become Christians by faith in Jesus Christ. How wonderful that Paul won a victory for salvation by grace through faith for every person to come directly to God. No one must become a Jew before becoming a Christian.

    2. The parable of new wine in old wineskins (Matt. 9:17). One not knowing the customs of the day might be misled by the word *bottles* in the King James Version. The reference, of course, is to containers for wine made from the skins of goats or kids. After a time the skins became hardened and more likely to crack. If the new vintage was put in an old wineskin, the skin would probably burst when the juice began to ferment. New wine is to be put in new wineskins.

        The new gospel of the kingdom of God is powerful like fermenting wine. The old Judaic wineskins could not hold it. No longer were animals to be sacrificed. "Behold the Lamb of God, which taketh away the sin of the world" (John 1:29). There was no more need for the observance of the Passover. "For even Christ our passover is sacrificed for us" (1 Cor. 5:7). There was no longer need of temple or Holy Place. Worship of God according to Jesus is not restricted to special places. Jesus said to the woman at the well, "Believe me, the hour cometh, when ye shall neither in this mountain, nor yet at Jerusalem, worship the Father. Ye worship ye know not what: we know what we worship: for salvation is of the Jews. But the hour cometh, and now is, when the true worshippers shall worship the Father in spirit and in truth: for the Father seeketh such to worship him. God is a Spirit: and they that worship him must worship him in spirit and truth" (John 4:21–24). The distinctions of ceremonially clean or unclean persons, foods, and vessels was completely gone (see Matt. 15:1–20). The distinction between priest and laity was no more. Jesus was now the High Priest, and he invited every person to come unto God by him. "The veil of the temple was rent in twain from the top to the bottom" (Matt. 27:51), because Jesus opened the way for every person to come to God.

Conclusion

The old covenant has been fulfilled in the new covenant. The Old Testament as authority has passed away by fulfillment in Jesus. In a wonderful passage, Matthew 5:17–20, Jesus said that "one jot or one tittle shall in no wise pass from the law, till all be fulfilled" (v. 18). He did not say, as some erroneously interpret, that nothing would pass away. He said that nothing would fail to be fulfilled in him. In the illustrations that follow in Matthew 5:21–48, Jesus makes it clear that nothing of permanent value in the old is lost but all is carried to a higher plane by fulfillment in him. A bud is fulfilled by becoming a rose. A baby is fulfilled by becoming an adult. Is the bud lost? Is the baby lost? Yes, if you mean they are no more. No, in the sense that they have fulfilled their intended purpose. This has the most important practical bearing. The Old Testament is valuable. It is the history of God's progressive revelation. It contains the prophecies that were fulfilled in Jesus. It has many great insights that abide, but it is an old wineskin; it is an old garment; it is as out of place for the expression of Christian experience as fasting at a wedding. It was good; Christ is better. The final answer to any great question is to be found in Jesus, who said, "All power is given unto me in heaven and in earth" (Matt. 28:18). "For Christ is the end of the law for righteousness to every one that believeth" (Rom. 10:4). His Father would admonish us, "This is my beloved Son, in whom I am well pleased; hear ye him" (Matt. 17:5).

SUNDAY EVENING, SEPTEMBER 28

Title: God's Faithful Few

Text: "And the LORD said unto Gideon, By the three hundred men that lapped will I save you, and deliver the Midianites into thine hand; and let all the other people go every man unto his place" (**Judg. 7:7**).

Scripture Reading: Judges 7:1–23

Introduction

This evening we will look at an Old Testament example of faithfulness exhibited in Gideon and his army. For seven long years, Israel was troubled by the Midianites who came to destroy the increase of the fields. We read, "And Israel was greatly impoverished because of the Midianites" (Judg. 6:6). So afraid and so impoverished were they that they lived in dens, caves, and strongholds (6:2). Why this trouble for seven years? We read, "And the children of Israel did evil in the sight of the LORD; and the LORD delivered them into the hand of Midian seven years" (6:1).

In their anguish, the Israelites cried to the Lord, and he heard their cry. Gideon was called to lead Israel out of their pitiful plight. He issued a call for men, and 32,000 responded. God told Gideon that 32,000 were too many because Israel would vaunt themselves against God and claim the victory by their own hand. All of the fearful in the army were told to return home, and 22,000 turned back (Judg. 7:3). The Lord said 10,000 were too many to fight the Midianite army, which numbered 120,000 (8:10). "The LORD said unto Gideon, The people are yet too many; bring them down unto the water, and I will try them for thee there" (7:4). The sifting of the Lord took place, and only 300 were left of the 10,000. Think of it, a band of 300 men was left to fight 120,000 men.

It is always God's faithful few who get the Lord's work done. Seldom do the masses of people serve him. Let us look further at Gideon and his 300 men, God's faithful few.

I. God's faithful few are endowed with great assets.

A. *God's faithful few are endowed with a call from the Lord.* "The angel of the LORD appeared unto him, and said unto him, The LORD is with thee, thou mighty man of valor" (Judg. 6:12). Later, "the LORD said unto Gideon, By the three hundred men that lapped will I save you, and deliver the Midianites into thine hand" (7:7). No one will do much in this world until he or she hears the voice of the Lord. Our service will be in proportion to our hearing of the voice of the Lord.

B. *God's faithful few are endowed with faithfulness.* The beautiful verse reads, "And they stood every man in his place round about the camp" (7:21). Consider the results we would have today if every Christian stood in his or her place. The crying need of the hour is faithfulness. Only those who trust implicitly stand steady and ready.

C. *God's faithful few are endowed with confidence in the Lord's help (7:15).* Gideon felt inadequate for the task the angel of the Lord had assigned to him. He said, "Oh my LORD, wherewith shall I save Israel? behold, my family is poor in Manasseh, and I am the least in my father's house" (6:15). Gideon asked the Lord to show him a sign or two. This the Lord did, and Gideon became convinced that the Lord would help him in routing the Midianites.

D. *God's faithful few are endowed with humility (6:15).*

E. *God's faithful few are endowed with obedience (7:17–18).* Gideon's men were told to follow Gideon's example, and they did.

F. *God's faithful few are endowed with togetherness and unity.* Gideon's men were as one man with one sword. This is the way to victory. It was so in the day of Gideon, and it is so today.

II. God's faithful few render great service.

A. *God's faithful few render great service by undertaking the impossible.* Whoever heard of a band of 300 men taking on an army of 120,000? Gideon and the 300 believed in undertaking the impossible. Some Christians would be shocked and surprised if anything out of the ordinary ever happened to them. They never take on the impossible task for their Lord. These people are usually spiritually bankrupt and sometimes corrupt.

B. *God's faithful few render great service by holding fast to their convictions.* Many people hold opinions, but few hold fast to their convictions. We are not held by opinions but by convictions. There were only 300 men, but "they stood every man in his place" (7:21).

C. *God's faithful few render great service by holding the trust committed to them.* The task assigned Gideon and his 300 men must be performed. The trust in them must not be violated, must not be profaned.

D. *God's faithful few render great service by showing that God's work can be accomplished.* Too often the faithless and unbelieving say, "You are asking too much; it can't be done." But the faithful few teach us it can be done.

III. God's faithful few teach marvelous lessons.

A. *God's faithful few teach us that the Lord is active in history.* For seven long years, Israel cowered before the Midianites. For seven long years, Israel hid in caves, dens, and strongholds. For seven long years, their possessions, their food, and their land had been taken over by the Midianites. For seven long years, it appeared as if the Lord were dead. But he was not dead. He was at work in answering prayer, in Gideon and 300 men. God is active in history. History is "his story"!

B. *God's faithful few teach us that success is not dependent on numbers.* Would God use 32,000 or 10,000? No, he would use 300! We do not need to be anxious about counting heads when we are sure we are in God's will and busy about his work! We do not need to count numbers but need to learn how to make numbers count. God's people need not fear being in the minority. God is not dependent on numbers, and neither is success!

C. *God's faithful few teach us that it is moral influence that counts for him in this world (8:33–35).* It is a tragedy when people turn away from God, his will, his way, and his work.

D. *God's faithful few teach us that he will use us when we are dedicated to him.* God used Gideon, and he used the 300. He did not use the 31,700. Why? Wasn't it because they were fearful, careless, indifferent, and selfish? Wasn't it because they were not dedicated?

Conclusion

Are you one of the faithful few the Lord is using today? How do you classify yourself? Will you become one of the faithful few and let him accomplish his work through you?

OCTOBER

■ **Sunday Mornings**

The theme for the Sunday morning messages this month is "The Great Claims of Our Lord." John's gospel records a number of metaphors by which our Lord described his mission and ministry. These messages have an evangelistic objective, and they can also encourage the saints.

■ **Sunday Evenings**

A series of eight messages based on the book of Joshua is in view in October and November on the theme "The Walk and Work of Faith."

■ **Wednesday Evenings**

Continuing with the theme "The Bible Speaks to Our Condition," certain great chapters of the New Testament are used for the midweek services. The theme verse for the month is "He that hath an ear, let him hear what the Spirit saith unto the churches" (Rev. 2:29).

WEDNESDAY EVENING, OCTOBER 1

Title: The Bible Speaks to Our Condition

Scripture Reading: Matthew 6

Introduction

In the Sermon on the Mount, the lecture by heaven's infallible Teacher, we find Jesus contrasting the righteousness of the ideal citizen of the kingdom of God with the righteousness of the law and with the righteousness of the scribes and Pharisees.

Each of us needs to sit at Jesus' feet and listen to the words that fell from his lips. God will speak to our condition today if we will but open our minds and our hearts to him who spoke as man had never spoken before—or since.

I. The motive for kingdom righteousness (Matt. 6:1–18).

To Jesus the motive for the righteous conduct of a kingdom citizen was of primary importance. Without the proper motive, there could not be proper conduct. In the illustrations that follow, our Lord is contrasting the desire for the approval of God with the desire for the approval of people as a basis for motivation in religious service.

It is important that we examine our motives. Whose approval are we seeking?

Where do we get our deepest satisfaction? Are we seeking to please God, or are we seeking to please people?

A. *True piety and righteousness toward others—almsgiving (6:2–4).* Some give merely to receive the applause of people. If we would be properly motivated, we must give to please God and minister to the needs of others. The desire for the approval of people is not a worthy motive for citizens of the kingdom of heaven as they practice generosity and philanthropy toward the needy.

B. *True piety and righteousness toward God—prayer (6:5–15).* In these verses, our Lord gives authoritative teaching concerning the art of effective praying. The primary thought behind it all concerns the motive that we have when we go into God's presence in prayer. Jesus is declaring that one can be so deceived as to be motivated by the desire for the approval of people even when bowing to offer petitions to God. If prayer is to be genuine, it must be a conversation between a needy child to the heavenly Father rather than a speech made for the ears and applause of people.

C. *True piety or righteousness toward self—fasting (6:14–18).* In our personal, private discipline designed to produce genuine piety, we must beware lest we put on a show. Do you read the Bible day by day in order to be able to report to others that you have read all the way through the Bible? Do you pray that you might have the reputation of a person who prays much? Jesus affirmed that the genuine disciple would make no public display of personal piety with a desire to receive the applause of people. He would encourage us to seek supremely the approval of our heavenly Father. Our motives are of supreme importance.

II. The kingdom attitude toward things.

Ideal citizens of the kingdom must be rightly related to the world in which they live. Christians are faced with two problems in the light of material things. They are tempted to trust in them or to worry about them. Their trust must be in God rather than in material things.

A. *Jesus issued a warning against faith in material values (6:19–24).* Our Lord sounds some serious warnings against trusting in material things, for material things are perishable and do not have permanent value. They have temporary significance only.

Jesus taught that earthly treasures will master Christians if they do not master things first. They will master their desires and affections. If they major on materialistic values, they will destroy their ability to tell right from wrong so that they cannot trust their own conscience. Earthly treasures will master their will and make slaves of them if they give them priority in their lives.

B. *Jesus encouraged us to trust implicitly in the heavenly Father (6:25–34).* The only genuine alternative to the agony of anxiety is for one to have an implicit faith in the generosity and benevolent faithfulness of the heavenly Father.

In these verses, our Lord has much to say about the foolishness of a life of worry.

1. Worries are pagan (6:24).
2. Worries are secondary and unworthy (6:25).
3. Worries are useless (6:27).
4. Worries are pagan (6:32).
5. Worries are injurious (6:34).

Conclusion

Instead of living a life of worry, our Lord makes three positive suggestions that can help us overcome the agony of anxiety.

1. He suggests that we evaluate ourselves (6:26). We need to listen to a sermon from the sparrows and take a lesson from the lilies.
2. He suggests that each of us accept ourselves (6:27). This will relieve a lot of pressure and a lot of anxiety.
3. He suggests that we dedicate ourselves supremely to the kingdom (6:33). This will take our minds and hearts off the cares that distress, disturb, and upset us. It will give us a proper scale of values and a proper set of priorities for life.

May the Lord give us hearing ears as we listen to his words.

SUNDAY MORNING, OCTOBER 5

Title: I Am That Bread of Life

Text: "I am that bread of life" **(John 6:48).**

Scripture Reading: John 6:5–13, 26–27, 48–58

Hymns: "Guide Me, O Thou Great Jehovah," Williams

"The Lord Is My Shepherd," Montgomery

"He Leadeth Me!" Gilmore

Offertory Prayer: Heavenly Father, from your bountiful hand many blessings have come. We thank you for life. We are grateful for forgiveness. We rejoice in the opportunity to serve. You have bestowed on us the privilege of labor and, today, as an act of worship, we bring to you the fruit of our toil. Bless these tithes and offerings for a ministry of mercy to the suffering and a ministry of redemption of the lost through Jesus Christ. Amen.

Introduction

Modern psychologists are emphasizing the importance of a person's self-image. What people think of themselves is extremely important. It may well mean the difference between success and suicide. It is never true humility to have a low self-image, nor is it always arrogant to think well of oneself. Jesus was the ultimate pattern of humility, yet he made extravagant claims for himself. He even claimed to be God in the flesh.

Our message is the first of our series based on the self-applied metaphors of Jesus as recorded in John's gospel. A metaphor is a figure of speech denoting literally one thing yet meaning another. We say, "He is a ball of fire," "She is a cyclone," or "He is a wolf." These are metaphors.

Jesus said, "I am … bread."

I. The need of the bread (John 6:5).

There was no question but that hungry people needed bread. Early in the Bible, God says to Adam, "In the sweat of thy face shalt thou eat bread, till thou return unto the ground; for out of it wast thou taken; for dust thou art, and unto dust shalt thou return" (Gen. 3:19). Since then people have needed bread. It is the staff of life. Nothing takes the place of bread.

There is the same basic necessity for the soul. People are made with a spiritual appetite; they have a built-in hunger of spirit. One scholar has reported that every civilization has had three things: jails, temples, and cemeteries. He observed that this is because all people sin, worship, and die. That every civilization has had its temples is evidence of the basic need of people for spiritual bread. It is said that people are incurably religious. This is debatable, but because people are made in the image of God, they do have a soul hunger for bread.

II. The identity of the Bread (John 6:48).

To people who were informed about temporal bread and who had eaten personal bread, Jesus declared that he was the real Bread. He does not just give it. He *is* it. There is a loaf-shaped vacancy in every heart until Jesus comes in to fill it. Jesus attributes to himself as Bread five unique qualities.

A. *He has a unique origin (vv. 33, 41, 50).* Jesus is the Bread that "cometh down from heaven." He came from no earthly oven. He was no ordinary man. His origin was not earthly; it was heavenly. He was divine. The Passover bread had spiritual significance but was earthly in origin. The loaves our Lord blessed just before this discourse were earthly. They were multiplied by divine miracle, but they originated with humans. They came from a boy's lunch basket and not down from heaven. Jesus was and is the "bread of heaven."

B. *He is Living Bread (v. 51).* Jesus is no packaged loaf. No inert ingredients lie stored in him awaiting the temporary fancies of people. Moving, speaking, healing, and teaching, he lives forever.

C. *He is available Bread (v. 51).* "If *any* man eat of this bread, he shall live for ever." Any person can afford Jesus, but no person can afford not to have him. The invitation to eat is "Whosoever will, let him come." God's prophet asked, "Why spend money on what is not bread, and your labor on what does not satisfy? Listen, listen to me, and eat what is good, and you will delight in the richest of fare" (Isa. 55:2 NIV). This is the operational basis of all missions. This is the optimism of our evangelism. This colors all our theology because our God is "God our Saviour; who will have all men to be saved, and come unto the knowledge of the truth" (1 Tim. 2:3–4). As long as there is one person on the earth who has not come to a knowledge of Jesus, there is an urgent task for those of us who do know him.

D. *He is preserving Bread (v. 51)*. "If any man eat of this bread, he shall live for ever." Temporal bread has temporal limits, but eternal Bread has no limitation except eternity. The fathers ate, even the manna in the wilderness, yet they died. The real Bread has a future. Because Jesus lasts forever and comes into us, we last forever. Because he *is* life everlasting, we *have* life everlasting. This does not mean that we "get saved" and forget it. Daily replenishment of our lives is a part of his eternal nature.

E. *He is consumable Bread (v. 51)*. "And the bread that I will give is my flesh, which I will give for the life of the world." As earthly bread does not exist for itself, so Christ does not exist for himself. Earthly bread loses its identity, is transformed into life itself, when received and eaten. It is so with heavenly Bread.

F. *Bread is rejected (v. 66)*. "From that time many of his disciples went back, and walked no more with him" (John 6:66). In our Lord's parable of the great supper, many rejected the feast although the table was spread. The rich young ruler went away from Jesus a pauper because this Bread of Life was refused. It is unthinkable that a drowning man would refuse rescue or a dying man would refuse medical help, yet starving people refuse the Bread of Heaven.

"You can lead a horse to water, but you cannot make him drink." You can lead hungry people to the Bread of Heaven, but you cannot make them eat. As the final refusal of earthly food means physical suicide, so the refusal of Jesus means suicide of the soul.

III. The comparison of the Bread.

A. *Similarities.*

1. Both the bread "in the wilderness" and the true Bread came down from heaven. Each was an act of God.
2. Both the breads were and are for personal consumption. One person does not eat bread for another. Each must partake for oneself.
3. Both were miracles. The manna of the wilderness was a miracle of God (Ex. 16:11–21). The virgin birth of Jesus was a miracle of God (Luke 1:28–56).

B. *Contrasts.*

1. The bread given in the wilderness was for the physical body. The true Bread is given for the spiritual bodies of people.
2. The bread given in the wilderness sustained life temporarily. The true Bread sustains life everlastingly.

3. The bread given in the wilderness was temporary. The true Bread is permanent.

Conclusion

The testimony of millions is that Jesus satisfies. The promises of the Scriptures assure us that Jesus is the Bread of Life. Therefore, if you have never received him, "Taste and see that the LORD is good: blessed is the man that trusteth in him" (Ps. 34:8).

If we have tasted and seen that he is good, let us share him with those about us who hunger for spiritual bread that satisfies.

"Blessed are they which do hunger and thirst after righteousness: for they shall be filled" (Matt. 5:6).

SUNDAY EVENING, OCTOBER 5

Title: Conquering by Faith

Text: "... arise, go over this Jordan, ... you and all this people, into the land which I am giving to them, to the people of Israel. Every place that the sole of your foot will tread upon I have given to you, as I promised to Moses" (**Josh. 1:2–3 RSV**).

Scripture Reading: Joshua 1:1–9

Introduction

One of the most encouraging books of the Old Testament is the book of Joshua. All of us need to know the power of faith so that we can be "more than conquerors." God's Word says that "this is the victory that overcomes the world, our faith" (1 John 5:4). We need to know that we can conquer the challenges of the day by faith.

Joshua's life is a beautiful illustration of the power of faith. Joshua teaches us the key to victorious living. The principles Joshua lived by and by which he was successful are the same principles we may live by to be victorious in Christ. The key principle is faith.

Who was Joshua? He was the man God used to fulfill his promise to his people regarding the land of Canaan. He was born as a slave in Egypt but experienced the supernatural deliverance from Egypt, the crossing of the Red Sea.

During the second forty years of his life, Joshua was a minister to Moses, assisting, leading in battle, and observing the ways of the Lord.

Now Joshua had come to the time of his appointment as leader of the Israelites following Moses' death. In Moses was the anticipation of the Promised Land; in Joshua was the realization of it.

Joshua's heart and life were prepared for this challenge. Numbers 27:18 says that he was "a man in whom is the Spirit" (RSV). He was controlled by the Spirit of God. Numbers 32:10–12 says that he was a man who wholly followed God in faith. He was victorious and obedient. Deuteronomy 34:9 says he was "full of the spirit of wisdom" (RSV). Joshua can teach us how to conquer by faith.

I. Faith's challenge (Josh. 1:2).

Verse 2 indicates that it is a challenge from God to accept his Word and act on it. Joshua's greatest challenge is to see what *God* will do! He had already seen God at work in other victorious experiences in Egypt, at the Red Sea, and against Amalek.

Joshua already knew what people could not do. Numbers 13 and 14 record the Kadesh-barnea experience and the bitter consequences of unbelief. And just as Israel suffered these consequences, so does unbelief disqualify us from service and God's success. A life lived according to self is like Israel wandering in the desert for an entire generation. It is a picture of the carnal life of a Christian.

Now God challenges Joshua to go into the land and possess it. It is a challenge to experience the victory God had already given. It is God's commission to him. This is our challenge: to experience the victorious life in Jesus Christ and to experience spiritual conquest in obeying the Lord's commission to us following his resurrection.

II. Faith's assurance (Josh. 1:5, 9).

God not only commands; he also assures fulfillment. His promises are ever ours to accept.

A. *The promise of divine authority.* All of God is behind his Word. God's "I will" is enough! As he commands us to service, so he obligates himself to see us through (John 15:16; Phil. 1:6).

B. *There is the promise of divine faithfulness.* Verse 5 states God's promise of his abiding presence: "I will be with thee." This is not just for Joshua; it is repeated elsewhere in the Bible, especially in Hebrews 13:5. This is God's eternal principle made real through the ministry of the Holy Spirit.

III. Faith's appropriation (Josh. 1:3).

As Joshua responded by faith, the promise would be fulfilled in every place that the sole of his foot would tread. Here is the principle of appropriation. He was to claim what God had already given. God promises to give the land, but the people must possess it. God provides, faith takes. God waited for them to believe his Word and claim the land for themselves. It was legally theirs from the moment God uttered his promise; it was experientially theirs when they entered the land to possess it.

All of God's provisions are waiting to be claimed today. After we have claimed salvation in Jesus Christ by faith, there are other vast spiritual possessions in Christ that we are challenged to claim in faith. When we do, we are wonderfully rich; when we do not, many of the Lord's riches remain unclaimed.

IV. Faith's victory (Josh. 1:5).

In verse 2, Joshua is told to "go over this Jordan." In verse 5, he is assured that not any man would be able to stand before him—nothing could stop faith in action. Verse 10 records that Joshua accepts the challenge and moves out according to God's Word. Verse 16 describes the people's response in obedience to God's command through Joshua. Victory is assured in God's word to Joshua. And the rest of the book of Joshua tells the story.

V. Faith's secret (Josh. 1:7–8).

Verses 7 and 8 teach that successful living is living by the principles of God's Word. It was God's purpose for Joshua that if he was to be a leader, he must have spiritual discipline in his life through the Word of God. There was also to be absolute obedience—obedience to the Word of God, the source of our strength and courage. If we are to experience God's secret to life, we must get into God's Word and meditate on it, allowing it to do its work in us.

Conclusion

How can you exercise faith today? You can accept God's challenge to you, whatever it is. You have some "land" to conquer. You can believe in Jesus Christ and receive him as your Savior and Lord. You can believe that God will never leave you nor forsake you. You can believe that God has an answer for your problem, your suffering, your circumstance. You can believe God's Word and begin today reading it, memorizing it, and meditating on it.

WEDNESDAY EVENING, OCTOBER 8

Title: The Bible Speaks to Our Condition
Scripture Reading: Matthew 7

Introduction

The great chapter from the New Testament through which we will let the Lord speak to us today is the concluding portion of the Sermon on the Mount. We see from the closing verses of this lecture from heaven's infallible Teacher that his purpose for us is a life that is stable and satisfying. He wants to deliver us from the storms and stresses of life that would destroy and disappoint.

I. A warning against improper judgments (Matt. 7:1–6).

Some people labor under the impression that our Lord forbids the use of our power to discriminate and to arrive at moral decisions. For him to do so would be to deny us the use of one of God's greatest gifts to humanity. Rather, our Lord forbids improper judgments, snap judgments, superficial judgments, unkind judgments, and untrue judgments.

In these words, he forbids our reaching a decision and pronouncing a verdict without considering all of the evidence. We must beware of and guard against the snap judgment that places someone else either in a very favorable or a very adverse light. He is suggesting that we treat others and judge others in the same manner and method by which we would want our own case to be considered.

The real focus of attention is on self-judgment. We could be more critical of ourselves than of others.

II. The habit of prayer is encouraged (Matt. 7:7–11).

The habit of prayer is encouraged. The nature of our loving Father God is the main basis on which we should have faith in the efficacy of prayer. God is good. He always will be good.

III. The golden rule (Matt. 7:12).

To practice the Golden Rule is to bring a foretaste of heaven into the present.

IV. Voluntary self-discipline is necessary (Matt. 7:13–14).

Our Lord believed that one must voluntarily discipline self in order to experience fullness of life. He points out that those who aimlessly drift live a life of mediocrity.

The broad way against which Jesus warns is not so much the road that leads to hell hereafter as it is the way that leads to a hell in the here and now.

To achieve significantly, one must choose the pathway of voluntary self-discipline and then follow that discipline. This leads to fullness of life in the chosen area of endeavor.

V. A warning against false teachers (Matt. 7:15–20).

We must beware of false teachers who come to us claiming to speak authentically for God. We must beware lest we listen to the many different voices in the world that would lead us astray. We each must do our own listening, because we each will do our own suffering if we follow a false way of life.

VI. Profession plus practice (Matt. 7:21–23).

It takes something more than a pious profession to satisfy the heart of a person. It takes something more than mere words to be pleasing to God. We can be sure of the genuineness of our profession only when it leads to a practice of the implications of our profession.

VII. Life built upon a rock (Matt. 7:24–27).

Are we building our lives on the shifting sands of time? Are we mere hearers of the Word? Is our religion merely the religion of our forefathers, or is it real to us? Do we listen responsively to the words of the Lord Jesus, and do we recognize his lordship? Only those who both hear and heed can be sure of a stable life when the storms begin to blow.

Conclusion

Jesus was an authoritative teacher. His authority grew out of his unique person, the absolute truthfulness of what he taught, and his purpose of love for us.

Today God wants to speak to our hearts through this portion of his Word. May we have ears to hear.

SUNDAY MORNING, OCTOBER 12

Title: I Am the Light of the World

Text: "I am the light of the world" (**John 8:12**).

Scripture Reading: John 1:1–9; 8:12

Hymns: "The Light of the World Is Jesus," Bliss

"We've a Story to Tell," Nichol

"Rescue the Perishing," Crosby

Offertory Prayer: Our heavenly Father, through the testimony of others we have learned of your great love for us. We thank you for the gift of salvation. Gratitude compels us to desire to share the good news of your love with a lost world. Today we bring our tithes and offerings that the ministry of preaching and teaching and healing and serving of Jesus Christ might be carried to all parts of the earth. Bless these tithes and offerings. To that purpose we pray in Jesus' name. Amen.

Introduction

Most of us have been taught that the sun is the center of our solar system and thus is the light of the world. The sun is 93 million miles from earth. If a baby should start flying to the sun at birth and travel 150 miles per hour, he or she would be nearly seventy-one years of age upon arrival. Astronomers estimate that the diameter of the sun is 109 times that of the earth. Its output of energy is 70,000 horsepower per square yard per minute. The temperature at its surface is about 10,000 degrees Fahrenheit. But the Light of the World is not the sun. It is the Son. Jesus declared himself to be such. It was he who made the sun, for he was coexistent with the Father in creation. With one bold stroke, Jesus declared, "I am the light of the world." Though it is beyond our grasp, let us reach out by faith and try to apprehend some of our Lord's meaning in this self-addressed metaphor of the Master.

I. Light is repulsive.

Immediately before Jesus proclaimed that he was the Light of the World, the scribes and Pharisees brought to him a woman taken in the act of adultery and demanded of him an opinion of her punishment in the light of Moses' Law. Jesus stooped and wrote on the ground. Then he said to them, "He that is without sin among you, let him first cast a stone at her" (John 8:7). Then he wrote again, and when he looked up, the accusers had fled one by one until only the condemned woman was left. The truth was that they did not like the light.

290

Turn over a log in the woods, and bugs will scurry everywhere, not because they fear you, but because light is repulsive to them.

Two chapters earlier, Jesus had preached the crowd away. This is foreign and unwelcome truth for our day. We want crowd getters. We want to "pack 'em in," but Jesus frequently thinned them out.

The gospel has always been a stumbling block. Paul declared, "But we preach Christ crucified, unto the Jews a stumbling block, and unto the Greeks foolishness" (1 Cor. 1:23).

It was this very quality of the light our Lord so vividly described. "And this is the condemnation, that light is come into the world, and men loved darkness rather than light, because their deeds were evil. For every one that doeth evil hateth the light, neither cometh to the light, lest his deeds should be reproved" (John 3:19–20).

II. Because light is repulsive, light is rejected.

"He was in the world, and the world was made by him, and the world knew him not. He came unto his own, and his own received him not" (John 1:10–11).

Can you easily think of a dying person refusing a doctor? Can you readily imagine a starving person rejecting bread? Can you comprehend a drowning person refusing rescue or a freezing person refusing a warm house, or the captain of a sinking ship spurning help? Yet the Light was rejected, and he still is rejected by many. Why?

A. *The nature of humanity is sinful.*

B. *Those who live in darkness do not want their evil deeds to be exposed.*

C. *Some people are ignorant of the blessing of the true Light.*

D. *The prince of darkness, Satan, rules in the hearts of unregenerated people.*

But woven into the fabric of all this divine truth is the fact that light is revealing.

III. Light is revealing.

A. *The Light reveals us to ourselves.* We never see ourselves truly until we see ourselves in the context of Christ. In that Light, Thomas saw himself and cried out, "My Lord and my God" (John 20:28).

In that Light, the woman of Samaria saw herself and said, "Come, see a man, which told me all things that ever I did" (John 4:29).

In that Light, the robber saw himself and asked, "Lord, remember me when thou comest into thy kingdom" (Luke 23:42).

B. *The Light reveals the identity of Christ to us.* The woman at the well saw herself, but she also saw Jesus and identified him: "Is not this the Christ?" (John 4:29).

The two who walked the road to Emmaus finally recognized Jesus in the light of his own revelation.

The Light shone, and John so recognized Jesus that he declared without hesitation, "Behold the Lamb of God, which taketh away the sin of the world" (John 1:29).

C. *The Light reveals the Father.* Philip voiced the yearning of many a disciple when he requested, "Lord, shew us the Father" (John 14:8). Beautifully and blessedly, Jesus claimed his own deity when he testified, "He that hath seen me hath seen the Father.... Believe me that I am in the Father, and the Father in me" (John 14:9–11). Clearly the Light reveals the Father. Hear him say, "I and my Father are one" (John 10:30).

D. *The Light reveals the way of salvation.* "He that followeth me shall not walk in darkness, but shall have the light of life" (John 8:12).

"I am the way, the truth and the life: no man cometh unto the Father, but by me" (John 14:6).

Never has so much light been thrown on any subject as when the Light of the World shone on his subjects, on himself, on the Father, and on the way of redemption.

IV. Light is refining.

Wherever Jesus has come into the hearts of people, there has been a refining, purifying, uplifting influence.

When Jesus came into the demoniac, the evil spirits went out. When he came into the heart of Simon, holy refinement followed. As sunlight purifies, so the Sonlight of God purifies wherever he shines.

V. Light is regulating.

The ordinary traffic lights that we encounter daily are regulatory. We stop, we go, we use caution, we turn, we observe signs because of lights. Landing lights at airports guide the giant metal birds through the night to safe landings.

In some comparable way, the great light of Jesus Christ regulates the traffic of life when he is permitted to do so. He tells us when to go and when to stop. He flashes the warning signals. He guides us through our nights to safe landings.

There is a simple story of a man who drove his team and wagon swiftly and safely on a road through a dark forest. Afterward he was asked how he knew where all the trees were along the road so that he could miss them as he drove the narrow road. He replied that he did not know where they were. He added, "I looked up at the opening between the treetops and knew that if I followed the light above I could be safe." Oh, that people might do so in their spiritual journey!

VI. Light is reassuring.

There is reassurance in the lights of the city as one comes home. There is comfort in seeing the light in the window of one's own house. The lights of the shore reassure as the returning ship approaches the harbor.

It is so with our Light. We are coming to our heavenly home, and the Light is shining gloriously there for us. Oh, what reassurance!

Conclusion

The Light of the World is Jesus. Let him reveal yourself, himself, the Father, and the way of life to you. Let us let him and his presence refine us and make us pure. Let us permit him to regulate every mile of the journey. Let us be reassured and encouraged that Christ shines forever for his own.

This Light is for every person. You can have him. Will you not take him and let him shine for you and through you?

SUNDAY EVENING, OCTOBER 12

Title: Crossing the Jordan

Text: "Joshua rose early in the morning; and they removed from Shittim, and came to Jordan, he and all the children of Israel, and lodged there before they passed over" (**Josh. 3:1**).

Scripture Reading: Joshua 3

Introduction

The book of Joshua is important to everyone who will listen to it. Chapter 1 describes God's challenge to Joshua and his assurances to his faith. Chapter 2 describes the two spies who were sent out to search the land secretly and how God provided for their deliverance through Rahab. Their report is stated in Joshua 2:23–24.

Joshua believed that surely it was God's will to cross into the land and possess it, so he wasted no time. Verse 1 indicates that he rose early in the morning and got the nation to begin moving. They moved from Shittim and came to Jordan.

Between them and the land of abundance was the Jordan River. Humanly speaking, to cross the Jordan was an impossibility. Verse 15 indicates that it was a time of overflow; the river was flooding. There were no bridges and only a few fords, and these were impassable during this season. How could they cross with the women, children, and baggage?

The historical fact is that the people did cross the flooding Jordan to enter the land. God had a plan, and in his power he performed it. What was God's plan to follow? Chapter 3 describes step by step how they were to move when the priests moved the ark. The priests were to lead the way before the people, and when they came to the Jordan, they were to stand still in it. What happened is described in verses 13–17.

Why was there such an urgency about this? Why was it necessary to go into the land at this precise time? Why not wait until the river was down and not flooding? There are several answers to these questions. For one, thing, it was God's timing, and God's timing is always perfect. It was also God's opportunity to demonstrate his power, as seen in verse 10. And it provided an opportunity for the Israelites to exercise their faith. Finally, it was God's way of magnifying Joshua, and this was very important to the people because Joshua was to be God's instrument for leadership. There are two truths to be shared from this experience.

I. The significance of crossing the Jordan.

For Israel the significance of crossing the Jordan was a definite historical experience in which the people left the desert life to enter into the land of abundance. The victory was miraculously given, and God magnified himself in his plan of conquering the land. The people showed commitment by going into the land and entering into warfare to possess the land and to enjoy its benefits.

For us, "crossing the Jordan" is not symbolic of entering heaven; it is symbolic of the Christian entering into the abundant life God has promised in Jesus Christ. It is not passing into eternity; it illustrates passing from one level of Christian experience to another level in the Lord.

Egypt in Israel's life was representative of sin and bondage. The deliverance from Egypt, miraculously, was representative of salvation—new birth and spiritual deliverance. The wilderness in the life of Israel was representative of the carnal life of Christians who live in self-centeredness, defeat, discouragement, and unbelief. Canaan was representative of the triumph that people experience. It included both conflict and rest, but it also had the abundant life that God had promised. Canaan was representative of the victorious Christian life.

Therefore, the Jordan River crossing is the gateway to the conquering life. It is the experience that leads to the obtaining of our spiritual possessions in Christ Jesus. Ephesians 1:3 refers to all the spiritual blessings that we have in heavenly places in Christ. "The crossing" is that moment of victory when we make our lives available to God, to cause us to possess all that truly belongs to us in Jesus Christ. It is that point when self-life and its control end and the Christ-life begins. It marks the separation between the carnal Christian and a Christ-controlled Christian.

II. The secret to crossing the Jordan.

How are we to do it? For Israel the secret of crossing the Jordan was listening to God's words and obeying them, as seen in verse 9. It was also by following the ark of the covenant in faith. This required cleansed lives, as in verse 5, and confidence in God's promises and power (vv. 5, 7, 11).

Chapter 3 contains ten references to the ark. According to this chapter, it was the key to the victory Israel had over the Jordan River. What was the ark? It was the most outstanding piece of furniture in the tabernacle. It represented the presence of God. It contained the two tables of stone on which the law was written by the finger of God, and it represented the awesome power, holiness, and presence of the living God. It resided in the Holy of Holies—God's continual dwelling place with humanity.

For us the ark is a type of the person of the Lord Jesus Christ. On the ark was a cover of gold called the mercy seat. This mercy seat represents Jesus Christ, who was God's propitiation through his blood. Just as the Israelites were to focus their attention on the ark, so are we to focus attention on Christ. We are not to focus attention on our frustrations, circumstances, or surroundings, but we are to keep our eyes on Jesus Christ.

The secret to crossing the Jordan, the spiritual victory over the self-life into a Christ-controlled life, is related to three steps to victory. First, we must desire sincerely to be victorious. Joshua 1:16 indicates that the people were willing and eager to enter into the land. How about you? The second step is to confess our sins and be cleansed (cf. 1 John 1:9). The sins of our lives must be confronted and God's cleansing experienced. The third step is to surrender by faith to Jesus Christ. Jesus Christ is God's plan of victory for us. As the ark led the Israelites to victory, so does Jesus Christ lead us.

Conclusion

It is not God's will for any person to live in Egypt spiritually. He is not willing that any should perish. Neither is it God's will for any Christian to live in the wilderness spiritually, because of all that is related to it—ignorance, unbelief, sin, and pride. It *is* God's will to enter into the land of Canaan spiritually, to cross over the Jordan, to experience the power of God in our lives and to make ourselves available to him now.

WEDNESDAY EVENING, OCTOBER 15

Title: The Bible Speaks to Our Condition

Scripture Reading: Matthew 8

Introduction

The great chapter through which we would let God speak to us today describes the diversity of the ministry of our Lord. He wants to come today into every type of situation to minister in mercy and in power. Each of us needs to let him work in us and through us.

I. The cleansing of a leper (Matt. 8:1–4).

The lepers were the untouchables of that day. Everyone else, but especially the leper, was surprised when Jesus reached forth his hand and touched him. Immediately he was cleansed.

Jesus will come into the midst of our situation today and give us the healing and cleansing touch of his grace and power if we will permit him to do so.

II. The prayer of an outsider (Matt. 8:5–13).

The centurion was no doubt a Gentile. He did not approach our Lord on the basis of his own faithfulness and his own moral merit. He approached our Lord on the basis of our Lord's compassion and power. He had faith to believe that Jesus had the authority to heal disease at a distance. Jesus did not have to place his hand on a person to impart healing. Our Lord was amazed at the greatness of the faith of this outsider.

Let us beware lest we put restrictions on the disposition of our God to hear and answer the prayers of those who have no relationship to him except that which his grace permits.

May we be granted the gift of faith and use it as did the centurion.

III. The healing of the sick (Matt. 8:14–17).

Our Lord is the great Healer. He heals all kinds of sickness—of the mind, body, and spirit. Let us invite him to come in as the divine Minister and Healer in every possible illness today.

IV. The priorities of life (Matt. 8:18–23).

Our Lord recognizes that many people live unsatisfying lives because they do not have the right priorities. He declares that if one is to be a true follower of God's will, material things must not have top priority. He also declares that God's will must have priority over the claims of family.

V. What to do in a storm (Matt. 8:24–27).

The storms of life are bound to come upon each individual, family, and nation. What will you do when the winds begin to blow and the waves begin to toss the ship of your life? The disciples turned to our Lord with a plea for help. Even though their faith was feeble, Jesus responded to their plea and commanded the winds to cease blowing and the waves to stop tossing.

When Christ is on board the vessel of your life, you will enjoy a degree of safety that is not to be found at any other place or time.

VI. Do you love pigs more than people? (Matt. 8:28–34).

This is a strange incident in the life of our Savior. It gives rise to many questions. It is interesting to note that seemingly the citizens of this village were more concerned about the pigs who had committed "hogicide" than they were for the welfare of the man out of whom the demons had been cast.

Which is more important, pigs or the lives of people in distress?

Conclusion

Surely we can hear the voice of God speaking to our condition through one of these incidents in the life of our Lord: "He that hath ears to hear, let him hear."

SUNDAY MORNING, OCTOBER 19

Title: I Am the Door

Text: "I am the door" (**John 10:9**).

Scripture Reading: John 10:1–10

Hymns: "Jesus! the Very Thought of Thee," Bernard of Clairvaux

"Saviour, More Than Life," Crosby

"Jesus Saves," Owens

Offertory Prayer: Holy Father, your Holy Spirit has come to dwell in our physical bodies to make us holy. Take now the substance of our hands and bless and use it for holy purposes. We pray this in the name of Jesus, our Savior. Amen.

Introduction

This is the third metaphor our Lord employed in revealing himself to his disciples. Types, symbols, and figures have always been used by God, but they have frequently been misused by people as they have cited these very figures to support their own pet theories and theological fabrications.

Let us be zealous to see all that our Lord sought to reveal, but let us be careful that our zeal does not warp our judgment to the point that we read into this figure more than was intended.

I. Pastorale.

The language of Jesus was more meaningful to the people of Palestine than it is to those who do not live in sheep country today. We are told that many flocks of sheep were brought to one sheepfold and enclosed for the night. Each of these flocks had its own shepherd. Each shepherd would bring his sheep in for the night and call for them the next morning. Frequently there was one common keeper of all the flocks through the night. It was a preventive measure to guard the sheep against their many enemies.

II. Pests.

Predators were always after the sheep. Then there were also thieves and robbers. Of these Jesus observed, "The thief cometh not, but for to steal, and to kill, and to destroy" (John 10:10).

In the spiritual realm, there were also those who came before Jesus; that is, those who claimed spiritual priority above Jesus. We must remember that Jesus spoke to the Pharisees (John 9:40).

It has been suggested that these very Pharisees made the simple way of salvation so difficult that they were as those who would "climb up some other way." Jesus may have been saying to them that instead of using the door, they preferred to use their own ecclesiastical ladders and their own religious inventions. This is likely an apt interpretation. If it is, then let it be observed that then as well as now there are scarcely any pests as pestiferous as religious ones.

III. Preeminence.

Jesus declared that he is *the* Door. The ark had but one door, and Dr. George Truett was fond of saying that the big elephant and the little ant both entered through the same door. He would then remind his congregation that the businessman and the child must come into the kingdom through the same door.

This singularity, this exclusiveness, this monopoly—all of these were packed tersely into the statement of Jesus, "I am the way, the truth, and the life: no man cometh unto the Father, but by me" (John 14:6). This same deep conviction prompted Peter to declare, "Neither is there salvation in any other: for there is none other name under heaven given among men, whereby we must be saved" (Acts 4:12). There is perhaps no more fatal heresy than the teaching that Jesus is an optional way of salvation.

IV. Porter.

We do not overlabor the figure if we suggest that the porter is the Holy Spirit. It is he who makes the door available. It is he who points to the door. He is the divine usher who attends the door. Just as he opens the door, he also closes the door. For those enclosed, the Holy Spirit guarantees complete safety.

Without the drawing of the Holy Spirit to the door, none may enter for salvation and life. And there is a time when the final offense against the Holy Spirit so grieves him that he closes the door.

V. Promise.

A. *The promise is universal.* "If any man" is the condition of the invitation.
B. *The promise is sure.* "He shall be saved" is the blessed assurance.
C. *The promise is for liberty.* "He shall go in and out" is the scope of freedom. As the use of earthly doors affords liberty and freedom in that which is beyond these doors, so the access to the divine door brings freedom indeed.
D. *The promise is for sustenance.* "He shall find pasture" is the guarantee. The Christian is alive, moving, going and coming, always strengthened by the pasture.

VI. Prescription.

The blessings of the door are received on one condition, and that one condition is that one "enter in." Doors are not primarily for decoration, although some are appealing. Their primary purpose is not to bear the name plates or the house numbers. Doors are for entrance and exit. Those who were saved from the flood were those who "entered in" to the ark. The six cities of refuge (Num. 35) afforded immunity and security to only those who would "enter in." Those who partook of the marriage feast were those who purposed to "enter in." This is the human side of salvation; it involves will, choice, and action. We never satisfy our hunger by admiring bread; we eat it. We are not cured by examining and analyzing medicine; we take it. So it is with the door. Unless we "enter in," it becomes but another wall.

Conclusion

Let us not be overcome by the spiritual pests that plague our way. Let us know, once and for all, that Jesus is the only Door. He is the entrance to salvation and the exit from many of life's perils.

We cannot afford to ignore the courteous, personal work of the Holy Spirit as he presides at the threshold of the door. May we claim the promises and find salvation, freedom, and sustenance for our souls. And let us act now!

SUNDAY EVENING, OCTOBER 19

Title: The Triumph of Faith

Text: "Now Jericho was straitly shut up because of the children of Israel: none went out, and none came in. And the LORD said unto Joshua, See, I have given into thine hand Jericho, and the king thereof, and the mighty men of valour" (**Josh. 6:1–2**).

Scripture Reading: Joshua 6

Introduction

Why was Jericho so important? Jericho was the key city to Israel's whole campaign in the land of Canaan. Once that obstacle was removed, the armies of Israel could spread out in all directions. Israel could not retreat. Behind them was the Jordan River overflowing its banks, the desert, the Red Sea, and Egypt. They had committed themselves to God's Word. Now it was time to begin possessing the land. Jericho stood in the way of possessing what God had promised and had potentially given to the Israelites.

Jericho was a strong fortress about three miles in circumference. It was strategically located, guarding all the passes to the interior of Canaan.

The fall of Jericho is a literal fact of history. Joshua is the first book of history to record it as such and describes in detail Jericho's previous conquests. Five hundred years later it was referred to when the city was rebuilt. And in New Testament times the fall of Jericho is referred to in the book of Hebrews. Also, archaeology confirms the fall of Jericho. Dr. John Garstang excavated the ruins of Jericho in the 1930s and found pottery and scarab evidence that the city had been destroyed about 1400 BC, coinciding with Joshua's date. He also found that the walls did actually fall down flat (v. 20). There were double walls fifteen feet apart. The outer wall was six feet thick, the inner wall twelve feet thick. The walls were thirty feet high and were linked together by houses built across the top. The outer walls fell outward, down the hillside, dragging the inner wall and houses with it. Verse 24 speaks of the city being burned with fire. Archaeologists have concluded that there are marked signs of conflagration and destruction.

The fall of Jericho is not only a literal fact of history; it is also a living spiritual lesson of the triumph of faith. Joshua does not say this pointedly, but its evidence is discerned throughout the experience. Hebrews 11:30 says that "by faith the walls of Jericho fell down."

All the progress and victories Israel experienced were victories God wrought by faith. Faith is a spiritual principle of life for us all. Faith is trusting God and his Word, relying on his promises and truth. Romans 4:20–21 reveals that Abraham's faith was the secret to his life and victories. The world does not understand faith, considering it foolish and illogical. Rather, it emphasizes human power. But faith rests in the power of God to fulfill his Word.

I. Faith's conflicts.

Jericho represents the opposition and conflict Israel would face in possessing the land. God, however, promised life to them. In possessing the spiritual blessings God has given us, we, too, confront spiritual conflicts. In the gospel of John, Jesus indicates that the world does not hate its own but that it does hate Jesus and his followers.

Verse 2 describes the victorious assurance that Israel had. Just as they experienced this assurance, so do we have peace through Jesus Christ (John 14:27; 16:33). Faith accepts the reality of conflict and claims God's victory. Christians have conflict with the world, flesh, and the devil—all of the invisible forces of the evil world—but Jesus Christ gives victory (Eph. 6).

II. Faith's obedience.

Victory over Jericho depended on the obedience of Israel to God's command. God spoke and Joshua listened, believed, obeyed, and acted. Victory was dependent on obedience to God's plan (vv. 3–5). The Israelites were to march around the city each day for six days and seven times on the seventh day. There was to be no noise made except for the blowing of rams' horns. This was God's plan. He did not tell why; they were merely to obey. Obedience is based on the faith that God is sufficient. We are to trust God to fulfill his purpose.

Faith disciplines itself in the silence that the people experience. There was to be no complaining, no suggesting, no frivolous talk; there was to be utter silence. In other words, keep silent and let God work. Victory is experienced in letting God give us triumph in his way (John 15:5; Phil. 1:6; 4:13).

III. Faith's secret.

The key fact of the procession was the ark of God, as it was when the people crossed the Jordan River victoriously. Eleven times the ark of God is mentioned in Joshua 6. God was undeniably with his people. We need Jerichos today to challenge our faith, to put us on our knees, to give God an opportunity to demonstrate his power. We need fresh experiences of faith for the new generation. The secret of faith is trusting God. *He* is our victory.

IV. Faith's patience.

The Israelites were to circle the city thirteen times in seven days, and all during this time the walls of the city were stout and forbidding. God required that they wait on him and demonstrate patience in his willingness to work. Possibly he is teaching us some quality that needs to be developed in us—that we are helpless within ourselves, that victory is his. Can you keep on trusting when outward results are not happening? Victory may be just moments away. When it was all accomplished, it was all God's victory. The Israelites were physically exhausted, and what resulted was the working of God's power. Sometimes faith demands that we rest in the Lord and wait patiently for him.

V. Faith's achievement.

Faith's achievement is symbolized in a shout of victory (vv. 16, 20). It came at the close of the last time around the city. Every step around the city was a step of the appropriation of faith. The city had to be circled thirteen times before the shout of victory was given. The shout was the outward expression of the people's inward faith in their omnipotent God. The walls were still intact immediately prior to the shout. There was a risk of everything upon God's faithfulness. Then it happened! The city was demolished, burned, and cursed. Faith had achieved the victory.

Conclusion

How are we to see God's supernatural power unless we let him give us a Jericho challenge? What is the Jericho in your spiritual life? Can you trust God to work today as then? God's will is for us to experience victory and power in our lives. Once we cross Jordan and yield ourselves to him and his will, he will give us victory in all of our spiritual conflicts.

WEDNESDAY EVENING, OCTOBER 22

Title: The Bible Speaks to Our Condition

Scripture Reading: Matthew 17

Introduction

The great chapter through which we will let our Lord speak to our condition today describes one of the truly great experiences in the life of our Lord.

I. An experience on a mountaintop (Matt. 17:1–8).

It is interesting to note that our Lord felt the need to go apart for prayer and communion with God. It is also interesting that he took several intimate friends with him for this experience of prayer and fellowship with God. It is significant that as he prayed there was an inward transformation that expressed itself in an outward transfiguration of his countenance.

In this prayer experience, Moses and Elijah came to communicate with Jesus, and I would assume, to encourage him as he faced the ordeal of his exodus, his death on the cross, his resurrection from the dead, and his ascension to the Father.

While on the mountaintop, Jesus' disciples heard a voice of identification and commendation from heaven. By this experience they came to a new recognition of his unique person and his divine authority.

It is possible today for us to have experiences with God that bring enlightenment and encouragement as we face great crises.

II. The suffering in the valley (Matt. 17:14–21).

The tremendous experience on the mountaintop was not designed to produce a mystical experience that would provide emotional satisfaction for the disciples. At the bottom of the mountain there is always a suffering, needy world that needs the ministry of those who have been on a mountaintop with God.

It is most interesting to note how our Lord responded to the faltering faith of a fearful father as he prayed for a helpless son. By this experience, our Lord would encourage every distressed father and mother to bring their needy children before God's throne of grace for help and for mercy in time of need.

III. Jesus speaks of his approaching death (Matt. 17:22–23).

The death of Christ on the cross was no accident in God's plan. Jesus lived and labored under the burden of Calvary long before the cross was ever placed on his shoulder. His love for us is an unmerited and sacrificial love as well as a suffering love. With a steadfast, unflinching dedication and determination, he moved toward his cross.

Paul prayed that he might know "the fellowship of [Christ's] sufferings." Most of us try to avoid this knowledge and experience.

IV. The payment of taxes (Matt. 17:24–27).

It is interesting to note that the conclusion of this great chapter, which has said so many significant things about the heart and life of the Lord of life, would also speak concerning his paying the taxes that were expected from every good citizen of the country. We have a responsibility toward our country that we fulfill only as we pay our portion of the taxes that are necessary for the function of government.

Conclusion

May the God of grace and mercy enlarge our hearing capacity to hear what he would have us to hear as we study a great chapter like this.

SUNDAY MORNING, OCTOBER 26

Title: I Am the Way

Text: "I am the way" (**John 14:6**).

Scripture Reading: John 14:1–6

Hymns: "Joyful, Joyful, We Adore Thee," van Dyke

           "Blessed Redeemer," Christiansen

           "The Old Rugged Cross," Bennard

Offertory Prayer: Heavenly Father, you have given your Son to die on the cross for us. You have given us the Holy Spirit to dwell in our hearts. You have given us eternal life, which causes us to hunger after you and to love you. Today we give ourselves completely to you. Accept our tithes and offerings as tokens of our desire to belong completely to you, through Jesus Christ our Lord. Amen.

Introduction

This is another metaphor of the Master that he employed in an effort to communicate to those nearest him. Webster has defined a metaphor as "the use of a word or phrase literally denoting one kind of object or idea in place of another by way of suggesting a likeness or analogy between them."

To those in darkness Jesus had affirmed, "I am the light." To the hungry Jesus had declared, "I am the bread." To the separated he had asserted, "I am the door." Now, to those so uncertain of where he was going and where they were going, he announced, "I am the way."

In the context of our Lord's announcement, let us observe:

I. An evident desperation.

"Lord, we know not whither thou goest; and how can we know the way?"

It was no ordinary hour for those about Jesus. The shadows of the cross came closer. The Last Supper had been observed with all its prophetic and unique meaning. Judas had made his historic exit from the supper and had committed or was on his way to committing suicide. Peter had made a bold but shallow assurance of his loyalty to Jesus, an assurance that would not last long or prove true. The disciples' plans were shattered. Their hopes were spoiled. Their fondest dreams had suddenly become a frightening nightmare. Their bright and promising future had quickly become a leaden gray. Their leader, on whose presence so much depended and in whose fellowship they so delighted, was going away. The sunshine of certainty yielded to the clouds of uncertainty and doubt.

Thomas voiced the frustration of the group when he said, "Lord, we know not whither thou goest; and how can we know the way?" They were not sure where their leader was going, so they were not sure where they were going. They knew only that they were going; where and how they did not know. Theirs was a bad outlook but good logic. It just makes good sense that if you do not know where you are going, you do not know how to get there. Routes and roads and maps do not mean much until destinations are fixed.

There is something of this desperation in our world. People find themselves confronted by enemies, amazed by politics, frightened by knowledge, confused by conflicting ideologies, and shaken by human performance.

In desperation millions ask, "How can we know the way?" In the face of such contemporary desperation, let us hear:

II. An exact designation.

"I am the way."

Jesus cannot be much clearer than that. Although the primary focus was on the cross, the resurrection, and the ascension of Jesus, a world of truth for this life and the next one is contained in his poignant statement.

A. *Jesus is the way to a victorious confrontation of sin.* There is no way around the cross. Nor is there any adequate salvation from sin apart from the cross.

B. *Jesus is the way of victory over death.* He had already told his disciples of his coming death. His assurance was projected to his postresurrection victory.

C. *Jesus is the way of truth.* He is the way of truth because he is the truth.

D. *Jesus is the way of life.* Again, Jesus is the way of life because he is life. It is not playing with words to affirm that because he is the way of life, he is the way to live, in time and in eternity.

In life's troubles, Jesus is the Way. In personal and social tensions, Jesus is the Way. In temptations all around us, Jesus, who was in all points tempted as we are, is the way to live victoriously.

In our tasks, Jesus who came with a sense of sentness to "work the works of him that sent me" is the way to accomplish our work objectives. Our generation has offered a depersonalized way of success. It is not straining the point to declare and to believe that Jesus does not simply have a way: He *is* the Way. Here also is:

III. A declaration that is exclusive.

"No man cometh unto the Father but by me."

The acid test of Christian theology is what a person does with Jesus Christ. There is no more dangerous indulgence than to reduce Christ to the equality of others and make him simply *a* way rather than *the* way.

We are not hesitant to accept absolutes in the natural world. We accept the absolutes of physics, chemistry, and all forms of scientific calculations, yet many are afraid of the divine dogma that Christ is the absolute in spiritual salvation.

To proclaim Christ as an optional way of salvation is to reduce his divinity to mere humanity. And a human Christ cannot lift us from human despair.

The Duke of Wellington was right when he said, "Education without God will fill our world with clever devils." And a salvation without a divine Savior will fill our world with demons, clever or dull.

It was this excellent exclusiveness that Peter preached. "Neither is there salvation in any other: for there is none other name under heaven given among men, whereby we must be saved" (Acts 4:12).

Conclusion

Let us come from life's deepest desperations to Jesus who is the Way.

Let us receive Jesus as the clear, simple designation of heaven for earth's afflictions.

Let us be consistent in giving Christ absolute authority and mastery over our lives.

Have you lost your way, dear friend? Hear him say, "I am the way." Asked the way to heaven, Bishop Wilberforce replied crisply, "Take the first turn to the right and go straight ahead." If you have not already done so, will you not do it now?

SUNDAY EVENING, OCTOBER 26

Title: How to Lose at Christian Living

Text: "But the children of Israel committed a trespass in the accursed thing.... Israel hath sinned, and they have also transgressed my covenant which I commanded them" **(Josh. 7:1, 11).**

Scripture Reading: Joshua 7

Introduction

Chapters 1 through 6 of Joshua teach us how to live victoriously; chapter 7 tells us how to lose at Christian living. Chapter 6 closes with a victorious statement; chapter 7 begins by introducing a dark cloud that covers Israel's life.

Verse 1 says that a trespass, a breach of faith, affected the whole nation. Verses 2 though 5 describe Israel's defeat by Ai. The people were overwhelmed, and their hearts melted and became as water. Verses 6 through 9 record Joshua's prayer, that he fell on his face before the ark of the Lord until evening, with a crushed and perplexed spirit. Verses 10 through 15 share God's answer to Joshua. God was not unfaithful; it was Israel who had sinned. Verses 16 through 26 describe how Achan was exposed and punished severely. We can learn at least three lessons from this chapter.

I. The reality of defeat in the Christian life.

As Israel was defeated in its conquest of faith to possess the land, so do we as Christians and churches sometimes experience defeat in the Christian life. Defeat may occur, but it is not necessary (1 John 2:1). Victory is always possible in Christ (1 Cor. 10:13).

Defeat may be related to two things according to this chapter. One is presumption (vv. 2–3). Because of the fewness of people, the children of Israel presumed to gain victory. Their pride was their undoing. A second fact related to defeat is prayerlessness. In this chapter, there is no evidence of God's promise of victory, and there is no evidence of prayer like there was before Jericho. Here is an experience of Joshua praying after defeat rather than before victory. How like our Christian living this is.

II. The root cause of a defeated life.

Why am I not experiencing victory in the Christian life? Why do I keep losing? Joshua's reaction was one of resentment, as reflected in his prayer. His attitude was that God had failed. *Why did God let this happen?* he wondered. The better question is, "What is God saying through this experience?" When I fail, it is not that God is unfaithful; it may be that God is saying something to me through the experience.

God gets to the root cause of the defeat of Israel as well as of our own. There was first a surface problem—something that was visible. Achan had stolen what belonged to God. It is not a trivial thing to steal God's devoted thing. The warn-

305

ing toward this was given in Joshua 6:18–19. However, the sin was committed. Many of God's people today are guilty before God in taking what belongs to him in tithes and offerings.

The root problem was that Achan's life was built on temporal values. He wanted to live for now rather than for eternity. What he could see was more important than the unseen. The root cause is found in verse 11 where the sin is described as a transgression against God's covenant. The root cause of every sin is to live life our way instead of God's. We try to live by our wisdom and reject God's principles. At the base of all our surface problems is resistance to God's way.

III. The remedy for spiritual defeat.

What is the remedy for spiritual defeat? God's way is the only way—through confession and repentance. Two things must be remembered. First, God truly discovers us. He knows all about us. He revealed to Joshua the very individual responsible—from tribe, to family, to household, to individual. God knows our actions, attitudes, thoughts, and motives; nothing escapes his eyes.

The second thing to remember is that the sin problem must be solved. The nation was delivered when the sin was confessed and judged. We experience victory over our sins through Jesus Christ. We receive forgiveness on the basis of his death on the cross. He is our sacrifice.

We claim victory over sin and the sins that defeat us through confession (1 John 1:9). To confess is to agree with God that we have sinned, and it is to claim by faith his cleansing and forgiveness because of Christ's death.

Cleansing is also related to repentance, a turning from sin in sorrow of heart to the way God intends for us to live. It also involves making restitution whenever necessary.

Conclusion

You may do something about your defeated Christian life. (1) Take a pen and paper and make a list of every known sin in your life that the Holy Spirit brings to your memory. (2) Across that list write the wonderful promise of 1 John 1:9. (3) When the list is completed, destroy the paper on which it is written. (4) Express thanks to the Lord that he has forgiven you. (5) Claim by faith God's promise to forgive and cleanse us from all sin.

WEDNESDAY EVENING, OCTOBER 29

Title: The Bible Speaks to Our Condition

Scripture Reading: Matthew 28

Introduction

The last chapter of Matthew's gospel focuses on the resurrection of the Lord Jesus Christ and on the Great Commission he gave to his disciples to publish to the ends of the earth his redemptive acts and their meaning for the heart of every person.

I. He is risen (Matt. 28:1–7).

Never did trumpeters sounding ten thousand trumpets speak with greater significance than did the angel when he said, "Do not be afraid, for I know that you are looking for Jesus, who was crucified. He is not here; he has risen, just as he said" (Matt. 28:5–6).

We have let the truth of the resurrection of Jesus Christ become so common that it is threadbare. In reality the overwhelming majority of his followers live somewhere between sundown on Good Friday and before dawn on Easter Sunday. We have not recognized and fully responded to the fact that ours is a living Lord.

II. Jesus met them (Matt. 28:9–10, 16–17).

Over and over again, our Lord revealed himself to his disciples following his conquest of death and the grave. There are at least ten different recorded instances of his appearance to his disciples—to individuals, to small groups, and to over five hundred at one time.

Our Lord wants to meet us today on life's highway. He wants to quiet our fears, open our minds to divine truth, and encourage us in service. He deserves our faith, and he merits our love.

III. Sharing the Good News (Matt. 28:18–20).

Our Lord tells us that God has invested him with authority both in heaven and on earth. He has received this authority because of his self-denying surrender to his redemptive mission and his willingness to suffer the agony of Calvary (Phil. 2:5–11).

Some have professionalized the Great Commission and applied it only to the clergy, and others have internationalized it and applied it only to the work of foreign missionaries. But the real imperative in the Great Commission is found in the phrase translated "Teach all nations." Jesus is literally saying, "Make disciples." The word translated "go" is a participle with the force of an imperative. It literally means, "In your going about from place to place, make disciples." This includes every disciple of the Lord Jesus Christ. All of us are to be sharers of the good news of both the redemptive acts of Jesus Christ and their significance for the heart need of every man, woman, boy, and girl.

IV. A wonderful promise (Matt. 28:20).

The Great Commission closes with the glowing promise of our Lord to bless with his continuing presence those who give themselves in obedience to his command to share the good news of his love with all people.

As he was with Abraham, Isaac, Moses, Joshua, Jeremiah, and others, so will our Lord be with us if we are obedient to him.

Conclusion

If we would please the crucified but risen living Lord, we must not be silent concerning what he has accomplished and what he has come to mean to us as individuals. May God grant to each of us hearing ears as we listen to these words that fell from the lips of our precious Lord.

SUGGESTED PREACHING PROGRAM FOR

NOVEMBER

■ Sunday Mornings

Begin a new series titled "Taking the Stew Out of Stewardship." After people have been led to put faith in Jesus Christ as Lord and Savior, there is probably no greater service that can be rendered to them than to lead them to become a joyful and sacrificial contributor to the work of God's kingdom. A series of messages emphasizing that it is more blessed to give than to receive can make a great contribution toward spiritual growth and the enlargement of the life of those who have trusted Christ as Savior.

On the last Sunday of the month, begin a series called "The True Spirit of Christmas."

■ Sunday Evenings

Continue with the theme "The Walk and Work of Faith" based on the book of Joshua.

On the last Sunday of the month, begin the series "The Missionary Message of Christmas." The obligation of each Christian to share the Good News is the recurring emphasis for the month.

■ Wednesday Evenings

Continue with the series "The Bible Speaks to Our Condition," using selected great chapters from the New Testament. The theme verse for the month is, "Thy word have I hid in mine heart, that I might not sin against thee" (Ps. 119:11).

SUNDAY MORNING, NOVEMBER 2

Title: Can a Man Rob God?

Text: "Bring ye all the tithes into the storehouse that there may be meat in mine house, and prove me now herewith, saith the LORD of hosts, if I will not open you the windows of heaven, and pour you out a blessing, that there shall not be room enough to receive it" (**Mal. 3:10**).

Scripture Reading: Malachi 3:5–10

Hymns: "We Give Thee but Thine Own," How

"Trust, Try and Prove Me," Leech

"All Things Are Thine," Whittier

Offertory Prayer: Heavenly Father, we recognize that we are always in your holy presence. Thank you for reminding us every day that you are a God who plans.

Now let us follow your plan by giving your tithe and our offerings to your work. In Jesus' name. Amen.

Introduction

How many attend your Sunday school class? For the sake of illustration, let us imagine that ten people attend regularly. You know all ten of them well, and you enjoy studying the Bible with them each Sunday. As far as you can tell, all ten of them are dedicated Christians.

You pick up the morning newspaper and read on the front page that eight of the ten people in your Sunday school class have been jailed for robbery! Would you be alarmed? Of course you would.

Did you know that far less than two out of ten Christians actually give a tithe (10 percent) of their income to God's work through their local churches? The Bible calls the nontither a robber!

I. The nontither robs God.

A. *God's wrath is declared on six categories of evildoers—sorcerers, adulterers, false swearers, oppressors, those who abuse the helpless, and those who do not fear God (Mal. 3:5–7).* Such people deserve destruction, but God's grace prevents such destruction. His patience is greater than his wrath.

B. *Even God's people stray from his teachings and break their covenants.* God bids them to return. In the spiritual darkness of their backsliding, many Christians blindly ask, "Wherein shall we return?"

C. *Most Christians who are not tithers never think of themselves as robbers who have strayed from God.* But Malachi leaves no doubt about this matter. Even though his name may not be entered on the local police ledgers, the nontithing Christian is guilty of robbery in the worst way (3:8).

II. The nontither denies God's ability to plan his universe.

God, the Master Planner, has left nothing to chance.

A. *The planets in our solar system range in distance from the sun from 36 million to 3,600 miles.* Each moves around the sun in exact precision, with orbits ranging from 88 days for Mercury to 249 years for the dwarf planet Pluto.

B. *Our earth, which makes its orbit in 365.25 days, rotates on its axis so accurately that a variation of one second in a hundred years would throw earthly life into unspeakable chaos.*

C. *It is said that the ink in an ordinary period contains more atoms than there are people in the world.*

D. *Scientists tell us that each atom contains its own individual solar system perfectly balanced with its protons and neutrons.* A scientist at the Argonne Laboratory near Chicago remarked, "My respect and admiration of God's handiwork grows with every passing day I spend in this lab."

F. *A watermelon has an even number of stripes on the rind.* There is an even number of segments in every orange and an even number of rows in every ear

310

of corn. Every stalk of wheat has an even number of grains. The waves of the sea roll into the shore at the rate of twenty-six times per minute in all kinds of weather. A limb grows as much as fifty feet from the trunk of a tree with no anchorage except the tree's trunk.

So we can see that God has a perfect plan for everything he creates. We can trust that he has a perfect plan for us.

III. The nontither denies God's ability to provide salvation for the lost.

A. *God plans everything.* God has proclaimed just one plan of salvation. Paul said, "God was in Christ, reconciling the world unto himself" (2 Cor. 5:19). Simon Peter said of Jesus Christ, "Salvation is found in no one else, for there is no other name under heaven given to mankind by which we must be saved" (Acts 4:12 NIV). "For whosoever shall call upon the name of the Lord shall be saved" (Rom. 10:13).

B. *God's missionary plan was expressed by Christ just before his ascension.* Jesus said to his disciples, "Therefore go and make disciples of all nations, baptizing them in the name of the Father and of the Son and of the Holy Spirit, and teaching them to obey everything I have commanded you. And surely I am with you always, to the very end of the age" (Matt. 28:19–20 NIV).

Conclusion

Would God, who has planned everything in such detail, leave the financial support of his work to chance? Not at all! In the Old Testament, the tithe was considered "holy unto the Lord" (Lev. 27:30). God's people were to pay the tenth of "all the increase" (Deut. 14:22). They were to bring the tithe "into the storehouse" (Mal. 3:10).

SUNDAY EVENING, NOVEMBER 2

Title: Principles for Spiritual Victory

Text: "And the Lord said unto Joshua, Fear not, neither be thou dismayed: take all the people of war with thee, and arise, go up to Ai: see, I have given into thy hand the king of Ai, and his people, and his city, and his land: And thou shalt do to Ai and her king as thou didst unto Jericho and her king: only the spoil thereof, and the cattle thereof, shall ye take for a prey unto yourselves: lay thee an ambush for the city behind it" **(Josh. 8:1–2)**.

Scripture Reading: Joshua 8:1–8, 30–35; 9:3–15

Introduction

The book of Joshua is a fascinating book describing how God's people possessed the land he had given them. It is a story of victories and defeats, of intrigue and war, of faith and supernatural power. It is a book of history, but it is more than that; it is a book of principles that apply to the Christian life, as the writer of Hebrews in the New Testament recognized.

Many key events in the life of Israel have spiritual meaning for our Christian lives. The children of Israel crossed the Jordan River into the land of Canaan. They experienced God's victory over Jericho. In doing so, they experienced the power of conquering faith in following God's leadership. Then there came unexpected defeat, humiliating defeat. Why? Because there was sin in the camp of Israel. Joshua 7 deals with this particular experience in their history and closes with the sin that caused defeat being punished. What would be next for Joshua and the people? The next chapters describe continuing conquest of the armies of God in possessing the land. Several principles of spiritual victory may be discovered.

I. Claim God's victory over sin.

The Bible teaches that any victory over sin involves confession, repentance, and restitution. Israel was defeated, and sin was exposed. Joshua was humbled in prayer, and in answer God revealed the problem. The sin was confessed and judged, and the guilt was removed. The nation returned to victory. The only way to experience victory over sin in our lives is found in 1 John 1:9: "If we confess our sins, he is faithful and just to forgive us our sins, and to cleanse us from all unrighteousness."

What does this say to us specifically? Whenever we take what belongs to God, we commit a dangerous sin. It may be stealing, covetousness, love of material things, or taking the tithe that belongs to God. Whatever it is, if we desire to find spiritual victory from the Lord, we must confess our need to God, become honest with him, and experience his spiritual victory in our Christian lives. We must claim God's victory in our lives today.

II. By faith follow God's directions for your life.

First, we are not to let sin defeat us and failure stop us. When God forgives our sins, he is ready to give us directions for victorious living. In Joshua 8:1, after the sin was cleared up, God commanded Joshua to move out to further conquests. There is no need to keep on living our failures and defeats once they are forgiven through Jesus Christ. Satan tempts us to keep thinking about them, but God commands us to walk in victory (see Rom. 8:28; Phil 3:13).

Second, accept God's leading. God gave to Joshua new orders for Ai. God had one plan for Jericho, another for Ai. The Lord does not always work the same way year after year. The method used here was not repeated for any other city or fortress in Canaan. This was God's new plan for Ai. Chapter 8 describes it as an intriguing ambush of the city.

Although God never changes in character and purpose, he does change his methods. He is not stereotyped in his working. First Corinthians 12 describes the diversities of ministries. God is creative, and he wants us to be creative in expressing spiritual freedom. The amazing thing today is how God is blessing so many varied ways of doing his work. We are experiencing a freshness that we have needed for many years. The principle that comes to me is that he will bless any of his people who make themselves available to him. God gives strategies to those who seek them and who are willing to attempt them by faith. Our goal should be to let the Holy Spirit lead us in the fulfillment of God's purpose.

III. Be prepared for spiritual conflict.

Chapter 9 describes the deception used by the Gibeonites. There are three lessons to be learned. (1) We are tempted to compromise God's principles. (2) We are tempted to live by our wisdom rather than God's. All that was done in chapter 9 was done without the counsel of the Lord. (3) Be alert for Satan. The Gibeonites worked like Satan does—deceptively. Satan battles with us in various ways, and we are warned in the Scripture "to be strong in the Lord." Ephesians 6:11 speaks of the wiles of the devil. Second Corinthians 2:11 describes how Satan disguises himself. First Peter 5:8 indicates that Satan is sometimes like a roaring lion seeking whom he may devour. He is doing everything he can to thwart God's purposes through us, but his power was broken two thousand years ago. We may claim the spiritual victory that God has for us in Jesus Christ.

Conclusion

The book of Joshua teaches us that God's purpose for our lives is a victorious one. It is his purpose to lead us and to fill us with his power. He knows that we will be faced with conflicts in our Christian lives, and he wants us to be prepared with his counsel of wisdom. Where can we get God's wisdom? God's wisdom comes to us from his Word. Proverbs 4:7 says, "Wisdom is the principal thing; therefore get wisdom: and with all thy getting get understanding." Wisdom is looking at life with God's point of view, and understanding is responding to life's situations as God does. If we want to be victorious, we must be willing to seek his wisdom and commit ourselves to living according to his way of life.

WEDNESDAY EVENING, NOVEMBER 5

Title: The Bible Speaks to Our Condition

Scripture Reading: Luke 15

Introduction

The opening verse in the great chapter for today reveals the attraction Jesus had for people of every class and condition. Particularly those who were normally considered as irreligious were attracted to him. In some respects, this is an indictment against the clergy of today and many of those who consider themselves to be the very best of Christians. This conclusion is reached because there is something about them that repels sinners rather than attracts them.

Jesus was accused of being a friend of sinners, and he gave a beautiful parable made up of three different stories to plead guilty to the charge. At least four important truths come shining through this great chapter.

I. The parable of lost things.

The entire chapter speaks of lost things—a lost sheep, a lost coin, a lost younger son, and a lost older son who stayed at home. The older son personifies the attitude of the Pharisees and the scribes toward sinners. He was critical and had no compassion for lost people.

II. The parable of God's sorrow (Luke 15:4, 8, 13).

The great God of heaven is not unconcerned about lost people. He suffers like a shepherd with a lost sheep; like a woman with a lost coin; and like a father with a wayward, rebellious, ungrateful son. God's heart is broken because of the lostness of people.

III. The parable of God's struggles (Luke 15:6, 8, 23).

God is the God of grace. God sent the Savior to seek and save the sinners. God goes out searching for the lost sinner like a compassionate shepherd seeking a lost sheep in the darkness of midnight. God works to find those who have become lost values, like a woman seeking a lost coin. God is like a brokenhearted father who practices generosity toward a son who proves to be unworthy and ungrateful. He grants the son the liberty to go to hell if the son is determined to do so. In the meantime, he builds a stall and feeds a calf so that he will be prepared to provide a banquet feast should the son come to his senses and return home.

IV. The parable of God's joy (Luke 15:6, 10, 22–24, 32).

The highest happiness ever known is the happiness of heaven over the safety of those who once were lost. God rejoices over the salvation of a sinner like a shepherd rejoices when he finds a lost sheep; like a distressed woman who finds a lost coin; like a grieving, brokenhearted father when he sees the long-lost son returning to the home.

Conclusion

This parable is often called the parable of the prodigal son. In reality it is the parable of the waiting father who lovingly longs for the return of a foolish, wayward, unworthy son.

There are still many lost over whom God yearns. We can enter into God's sorrow and God's struggle to save. To the degree that we do so, we can enter into God's joy over the salvation of the lost.

SUNDAY MORNING, NOVEMBER 9

Title: Did Jesus Teach Tithing?

Text: "Woe unto you, scribes and Pharisees, hypocrites! for ye pay tithe of mint and anise and cumin, and have omitted the weightier matters of the law, judgment, mercy, and faith: these ought ye to have done, and not to leave the other undone" **(Matt. 23:23)**.

Scripture Reading: Mark 12:41–44

Hymns: "I Gave My Life for Thee," Havergal

"More Love to Thee, O Christ," Prentiss

"My Jesus, I Love Thee," Featherston

Offertory Prayer: Heavenly Father, we thank you for your love expressed in Jesus Christ. We praise you for his love, which caused him to suffer hurt for our sins. Now may your love for us through Christ constrain us to give until it hurts. In Jesus' name. Amen.

Introduction

Did Jesus tithe? If he did not tithe, surely the Pharisees would have openly criticized him as they did when he violated their Sabbath regulations.

Did Jesus teach tithing? Since Jesus must have assumed that the Christian would tithe, he did not spend much time talking about this subject. However, he commended the practice of tithing when he said, "Ye pay tithe of mint and anise and cumin, and have omitted the weightier matters of the law, judgment, mercy, and faith: these ought ye to have done, and not to leave the other undone" (Matt. 23:23).

I. Jesus commended tithing.

A. *Christ commended the scribes, Pharisees, and hypocrites for tithing, but he condemned the motive and manner in which they tithed.*

B. *The Pharisees were careful to pay the tithe on the smallest of garden herbs—mint, anise, and cumin.* They were giving their tithe instead of their lives. What about being just in their dealings with others (judgment)? What about being merciful toward the unfortunate (mercy)? What about loyalty to God and honesty in their business dealings (faith)? They had omitted these, thinking somehow that their tithing would substitute for their unethical practices.

C. *Tithing is no back door to dedication.* You do not become a better Christian by tithing. Tithing is an outgrowth of dedication—not a substitute for dedication. Paul indicated the proper order for stewardship of possessions when he spoke of the liberal giving of the Macedonian Christians who "first gave their own selves" (2 Cor. 8:5). God gets your money not to get you; he gets your money *when* he gets you! The proper order is self before substance.

II. Jesus condemned impure tithing motives.

Behind the tithing of the Pharisees were impure motives. What should our motive be when we tithe?

A. *What about the motive of fear?* "I tithe because I am afraid not to tithe," say some well-meaning Christians. Tithing completely motivated by fear leads to the conclusion that God can be "bought off."

B. *"I like to pay my way because I just don't like to be a Christian freeloader," says the motive of duty.* There is a sense in which tithing is a Christian duty, but

315

tithing wholly motivated by duty reduces Christian stewardship to mere bill paying.

C. *What about the motive of self-respect?* Some say, "I'll give as much as the next fellow." It *is* surprising that many churches collect more money when more people know who is giving it. Someone has justly claimed that it would be surprising how little might be done in some churches if we did not care who got the credit. Self-respect falls far short of the proper motive for tithing.

D. *What about the motive of reward?* Does tithing really pay? God certainly promised to protect Israel's crops and make them a delightsome nation. But was God blessing tithing or the spirit that was behind tithing?

Tithing *does* pay—but not always in financial blessings. In fact, some tithers face more hardships than nontithers. The greatest blessing in tithing is found in the heart of the Christian who knows that he or she is cooperating in God's plan for financing the most important work in the world.

E. *A pastor went visiting with one of the men in the young married people's department of his church.* As he climbed into the old car, he noticed that the right front fender was badly damaged. The young man started the car and pulled away from the church. From the sound of the motor, the pastor noticed that it was badly in need of repair. Before the evening was over, the young man said, "I know this car isn't much. We would have bought a new one before now if we had not decided to tithe this year. We are happy to drive this 'rattletrap' a few more miles until we feel that we can buy a new one without having to take the payments out of our tithe."

III. Jesus conveyed the proper motive for tithing.

A. *Certainly the elements of fear, duty, self-respect, and blessing are involved in Christian stewardship.* But the underlying motive behind tithing ought to be love. God so loved that he gave (John 3:16).

B. *Our love for God and others will not let us spend God's tithe on a house, car, vacation, furniture, golf clubs, rifle, boat, water skis, TV, or dinner out.* There is nothing wrong with owning these things, but Christian love will let us buy them only after God's tithe has been taken from our paycheck.

C. *God's knowledge of our stewardship means more than that he sees how much we drop into the offering plate on Sunday.* God asks more than, "Did you give today?"

Conclusion

How do you earn your money? Do you work for it? Is your occupation honest? Are you honest within your occupation? Do you hurt others to make your living? What is your attitude toward your money? Are you depending on money to bring happiness? Would you depend more on God if you did not have as much money as you now have? Are you more dedicated to money making than to your family, health, church, and God? How much of your money do you give to God's work through the storehouse of your local church? How much do you keep for yourself? Do you spend wisely what is left after giving your tithes and offerings?

The tithe is the beginning place in Christian stewardship. Have you begun to give yet?

SUNDAY EVENING, NOVEMBER 9

Title: Growing on in Christ

Text: "So Joshua took the whole land, according to all that the LORD said unto Moses; and Joshua gave it for an inheritance unto Israel according to their divisions by their tribes. And the land rested from war.... Now Joshua was old and stricken in years; and the LORD said unto him, Thou art old and stricken in years, and there remaineth yet very much land to be possessed" (**Josh. 11:23; 13:1**).

Scripture Reading: Joshua 11:23; 13:1; 14:6–15; 18:1–5

Introduction

The book of Joshua describes how Israel conquered Canaan by faith. It also shares spiritual lessons on how to conquer the Christian life by faith. Israel had seen God's miracles at work in their crossing the Jordan and in conquering Jericho. They had also seen disobedience by Achan, defeat at Ai, and deceit by the Gibeonites. In it all, they were marching on in conquest of the land. But what next?

Their work was not finished. God's will, as revealed to Joshua, was to go over the Jordan and inherit the land he had sworn to give to their fathers. After Jericho and other experiences, Joshua 11 describes what happened. Joshua took all of the land and waged war for a long time. The land was taken according to God's Word. Then in verse 23 we read that the land rested from war. Joshua was going on in the conquest of the land. This is exactly what God wants us to do. Once we have Jesus Christ in our lives and we are committed to his victory in Christian living, he wants us to *grow* on in Christ. We are not to cease maturing in our relationship with him. Three truths come from this section of Joshua.

I. God's rest.

God's rest is described in Joshua 11:23, "And the land rested from war." The Bible speaks of rest when it describes Israel experiencing rest in the conflict and conquest of Canaan. Hebrews 4:1, 9 also refer to rest in the Christian life. For the Christian, rest is a marvelous reality. It is God's will that we know this rest and experience it. This passage is not speaking of physical rest; it is speaking of spiritual rest, rest from turmoil and strain in the Christian life, rest from the worry of trials and troubles, rest from frustration and discouragement. Jesus described rest in Matthew 11:28–30—the rest of forgiveness of sins and also the rest of submission to Jesus Christ. When we are yoked to Christ, we experience life under his control. This is abundant life — rest indeed!

II. God's challenge.

God's challenge is described in Joshua 13:1. God told Joshua, "There remaineth yet very much land to be possessed" and challenged Joshua to go on to possess the land. Two words need emphasis. One is "inheritance," a word used to refer to the land as God's gift to Israel (v. 23). The second is "possess" in verse 1. This was the action Israel was to take to make the land their actual inheritance.

Inheritance is what God provided; possession is what they took. God gives, but we must possess all that belongs to us.

The chief lesson for us is that God has a rich spiritual heritage for us in Jesus Christ (Eph. 1:3). God has given spiritual blessings in Christ, but we must possess them by faith. God gives by grace; we must claim by faith. The challenge for us, then, is to grow in Christ, to go on to maturity (Heb. 5:11–14; 6:1; 2 Peter 3:18).

It is not God's will that we fail to grow spiritually or that we be defeated, fruitless, miserable Christians. He challenges us to grow on in Christ.

III. Our response.

What will be our response to the challenge of spiritual growth, or to possess our spiritual heritage in Christ? Two illustrations in Joshua point out two responses that we may make. First, in Joshua 18:1–3 is the attitude of slackness to do what God wills us to do. To be slack refers to slothfulness in Christian growth. The Bible has a lot to say about slothfulness (see Judg. 18:9; Prov. 10:4; 15:19; 18:9; 21:25; 24:30).

This is one attitude that we may take toward spiritual growth — being slothful, spiritually lazy toward God. When we have this attitude, it prevents appropriating the victorious life and hinders fruitfulness.

The second attitude is found in Joshua 14:6–15 against the background of a noble person named Caleb. He is one of the truly beautiful characters of the Bible. He is referred to in Numbers 14:8–9, 24, where the qualities of his life are seen. Numbers 32:10–12 describes his faith and his fullness of the Spirit. In this passage, he is eighty-five years old yet full of daring. He is both physically strong and spiritually courageous. He is facing the greatest challenge of his lifetime and is definitely not ready for retirement. The keys to Caleb's life are found in Joshua 14:10, where he says, "The LORD hath kept me alive." He had the constant assurance of the presence and power of God. He was constantly walking in the Spirit. Also, verses 8, 9, and 14 say that he "wholly followed the LORD." Caleb was not concerned about comparing himself with others; he wanted God's best for his life.

There was a burning desire in Caleb's heart to get into the battle. His one great request was "give me this mountain." He was hungering and thirsting after righteousness, and consequently he was completely satisfied in his relationship with God.

Conclusion

Growing on in Christ means that we must not be slothful toward the spiritual heritage that God has given us in Jesus Christ. Rather, we must be spiritually zealous for God to fulfill his ministry through us.

We must claim God's victory in our lives by faith. Let us believe that he will give his victory. As Jesus said, "According to your faith be it unto you" (Matt. 9:29), and as Paul said, "I can do all things through Christ which strengtheneth me" (Phil. 4:13). Growing on in Christ is the continual step in fulfilling God's purpose for a victorious life.

WEDNESDAY EVENING, NOVEMBER 12

Title: The Bible Speaks to Our Condition

Scripture Reading: Luke 18

Introduction

The Bible was not written merely that we might have a historical record of the past. The Bible is a revelation of God in action, portraying his nature, his purpose, and his will for our lives. On every page, in every incident, in every conversation recorded in Holy Scripture, God speaks to our condition today.

I. Persistence in prayer is encouraged (Luke 18:1–8).

Jesus spoke a parable to the intent that people ought always to pray and not to faint. We must develop the habit of prayer and not break that habit. To neglect this spiritual discipline is to faint and cave in when times of stress come. A contrast is drawn between an unjust judge who finally grants the plea of a poor widow and the God of heaven who is eager to bless his children.

II. Beware of strutting into God's presence (Luke 18:9–14).

Human nature is deceptive. It is easy for people to assume that they merit a position of preference in the presence of a holy God. The proud Pharisee was filled with conceit even in God's presence. He went through a ritual that he thought was prayer but in reality was nothing more than a conversation with himself.

The publican, hated and despised by the citizens of his country, feeling cut off from those about him, enjoyed an audience with the eternal God because he came in an attitude of humility, reverence, and confession of sin. He made a plea for pardon, and our Lord declares that he received a position of acceptance in the presence of God on the basis of his plea growing out of his faith.

III. A lesson from the children (Luke 18:15–17).

Our Lord loved little children, welcomed them, and prayed for them. He used their open attitude of humility, trust, and willingness to receive truth as a method of teaching great truths to people who stumbled over the simple way of salvation.

IV. The worship of material things (Luke 18:18–30).

The ruler who came to our Lord asking for the way of life was a prisoner of perishables. He had wrapped his heart and life around the physical things he held title to. In reality things owned and dominated him.

His question to our Lord concerning the way of life revealed the unsatisfied hunger of his soul. He who worships a false god will ultimately be disappointed by the object of his worship.

Jesus perceived the man's real problem and dealt decisively and radically with the man's worship of material things. The man was unwilling to repudiate his false god in order to become a follower of Jesus Christ.

V. The way to the cross (Luke 18:31–34).

With a steadfast commitment to the will of God, and with an indescribable love for lost people, our Lord moved steadfastly to the cross. He was willing to suffer to glorify God and to bless humankind. To what degree are we willing to spend and be spent that our God might be lifted up in the hearts of other people?

VI. The gift of sight (Luke 18:35–43).

On the way to his crucifixion, our Lord tarried for a moment that he might bestow the gift of sight to one whose eyes were blind. This incident reveals his infinite compassion and his attention to the personal needs of those about him.

Conclusion

This chapter speaks words of encouragement and words of warning to each of us. Each of us needs to communicate with God more often. Each of us could be humbler in God's presence. Each of us needs to beware lest we worship things unworthy of worship. God will grant to us sight and insight if we will but trust and obey him.

SUNDAY MORNING, NOVEMBER 16

Title: Investing in Heaven

Text: "Lay not up for yourselves treasures upon earth, where moth and rust doth corrupt, and where thieves break through and steal: But lay up for yourselves treasures in heaven, where neither moth nor rust doth corrupt, and where thieves do not break through nor steal: For where your treasure is, there will your heart be also" (**Matt. 6:19–21**).

Scripture Reading: Revelation 7:9–17; 11:15

Hymns: "O That Will Be Glory," Gabriel

"O They Tell Me of a Home," Alwood

"My Saviour First of All," Crosby

Offertory Prayer: Our heavenly Father, we thank you for the assurance that your children will dwell with you in heaven forever. While we are on earth, help us to think of heaven. May we give today as though we were laying up treasures in heaven. In Jesus' name. Amen.

Introduction

A little girl, blind from birth, knew the beauties of the earth only from her mother's lips. A noted surgeon performed a successful operation. When the last bandage was removed from her eyes, she ran from the doctor into the arms of her mother. Then she ran to the window and looked out at the world for the first time. For the first time, the glories of the earth rolled into her vision. She ran to her mother and screamed with joy, "Oh, Mama, why didn't you tell me it was so beautiful?" As the mother wiped the tears from her eyes, she said, "Precious child, I tried to tell you."

We read much about heaven in the book of Revelation, but when we get to heaven, we too will scream with joy, "John, why didn't you tell us it was so beautiful?" Perhaps John will say, "I tried to tell you in the last book in the Bible."

What is heaven like? In the last two chapters of the Revelation, John says that heaven is like a tabernacle, a city, and a garden.

I. Heaven is like a tabernacle (Rev. 21:1–5).

A. *In the Old Testament, the tabernacle was a place of fellowship with God.* In heaven Christians will fellowship with God in a way that humans have never known.

B. *John says that in heaven there is "no more sea" (Rev. 21:1).* The sea is a symbol of separation (Rev. 4:6). There will be nothing in heaven to separate one from God. John also referred to the tabernacle experience of the Christian in heaven in an earlier part of his book (7:9–17). He pictures Christians of all races standing in God's presence dressed in the white robes of purity with palms in their hands. Soldiers carry spears to war, but those who celebrate the victory of battle wave palm branches!

C. *The Christian will enjoy heavenly fellowship with God without the distressing presence of grief.* John pictures heaven as a place where God is served day and night "in his temple" (7:15). He pictures heaven as a place where there is no hunger or thirst and where God wipes away the tears.

D. *Illustration:* After Dr. Wayne Ward, former professor of theology at Southern Baptist Theological Seminary, preached a sermon on heaven, a ninety-year-old blind man approached him with these words: "Brother Wayne, I want to *see* you."

He ran his fingers over Dr. Ward's face. Then with tears streaming out of sightless sockets, he said, "When I open my eyes for the first time, you know who I will be looking at, don't you?" Dr. Ward said, "Yes, you will be looking at Jesus."

Then, with a cry of joy, the blind man said, "Brother Wayne, it is worth being blind for ninety years to know that the first time I open my eyes, I will be looking at Jesus!"

II. Heaven is like a walled city (Rev. 21:10–14, 21–27).

A. *In Old Testament times, the walled city was the city of protection.* In times of trouble, people made their way to the walled cities. Heaven is a place of perfect protection!

B. *Illustration:* A little girl who was spending her first night away from home with a girlfriend was heard to cry in the night. The mother of the house went to her bedroom and said tenderly, "Honey, what is the matter? Are you homesick?" The little girl said, "No, I'm here-sick." Christians often get sick of living in a world where the threat of war and destruction hang overhead. But they can rest assured that, in heaven, there is perfect protection.

C. *A preacher said to a dying pauper, "I am sorry for you!"* The poor man said, "Sorry, for me? Just look at the prospects!"

III. Heaven is like a beautiful garden (Rev. 22:1–5).

A. *John paints an unforgettable picture of a garden where there is plenty of water and vegetation.* In the garden of heaven, everything we need is provided. Heaven is not only like a tabernacle where we have perfect fellowship with God and like a city where we have perfect protection, it is also like a garden where we have perfect provision.

B. *The drama of redemption in the Bible revolves around three gardens.* Man is cast out of the garden of Eden because of sin. In the garden of Gethsemane, man finds his way back to God and forgiveness for sin. In the garden of heaven, man's redemption from sin is complete!

IV. Heaven has pearly gates (Rev. 21:21).

A. *But how does one get to heaven?* Only through Jesus Christ! John indicated that those who stand before God's throne in heaven stand there because their robes have been made white "in the blood of the Lamb" (Rev. 7:14). John pictures the wall around heaven with twelve tremendous gates, and each gate is one huge pearl.

B. *A pearl is formed when a piece of foreign matter such as a grain of sand gets into the shell of an oyster.* The wounded oyster's body secretes a milky liquid that forms a hard cover around the piece of sand. The oyster is suffering during the whole process. Finally, the hard cover builds up around the piece of painful sand and forces it out of the shell.

C. *How wonderful!* The entrance to heaven is pictured as pearly gates! We could not walk through the gates of heaven on our own merit. Our entrance to heaven is gained through the suffering of our Lord and Savior, Jesus Christ. Jesus said, "In my father's house are many mansions.... I am the way" (John 14:2, 6).

Conclusion

We *shall* inherit heaven. But what treasures are we laying up there now? A Texas oilman said, "The best way I know to lay up treasures in heaven is to invest my money in people who are going there." Won't heaven be great! Invest your money, time, and talents in your church. It is in the heaven-going business!

SUNDAY EVENING, NOVEMBER 16

Title: The Faithfulness of God

Text: "And, behold, this day I am going the way of all the earth: and ye know in all your hearts and in all your souls, that not one thing hath failed of all the good things which the LORD your God spake concerning you; all are come to pass unto you, and not one thing hath failed thereof" **(Josh. 23:14)**.

Scripture Reading: Joshua 23

Introduction

In Joshua 23, the great leader of the people of Israel has reached old age and is stricken in years. The final two chapters record his last words to the people. To the end, he remained full of faith and full of the Spirit. He knew what it meant to conquer by faith and to possess God's inheritance.

There is one great keynote found in chapter 23. Although the word itself is not used, the truth undergirding all that Joshua says in this chapter relates to the faithfulness of God. Some of the verses sound this encouraging note. Verse 3: "For the LORD your God is he that has fought for you." Verse 5: "Ye shall possess their land, as the LORD your God hath promised unto you." Verse 10: "The LORD your God, he it is that fighteth for you, as he hath promised you." Verse 14: "Not one thing hath failed of all the good things which the LORD your God spake concerning you." What a faithful God Joshua had!

The faithfulness of God is one of the great truths of Scripture and life. Just as Joshua was able to conquer through God's faithfulness, so do we as we live victorious Christian lives. Three words stand out in understanding the faithfulness of God.

I. Reliance.

Just as Israel conquered the land of Canaan by relying on God's faithfulness, so may we rely on his faithfulness for the victorious Christian life. It is utterly impossible for us to rely on ourselves. We must depend on God's trustworthiness. Certain Scripture passages will build our faith regarding God's faithfulness. One such passage is 1 Corinthians 10:13, which indicates that God does not allow Christians to be tested beyond his willingness to provide a way of escape. Another is 1 Thessalonians 5:23–24, which states that God is faithful to keep us to finish what he has set out to do. Second Thessalonians 3:3 says that God is faithful to give us stability and protection against all that is evil. First John 1:9 says that God is faithful to forgive us and cleanse us of all our sins. And Hebrews 10:23 and 11:11 tells us that God will be faithful to keep his promises to us. Whatever he has promised he will fulfill.

II. Responsibility.

Just as there are rewards and assurances, there are warnings and responsibilities. In Joshua 23:7–8, the people are warned against becoming like their surroundings. So are we to live a separated life by not copying the world (Rom. 12:1–2) and by not making alliances with sinners (2 Cor. 6:14).

In verse 11, the Israelites were to love God with a deep love. This is not just human love; it is God's kind of love—an undivided love in our hearts for him.

III. Retrogression.

In verses 12–13, we are warned that we are not to fail to go on in faith. Turning back was being willing to give up the Canaan life for the old life. It meant to turn against God and his will and to live for self-will. The challenge is to keep going forward (Heb. 12:1).

The warning is a very real one, because it is possible to retrogress in the Christian life. When we do, there are three losses, as seen in Joshua 23. One is the loss of power (v. 13). God removes his power when we do not honor him and his will for our lives. Samson is a testimony to this truth. When we resist the ministry of the Holy Spirit for our lives, we experience powerlessness. Therefore, there is an inability to bear fruit. According to John 15, we must abide in Christ if we are to be fruit-bearing Christians.

A second loss is the loss of comfort, also found in verse 13 when it refers to snares and traps, scourges and thorns. Israel's enemies would be like all of these to them. When we resist and reject God's principles for our lives, our lives, too, are filled with all types of conflicts. God does not leave us comfortable. He warns and probes and pricks our conscience. If our conscience is not troubled when we win wrongly, then we are in danger.

The third loss is the loss of capacity. This is also found in verse 13, when the people were told that they would perish from the land if the rejection continued. When we turn back from God, we experience a progressive loss of capacity. It may not all happen at once, but we will follow a downward pattern of life (see Ps. 1).

Conclusion

Reverse this trend of thought from the negative to the positive. Determine in your heart to go forward in Christ instead of backward by relying on the faithfulness of God. How can this be done? Five things will keep you moving. (1) Read the Word of God faithfully, (2) pray daily, (3) fellowship with other Christians, (4) witness for Christ, and (5) be obedient to God's Spirit in your life.

WEDNESDAY EVENING, NOVEMBER 19

Title: The Bible Speaks to Our Condition

Scripture Reading: John 1

Introduction

The gospel of John is the favorite gospel of millions of followers of the Lord Jesus. John is known as the apostle of love. Many believe that he is the apostle who leaned on the bosom of our Lord on the night when he instituted the Lord's Supper.

The great chapter from the New Testament through which we will let God speak to us today is both profound and simple.

I. The Eternal One enters time (Gen. 1:1–14).

There is some similarity between this chapter and the first chapter of Genesis. Genesis 1 speaks of how in the beginning God created the heavens and the earth. John 1 tells us how the eternal Creator clothed himself in human flesh and entered time.

The eternal Word of God clothed himself in human flesh and came to live with and to speak to the hearts and minds of people. John was one of those who had beheld Jesus with his eyes, felt him with his hands, and heard him with his ears. He declared that his Lord had come "full of grace and truth."

II. The witness of John the Baptist (Gen. 1:15–34).

John the Baptist was a servant of the Lord whom God appointed to be the forerunner of our Lord Jesus Christ. John came as a voice, as a witness, preaching to the multitudes to repent. He proclaimed the early arrival of the Messiah.

Over and over the ministry of John the Baptist is described in terms of giving a witness, giving a testimony, establishing an official record concerning the coming Messiah. Instead of calling attention to himself, we find John directing the attention of his disciples toward Jesus: "Behold the Lamb of God, which taketh away the sin of the world" (John 1:29).

John was careful to give testimony only to what he knew personally about Jesus Christ. Each of us should follow his example. God does not expect us to give anyone's testimony concerning Christ except our own personal testimony.

III. A continuing invitation (Gen. 1:35–40).

When two of John the Baptist's disciples followed the Lord Jesus with genuine curiosity, they received a gracious invitation that continues to be relevant for those who want to know more about Jesus Christ. Our Lord said to them, "Come and see" (1:39). The conversations of that visit would be interesting if we could but listen in.

IV. The example of Andrew (Gen. 1:41–42).

After Andrew recognized Jesus as the Messiah, he sought his brother, Simon Peter, that he might introduce him to Jesus. Later we find Andrew bringing a boy with his loaves and fish to Jesus (John 6:8–9). It was also Andrew who brought the Greeks to see Jesus shortly before the end of his ministry (John 12:20–22).

In the three instances in which Andrew is described as being active, he is described in terms of bringing someone to Jesus.

Conclusion

The Eternal One who entered time has reentered eternity and yet dwells within the hearts of those who have trusted him as Lord and Savior. We should follow the example of John the Baptist and give our personal testimony to those about us concerning this wonderful Lord. We would be wise to follow Andrew's example and bring as many as we can to meet the Lord Jesus Christ.

SUNDAY MORNING, NOVEMBER 23

Title: Giving More Than Thanks

Text: "For we shall all stand before the judgment seat of Christ" (**Rom. 14:10**).

Scripture Reading: Romans 14:7–12

Hymns: "Come, Ye Thankful People, Come," Alford

"Thanksgiving Hymn," McNeely

"Now Thank We All Our God," Rinkart

Offertory Prayer: Our heavenly Father, at this Thanksgiving season we engage in thanks-living. Help us to *be* thankful and to *act* thankful. In Jesus' name. Amen.

Introduction

Daniel Webster once said, "The most serious thought of my life is that I, as an individual, am accountable unto God." In Romans 14:10, Paul says, "We shall all stand before the judgment seat of Christ." In verse 12, he adds, "Every one of us shall give account of himself to God."

I. Total stewardship involves the total person.

A. *We will give an account to God of how we spend our time.* We will be held accountable for how much of our time we gave to witnessing to the lost. We will give an account of how much time we spent in helping those in need and visiting those who were sick. In Ephesians 5:15–16, we read, "See then that ye walk circumspectly, not as fools, but as wise, redeeming the time, because the days are evil."

B. *We shall give an account of how we have used our tongue.* "Every idle word that men shall speak, they shall give account thereof in the day of judgment" (Matt. 12:36). Every day each of us speaks enough words to fill a book. So much is said that could and should go unsaid. Our gossip, our lies, the hurtful things we have said about another person, even if true, will all be witnesses against us in the day of judgment. We are always to speak in a Christlike manner. "To him that ordereth his conversation aright will I shew the salvation of God" (Ps. 50:23). We will give an account of the good and bad we have spoken.

C. *We are all charged with the responsibility of using the talents that we have been given by God.* Some people can sing beautifully, and some can teach. Some can preach, and others are given the talent to witness. Some are given the talent of intercessory prayer. We are all given some talent, and we will all be held accountable for how we use our talent.

D. *We will give an account of how we have used the opportunities to witness that have opened to us.* Some Christians witness whenever the opportunity presents itself. They speak of Christ at the hair salon or gym. They invite people to come to church while they do their grocery shopping. Some tell of the love of Christ over their fishing rods and around the campfire at deer camp. They take every opportunity to use their talent for witnessing. But many do not. Many find themselves talking about anything other than God's work.

II. Giving money to God's work is thanks giving.

Christian stewardship involves more than just dropping money into the offering plate. It involves our position behind the offering plate, above the offering plate, in the offering plate, and beyond the offering plate. We are not good stewards until we have fulfilled our responsibility to God in all four of these aspects.

A. *Behind the offering plate.* God is concerned with how we earn our money. He expects us to work for our money at a legitimate trade. "Six days shalt thou labour, and do all thy work" (Ex. 20:9). "If any would not work, neither should he eat" (2 Thess. 3:10). When you consider earning money in a manner that pleases God, ask yourself these questions:

1. Is it legal? God will not honor money made by gambling, narcotic sales, prostitution, dishonest advertising, and shady business deals even if we give 90 percent instead of 10 percent.

2. Is it helpful? If the money is earned by the sale of obscene material, drugs, alcoholic beverages, and other detrimental products, it will not be pleasing to God.

3. Is it fair to everyone concerned? One can be in an honest vocation and still be dishonest and unfair.

B. *Over the offering plate.* God also wants to know if you have the right attitude toward your money. "For the love of money is the root of all evil" (1 Tim. 6:10). Before you can change your attitude toward money, you must ask yourself several questions.

1. Would I be just as happy without as much money? You must come to the place where you would be willing to take a job even with less pay in order to have time to attend the Lord's house on the Lord's Day.

2. Would I depend on God more if I did not have as much money? It is

easier to trust God when finances are scarce. As we become more affluent, we have a tendency to depend on our own resources and less on
God.

3. Do I put money before my God, my church, and my family? Jesus said,
"Seek ye first the kingdom of God, and his righteousness; and all these
things shall be added unto you" (Matt. 6:33).

C. *In the offering plate.* As you hold your money, ready to drop it in the offering
plate, God asks another question, "Why are you giving this money?" Your
gift to God's work should be from a heart of love and a desire to serve him.
It should not be given out of fear or duty. It should not be given to receive
reward or praise from people. Jesus rebuked the Pharisees and scribes
and said of them, "Everything they do is for people to see" (Matt. 23:5
NIV). Your tithe and offerings should not be given to make up for failures
in other areas of your Christian life. Giving is an outgrowth of dedication,
not a substitute for dedication.

Christians are also accountable for what they put into the offering
plate. When God asks, "How much did you put into the offering plate?"
he is not talking about dollars, he is talking about percentage.

God asks for 10 percent of our earnings. That is the least that we can
give. But God desires that we go beyond the tithe as soon as we can. "Upon
the first day of the week let every one of you lay by him in store, *as God hath
prospered him*" (1 Cor. 16:2, emphasis added). If God has prospered you and
blessed you to a great extent, then you are to give proportionately as God
has blessed you.

D. *Beyond the offering plate.* Christian stewardship also involves our money
and possessions beyond the offering plate. God wants us to be wise stewards of the money that we have left after paying our tithe and giving our
offerings. Charles Haddon Spurgeon said, "A fool can make money, but it
takes a wise man to spend it." It follows that the art of acquiring money is
subordinate to the art of using money.

So often the possessions that are left at death cause headaches and
heartbreak among the loved ones that remain. Do you know, before
death, exactly how your money will be used after your death? All Christians should pray about this and let God help them decide what percentage of their estate will go to the work of the Lord. Christians' stewardship
of possessions is not over until they have decided here on this earth before
they die how their estate will be used after they die.

Conclusion

We must gather all the facts and information that God has given us concerning stewardship so that we can wisely evaluate our accountability to God. The
stewardship of money is just one part of the total picture of our accountability to
God. As we give our money, we need to realize that God looks behind the offering plate, over the offering plate, in the offering plate, and beyond the offering
plate. Let us give more than thanks this Thanksgiving!

SUNDAY EVENING, NOVEMBER 23

Title: Victorious Christian Commitment

Text: "And if it seem evil unto you to serve the LORD, choose you this day whom ye will serve; whether the gods which your fathers served that were on the other side of the flood, or the gods of the Amorites, in whose land ye dwell: but as for me and my house, we will serve the LORD" **(Josh. 24:15)**.

Scripture Reading: Joshua 24

Introduction

Joshua 24:1 describes an awesome scene: all the tribes of Israel; their elders; their heads and their judges; along with Joshua, their leader, presenting themselves before God. It is the occasion when the respected and loved leader gives his farewell message to the nation. It is a message of God's miraculous works and Joshua's personal commitment. This occasion was to become a decisive moment for Israel that would result in continuous victory for years to come. It was an experience in which the Lord was enthroned and self was dethroned and victory assured.

Christian life is all about salvation. The Lord saved Israel from Egyptian bondage, and he has saved us from sin's bondage. Just as God promised the abundant land for Israel, so he has promised abundant life for all who are in Jesus Christ. And just as Israel had failed to experience victorious life because of unbelief, we too will live in failure, defeat, and frustration if we trust in our own efforts to live like Christ. But Israel entered the land by faith and experienced great victories. It is not God's will that we be defeated; rather, we are to experience daily victory through Jesus Christ our Lord.

Chapter 24 describes that moment in the life of Israel when they made a commitment that was to continue for years to come. This chapter gives insights on how to continue living victoriously by means of an overcoming Christian commitment. Such a commitment does at least two things.

I. It rests confidently in God.

This is described in verses 1–13, where God's sufficiency is proclaimed. Great moments in Israel's history are referred to, but all of them are God's doing. They were unmerited and came only by God's grace. All that we are is also by God's grace, according to Ephesians 2:8–10. All that we are spiritually now is God doing it, according to Philippians 2:13. How is this made real to us? It is by faith. The purpose, power, and faithfulness of God calls for faith in him. Just as the Israelites experienced the sufficiency of God by faith, so every Christian experiences victory by faith. We are saved by faith; we walk by faith. By faith we accept God's salvation, and by faith we accept God's victory. The same faith that saves us is the faith that makes us victorious.

II. The victorious Christian commitment responds to God decisively.

Victorious Christian commitment is described in verses 14 through 28. Verse

14 begins, "Now therefore...." On the basis of what has been said in the previous verses, a commitment is called for. The Israelites were to respond, to act, to choose. What are the marks of this response as described in this chapter? The first mark is to fear the Lord (v. 14). This is not a cringing fear of God but a reverent trust in him. Fear is an awareness of the presence of God. The first step of wise living is to fear God. Proverbs 1:7 says, "The fear of the LORD is the beginning of knowledge." Jesus said, "Fear him which is able to destroy both soul and body in hell" (Matt. 10:28). Acts 2:43 says, "And fear came upon every soul." Commitment that is worth anything at all has an element of fear in it, an element of God-consciousness, reverence, and trust in him.

A second response is availability. Verse 14 says, "Now therefore fear the LORD, and serve him." The heart of a victorious response is making ourselves available to Jesus Christ. It is not our ability that is important but our availability. We are to live the Christian life in the arrangement of the book of Romans. Romans 1 through 11 describes all that God has done for us. Romans 12 begins with a plea for Christians to yield themselves to God, making possible true service. Victorious service is allowing God to work through us. We may have been told all of our lives to do things for God, but very few have really told us to first make ourselves available to him for him to be and do in us what he desires. When you arrive at this point in your life, service becomes meaningful and joyful without pressure.

III. A decisive commitment involves a cleansed life.

In verse 14, Joshua challenges the people "to put away the gods which [their] fathers served on the other side of the flood, and in Egypt." God did not allow his people to worship other gods. They were to turn away from these false gods that could destroy their relationship with *the* God.

Verse 23 says, "Now therefore put away ... the strange gods which are among you, and incline your heart unto the LORD God of Israel." Anything that inclines your heart away from the Lord is a strange god and is sinful; it must be put away. Anything in our lives—attitudes, thoughts, actions, habits—that causes us to drift away from God is sinful and must be put away from us. A cleansed life is essential to victory in the Christian life.

IV. A mark of a decisive commitment is a yielded life.

In verse 15, Joshua says, "Choose you this day whom ye will serve." We cannot be neutral. We must progress or retrogress in our relationship with God. To go on in victory we must choose the Lord. This describes Joshua's yielded life. He first speaks as a person, a man, and an individual, then as a father willing to become God's spiritual leader for his home. There is no greater combination than this personal life related to the family.

This is life under new management—under God as Lord. Joshua said, "As for me and my house, we will serve the LORD."

Conclusion

A man shared with me that he had wandered for forty years in his Christian life, trusting Jesus only as Savior, but only this year had come to experience the living truth of two additional words — "and Lord." Jesus is both Savior and Lord. Victorious Christian commitment recognizes both.

WEDNESDAY EVENING, NOVEMBER 26

Title: The Bible Speaks to Our Condition

Scripture Reading: John 10

Introduction

The great chapter of the New Testament for today has been called the "Good Shepherd" chapter. In these words, our Lord used a familiar figure of that day to communicate great truths concerning his relationship to his people and their relationship to him.

It is said that even though Jesus used the parable of the good shepherd and the sheepfold, some of those to whom he spoke did not understand him (10:6). We must have hearing ears if we are going to hear the Lord speak authentically to our condition.

I. The Lord is the Good Shepherd.

Our Lord describes himself as the Good Shepherd who provides for his sheep. He also describes himself as the door of the sheepfold, which is symbolic of the security he provides for those who hear his voice and follow his leadership. The good shepherd is described in a number of different ways.

A. *He calls his sheep by name (10:3).*
B. *He leads his sheep (10:3).*
C. *He describes his purpose for coming into the world in terms of making the abundant life possible for his sheep (10:10).*
D. *He lays down his life for the sheep (10:11–18).* By laying down his life, he reveals his love for the sheep and for the Father.
E. *He knows his sheep (10:27).*
F. *He gives his sheep eternal life (10:28).*

II. The sheep of the shepherd.

A. *They know the good shepherd (10:14).*
B. *They hear the shepherd's voice (10:3).*
C. *They follow the good shepherd (10:4, 27).*
D. *They refuse to follow a stranger (10:5).*

Conclusion

There were various reactions to the person and ministry of Jesus Christ, who described himself as the Good Shepherd (10:19–21, 31–39). Some repudiated his claims and refused to examine his works or consider his words. They rejected him as a blasphemer.

Because of the testimony of John the Baptist, many put their faith in Jesus as the Good Shepherd who could lead them to the home of the heavenly Father.

Even at this point, our Lord was eager to have all of his sheep in the same fold. Perhaps this is a reference to the conversion of the Gentiles at a later time. Our Lord came into the world that he might provide forgiveness of sin, new life, and the spiritual security that comes as a result of being safe in the hand of our Father God (10:29–30).

It is wonderful to know the Good Shepherd. As the sheep of his pasture, we should know him, love him, hear his voice, follow him, and refuse to follow any strange voice that would lead us astray. May the Good Shepherd grant us ears to hear his message of comfort for us today.

SUNDAY MORNING, NOVEMBER 30

Title: They Shall Call His Name Immanuel

Text: "The virgin will be with child and will give birth to a son, and they will call him Immanuel"—which means, "God with us" (**Matt. 1:23 NIV**).

Scripture Reading: Matthew 1:18–25

Hymns: "O Little Town of Bethlehem," Brooks

"Joy to the World," Watts

"O Come, All Ye Faithful," Latin hymn

Offertory Prayer: Our heavenly Father, we thank you for many wonderful names, but today our minds are focused especially on the name Immanuel. The reason we so turn our hearts is because this is the season when we place special emphasis on the birth of Jesus. We thank you that you are with us today. Help us to give, conscious of your presence, and with the purpose of making Jesus known to others. We pray in Jesus' name. Amen.

Introduction

What is in a name? Almost any name one can call will immediately bring to mind something other than the name and/or person. The name Herod stands for cruelty. The name Alexander stands for conquest. Demosthenes stands for eloquence, and Beethoven stands for music. Milton suggests poetry, and Judas stands for treachery. Other names, such as Hitler, Mussolini, and Stalin, stand out in the minds of many for barbarity and atheism. But there is a name that is higher and stands for much more than any of these. It is the name of the one whose birthday is celebrated at Christmas.

He bears several different names. His name is Jesus, and the word itself is a contraction of words meaning "Jehovah is helper," thus the name Jesus means Savior, Redeemer, Comforter, and Friend. His name is Christ, which means Anointed One. His name is Teacher, which suggests Truth. His name is Friend, and he sticks closer than a brother.

The name that is being used in this message is "Immanuel," the name given by the angel of the Lord (Matt. 1:20–23) and prophesied by Isaiah (7:14). It is a name that has meaning today. It means that God is in touch with his creation right now.

I. The name Immanuel—God with us—is the way God saves the sinner.

A. *Every lost sinner is in despair, and apart from God's being in reach of him, there is no hope.* The Bible tells us that people hunger and thirst for righteousness. This is especially true when they are without Christ. This is true because life without Christ is incomplete. A Christless life is one without a compass. It is an unhappy life of straying feet and condemning conscience. It is a life that is condemned, lost, and wretched. The soul of the lost sinner cries out for redemption.

B. *Every lost sinner has hope in Immanuel.* The presence of God serves as a standard to show people they are sinners. The presence of God leads people to salvation. When God became a person, it was then that he paid the supreme price for sinners' salvation.

II. The name Immanuel—God with us—enables God to comfort the sorrowing (Luke 4:18).

A. *Sorrow is universal.* It is a common denominator, a ground leveler. Sooner or later each person experiences it one way or another. The world is full of griefs and graves. The very air seems heavy with farewells. The people of the world are weary and heavy laden.

B. *People go about alleviating this sorrow in a number of ways.* They try withdrawing from activity, people, places, and things, but this gives very little, if any, relief. They attempt living in the future. They seek to use activity, but these efforts become futile.

C. *In the person Jesus Christ, whose name is Immanuel, there is real comfort.* His presence provides real compassion. His presence gives comfort, and he has the will to comfort.

III. The name Immanuel—God with us—serves as a constant inspiration for God's children.

A. *Servants of God need inspiration and encouragement.* The road seems full of unappreciative people. It seems crowded with criticism. The road of life is difficult. It is demanding, trying, and time-consuming. It is full of doubts and despair. In order for one to continue at one's best, one must find strength and inspiration, and it is available.

B. *Servants of God find the inspiration in the presence of God—Immanuel.* "It is God that girdeth me with strength, and maketh my way perfect" (Ps. 18:32). The word *strength* means twisted together, and God becomes entwined with his people.

IV. The name Immanuel—God with us—tells us that God is present in time of death.

Death is cold, dreaded, and universal. It is a deep, dark, uncertain mystery and is feared by many. There is only one light that will continue to burn through the valley of death. It is God, who is light and whose light darkness cannot comprehend. It is Immanuel (Rev. 21:2–4).

Conclusion

You may anticipate the celebration of Christmas in many different ways, but if you have never experienced the presence and power of Jesus Christ in your life, then give your heart to him now and you will have your greatest Christmas ever. It is then that you will come to know the true meaning of the name Immanuel. It is "God with us."

SUNDAY EVENING, NOVEMBER 30

Title: The Contemporary Missionary

Text: "In this work, we work with God" (**1 Cor. 3:9 PHILLIPS**).

Scripture Reading: 1 Corinthians 3:1–9

Introduction

As a child between ages seven and twelve, I received an indelible impression of what a missionary was. My home church sponsored one of our pioneer missionaries in Brazil. Every three years, this man of God would return to his home community and share his mission field experiences. I got the impression from listening to him that a missionary is somebody who leaves home and his home church and goes far, far away, to come back every three or four years to tell stories about people in strange lands and what God is doing in their lives.

A bit later in my spiritual pilgrimage, I discovered 1 Corinthians 3:1–9. I read this passage anew in J. B. Phillips' translation, "In this work, we work with God." I discovered for the first time that I was included by the grace of God as a missionary.

The professional understanding of a missionary is neither biblical nor practical for our time. God intends mission accomplishment from each redeemed person. Rightly considered, the Word of God teaches that a missionary is a redeemed person living under the lordship of Christ, on mission in a particular setting.

A Christian seriously concerned about personal mission can be moved to commitment by the factors of personal setting, sense of sensitivity for others, and response in commitment to daily leadership of a living, loving Lord.

I. Perception: Contemporary missionaries are perceptive of their setting.

Paul points to the incompleteness of the concept of "professional missionary." The Corinthian congregation found itself greatly divided by an attempt to determine leadership. Some felt Apollos was the complete missionary; others felt Simon Peter was the divine example; and still others looked backward to their experiences with the apostle Paul. "In this work, *we* work with God." It is not a matter of associated Christian action. Redeemed persons have diversity of gifts, diversity of available time, diversity of endowment of talent, and diversity of economic possessions, but each Christian is on mission in his or her setting.

Contemporary missionaries begin with the inward look. Questions about self, time use, divine endowments, and material resources are appropriate for self-inventory. The early Christians were scattered abroad in a limited world for their time. The book of Acts wonderfully tells the experience of Christians who were scattered but who saw themselves perceptively as missionaries.

Contemporary missionaries are perceptive of their immediate setting. Urban patterns keep pointing us to the diversity of community, diversity of socioeconomic backgrounds, diversity of churches, diversity of lifestyles, and especially a great diversity of geographical location. New York City is not Albany, Georgia; Louisville, Kentucky, is not Los Angeles; and Texarkana, Texas, is not Buenos Aires, Argentina. Characteristics of lifestyles and daily patterns for living are being determined by socioeconomic circumstances, the crush of population, and daily human encounter in personal life situations. Modern Christians begin well to be missionaries when they are alert and perceptive of the people who daily surround them and of their life patterns. What are the needs of people with whom I am cast? What are their problems? What are their hang-ups?

Effective mission service seldom begins with a program. The excitement and joy of the Christian life are generated by personal relationships with other people. Contemporary missionaries can find a new joy and a delightful partnership with God and other believers by seeing their immediate setting realistically. Some reside in the inner city of great metropolitan areas. Some are factory workers, others live behind a desk. Wherever we are, God still says, "You shall be my witnesses."

II. Sensitivity: Contemporary missionaries are daily involved in the process of sensitivity.

The last visit of Jesus to Jerusalem is prefaced by an emotional display that produced tears. Luke tells us, "And when he was come near, he beheld the city, and wept over it" (Luke 19:41). This is a modern parable of sensitivity. There are many things that Jesus saw in his immediate setting that produced his tears. He saw their false peace. He was perceptive of the failure of the things that produced their insecurity, and he was sensitive to their human plight.

The tears of Jesus were not tears of failure or emotion. He was able to catch the feeling of people in his immediate setting. Jesus knew what was in people. His sensitivity was alerted at what he saw in the immediate setting of the beloved city of Jerusalem. By personal relationship with others, missionaries today not only will see their setting perceptively but will be consciously sensitive to the plight of real people.

Contemporary missionaries will understand the emotions and trauma of real people. In recent years, many pastors, some great churches, and too many of the Lord's people have pulled away from any personal commitment to certain kinds of people. Our Lord saw people who had moved too much toward self and ignored others, who were caught in the circumstances of life that produced fear, guilt, inferiority feelings, and hate. Contemporary missionaries will be sensitive to the problems that produce these behavior patterns in the lives of millions of real people. They will be sensitive to human need and be alert to relate themselves, by the love of God, to those who seek redemptive relationships.

III. Commitments: Contemporary missionaries will move toward decision in the challenge of mission for their personal commitment.

The theme of the public ministry and life of our Lord tells the story of God come down to humanity, as he became man and gave himself for what he found in humanity. Indeed, he was a "man for others."

Jesus taught his disciples the art of servanthood, the joyful necessity of giving self away to others. He not only told his disciples this necessity, he demonstrated it by a cross.

When redeemed people are perceptive of their world, sensitive to the plight of others, they come to decision time. Only they can make that decision. The major question at this point is, "Can I be this kind of person?" Contemporary missionaries will see themselves on mission in their domestic settings. A good place to begin to be a missionary is in our own home and family circle. God seeks dedicated Christian missionaries at the level of parenthood. The businesswoman may see herself on mission in her setting, the tradesman as he plies his trade. Contemporary missionaries will see themselves on mission where they are and whenever they are involved in personal relationships with others.

Involved in the decision for commitment to personal mission are at least these factors: (1) What is my first loyalty? Who is my Lord? (2) How important, really, is one individual person? (3) I am not really alone on my mission, am I? ("In this work, we work with God.") (4) What is the significance of God's commission to each disciple ("Ye shall be my witnesses")?

Conclusion

The basic task of contemporary missionaries is one that involves an understanding of communication. Basic to providing communication is relationships. There is a creative excitement loose in our world for redeemed people under the lordship of Christ and committed to personal mission in their setting. The next-door neighbor and his family, the kids on the playground or in the park, and the community in which a believer lives (whether inner-city, ghetto, or suburbia) will have new significance for the Christian on mission in our time.

DECEMBER

- ## Sunday Mornings

    Complete the series "The True Spirit of Christmas."

- ## Sunday Evenings

    Complete the series "The Missionary Message of Christmas."

- ## Wednesday Evenings

    Complete the series "The Bible Speaks to Our Condition." The theme verse for the month is "Thy word have I hid in mine heart, that I might not sin against thee" (Ps. 119:11).

    A New Year's Eve message is provided for the last Wednesday evening of the month.

WEDNESDAY EVENING, DECEMBER 3

Title: The Bible Speaks to Our Condition

Scripture Reading: John 14

Introduction

Jesus spoke the words recorded in our chapter for today on the night before his crucifixion. This passage of Holy Scripture has spoken to the hearts of multiplied millions of believers through the centuries, bringing comfort and courage for living in difficult times. Surely God will speak to our hearts this day as we prayerfully consider this great chapter from the New Testament.

I. The secret of the untroubled heart (John 14:1–3, 27–31).

Our Lord had announced to his disciples that the time for his departure had arrived and that he was returning to the heavenly Father. We can easily imagine how this must have distressed them. Our Lord encouraged them to face the future with faith. He encouraged them to believe that the secret of tranquillity and inward poise in a time of stress would be found through faith.

    A. *We must believe Jesus' words (14:10).* There is no way to face the future with poise and inward peace if we do not trust implicitly in the truthfulness of the words of the Lord Jesus Christ.

    B. *We must believe in Jesus' works (14:11–14).* Our Lord was not only a speaker, he was a worker. He encouraged his disciples to put their faith in him on the basis of his good works in the name of the Father. He was not a silent, inactive spectator. He worked the works of God while he was here on the earth. He declared that he was going to depart and be with the heavenly Father in order that his disciples might be able to do even greater works than he did.

With implicit faith in the words and promises of our Lord, and with confidence in his activity on our behalf, it is possible for us to experience the untroubled heart—inward peace and poise in the midst of circumstances that might otherwise terrify us.

II. The revelation of the heavenly Father (John 14:4–11, 20–24).

Jesus spoke to his disciples concerning one of the major purposes for his ministry in the world. He declared over and over that he came to reveal the Father. He affirmed that he is the only way to the Father (14:6). We can discover the power of God by studying nature and the physical world about us. But we come to experience God as heavenly Father only through faith in Jesus Christ.

Jesus Christ is more than just the best man who ever lived. He is more than just a heavenly inspired teacher who lived an unselfish life. Jesus Christ is the eternal God who came in a human body. If we would come to understand and know God, we can do so only as we look into the face of Jesus Christ. He is a revelation of the nature and purpose of the loving Father God (14:8–11).

III. The promise of the Holy Spirit (John 14:12–19, 25–27).

Our Lord sought to tranquilize the hearts and dissolve the fears of his disciples by promising them "another comforter" who would abide with them forever. There are several significant words in verses 16–18 of this great chapter.

A. *"Another" means "another of the same kind."* There is another word that Jesus could have used that means "another of a different kind."

B. *"Comforter" means "one called to walk by the side of."* Jesus had walked with his disciples and talked with them for three and a half years. They were distressed at the thought of being deprived of his presence.

C. *The Holy Spirit is to abide with Jesus' followers forever.* This is in contrast to the three and a half years of the ministry of our Lord.

D. *In the phrase "whom the world cannot receive," Jesus was saying that the Holy Spirit would not be subject to arrest and crucifixion as he was to be arrested and crucified.* The word translated "receive" can also mean "to seize," "to arrest." Jesus was declaring that no one would be able to crucify the Holy Spirit, because he is invisible and spiritual. He would not be tangible and limited to a human body as the Savior was.

E. *The Holy Spirit is to dwell within Jesus' followers permanently.* Our Lord declared that he would not leave his followers desolate and forsaken as if they were orphans. He said, "I will come to you."

Conclusion

This chapter speaks of God the Father, God the Son, and God the Holy

Spirit, a perfect unit expressing itself in trinity. God the Father expressed his love through God the Son in a dramatic and unique manner. God continues to manifest himself through the person of the Holy Spirit who is in the heart of each believer and who is in the world to impart faith and life to those who will trust the Lord Jesus Christ.

SUNDAY MORNING, DECEMBER 7

Title: Why the Christ Child?

Text: "Therefore the Lord himself shall give you a sign; Behold, a virgin shall conceive, and bear a son, and shall call his name Immanuel" **(Isa. 7:14).**

Scripture Reading: Isaiah 53:1–12

Hymns: "Hark! the Herald Angels Sing," Wesley

            "The First Noel," Old English Carol

            "Come, Thou Long-Expected Jesus," Wesley

Offertory Prayer: Heavenly Father, babies have been blessings throughout our lives, but the one baby who has meant more to us than all others is the Christ child, whose birth we commemorate during the Christmas season. We thank you for what he has meant to us as individuals and to all the world. Help us to honor him with our lives and our gifts, as we pray in Jesus' name. Amen.

Introduction

Most of the major doctrines of Christianity can be found in the Christmas message. Those that are not specifically found are implied. A few examples can illustrate the many. The thought "God with" is the doctrine of omnipresence. "His name, Immanuel" is the doctrine of justification. The Lord Jesus satisfies the demands of both humanity and God. "He gave his only begotten son" illustrates God's love. The baby Jesus points out the doctrine of humility.

The hymns that are sung around Christmastime are good phrases to help one understand the real Christmas message. The hymn "Hark! the Herald Angels Sing" is used as the basis for this message.

I. The phrases "Jesus, Our Immanuel," and "Veiled in flesh, the godhead see," are the very center of the Christmas thought.

    A. *Two passages of Scripture (Isa. 7:14 and Matt. 1:23) use the word "Immanuel."* This word is a derivative of three Hebrew words — *im* means "with"; *anu* means "us"; *el* means "God." Combine the three, and you get the name *Immanuel*, which means "God with us."

    B. *The lesson derived from this thought is most helpful.* God is identified with the total self of each person. By being born as a baby, he is identified with the birth of other babies. By living on earth, he is identified with the normal life of all people. By dying on the cross, he is identified with the death of all. By rising from the grave and ascending to heaven, he is identified with the hope of all.

Second Corinthians 5:21 says, "He hath made him to be sin for us, who knew no sin; that we might be made the righteousness of God in him." The passage shows each sinful person how God is identified with his temptation and sin and how he removes sin.

God is ever present to protect, help, and guide his people.

C. *This identity makes the Lord Jesus a just king to reign over his people.* No king can be a good king apart from an identity with his people. But the King of Kings who is the Lord Jesus is the perfect King. He knows his people and never makes a mistake in regard to them.

II. Another phrase in the familiar hymn is "God and sinners reconciled."

A. *This is Jesus' mission into the world.* The meaning of the word *reconcile* is to reunite, to cause to be friendly again, or to bring back to harmony. A definition of this nature immediately implies a break—humanity's break with God. This is humanity's sin. Sin causes estrangement. The estrangement is on our part, not God's. The one greatest need today is to be brought into harmony with God. Humanity's lack of harmony explains the unrest, evil, and problems of the world today.

B. *A phrase in the hymn that suggests what happens to people in this reconciling process is "born to give them second birth."* John's gospel says, "You must be born again" (3:7 NIV). This is the making of a new life. A new emphasis on the doctrine of the new birth would be of help in these troubled times.

III. The third phrase is "Hail the heaven-born Prince of Peace."

A. *The Prince of Peace came to establish peace on earth, yet the world seems to be a long way from it.* Genuine peace starts with the new birth. It starts with the right relation to God on an individual basis. One person at a time surrenders to Jesus for salvation and becomes a new creature in Christ Jesus. The peace Jesus came to establish on earth will become a reality as a life of righteousness is lived by each of the children of God. Righteousness is right living, and peace among people will become a reality when God's people live right.

B. *It is the privilege and responsibility of each Christian to join with the angelic host and proclaim.* The only hope of peace is the true reign of God in the hearts of all. This can be done as each person who has been born again lives in a godly manner. One of the greatest promises in the Bible is "If my people, which are called by my name, shall humble themselves, and pray, and seek my face, and turn from their wicked ways; then will I hear from heaven, and will forgive their sin, and will heal their land" (2 Chron. 7:14). This is a firm commitment on God's part to heal a sin-sick world when the world meets the conditions of a righteous, loving God.

Conclusion

Where do you fit into a message of this nature? You need to personally place yourself in the will of God. If you are not a Christian, you need to unashamedly confess him before people and live for him.

Christmastime is a time of rededication for all God's children. This Christmas rededicate yourself to Christ, die to self, and let the Holy Spirit live through you.

SUNDAY EVENING, DECEMBER 7

Title: Do We Look for Another?

Text: "Now John sent two of his disciples, and said unto [Jesus], Art thou he that should come, or do we look for another?" **(Matt. 11:2–3)**.

Scripture Reading: Matthew 11:1–6

Introduction

Life without purpose is an empty shell. A purposeless life is flabby and subject to fluctuation. It is no problem to discover the purpose God gave to all other of his creation. People have purpose too, but purpose must be discovered and personal commitment be made to the highest reason for life. This message deals with the interplay of relationships between John and Jesus. These men were highly motivated by a realization of purpose. They were in this life for reasons assigned by God!

John knew his mission and fulfilled it. The coming of John into this world is a preface to the coming of Jesus. A boy child was born to Zechariah and Elizabeth. The proud parents suffered a traumatic experience when Zechariah became mute. With the coming of the son and Zechariah's naming him John, his speech returned. This couple was dedicated to the things of the temple. The announcement of the coming child was brought to the father by an angel of the Lord. He would be a child promised by the Lord, and he would be the one who would announce to the world the Holy One of Israel.

There were no shepherds, no wise men, no bright stars in the East, and no heavenly chorus when John came into the world. The child grew and waxed strong in spirit and was in the desert until the day of his appearance to Israel. As John preached, the echoes of his message ran across Israel. John called people to repentance and insisted that people bring forth fruit indicating their repentance.

I. Scene I: John the Baptist and Jesus.

John's highest moment had come. John was involved in a baptismal service at the Jordan when he saw Jesus in the crowd. It was time for the great announcement: "Behold, the Lamb of God." John had lived for this minute and for this epochal announcement.

See how John did it! There was no great fanfare. He planned no promotional events. John stood last in the long line of prophets that had spanned many years.

Other prophets before him had the privilege of saying, "He will come." John had the privilege of shouting, "Here he is!" The Anointed One promised by God and looked for by his people had now been provided to the world.

John denounced himself in favor of Jesus. He said, "I am not worthy to carry his sandals" (see Matt. 3:11 NIV). John's purpose was to introduce Jesus as the Messiah of God. He fulfilled his mission and faded into the background.

Later Jesus evaluated the role of John the Baptist in the ranks of the prophets. He was no reed shaken by the wind, a man clothed in soft raiment. He was a prophet of the Lord, and Jesus said that there was none greater than John. He was a man with a mission, and the mission was realized in Jesus.

II. Scene 2: John in prison.

John was put in prison. The walls were high, and he was shut off from outside developments. No reports had come to him about Jesus' activities. Often he wondered, *How are things going with Jesus? What are his activities? What are his methods?* He eagerly waited to hear word of Jesus' inauguration as king. That word never came.

Patience sometimes wanes when a person is cut off from friends and his activities are stymied. He sent word through two of his disciples to Jesus: "Are you the one who is to come, or are we to expect another?" Is this a question from depression, a result of isolation, or evidence of inactivity?

The reports John had been receiving about Jesus' activity did not seem consistent with his personal expectations. Here was a very human trait in even the finest of disciples. Was John trying to set the guidelines for the mission God had for the life of another? The text does not suggest just what John's expectations were. Was he expecting Jesus to shake this world mightily in force and power? John was really seeking some affirmation of his personal mission. Had he made a mistake? He wanted an answer. Wisely he directed it to Jesus.

Jesus affirmed the mission of John. "Go thy way," he said to John's disciples, "tell John what things you have seen and heard; how the blind see, the lame walk, the lepers are cleansed, the deaf hear, the dead are raised up, the gospel is preached to the poor" (Matt. 11:4–5). Jesus told John that he would find his answer where he found his question. John went to his death. He probably never received satisfaction for his question. Strangely enough, neither John nor Jesus was received by people. Both of them went to their death, but the joy of life is demonstrated in the realization each of them had for his personal mission in this world. They lived and died for the mission given each of them by God.

III. Scene 3: Across two thousand years the same question is asked: "Shall we look for another?"

Is it all a sad mistake? Have we wasted our years? Is Jesus done? Did we join a losing cause? Is it worthwhile to make personal commitments of heart and time and service to Jesus? John said that he is "the Lamb of God, which taketh away the sins of the world." We certainly need that, but still there is the question, "Are you the one … or should we expect someone else?" (Matt. 11:3 NIV).

If Jesus is not the one, where shall the one be found? What do we want him to be? What is he to be doing? Where shall we look for evidences of the "taking away the sin of the world"?

Some want to look to great government. What has great government ever produced for the souls of people? History tells this story well. The governments of Egypt, Greece, the Roman Empire, Germany, France, and Spain were at one time first-rate world powers. Government cannot produce human values. Government is usually intended to serve people, but government standing alone usually produces an arrangement where people become its servant.

Social reform can never "take away the sins of the world." Thousands of years ago, Josiah discovered that social reform can help people to walk on this earth but cannot help people to live as complete persons.

Where shall we go if not to Jesus? Jesus came to bear the sin of the world! His death on the cross is his credential. His victory over the tomb is the seal of his heavenly qualifications.

IV. Final scene: This very day and this very life.

John's problem was that he seemed to want to describe how God's mission would be realized in Jesus. He wanted things to happen as they had happened to him. The balance of the story and the progress of Christian history tells us another great truth: What God does in Jesus is a lot better than what we think he ought to do!

John and Jesus were certainly not exceptions to the necessity for realization of personal mission in redeemed lives. My life and yours are here for reasons known by God. We are to be "on a mission." That mission is the mission of God through life. Discovery of that reason is something of what Jesus meant when he described life in him as the "abundant life."

God is constantly at work in the world. He works in and through redeemed persons who will commit time, talent, and total personality to those purposes that are discovered through prayer and involvement with others.

Conclusion

The Christmas story has a deep missionary theme. John was sent from God. Jesus was sent to the world. The commission of Christ is to redeemed persons who will commit time, talent, and total personality to those redemptive purposes that are discovered through prayer and involvement with others.

WEDNESDAY EVENING, DECEMBER 10

Title: The Bible Speaks to Our Condition
Scripture Reading: John 21

Introduction

To receive strength and guidance from the Holy Scriptures, each of us must put ourselves solidly and completely into a situation and let God's Word speak to our minds, our hearts, our sins, and our potential for good.

The great chapter for today shows that our Lord revealed himself time and time again to his disciples. There are at least ten recorded instances in the Scriptures of the appearance of the risen Lord before his ascension. Often he was not recognized at first (21:4).

Scripture teaches that the Christ of history becomes our contemporary through the Holy Spirit. He has promised his disciples his abiding presence as long as the ages roll. He comes to those who have faith and are willing to be responsive to his leadership.

I. The importance of obedience (John 21:5 – 11).

All night long the apostles had labored in vain. Their nets continued to be empty. This is a parable of the life that is lived on the level of human skills and resources alone.

The risen Christ approached, and after asking a question, issued a suggestion. Without knowing who the unique person on shore was, the fishermen followed his suggestion and caught a net so full of fish that they were unable to pull it to the shore. We are not spiritualizing this passage when we draw the conclusion that to live the life of obedience is to experience a life that is full of the resources that God makes available to us. Faith and obedience are the twin tracks that lead to fullness of life.

II. The restoration of an apostle (John 21:12 – 20).

Many significant lessons can be drawn from this experience in the life of the apostle Peter. The major purpose of these three pointed, painful questions probably is the desire of the Good Shepherd to find, to restore, and to recommission one who had disappointed his Lord and who had lost his self-confidence by his shameful threefold denial of the Lord during his trials. After each question and answer, our Lord gave Peter a command that was in reality an assurance of forgiveness and a recommission to service.

Each of us has disappointed our Lord and disappointed ourselves. In so many ways, we have fallen short and missed the mark. There is forgiveness with the Lord and there is a better tomorrow if we will but trust him and obey him.

III. A definition of discipleship (John 21:21 – 22).

In the words of our Lord to Peter, "Follow me," which were repeated twice in this passage, we have an excellent definition of what it means to be a good disciple of the Lord Jesus.

We need to follow him in the matter of discovering and accepting his attitudes. And we need to follow him at the point of discovering his affections and accepting these same objects of love and purpose of love as our own.

We need to discover what the compelling ambition of our Lord was and let his ambition become our ambition.

Conclusion

The risen Lord approaches each of us in the situation where life finds us today. He comes with purposes of love. He is eager to restore the drifter and the one who has failed. He is eager to lead us to the pathway that leads to a full net, and the full net must not be identified with financial affluence. We can discover the fullness of life that God has planned for us by following him all of the way throughout all of our days.

SUNDAY MORNING, DECEMBER 14

Title: The Christ of Christmas

Text: "But when the fulness of time was come, God sent forth his Son, made of a woman, made under the law" **(Gal. 4:4)**.

Scripture Reading: Galatians 4:4; Ephesians 1:10; 1 Timothy 2:6; Titus 1:3; Hebrews 9:26

Hymns: "While Shepherds Watched Their Flocks," Tate

"Gentle Mary Laid Her Child," Cook

"Silent Night! Holy Night!" Mohr

Offertory Prayer: Dear heavenly Father, you are good to us all the time, but at Christmas time we take special note of your goodness. Now we want to thank you especially for the Christ of Christmas. We thank you and love him for all he has done for us and for what he means to us. We thank you for his birth, and we thank you for his intercession. Help us in our giving that we may give in accordance with your will. In Jesus' name we pray. Amen.

Introduction

As a whole, people look forward to Christmas with more anticipation than any other season of the year. It is truly a time of rejoicing, bright eyes, giving and receiving of gifts, much delicious food, and visiting of relatives and friends. However, Christmas would have very little real depth of meaning apart from the Lord Jesus Christ. It is his birth date that we celebrate this season of the year, and it is the Christ of Christmas that is the subject for this message.

I. The Christ of Christmas from birth to his present status is a revelation from God.

A. *In Christ's birth, one can see the power of God to rise above the natural and manifest himself in a miraculous way.* The Babe in Bethlehem was one of the greatest miracles of all times. He was the preexistent one now in earthly existence. He was the eternal God in the form of a fleshly child. No one but an omnipresent God could do this.

The Babe in Bethlehem was born of a virgin without an earthly father. This also reveals God at work in an unusual way. Only one who had all power would be able to break a natural law and bring one into the world as God did Christ.

345

The Babe in Bethlehem is a proof of God's fulfillment of prophecy. Hundreds of years before the birth of Jesus, God had promised such an event with many little details spelled out. This is a revelation of God's knowledge and of his ability to carry out plans.

B. *In Christ's life, one can see the nature and characteristics of God at work.* The Bible speaks of God as love, and no greater revelation of love can be found and/or manifested than in Jesus Christ. He loved all. This all is all-inclusive regardless of how people might be cataloged or characterized. There are no exceptions.

The Bible speaks of God's being no respecter of persons. In the life of Jesus, one can see the validity of such a statement. In him the worth of each person is emphasized.

The Bible also speaks of Jesus as a God of compassion, and his very movements while on earth manifested God as a God of compassion.

C. *In Jesus' death, one can see the sacrifice of God to redeem lost people.* In Jesus, God died physically and spiritually to pay the price of sin. The wages of sin is death. This death is physical, but it is also separation from God, and Jesus paid the full price.

Jesus shed his blood for the remission of sin. From the beginning of time, blood sacrifices played a major role in the atonement for sin. But when Jesus died, his was a sacrifice once and for all, and apart from his sacrifice, there is no remission of sin.

D. *In his resurrection, ascension, and intercession, one can see God as mighty, ruling, and victorious.* The resurrection reveals power over enemy number one—death and the grave. When Jesus arose from the grave, he broke the power of death and the grave, and so he reveals God. The ascension reveals God's power over time and physical laws. The intercession reveals God and his concern for all people of all time.

E. *In Jesus' coming again, one can see the cleansing and ruling Christ.*

II. The Christ of Christmas is worthy of a lofty place in the lives of all people.

A. *He is worthy of worship, and people do worship him.* To worship Christ aright— in spirit and in truth—we must surrender our lives to him for salvation. Then Jesus becomes a personal Savior, and this is his purpose of coming into the world.

Christ is to be worshiped privately the year around. He is to be worshiped publicly in the church throughout the year.

Christ is to be worshiped in adoration. Everyone ought to see him as God and as Savior and manifest reverent admiration for him.

Christ is to be worshiped in praise. All Christians are to praise his name, his works, his love, and his redeeming grace. Christ is to be exalted because of love for him and appreciation to him.

B. *Christ is worthy of one's life and possessions.* In him one's life is its very best,

346

and apart from him it is inferior. In him a life is what it ought to be, and apart from him it is less than the best. In him one's possessions are sanctified, cleansed, and multiplied for good.

C. *Christ is worthy of recognition and consultation by the entire world.* It is natural to want to share Christ, and it is beneficial to consult him in every facet of life.

Conclusion

This is the Christmas season. In your buying of gifts, do not forget Christ. Think of missions. Think of the church and include Christ in the expenditure of money. In your seeking of happiness and a good time, take him into your lives, and he will give supreme happiness.

SUNDAY EVENING, DECEMBER 14

Title: God Is Ready When You Are

Text: "But when the fulness of the time was come, God sent forth his Son, made of a woman, made under the law, to redeem them that were under the law, that we might receive the adoption of sons" (**Gal. 4:4–5**).

Scripture Reading: Galatians 4:1–7

Introduction

The title of this message is "God Is Ready When You Are." The apostle Paul in his writing to the people of God in Galatia reviewed the providence of God across many years to a given point in history. Then he said that when the world was ready, God was ready. It was at that moment that Jesus came.

There is a truth about the ways of our Lord that can never be matched by the ways of humanity. It has to do with patience; what God does in his purposes, he does in his own time, and he is in no particular hurry to do it. To the contrary, what people do, they want to see accomplished in their own time. First the seed, then the sapling, and then the sturdy oak.

People formulate their plans and expect tomorrow to see their plan completed. Paul pointed out to the Galatian Christians that when the world was ready, but most of all when *God* was ready, Jesus came. Jesus came to this world as a baby, lived among people for approximately thirty-three years, died on a cross, and rose from the dead according to the purposes of God. And Paul summarized in the fullness of time — God was ready for the redemption of the world, and when it was just exactly the right time, Jesus came.

I. The world was ready for Jesus!

A. *Politically.* The dominating feature of the world to which Jesus came was "unification." This was the outstanding accomplishment of the Caesars. It was a new world; there were new horizons. There was no conglomerate of antagonistic national coalitions looking across giant barriers. The world, at the coming of Jesus, was a Roman world. The roads were Roman roads. From east to west and north to south ran the great roads of Rome. The road builders were paving the way for the industries, for the movement of the merchandising processes of Rome. Little did they know that they were paving the way for the coming of the Son of God.

The language barrier was eliminated. The Greek language was spoken and understood at this time around the world. Communication between people has been, is now, and will always be a problem.

B. *Economically.* Underneath the magnificence and splendor of the Roman world was *unrest* and *poverty.* Two of every three men on the streets of Rome were slaves. When the poets of Rome wrote of the Golden Age, they were writing of the past and not of the present. There was an economic affluence but a deep moral vacuum.

C. *Morally.* Nineteenth-century poet Algernon Charles Swinburn said that "Jesus has taken all the gaiety and great spiritedness of Rome away." Any idea that the ancient world was a happy, lighthearted one and stood at peace in the spiritual realm is neither historically or practically accurate. Paul speaks of this at length in the first three chapters of Romans. Rome had sinned its youth away. All the freshness of youth was gone, and the worm and canker of grief was at work producing the spiritual vacuum.

D. *Spiritually.* The old gods of Rome were dead or dying. There were two alternatives that seemed obvious. One, a new batch of gods were imported from the East. Mystical religions and oriental deities were brought in to stimulate the decayed souls of Rome. Among the philosophers who overcrowded Olympus, the place where the gods lived was an outstanding joke! The other alternative for a supply of gods was the Caesars themselves. Caesar worship appeared. The emperor himself was accorded divine honor. His image was erected in every town square and government building.

In the backdrop of all of this was Jewish expectation of the coming Messiah. He would come to save God's people from their sins.

It is not difficult to move these truths to the present tense. The year 2014 says again to us that the world is ready for Jesus. The political needs, the economic enigma of our time, the moral vacuum, and the dearth of religious commitment speak firmly to us that the world is ready for Jesus.

II. Our world is ready for the Spirit of Christ Jesus.

A. *Politically, a new world has appeared for our time.* The drastic transitions that are happening in the great national and international power structures of our world speak to us of the inability of political systems to structure any kind of design that has satisfactory human consequences.

B. *Economically, never has our world had so many consumer goods and yet so little personal human fulfillment.* Materialism has swept around our world. Commercialization is more obvious at this particular season of the year than at any other time. It is not difficult for one to point up the paradox that exists between the contents of the songs that are sung, the carols that are played, the dramas that are presented, and the decorations of the stores, the anxious looks on people's faces, and the behavior patterns displayed these days.

C. *Our world needs to turn to Jesus for a basis for moral integrity.* The coming of Christ into this world provided once and for all a basic foundation for determination of personal and interpersonal moral relationships. By the coming of Jesus into this world, we can have a basic foundation on which we can raise not only the question, "What do I think?" but also, "Lord, what would you have me to do?"

God is ready. The world is ready too.

III. The human paradox.

Christmas is a time when we emphasize the joy of giving. The Bible says, "It is more blessed to give than to receive." But there is a sense in which Christmas depends on the joy of receiving.

The purposes of God today are surely concerned with politics, economics, morals, and religion. God is concerned with the falling apart of nations, with the downward trend in human values, and with the degeneration of lives to useless goals. God is ready, and the world is ready. Now the question is whether his people are ready to receive this gift of God today.

A. *Are you ready for the faith promised in Jesus?* Faith is an ability of every life. When Jesus came, he brought to this world the realization of faith and what it really is and does. The writer of Hebrews insists, "Without faith it is impossible to please [God]" (Heb. 11:6). He describes a faith that makes the impossible possible, a faith that asks us to do what we cannot do, a faith that produces consequences for human life that cannot be produced by another.

B. *Are you ready for hope?* Hope expresses the circumstances of yesterday in terms of fulfillment in positive tones tomorrow. Hope takes our faith in yesterday and moves it as a reality into tomorrow. Hope lives in expectation and in expected fulfillment. People must dream their dreams. Self-pity and pessimism produce a dormant life. Jesus brought to this world, once and for all, a vital living hope. Are we ready to receive it?

C. *Jesus brings this world love!* Are we ready to receive it? An eminent minister of yesterday was asked to define Christianity in a single sentence. He replied with the words of a beloved children's hymn: "Jesus loves me this I know, for the Bible tells me so."

Conclusion

Surely the world is ready for faith, for hope, and for love. Political science, social science, educational techniques, material affluence—all of these can produce some value for people in our time. But the vacuum is too heavy and the breach is too broad for life that has no reality in faith, hope, and love. The question for our world today is this: Are you ready to receive the gift of God's Spirit and reflect it to our world? God is ready when you are.

WEDNESDAY EVENING, DECEMBER 17

Title: The Bible Speaks to Our Condition

Scripture Reading: Revelation 1

Introduction

The great book of Revelation is perhaps the most neglected, the most mistreated, and the most misunderstood book in the New Testament. Many have given up any attempt to try to come to understand this mysterious last book of the Bible. They have done so to their own spiritual impoverishment.

This last book is described as "the revelation of Jesus Christ." It is a revelation *from* Christ as well as a revelation *of* Christ. To properly understand this book, we need to know as much as possible about the political and religious conditions that faced the early church in the last decade of the first Christian century. We also need to understand the nature of and the uses of apocalyptic literature as a means of communicating truth. We also need the guidance of the Holy Spirit so that we might understand what we read.

A blessing is pronounced on those who read and hear and keep the teachings of this book (1:3). This particular book of the New Testament comes from John, from the Holy Spirit, and from the Lord Jesus Christ. Our Lord is described as the victorious Christ who will one day return to the earth in triumph and victory (1:8).

By the words "I was in the Spirit on the Lord's day," John describes his attitude of reverence and worship and openness to the truth of God while in a very difficult and dangerous situation. He had been exiled to the Isle of Patmos during a time of severe persecution, when it seemed as if Christianity would be obliterated by the policies of Domitian, the Roman emperor.

I. The vision of the glorified and exalted Lord (Rev. 1:12–16).

In these words, we have a description of John's vision of the risen Lord that equipped the elderly apostle to begin a unique ministry as a prophet of God in a very difficult time. God had appeared to Moses, Amos, Hosea, Isaiah, Jeremiah, Ezekiel, and the other prophets and had called them into a unique relationship with himself. He had also equipped them for significant service. In this vision, John reveals that he experienced something similar to the great prophets of the Old Testament.

John saw the Lord—alive, triumphant, victorious, and clothed in indescribable garments. An examination of the apparel of the risen Christ seemingly is a combination of the robe of the high priest of the Old Testament, the robe of a prince or a king, and even the garment of a messenger of God.

As a priest Christ had access to God, as a king he had royal authority, and as a prophet he spoke a message from God.

II. The reverent awe of the apostle (Rev. 1:17).

Like the prophets of the past, John fell on his face as though he were dead as he experienced the presence of his God. The vision of God always humbles.

III. The triumphant announcement (Rev. 1:17–18).

John heard the risen Christ speak with a voice of triumphant authority concerning his victory over death and the grave and his authority over death and the abode of the dead. This vision of a triumphant and ever-present Christ was desperately needed in a time when the disciples were filled with great perplexity concerning their status and their future.

IV. The message of the Lord (Rev. 1:19–20).

The purpose of this apocalyptic vision of the glorified Lord was to communicate an indelible impression to John's mind and equip him with a message for the churches of that day and time. This was no mystical experience that exalted the emotions of the apostle for his own enjoyment. It was purposeful and was intended to ready him for the ministry.

Conclusion

The overall impression of this experience on John was to give him a vision of the Christ as alive and triumphant over sin, death, and the grave. He was assured that Christ would be eternally victorious over all world conditions. He aslo recognized that the Christ was spiritually present with sovereign power. Moreover, he became convinced that Christ and his church would be ultimately victorious in the present terrible crisis.

We need today a vision of our risen and exalted Lord, who is ever present with us to meet the deepest needs of our lives. May each of us pray for open eyes and hearing ears as we seek to let our Lord speak to us through this great chapter.

SUNDAY MORNING, DECEMBER 21

Title: God with Us

Text: "Behold, a virgin shall be with child, and shall bring forth a son, and they shall call his name Emmanuel, which being interpreted is, God with us" (**Matt. 1:23**).

Scripture Reading: Matthew 1:18–23

Hymns: "Thou Didst Leave Thy Throne," Elliott

"One Day," Chapman

"I Heard the Bells on Christmas Day," Longfellow

Offertory Prayer: Father, you have given us many gifts, but the greatest of all is your Son, our Savior, Jesus Christ. We thank you that in Jesus you became identified with us. Thus you know and understand us. As we have entered this Christmas season, help us to realize your presence more than ever before, and as we worship you in giving, accept our gifts with the purpose we give them. Use them to bring other people to a knowledge that "God is with us." In Jesus' name we pray. Amen.

Introduction

People use a number of words to describe God. One is *transcendent*. This simply means that God is above or beyond the earthly. He exceeds the human. Another word used to describe God is *omnipresent*, and this means God is everywhere all the time. Still another word used to describe God is *imminent*. This means that God is present with us.

The words *imminent* and *Emmanuel* mean practically the same. Emmanuel means "God with us." This is the meaning found in the text.

The one prominent thing about the birth of Jesus is that God was making himself a human being. God was becoming identified with his creation. That is the meaning of the word *incarnate*. It means God in flesh.

I. During the earthly life of Jesus, he was God identified with humanity.

A. *Jesus was tempted as a man.* Hebrews 4:15 says, he "was in all points tempted like as we are, yet without sin." Humans have never nor will they ever, suffer a temptation that was not Jesus'. This identifies Jesus as a person within reach by sinful, struggling human beings. He knows all the struggles, weaknesses, and problems of those with whom he came to be identified.

By such coming, Jesus became Savior. He suffered temptation but never yielded; therefore he was able to offer himself as a perfect sacrifice for the sinner's sin.

B. *Jesus was called the Man of Sorrows.* Several hundred years before his birth, it was prophesied that he would be a "man of sorrows" (Isa. 53:3). In Luke (19:41) one sees him fulfilling this prophecy. Here he is pictured weeping over the city of Jerusalem. He was identified with the sin, and it caused much sorrow.

All during Jesus' earthly life, he grappled with the problems with which human beings are confronted.

C. *Jesus was involved in human situations.* When someone was experiencing physical or emotional pain, he was right there dealing with it.

The gospel of Matthew tells of Jesus healing a woman diseased with an issue of blood for twelve years. The same chapter also tells of his opening the eyes of two blind men and enabling them to see. The gospel of Luke tells of Jesus' healing a man with palsy and enabling him to take up his bed and walk. The gospel of Mark tells of Jesus laying his hand on an untouchable leper and cleansing him of the dreaded disease. Jesus was also found ministering to those with mental disorders and emotional disturbances.

Matthew (8:28) tells of two men, possessed with demons, being healed. The same gospel (9:32) gives a similar instance, and there Jesus gave the man ability to speak.

When there were social differences, Jesus dealt with the issues in a redemptive fashion. He made no distinction in people. He went through Samaria the same as he went through Judea. In doing so, he dealt with an outcast. He ate with a hated tax collector and showed his interest in the unlovely.

When there were economic problems, Jesus was equally concerned. He kept himself busy helping the poor. He gave parables to teach human relations in the economic world.

When there were religious problems, Jesus was in the middle of them seeking to find a solution.

When there were domestic problems, Jesus gave sound advice and helpful suggestions, as well as resourceful strength to deal with them.

When there was sin and guilt, Jesus forgave the sin and removed the guilt.

When there was joy in the hearts of the people, Jesus rejoiced with them and added to the joy.

Thus, one can see that when Jesus was born in Bethlehem of Judea, he was "God with us" in every human need.

II. God is equally identified with humans today.

A. *Just as God was identified with humans in the person of Jesus Christ, he is now identified with humans in the person of the Holy Spirit.* There is not one thing that can happen to any person today but what God is right there. No problem is ever faced but what God is present and ready to help deal with it. No heartache has ever been overlooked or ignored by the ever-present God in the person of the Holy Spirit. He is truly everywhere now as he was at the time when Jesus was born.

B. *There is a difference in God's presence in the Holy Spirit and in the Son.* In the Son, God took on self-limitations, whereas, in the Holy Spirit, there are no limitations. This is true geographically, time wise, and in regard to circumstances.

Conclusion

This is the time of year when special attention is given to God's identity with us. If you know Christ as your personal Savior, recommit your life to him for joys and victories. Lean on him for the strength you need. If you have not received him as your Savior, let this be the greatest Christmas you have ever experienced by trusting him now and letting him have complete control of your life.

SUNDAY EVENING, DECEMBER 21

Title: And Jesus Begat

Text: "He came unto his own, and his own received him not. But as many as received him, to them gave he power to become the sons of God, even to them that believe on his name" (**John 1:11–12**).

Scripture Reading: Matthew 1:1–14

Introduction

In a Christmas story of yesteryear, a group of English school children constructed a manger scene in one corner of their classroom. They built a barn and covered the floor with hay. The figures of Mary, Joseph, the shepherds, the wise men, and the animals faced the cradle. A tiny doll represented the baby Jesus. The children were all excited, but one little fellow seemed troubled. He kept returning again and again to the corner of the room to study the manger scene. Finally, the teacher asked if something was wrong. Revealing wisdom typical of a child's ability to confound the wise, he said, "What I would like to know is—where does God fit in?" This is an important question.

There are four books that begin our New Testament. Three of these set forth to introduce Jesus in the backdrop of a genealogy. The genealogy in Matthew's gospel is usually read quickly and taken quite lightly. There is a repetitiousness involved. Matthew keeps reminding his readers of the fact that certain people came and did certain things and "begat" other people and did other things. John's gospel goes right to the core of the spirit of the incarnation and identifies Jesus as the one who was from the beginning, who was with God, and was God, who became flesh and lived among us, who influences life eternally. The genealogy in Matthew's gospel points up the historical continuity of people relating to other people. These people, whose names for some of us are almost unpronounceable, are bound together by the word "begat," but the continuity moves forward toward the coming of Jesus. When Matthew gets to the place where he points out the continuity that begat Jesus, there is no further use of the word. However, as we look back across history and into the details of personal lives today, it is not difficult for us to recognize that there are some things that Jesus has begotten also. Jesus was never married and had no sons or daughters, but he did beget—the word itself means "bring to life."

I. Jesus begat his church.

It would take a great amount of time to go into the detail of this genealogy. Wiping away all the clutter of names, Matthew is tracing the story of a covenant God had with Abraham, continued through David, and now fulfilled in Jesus, who Matthew says is the Messiah of God. This covenant essentially says, "If you will be my people, I will be your God." Jesus begat a covenant people—the people of God.

The gospel is specific about what Jesus begat. He touched people of every walk and level of life from the person on the top rungs of the ladder of life to those on the lowest. Jesus paid attention to them. He saw them, he called them, he touched them, he helped them, and he blessed them. Out of these ranks came his disciples, the chosen ones, the holy people of the Lord. When we get to the last pages of this gospel, we get to see again what Jesus has begotten. He is in his resurrected body, and he is surrounded by people. He speaks: "All authority in heaven and on earth has been given to me. Therefore go and make disciples of all nations, baptizing them in the name of the Father and of the Son and of the Holy Spirit, and teaching them to obey everything I have commanded you. And surely I am with you always, to the very end of the age" (28:19–20).

Jesus begat a people of a covenant, a people of redemption, a people with God in their hearts and a message for their world. This is his church. He expressed the divine intention for the church to be on the cutting edge to bring to pass the kingdom of God.

Jesus gave his church something brand-new and has never taken it away from her. He gave his church a divine presence—the Holy Spirit. He gave his church a new day—the Lord's Day, the celebration of his resurrection. He gave his church two new ordinances—baptism and the Lord's Supper—covenant relationships internally with an external expression for the people of God. And he gave his church a glorious hope—"Surely I am with you always, to the very end of the age."

By this time in our century, our loyalty to God and his church is whittled down to one determined by attendance in services, giving in the offering plate, and the performance of a few benevolent deeds. But Jesus begat a people who claimed him the Lord of their life! These people count loyalties in terms of a commitment to a Christ who lives in their hearts and provides a guidance and a presence that cannot be produced by loyalties other than divine lordship in Jesus.

Sometimes we are inclined to think of goodness among the Lord's people in terms of specific congregational loyalties. It is not unusual to hear it said of certain persons of the fellowship, "This person has served the church for thirty years!" The response of the gospel to such an understanding is one of shame and wasted life. Basic to the claims of a total life is a primary loyalty to Jesus Christ, who came that we might have life.

Christ begat a brotherly fellowship. The children of God are redeemed people who have compassion for one another. The vertical dimension of relationships of an individual with God corresponds always in an outward expression of horizontal relationships of that total life and personal mission to others. The mere erection of buildings and planning of programs can never replace the commitment of a total personality bound together in mutual relationships of Christian love. The first one hundred years of the church were vital, vigorous, and victorious. The spirit of Christ permeated their presence. The dark years of the medieval ages were dark indeed in the loss of a vital relationship that God intends in a redemptive fellowship.

II. And Jesus begat a divine discontent with things as they are.

When Jesus came to this earth, he ran head-on into the religious world of his day. He was divinely discontented on two specific counts.

A. *The way religious people handled their precedent.* They made the law, the prophets, and the spiritual values an end in themselves instead of a means to an end. They forgot the covenant and worshiped the system.

B. *The way the religious people treated others.* They could not accept this one from Galilee. They said he kept paying attention to the lower classes of humanity. In answer to this accusation, Jesus gave them a parable about a fellow who was away from his father and living with pigs, and when he came home, he was welcomed into the open arms of a father who loved him. Jesus was no avowed rebel. He loved people and wept over a whole city, but he would not bend to the kind of religious living that would pass by on the other side.

III. Jesus begat a new hope.

When the life of every man great and small is written, it usually closes — "and he died!" But this is not true in the life of Jesus. Joseph Ernest Renan, a wise nineteenth-century French philosopher, wrote one of the lovely stories of the life of Jesus. When he told the story of the cross, he wrote on that last page, "*Finis.*" Renan could not see the hope that had been begotten eternally for the world by Jesus. The grave is not the end. James came forth from the tomb. The words spread like wildfire around the province: "He is not here — he is risen!" And because Jesus rose from the dead, he assures us of a glorious hope of tomorrow.

Conclusion

The Christmas story is a prelude to Jesus' death and resurrection. Through these events Jesus begat a new people. He gave birth to an astounding movement and gave his church to the world. He set the pattern for divine discontent with things as they are, and he continues to give redeemed people a glorious new hope.

When we come to the conclusion of our annual celebration of the coming of Christ into this world, we must recognize dramatically and conclusively that we have not really come to a conclusion of the meaning of Christ for life. The purposes of God are eternal, involving all persons of every kind in every generation. There are things beyond today that our minds cannot understand. There are things beyond today that our being cannot comprehend. There are things beyond today that will not be the same tomorrow as we have found them today. Beyond today is the vital necessity of the glorious reality of a Christian hope through Jesus Christ.

WEDNESDAY EVENING, DECEMBER 24

Title: The Bible Speaks to Our Condition
Scripture Reading: Revelation 22

Introduction

In this Christmas season when the thoughts of Christians are focused on the birth and first coming of our Lord, we should also let him speak to us concerning his final victorious return to the earth.

I. "Behold, I come quickly" (Rev. 22:7, 12, 20).

In the last chapter of the last book of the New Testament, we find three clear promises from our Lord that he will return to the earth. He spoke these words with greater determination and with greater authority than did General MacArthur when he left the Philippines during the Second World War with the promise, "I shall return." It is the clear teaching of the New Testament from our Lord, from angelic messengers, and from all of the apostles that one day the Lord Jesus Christ will return triumphant and victorious for his own.

II. Eden restored (Rev. 22:1–5).

It is interesting to note that humans began their earthly existence in a garden that God had prepared for them. In this final chapter, we find a picture of the redeemed in the garden of God enjoying that which God had prepared from the beginning and which humanity had forfeited because of sin. Everything that sin wrecked, grace has restored. The activity of the redeemed is described: "His servant shall serve him." Heaven will not be a place where we sit and rust; it will be a place where we serve and worship and praise.

III. The great final invitation (Rev. 22:17).

The last chapter of Revelation contains one of the greatest invitations from the heart of God to the hearts of people. It is like our gracious God that, after extending so many invitations to the hearts of sinful people, he would not let the Holy Book come to a close without extending this most intensive invitation to humanity.

As individual Christians and as congregations, it is our task to make this gracious invitation from God known to those about us. Let us not neglect our opportunity and responsibility.

IV. The rewards of the Lord (Rev. 22:12).

Forgiveness is full and free by the grace of God. Eternal life is the gift of God through faith in Jesus Christ. We do not merit a position of favor in the sight of God either by observing religious ceremony or by keeping the law. We become the children of God by God's pure grace through faith.

It is the plan and purpose of God to bestow rewards on his servants who labor faithfully and unselfishly. Let each of us pray that we might respond to God's grace and to God's commandments in such a way that he will be pleased with our stewardship and have words of commendation to bestow on us at the end of the way.

V. Our abiding hope (Rev. 22:20).

Some dread to even think of the second coming of Jesus Christ. In this last chapter of the Bible, the beloved apostle John reveals his attitude toward the return of Jesus in the words, "Even so, come, Lord Jesus." If the Lord's victorious return is properly understood, this will be the joyous and abiding hope of every living believer. There could be only one reason why we would not want him to come immediately: some are not ready.

Conclusion

Let us thank God that Christ came the first time. Let us rejoice in the promise of his return. Let us respond to that promise by giving ourselves in service to him that others might let him be born within their own hearts and lives today.

SUNDAY MORNING, DECEMBER 28

Title: Retrospective and Perspective

Text: "Surely I am with you always" (**Matt. 28:20 NIV**).

Scripture Reading: Matthew 28:18–20

Hymns: "O God, Our Help in Ages Past," Watts

"The Nail-Scarred Hand," McKinney

"Lead On, O King Eternal," Shurtleff

Offertory Prayer: Holy Father, you have blessed us in a bountiful way in the year that is about to come to a close. We thank you for each blessing. As we make our offering today, help us to particularly express our love and appreciation for the multiple blessings that have been ours. Then take the offering and use it to bring similar blessings to people all over the world. In Jesus' name we pray. Amen.

Introduction

This is the last Sunday in 2014. We cannot come to the end of a year without reflecting on the past. Neither can we project our thoughts into the incoming year without thinking what it holds for us.

Whether we reflect on the past or project into the future, we can be assured of God's presence with us. He is with each of his children always, even unto the end of the age.

I. The word *retrospective* is used to define looking backward on the year that is coming to a close.

A. *There is a group of words that deals with the physical and psychological aspects of our lives.* Paul uses the word *forget* (Phil. 3:13). He says to forget those things which are behind. To make one's reflections on the past fruitful, forgetting must be thought of in two ways — positively and negatively. The thought here is to forget the things that are bad. Every person needs to forget the unpleasant and unhappy. Such experiences as defeat, disappointment, and guilt are things that should be forgotten. This can be done by an unconditional surrender to Jesus for forgiveness and cleansing (1 John 1:9).

Each person needs to forget the attitudes that make for pride and egotism. The Bible says that "pride goeth before destruction" (Prov. 16:18). The Bible also says that "every good gift and every perfect gift is from above, and cometh down from the Father of lights" (James 1:17).

The word *remember* is used many times in the Bible and is also helpful as we seek to be retrospective. To make the past productive, it is necessary to remember that we are dependent on God for all that he has and is. We also need to remember the blessings and opportunities of the past year.

Another word that ought to be prevalent in the mind of each person as we reflect on the past is *learn*. Most honest and/or intelligent persons learn from mistakes. They also learn from their achievements and use these lessons to build the future.

Look is another word that will aid the retrospective mind. We need to look at what has happened in the past and use that knowledge. A good hard look at the past and an intelligent analysis of it is profitable for every person. The same thing is true of what could have happened.

B. *There is another group of words that applies to the spiritual aspects of our lives.* Reflecting on God's past dealings with us will cause us to stand in *awe*. We are amazed when we come to realize how sinful we really are and how merciful and longsuffering the Lord is toward us.

Then the awe leads to repentance. Conscientious people will turn from their wicked ways after reflecting on the past. To behold our sinfulness and God's goodness in our past will provoke repentance.

One of the greatest words in the Christian's vocabulary is *forgiveness*. The Bible assures every sinner of forgiveness when we confess our sins. It is indeed a spiritually healthy experience to be retrospective and realize that we are forgiven of all our sins.

II. The word *perspective* is used to project one's thought into the future.

A. *There are some helpful words that apply to the physical.* The word *vision* looms high in our minds as we think of the future. Proverbs 29:18 says, "Where there is no vision, the people perish." This applies to individuals and churches. It applies to the physical as well as the spiritual.

One word that is prevalent in the minds of many on the eve of a new year is *resolution*. This word implies purpose. For adequate plans to be made and for motivation to expedite them, there must be purpose.

Closely related to resolution is the word *determination*. This puts firmness into resolutions. Before much can be accomplished in the incoming year, determination is necessary. This will involve planning, work, sacrifice, and dedication.

To be truly successful in the coming year, we must feed into our subconscious the thought of victory. The Christian religion is a triumphant, victorious religion. Jesus came to triumph over evil. He is victorious, and his followers have the same assurance.

B. *There are some words that apply to the spiritual realm that are applicable to perspective attitude.* Paul says, "Be filled with the Spirit" (Eph. 5:18). This means to be controlled by the Holy Spirit and is a must for great accomplishments in kingdom work and personal aggrandizement.

Paul also says, "Pray without ceasing" (1 Thess. 5:17). "Prayer is like a vast continent, the shores of which one can touch from many directions, but a lifetime of exploration will not reveal its secrets" (Bruce E. Mills, *Help in Troubled Times* [Valley Forge, Pa.: Judson Press, 1962], 139). Prayer takes on the aspects of eternity and is also a must to make the incoming year a fruitful one.

Obedience to the will of God is the one greatest desire for next year. Whatever he says, do. Wherever he leads, follow. Complete obedience is our assurance of a full and meaningful life.

III. There is a word that stands between *retrospective* and *perspective*, and that word is *now*.

Now is between the past and future. In order to use the past and anticipate the future, we need to act now. The past is gone, and the future is yet to come. We must learn our lessons from the past and start trying now to be ready for the future. God has spoken in the past and has worked in the past, but he also has plans for the future. Now is the time to respond to the touch of his Holy Spirit.

Conclusion

As you reflect on the past year and on God's goodness to you, give him your thanks. As you look forward to the year just ahead, surrender your life to him. Place your hand in his nail-scarred hand and say, "Lead on, O King eternal."

SUNDAY EVENING, DECEMBER 28

Title: You Can Take It from Here

Text: "Therefore go and make disciples of all nations, baptizing them in the name of the Father and of the Son and of the Holy Spirit, and teaching them to obey everything I have commanded you. And surely I am with you always, to the very end of the age" **(Matt. 28:19–20 NIV)**.

Scripture Reading: Matthew 28:16–20

Introduction

Very appropriate to the concluding Sunday service of a year is the scene in the last verses of Matthew's gospel. Jesus gathers his disciples closely about him, reviews for them their base of authority, and gives them their marching orders into the world. At no other place in the history of the world is it more obvious that our Lord has committed the gospel to his church. We have a fourfold account of the great commission of our Lord. Matthew declares that the content of the gospel is "good news" and instructs his disciples to cross the barriers of geography, socioeconomic disparities, cultural and racial differences, and interpersonal relationships by the good news of God in Christ Jesus.

It is further appropriate that in the concluding Sunday evening service of this year we be reminded of the three great missionary motives: the command of Christ to go; the inner compulsion of the spirit that says, "I must go"; and the voice from God that keeps saying, "Go!" The needs of the world are obvious. The mission task of the people of God is not a matter of emotion or feeling. It is not a work to be carried on at our convenience. We are under orders of the Lord. He said, "You take it from here!"

There are at least three characteristics of this command of our Lord:

I. The authority of the command.

A religion that has no authority is a worthless one. Some have emphasized the autonomy of the individual to ridiculous extremes. In the backdrop of this principle, we might conclude that things pertaining to the Christian life are arbitrary or optional. We can do them or not do them as our souls command. But the flip side of that record is the authority of Christ, and Jesus leaves no question. "All power is given unto me in heaven and in earth." These are the orders of our King. If the church asked you to do it, you might have wavered; if the preacher asked you to do it, you might have made a decision; if the only reason we had for our missionary enterprise was that other churches were doing it, we would question. But our Lord, whose authority is beyond question, has given this command. Forever the principle is established!

This is the authority of the King. The task of the church and the task of the minister is to show people who God is in Christ Jesus. The one who left the glory of heaven and came among humans, who lived as a man, who gave his life sacrificially on Calvary's cross, who demonstrated the power of God over death and the grave by his glorious resurrection — it is he who says, "The authority belongs to me." This is the one who so majestically and regally certifies his work. He is the one who so royally stands by his disciples and gives them marching orders. The cross was behind him, the resurrection was the sealing bond. He lived, he loved, he taught, he served, and he died for people of all time. He has a right to say to his church, "Go make disciples."

II. A steady task.

Our Lord has not merely given us something to believe but something to do. Here in a few sentences is the scope of our task. The command leaves no question. What is the business of the church, the business of the Christian? It is to bring people to God through Jesus Christ. It is to baptize those who are won; it is to teach the way and the work and the purposes of our Lord. It is written indelibly in the history of the church that a Christian thrives spiritually when passing on his or her faith to others.

Significant and appropriate for the needs of our world is an individual review of personal mission. The mission God gives us is expressed in personal terms. It is not meant to be done by professionals; it is meant to be an expression of the faith and hope and love of an individual found in personal relationships with Christ Jesus. It is the task of each Christian.

A church may have some admirable characteristics. It may be financially successful, physically attractive, organizationally complete; but if it does not reflect a flame of missionary zeal, surely "the glory of the Lord" has departed from it.

There are more than 220 giant metropolitan areas of our nation in which individuals are groping, seeking, and longing for the filling of a spiritual vacuum. Personal face-to-face encounters by the people of God can provide the good news of God through Christ Jesus. These areas are full of domestic problems, youth dilemmas, economic anxieties, and social and cultural chaos. Great barriers exist in the minds and behavior patterns of tens of thousands of persons. Jesus himself said, "I am the way, the truth, and the life; no man cometh unto the Father, but by me" (John 14:6). In these concluding days of a year when we review our yesterdays, let us take a new look at tomorrow and understand that God is saying in Christ Jesus, "As you go, make disciples."

III. A divine presence.

Jesus expressed his authority for this mission, defined the continued and steady task of personal relationships with others, and concluded his commission with a promise: "Surely I am with you always, to the very end of the age." One of the traumatic experiences of personal relationship is the moment in which you must say good-bye to a dear friend. It is difficult to express feelings in a moment like this. Sometimes we say, "I will be thinking of you." By this, we mean that in spirit we will be sharing our friend's experience, helping, sustaining, and encouraging our friend in his or her new venture though separated physically. Certainly it does help to know that we are not forgotten, and continuing relationships can be maintained by correspondence and phone calls.

But our Lord goes farther than that. He says, "I will go with you." The promise of the living Christ is not just a dream. It is the promise of a very real presence. John expresses this truth in chapters, 14, 15, and 16 of his gospel.

Always is the word that Jesus uses. This means all the days of summer, winter, spring, and fall—the sunny days and the cloudy days, the days of storm and the days of joy, the days of faith and the days of doubt, the days of victory and the days of defeat, the days of strength and the days of weakness, the days of peace and the days of war, the days of youth when significant decisions are made and the days of midlife when decisions are being carried through, the days of life and, yes, even the days of death and the years of eternity. God meant it when he said, "I will be with you *always!*"

Conclusion

Here then is the final word of our Lord to his people: "You take it from here." At the highest moment in Jesus' ministry, he expressed the royal authority of King. It is by the authority of heaven and the authority of the earth entrusted to him that he says to every Christian, "You take it from here."

WEDNESDAY EVENING, DECEMBER 31

Title: Looking Backward and Forward

Text: "Grace and peace be multiplied unto you through the knowledge of God, and of Jesus our Lord" **(2 Peter 1:2)**.

Scripture Reading: 2 Peter 1:1–11

Introduction

As we come to the end of one year and approach the beginning of a new year, it would be profitable to take a look backward and count our blessings and then take a look forward and make our plans to cooperate with the Lord.

The first few verses of Peter's second epistle provide us with an opportunity to look at some of the blessings God has bestowed on us in the past. It also provides us with some words of instruction and encouragement to live a life in which we are growing spiritually and serving significantly.

Peter addressed his message "to them that have obtained like precious faith with us through the righteousness of God and our Saviour Jesus Christ" (v. 1:1). He wrote from the perspective of an aged pastor who was living on the edge of eternity. He spoke of his body as a tabernacle, or tent, from which he would soon depart. He referred to his approaching death as his "exodus," or departure—the word used for the departure of the children of Israel from Egypt.

I. The blessings of the past (2 Peter 1:3–4).

The apostle called to the attention of his readers the exceeding great and precious gifts from God to them through Jesus Christ. These two verses are a spiritual treasure chest that reveal the blessings that God has bestowed on believers through Jesus Christ. The generosity of God's provisions for his children is magnified and emphasized.

A. *"All things that pertain unto life and godliness."* In Christ Jesus, believers have received everything necessary for experiencing the abundant life. It is unnecessary for them to turn to any other teacher or discipline in order to be all God would have them to be.

B. *"Through the knowledge of him that hath called us to glory and virtue."* Through the beauty and the glory of the life and character of Jesus Christ, God calls all people to himself. The initiative belongs with God. Salvation is of the Lord. The human response to the gospel is a voluntary commitment of faith that makes possible the bestowal of these divine gifts.

C. *"The exceeding great and precious promises."* The Bible is a record of God's promises to his people. The Old Testament contains a continuing series of promises concerning the Messiah who was to come. Peter had witnessed the fulfillment of these exceeding great and precious promises in the person and life of Jesus Christ.

Jesus made many promises to his disciples. We will greatly enrich our spiritual life and deepen our faith if we will discover these promises, claim them for our own, and move forward depending on the Lord to keep his promises as people of faith have done in the past.

D. *"That by these ye might be partakers of the divine nature."* Faith in the promises of God makes possible the new birth. The new birth does not produce a divinity in people, but it does mean that the divine character, the divine nature, has been imparted in embryonic form. This new nature provides the believer with the possibility of experiencing and demonstrating the holiness, the tenderness, the gentleness, and the power of God.

By every means at our command, we should cooperate with the Holy Spirit as he seeks to develop the new nature that came to us in the miracle of the new birth.

E. *"Having escaped the corruption that is in the world through lust."* Through their experience with Jesus Christ, believers receive the potential for complete deliverance from the powerful evil forces that work in the world. Christ has granted forgiveness from sin. He provides spiritual power to overcome the contaminating presence of evil in the world. Through faith in him and through obedience to him, we can be victorious over the assaults of the devil.

II. The opportunity of the future (2 Peter 1:5–7).

The gift of new life has been given to those who had put faith in the promises of God. This new life is like a divine seed that needs to be developed by earnest care. Spiritual growth will not take place automatically or accidentally. Peter encouraged his readers to hasten with all diligence to cooperate with the Spirit of God in developing the beautiful graces that are associated with spiritual maturity.

As we enter a new year, we should give careful consideration to these words of encouragement from the apostle Peter.

A. *"Giving all diligence, add to your faith."* Faith is the human response to God's grace that makes possible the gift of new life. Faith is the basic foundation for all spiritual growth and service.

Peter challenged his readers to supplement their faith with the Christian graces that are needed for fruitful Christian living. Seemingly, each of the graces mentioned grows out of the preceding grace. The word translated "add" probably would be more correctly translated by the word "supply." This word was used by the Greeks to describe the actions of those who provided financial resources for the production of the great plays and dramas. It was also used for the action of furnishing the provisions and supplies for an army. Peter declared that Christians are to supplement their faith with these virtues, which are actually the pieces of equipment needed for the living of a genuine Christian life.

The apostle gives us a blueprint for spiritual progress.

B. *In your faith supply virtue.* Faith makes possible the power by which virtue is to be developed. The word *virtue* means courage, moral excellence, noble character. It is not tame and passive; it is active, aggressive, and on the march.

C. *To virtue supply knowledge.* In the practice of virtue an effort is put forth to gain knowledge, which is practical skill in choosing the right and refusing the wrong. To secure this knowledge, one must make a diligent study of God's Word.

D. *To knowledge supply temperance or self-control.* Self-restraint enables a person to curb his evil impulses and resist the lures of sin in the world that surrounds him. Each person must be in command of his own moods and impulses, or his life will end in ruin.

E. *To temperance supply patience.* The grace needed is endurance, steadfastness, fortitude, perseverance. Patience is that attitude of determination that enables a person to stay under the load until the victory is won.

F. *And to patience add godliness.* Godliness is that trait that characterizes the life of a person who lives continually "as seeing him who is invisible." Perhaps this grace refers to the growth of the divine nature received in the new birth.

G. *To godliness supply brotherly kindness.* The life of reverence for God is issued in brotherly kindness. The genuine worship of God will affect one's attitude toward fellow human beings (1 John 4:20).

H. *To brotherly kindness supply love.* The crown of Christian graces is love. Paul affirmed that love is the chief gift of the Holy Spirit (1 Cor. 13:13). It was concerning Peter's love that the Lord had inquired (John 21:15–17). Peter recognized and commended the believer's love for Christ (1 Peter 1:8) and encouraged love within the Christian brotherhood (1 Peter 1:22).

Conclusion

The apostle Peter was concerned that his readers experience the benefits that flow from spiritual maturity. He was eager that they escape the tragic results of persistent immaturity (1 Peter 2:8–9).

By adding Christian graces, believers will be assured that they can avoid both idleness and unfruitfulness in their experience of salvation through Christ. Peter declared that he who does not put forth a sincere effort to grow toward Christlikeness is blind. This term most likely refers to a state of mind that is alienated from spiritual reality. The phrase "cannot see afar off" refers to a condition of shortsightedness. The picture is that of a man who is squinting his eyes because of the light. Consequently, he is greatly limited in forming a true perspective concerning the things that really matter. In contrast to these conditions, it is inferred that the believer who strives for growth will experience meaningful activity, fruitful productivity, and spiritual insight into the meaning of life.

We are approaching the end of another year in the journey of life. The past is gone. Nothing can be done concerning the past except to admit and to confess past failures. The future is before us. With God's help, let each of us respond to the apostle's challenge for the future.

MISCELLANEOUS HELPS

MESSAGES ON THE LORD'S SUPPER

Title: The Lord's Supper: On Being Involved

Text: "And he said to them all, If any man will come after me, let him deny himself, and take up his cross daily, and follow me" **(Luke 9:23)**.

Scripture Reading: Luke 9:23–26; 1 Corinthians 11:26

Introduction

In Luke 9:23–26, we find only one of many places in which Jesus told what it meant to be involved as one of his disciples. He often warned people to count the cost of such involvement, but he also warned against overlooking the cost of not becoming involved.

In Matthew 10:32, Jesus warned against the high cost of noninvolvement. On another occasion, Jesus remarked that those who were not with him were against him. The Lord's Supper speaks to us about involvement.

I. The cross of Christ is God's involvement (Luke 9:23).

The cross reminds us that God was not content merely to create a world and to create people but was concerned about the welfare of his creation. God became involved in the affairs of people on many occasions in the course of history in order to redirect them to the only way of life. The supreme involvement came as the Word became flesh and dwelt among us, full of grace and truth. The involvement of our Lord in the problems of people found its zenith at the cross of Calvary. The cross reminds us that a Savior who is willing to become involved at the point of death can never be content with disciples who are uncommitted.

II. Discipleship is our involvement (Luke 9:23–24).

Somehow the tragic heresy has entered the minds of some people that says a person's soul can be saved without his or her life becoming involved in daily discipleship. No such alternative is offered. Conversion is equivalent to involvement with Christ as Savior. This is why Christ said to his disciples, "I am the way, the truth, and the life."

Three years ago in New York City when I was wanting to know the way back to my hotel, I asked a man for directions, and he obligingly chose rather to show me the way himself. He led me to the proper bus stop and missed his own bus in order to stay there and help me get on the right bus. Rather than give me directions that would have been hard to follow, he became my way. So it is with Jesus. He becomes our Way into life.

III. Communion is joint involvement.

We have often shied away from the word *Communion* when speaking of the Lord's Supper, but it is a perfectly valid biblical word that is used to speak of genuine Christian fellowship (*koinonia*). A part of our gathering at the Lord's Table is involvement.

A. *Involvement by identification.* One of the darkest moments in the life of Simon Peter was when he denied his involvement with Christ. Gathering at the Lord's Table identifies each of us as one who is involved with Christ and what he stands for. This is why the Lord's Supper is for Christians and has no meaning for anyone else.

The Lord's Supper is an identification with the message of the gospel. First Corinthians 11:26 says that as often as we do this we "proclaim the Lord's death." This is why we believe that the Lord's Supper is for those of like faith who proclaim the same gospel and mean the same things by it.

B. *Involvement by way of reminder.* After World War I, some people found a French soldier obviously suffering from amnesia. When they picked him up at a railway station, he looked at his questioners blankly and kept saying, "I don't know who I am. I don't know who I am." Because he had been disfigured by facial wounds, three different families claimed him as belonging to them. He was taken to one village after another where these different families lived and was allowed to walk around by himself. When he entered the third village, a sudden light of recognition came into his eyes. He walked unerringly down a side street, through a small gate, and up the steps of his father's home. Like a prodigal son, he had "come to himself." The old familiar surroundings had restored his mind. Once again he knew who he was and where he belonged.

Conclusion

So we come to the upper room like amnesia victims in a shell-shocked world. We have often forgotten who we are and where we belong. Let us, with minds of faith, make our way down a side street and up a flight of stairs to a room in old Jerusalem and thus find our way home. Here it is that we shall find our way back to God, restored in mind and heart. Here is the promised land of our souls (Leonard Griffith, *The Eternal Legacy from an Upper Room* [New York: Harper and Row, 1963], 77).

Title: The Atmosphere of the Lord's Supper

Text: "They began to inquire among themselves, which of them it was that should do this thing. And there was also a strife among them, which of them should be accounted the greatest" **(Luke 22:23–24)**.

Scripture Reading: Luke 22:22–38

Introduction

We are familiar with the meaning of the wine and the bread in the Lord's Supper. They symbolize the body and the blood of Christ, which made forgiveness of sin a reality. Jesus is not present in the wine and the bread as some believe, but the wine and the bread are here to remind us that Jesus is present with us. It is a time when we realize in a special way our heritage and the faithful ones who have preceded us. As the writer of Hebrews said, "We also are compassed about with so great a cloud of witnesses" (12:1). I would like for us to think together about the atmosphere that surrounds the Lord's Supper and let that atmosphere speak to us.

I. The atmosphere says a word about betrayal (Luke 22:22).

The disciples were struck with awe at the Lord's words that someone was to betray him. Betrayal is always present in our world, and few are the Christians who have not felt betrayed at some time. We too need to be awestruck by the possibility that we might in some way betray our Lord even as did Simon Peter in his denial, or even as did Judas in his disillusionment. This word about betrayal reminds us of the power and the pull of the world on us. It reminds us of the possibility of letting that which can be seen overcome in our own lives that which cannot be seen.

II. The atmosphere has a word about greatness (Luke 22:24–25).

It is rather shocking to find that in the midst of the Lord's Supper activities the disciples had an argument about who was the greatest: "And there was also a strife among them, which of them should be accounted the greatest." Jesus reminded them that his kingdom is not like earthly kingdoms: "The kings of the Gentiles exercise lordship over them; and they that exercise authority upon them are called benefactors. But ye shall not be so: but he that is greatest among you, let him be as the younger; and he that is chief, as he that doth serve."

In World War I, one of the most savage sections of the Western Front was the Ypres Salient. For weeks and months it was the center of monotonous, rugged trench warfare. In this British sector of the Allied fortifications, there was erected a wooden hut a few miles back from the front line. It was named Talbot House and was the meeting place of men going up to the trenches and men coming down. Over its entrance door was carved the inscription: "Abandon rank all ye who enter here." Every night the Lord's Supper was observed in the loft overhead, literally a last supper in an upper room for many men. Thousands had knelt in that room. The survivors never forgot it. When a soldier trudged upstairs to the loft, the abandoning of rank was a necessity for that kind of fellowship. Talbot House was only a tarrying place, a way station on the road from the rear billets to the front line. There men had a chance to take time out before they entered the muddy trenches and the battle (James Cleland, *Wherefore Art Thou Come? Meditations on the Lord's Supper,* 116–18 [first published 1961]).

The Lord's Supper is very similar. It is a place where we tarry from time to time to remember some things and to gain a new strength as we go on to face the conflict into which Christ has called us. The first Lord's Supper was just a stopping place on the way to the cross, and ours must always have about it this aspect. There must be a setting aside of all classes and ranks and human categories as we gather together here at the Lord's Table and realize that greatness is found only in humble service and that in the kingdom of God there is no lording it over others.

III. The atmosphere has a word about purpose (Luke 22:29).

Jesus mentions that each of those present is indeed appointed to a kingdom, and he also mentions the necessity of serving in this world. The atmosphere of the Lord's Supper has a great deal to say to us about the real purpose of life that is so often lost amid our confused activity. There are times when it seems that what we do has no purpose. The story is told of a group of laborers who were given the meaningless task of digging holes three feet deep and filling them in again. During lunch hour they delegated one of their number to approach the foreman. "We quit!" he announced. "We're tired of just digging holes." The boss replied, "Well, that's the only way to find a broken pipe." The man walked over to the others, conferred with them for a moment, then came back to the foreman and said, "All right, where do you want us to dig?" Once the men knew there was purpose in their work, they were willing to go on with it. The Lord's Supper reminds us that though at times it may seem like we are digging holes and filling them in, there is purpose behind trying to witness to people on behalf of Christ.

The Lord's Supper reminds us that into our hands have been committed certain problems of life. People everywhere about us are bound by sin, and God has chosen to set us in this world as a witness and a help to these people. This is not something we can hand over to someone else. The task is ours. In one of his novels, Dickens presents a despicable character named Mr. Skimpole, a human parasite who specializes in passing his problems to other people. We all have something of this in us, but at the Lord's Supper we are reminded that they are our problems under God (Leonard Griffith, *The Eternal Legacy from an Upper Room* [New York: Harper and Row, 1963], 165–67).

IV. The atmosphere has a word about the world (Luke 22:35–38).

Note the strange words of Jesus: " 'When I sent you without purse, bag or sandals, did you lack anything?'

" 'Nothing,' they answered.

"He said to them, 'But now if you have a purse, take it, and also a bag; and if you don't have a sword, sell your cloak and buy one.' "

The key to this passage is in Jesus' admonition to buy a sword. The hallmark of an outcast was that he carried a sword. "Buying a sword" was a symbolic phrase in that day for equipping oneself for an outcast's life. If a man criticized the government, his friend would jokingly say, "You had better go and buy a sword." For any civilian to carry a sword in Jerusalem at Passover time was a criminal offense.

Jesus knew that he was now an outcast and that his disciples would no longer be looked upon as conventional peace-loving citizens. Thus he said, "Buy a sword, for you are now outcasts from prevalent society." When the disciples told Jesus that they already had two swords, he said, "It is enough" (v. 38). This was Jesus' way of saying that he did not mean a literal sword and that his disciples had again completely misunderstood him.

What Jesus was saying to his disciples is that now they had to make their own way in the world. They were to take their purse and their scrip and no longer depend on the world for provisions. The world will not support Christ's movement, nor should it. God's people must support their own campaign for the Lord, for if the world pays the check, the church will lose power.

Conclusion

The Lord's Supper reminds us that we live in an alien world and must therefore depend on our Lord. We must plan to make sacrifices. We must plan to pay the cost of our campaign. We go forth from this moment today to go our separate ways, but each must somehow go by way of the cross. We must walk from this place with the realization that outside we will face the conflicts of the world about us.

MESSAGES FOR CHILDREN AND YOUNG PEOPLE

Title: The Temptations of a Young Man

Text: "She caught him by his garment, saying, Lie with me: and he left his garment in her hand, and fled, and got him out" **(Gen. 39:12)**.

Scripture Reading: Genesis 39:1–20

Introduction

William James said, "No man has matriculated in the university of life till he has been well tempted." Everyone is tempted. Everyone who has a body to live in will be tempted through it. Everyone who has a mind will be tempted through thoughts.

I. Who is attacked by temptations? (Gen. 39:2–3).

Temptations always attack those who are trying to do right. We learn that "the LORD was with Joseph ... and his master saw that the LORD was with him" (Gen. 39:2–3). Temptations attack the young person who is trying to live the Christian life, trying to do what is good and honorable and respectable. Those who are not seeking to do right have already succumbed to temptation, and their struggle is over. We learn early that Satan travels God's roads and appeals to us in an attempt to twist and pervert all the good appetites God has given us. Therefore every person needs to treat temptations with respect.

II. When do temptations attack? (Gen. 39:6).

Temptations come with every new liberty that is given. It was when the total welfare of the household was left in Joseph's hand that his greatest temptation struck. This is what makes liberty so dangerous. Joseph was entrusted with every-thing in Potiphar's household. A man is never tempted to take money from some-one's cash register until he first has been given access to it. This is the liberty of grace that the Scripture warns us about. We are never to use our liberty as an occasion through which the flesh can destroy us.

III. What are the earmarks of temptation?
  A. *Temptations appeal to one's pride.* Temptations often come to us in the form of flattery. They make us feel wanted, important, masterful. Joseph was merely a slave. Slaves were never looked upon by women of position and wealth, yet a beautiful woman threw herself at Joseph.
  B. *Temptations make refusal embarrassing and often dangerous.* Joseph no doubt knew the danger of scorning such a woman as Potiphar's wife, who was in effect his employer. A weaker person would have justified his sin by saying that he was obeying the command of his master and that disobedience could be met with the death penalty. It could be embarrassing for a girl to have to slap a boy's face and get out of a car and walk home. It could be equally embarrassing for a boy to have to tell a girl that she is being too forward.
  C. *Temptations appeal to a natural desire.* The attraction of a man for a woman is part of the handiwork of God. The day would come when Joseph would take a woman for his wife and enter into all the relationships of mar-riage made holy by God. But here the temptation was to become soiled by sexual immorality. The apostle Paul warned his readers to stand against temptation "lest Satan should get an advantage of us: for we are not igno-rant of his devices" (2 Cor. 2:11).

IV. How serious are temptations? (Gen. 39:9).
  A. *They lead us to sin against God.* Joseph was a young man for whom God had great plans. One moment of weakness could ruin those plans. As a young-ster growing up on a farm, I remember several occasions when I stood and watched a gathering storm cloud, filled with rumbling thunder and criss-crossed with lightning, its ominous green color revealing the presence of destructive hail. I knew that it threatened all the labor of the past year as it swept down on the fields of ripening wheat. Similarly sin can ruin an entire life.
  B. *Temptations lead us to let others down.* Potiphar, Joseph's employer, had placed supreme trust in his hand. Joseph was not aware of it at the moment, but his own father and brothers, who were to become the nation of Israel, would in the years to come depend on his faithfulness in the plan of God. There would come a time when Joseph would be used to bring his people together in deliverance, and the temptation he faced could ruin all of that.

V. How are temptations overcome? (Gen. 39:12).
  We overcome temptations by fleeing from them. We must never suppose that

we can toy with them and enjoy them without yielding to them. This is not to say that temptations are easily overcome. Because Joseph stood true to his faith, he found himself falsely accused and cast into prison. Only after much suffering would he be vindicated. Yet the time would come when his faithfulness, and the wisdom of his choice, would be manifest. Charles Spurgeon once said, "No man can keep the birds of passion from flying about his head; the trouble is when he allows them to begin building nests in his hair." To fight temptation we must learn the secret of watching and praying. Watching refers to the human side and praying refers to the divine side. As we cooperate with God, we overcome our temptations.

Conclusion

Temptation cannot overtake you by its own power. Temptation can win only with your help. There is only one knob to the door of a person's life, and it is on the inside. The door never opens except when you open it. God is more powerful than Satan, and if we are willing to look to God, he will give us the strength to overcome every temptation (1 Cor. 10:13).

Title: An Unlikely Disciple

Text: "And after these things he went forth, and saw a publican, named Levi, sitting at the receipt of custom: and he said unto him, Follow me" (**Luke 5:27**).

Scripture Reading: Luke 5:27–32

Introduction

Because of God's nature, he is always doing the impossible and dealing in unlikely places with unlikely people. From the human standpoint, calling Matthew as an apostle was very unwise. It might be likened in our day to electing a man just released from prison for embezzlement as a community fund chairman. The calling of a man like Matthew for a helper did not bespeak a bright future. Matthew truly was un unlikely disciple.

I. Notice the difficulties involved (Luke 5:27).

Matthew was a publican, or tax collector. There were few better ways of becoming financially independent than becoming a tax collector. By pulling strings and with much effort, Matthew had at last secured the position. His bid had been accepted for the portion of the taxes he was to render to Caesar, and of course everything he collected above that amount became his.

When Matthew gained his position as a tax collector, he at the same time closed the doors to the homes of his Jewish friends. No respectable person would have him as a guest. His money was not even acceptable in the synagogue. By Jewish law a tax collector was barred completely from the synagogue and was categorized with unclean things and beasts. He could not be a witness in any court case. Robbers, murderers, and tax collectors were all classed together by the Jewish people.

II. Notice the demands of the bargain (Luke 5:28).

As Jesus of Nazareth came by the customs place where Matthew worked, he challenged Matthew to give up all his worldly opportunity and to become a Christian. To the amazement of all, Matthew arose from his table of customs, gave up his world of opportunity, and became a Christian.

Matthew lost everything he had labored for years to achieve. He lost a comfortable job, a good income, and the security worldly wealth can bring with the approaching of old age. He lost his ability to provide anything his family wanted in the way of worldly goods. He gave up everything our world calls success in order to have honor, to become an heir to the riches of Christ, to be a man on a thrilling adventure pursuing the will of God, and most important of all, to be a man who now had a destiny.

III. Notice the talk (Luke 5:30).

Broadly speaking, in Palestine people were divided into two groups. There were the orthodox who rigidly kept the law in every petty detail and regulation; and there were the people who did not keep the petty regulations of the law. The second group were classed as "people of the land," and it was forbidden for the orthodox to go on a journey with them, to do any business with them, to give anything to them or to receive anything from them, to entertain them as guests or to be guests in their homes. By associating with people like this, Jesus was doing something the pious people of his day could never have done. The self-righteous said it was a disgrace for such people to meet together and propose to discuss religious matters.

Jesus answered by saying that people who claim that they are whole and have no sin are in no frame of mind to accept a physician. Jesus said, "I am coming to call those who will admit their sin and admit their sickness and out of this be willing to repent."

IV. Notice the outcome.

Matthew may have been an unlikely prospect, but when the power of God is considered, there are no unlikely prospects. Matthew immediately called his fellow tax collectors together that they too may meet Jesus. This is the fundamental principle of Christian growth. A person begins to grow when he begins to become concerned about helping other people find Christ. This is the fundamental principle Alcoholics Anonymous has come to use. An alcoholic is on his or her way to recovery when he or she can become responsible for helping another alcoholic.

Levi the tax collector became Matthew the disciple. I think it is significant that the name Matthew itself means "Gift of God."

How did this unlikely prospect turn out? Weeks later, when after a night in prayer Jesus chose twelve to be apostles, the list included Matthew.

The first book of the New Testament bears Matthew's name. Alexander Whyte has said, "When Matthew rose up and followed Jesus, the only thing he took with him was his ink and pen, and it is well for us that he did since he made such good use of them."

The last words in Matthew's gospel are, "Lo, I am with you always, even unto the end of the age." The tax collector once shut out from the congregation of Israel was never shut out from the fellowship of the Lord Jesus Christ. Christ remained with him always.

Conclusion

It is significant that in the building of the church our Lord used moral rubbish—a tax collector, a traitorous Simon Peter, and a fanatical zealot. The reason God can use such material is found in 2 Corinthians 5:17 where we read, "If any man be in Christ, he is a new creature: old things are passed away; behold, all things are become new."

Title: A Man Who Forgot God

Text: "In the same hour came forth fingers of a man's hand, and wrote over against the candlestick upon the plaster of the wall of the king's palace: and the king saw the part of the hand that wrote" **(Dan. 5:5).**

Scripture Reading: Daniel 5:1–31

Introduction

Picture, if you will, a successful businessman who has learned to take what he wants, say what he pleases, live as he chooses. Suddenly a tragedy envelops him. There is no reason to be too specific—whether a heart attack, a blinding crash on the highway, or some other tragedy—the result is the same. He suddenly is confronted by his mortality. He has an overwhelming sense that the God who has been ignored has drawn near in judgment.

Such is the setting for our Scripture. Though Belshazzar lived centuries ago, he was as modern in his outlook as tomorrow. We look into his life at a very crucial moment and discover a man who had completely forgotten God and chosen to live as if there is no God. This not only happened in far-off, forgotten Babylon. But it happens today, tonight, tomorrow!

I. Belshazzar's secularized life (Dan. 5:1–4).

We find in Belshazzar a totally secular outlook. The word *secular* has come to denote a kind of "this age-ism." It is not that Belshazzar did not believe in the possibility of another life beyond this one; it is merely that he chose to consume himself with the present moment.

It is strange indeed that people have feasts in the presence of great peril. Just outside the city's walls was encamped the army of Cyrus. Belshazzar felt secure within his walled city because he supposed it to be impregnable. It is said that the walls of Babylon were wide enough at the top for six chariots to race abreast. What he did not realize was that under the cover of darkness the enemy was quietly diverting the Euphrates River into an overflow canal that had been built years before and was in disuse. Once the waters had been so diverted, the enemy would be able to slip in under the walls of the city through the dry riverbed. One hundred and fifty years before, Isaiah had prophesied that Babylon would fall to Cyrus (Isa. 13:17–22; 45:1–2).

II. Belshazzar's interruption (Dan. 5:5–6).

The banquet was at its peak. The king, together with his leading nobles, was seated at one end of the great banquet hall on an elevated stage. The great candelabra illuminated the hall and cast shadows on the glistening white plaster of the walls. Suddenly God interrupted the party: "In the same hour came forth fingers of a man's hand, and wrote over against the candlestick upon the plaster of the wall of the king's palace: and the king saw the part of the hand that wrote" (Dan. 5:5).

Guards can shut out human intruders, but God cannot be shut out. No matter how hard we try to shut out all crises from our life, they at last descend on us with the suddenness of a summer storm.

III. Belshazzar's blindness (Dan. 5:20–24).

If anyone would have told Belshazzar that he would invite the preacher to his great feast, he would have laughed in his face. But now the situation had changed. It was Daniel who then reminded him of some of the handwriting that he should have heeded long before. One episode written on the walls of time before the very eyes of Belshazzar had to do with Nebuchadnezzar, a relative of Belshazzar. Daniel reminded the king that Nebuchadnezzar had once been the most powerful monarch in the world. He had held in his hand the power of life and death over many people. Yet there came a time in his life "when his heart was lifted up, and his mind hardened in pride" (Dan. 5:20). It was the living God who deposed him from his throne and took his mental powers from him, causing him to live like a beast of the field.

IV. Belshazzar's judgment (Dan. 5:25–30).

In this vivid account, we find the fate of every person who shuts out the supernatural and chooses to know only a half existence — a half life. Belshazzar's judgment awaits every person who leaves God out of his or her life. Daniel announced to the great potentate that the word *Mene* indicated that God had numbered the kingdom. In other words, God had announced: "Time's up!" God had allowed Belshazzar to run his course, and now the course had ended. There would be no further opportunity, no other chance. Time was up!

The next word in the mysterious writing was *Tekel*. It means: "Thou art weighed in the balances, and art found wanting." Thus Belshazzar's whole life had been weighed by a divine standard. "The LORD is a God of knowledge, and by him actions are weighed" (1 Sam. 2:3). The customs of ancient warfare were that when a monarch had been defeated, all his prized possessions were weighed and divided among the conquerors. Therefore, to be weighed was to be defeated. It was to lose all one's power. It was to be deposed from the throne forever (Albert Barnes, *Daniel,* vol. 1, and *Notes on the Old Testament* [Grand Rapids: Baker, 1957], 229, 300).

The third word of the writing was *Peres.* It meant that the kingdom of Belshazzar was to be divided and given to the Medes and the Persians. Opportunity had indeed vanished. The kingdom would be no more.

Ancient history tells us that the army of Cyrus did indeed divert the channel of the river and slip under the great iron gates by means of the dry riverbed. While the town slept, while the king reveled amid his banquet guests, the enemy was slipping quietly into the city to take it.

Conclusion

So we look into the life of a man who did not deny God but who lived as though God were not important.

It is almost an afterthought, almost an anticlimax, for Daniel to tell us in the following few verses: "And that night was Belshazzar the king of the Chaldeans slain" (Dan. 5:30). His death that night was not the real tragedy. It was his failure at life that was the tragedy.

FUNERAL MEDITATIONS

Title: Mixed Emotions

Text: "For thou hast delivered my soul from death, mine eyes from tears, and my feet from falling" **(Ps. 116:8).**

Scripture Reading: Psalm 116

Introduction

Any time a group of people are gathered around the body of a Christian loved one, there are mixed emotions. This is the subject for this message.

I. There are emotions of sorrow because a friend or loved one has departed in death.

A. *Any human finds it difficult to give up a loved one.* Often the survivors have seen the deceased loved one suffer long and much in life and perhaps just prior to death. They have observed a gradual failing of health for an extended time. They have known the anxiety that death was inevitable. Now that death has occurred, there is assurance that the loved one is in an eternal place of rest and freedom from earthly troubles. Yet even with this assurance, there is still sorrow in seeing one go.

B. *Any friend has grief in the departure of a friend.* This friendship may be a business associate, a fellow church member, or a neighbor. Once friendship has been established, it is a traumatic experience to part.

II. There are emotions of joy because of the eternal welfare of the deceased who is a Christian.

A. *Death for a Christian is a glorious thing.* It is a transformation from a sickly, frail, suffering body to a glorified body.

The Bible gives assurance of the wonderful state now (Rev. 21:1–4).

B. *Death for the Christian is a blessed experience.* "And I heard a voice from heaven saying unto me, Write, Blessed are the dead which die in the Lord from henceforth: Yea, saith the Spirit, that they may rest from their labours; and their works do follow them" (Rev. 14:13).

This passage gives assurance of another life after this one. Jesus told the sister of Lazarus, "I am the resurrection, and the life; he that believeth in me, though he were dead, yet shall he live" (John 11:25).

"And have hope toward God, which they themselves also allow, that there shall be a resurrection of the dead, both of the just and unjust" (Acts 24:15).

C. *We have emotions of joy because of the promises of God.* "But God will redeem my soul from the power of the grave: for he shall receive me" (Ps. 49:15). "Verily, verily, I say unto you, the hour is coming, and now is, when the dead shall hear the voice of the Son of God: and they that hear shall live" (John 5:25). "We know that the one who raised the Lord Jesus from the dead will also raise us with Jesus and present us ... to himself" (2 Cor. 4:14 NIV).

Conclusion

If you are in grief because of your loved one's death, then do not be ashamed of it. Thank God that you have human feelings, but then also thank God that he has provided for your loved one in death and that your loved one is now realizing this provision.

Title: Blessed Are the Dead Which Die in the Lord

Text: "Then I heard a voice from heaven say, Write this: Blessed are the dead who die in the Lord from now on." "Yes," says the Spirit, "they will rest from their labor, for their deeds will follow them" (**Rev. 14:13 NIV**).

Scripture Reading: Psalm 23

Introduction

Funeral services are designed to be of help to the loved ones of the deceased as well as to memorialize the one who has died. That is the purpose of this message.

I. What does it mean to die in Christ?

A. *To die in Christ simply refers to the death of a Christian.* This passage says that Christians are blessed at death. The word *blessed* means happy. So the Bible is confirming that death for a Christian is a happy experience. There are two reasons for this joy.

One reason is that they "rest from their labor." For a person who labors and toils all of his or her life, it is a great joy to look forward to rest. The idea of rest implies refreshment. Thus, when a Christian dies, he or she is refreshed from the toils of life.

The other reason for happiness in the death of Christians is that "their deeds will follow them." Those who have devoted their life to helping the helpless, ministering to the poor, serving in the name of Christ, and simply being a friend, have works that follow them long after they are dead.

B. *The Bible uses some terms for death that are of help in time of sorrow.* For example, death is referred to as sleep. For a tired, worn-out person, nothing is more meaningful and helpful than sleep. One goes to sleep with the anticipation of arising rested and refreshed for a new day. This is what death is for a Christian—going to sleep in the earthly world, exhausted from days of toil, to awake in the heavenly world refreshed for the new day.

Another term is used that refers to the unyoking of an animal. This term is almost obsolete for many people today, but it, too, is a word description of laying down burdens. It is the removal of the things that gall and make uncomfortable. It is the cessation of burden bearing. Another term found in the Bible in reference to death is a release from bonds. In this life, a person is shackled with the weakness of the flesh. He or she is imprisoned by fleshly limitations. Death breaks the shackles, destroys the prison walls, and frees the Christian from all limitations forever.

Still another biblical concept of death is loosening the tent rope and striking camp. The idea here is that of changing residence. Christians change their place of abode in death. They move from one dwelling place to a better one. Closely associated with tent ropes are mooring ropes of a ship. One loosens the mooring ropes and sails the deep waters into the presence of God.

Other concepts that help us understand the blessedness of death are coronation and moving from one room to another. The only way God can crown his own in the way he desires is by taking his own from this life into the greater one—moving them from one room to another by means of death.

II. The heart of the matter is that all these terms apply to a Christian.

A non-Christian cannot expect such blessings. Death serves as a motivation to cause all people to want to become Christians.

Conclusion

A word to you who are in sorrow because of the home-going of your loved one: recognize that you are hurt and make no pretense of it. Then turn your face toward the heavenly Father and thank him for the wonderful provisions he has made for his own in death.

A word to anyone present who is not a Christian: Take comfort in God's love for you. Then surrender to him for eternal life.

Title: Areas of Comfort

Text: "I will not leave you comfortless: I will come to you" **(John 14:18)**.

Scripture Reading: John 14:1–27

Introduction

We never need comfort more than when death claims a loved one. Death is one of the deepest hurts human beings suffer. This is the experience of the day. This is the purpose for our gathering. A loved one has died, and we are grieving. Where can we go for comfort? Comfort comes from three directions.

I. Comfort comes from God.

A. *The greatest source of comfort anyone can have is the Holy Spirit.* This is the Comforter mentioned in our text. John 14:16–17 tells the bereaved of the abiding presence of the Holy Spirit and tells of the believer being indwelt by the Holy Spirit. John 14:26 speaks of the Holy Spirit's teaching ministry and of his calling everything to remembrance.

Each of these verses is an identity of the all-loving, ever-present God, ministering to a deceased person's loved ones.

B. *God has also provided comfort for the bereaved in Christ, his Son.* The real comfort here is redemption from sin. When a person has been redeemed from sin, he or she has eternal blessedness with God in heaven. To know that a loved one is forever with the Lord because of the work of Christ is a comfort only God can provide.

II. Comfort comes from friends and family.

It has been said often that one does not know how many friends one has until a crisis situation arises. This is especially true when death invades a family and removes a loved one. Tokens of friends' comfort are seen in flowers, presence in the home, at the funeral, and in places of need. Friends use soft-spoken words of comfort and lend a helping hand. The many acts of kindness that friends bestow on the bereaved are true sources of comfort.

III. Comfort comes from within oneself.

A. *Each Christian is indwelt by the Holy Spirit.* For this divine Holy Spirit to adequately fulfill his role as a comforter, one must depend on him. One must pray to him and seek his leadership.

B. *Each Christian can recall memories.* The reason death hurts is because it separates the survivors from the deceased, but there are many wonderful memories of a loved one that can bring comfort. As each person relies on memory, he or she can find comfort.

C. *Prayer is a wonderful source of comfort.* Regardless of the thought, each person can tell God about it. His ear is always bent to hear. It is always uplifting to talk to God and listen to him. Prayer is one of the bereaved's main sources of comfort.

Conclusion

You who suffer sorrow now because of a lost loved one, look for sources of comfort. You will find them from God above, from friends without, and from yourself within.

WEDDINGS

Title: The Permanence of Love

Text: "In this life we have three great lasting qualities—faith, hope and love. But the greatest of them is love" (**1 Cor. 13:13 PHILLIPS**).

The minister performing the ceremony should read 1 Corinthians 13 from a modern version of the Scriptures. Preliminary remarks could include a review of the importance of Christian love, the nature of Christian love, and the permanence of Christian love. The minister could point out that while romantic love is important for the achieving of happiness in marriage, Christian love—that is, a persistent unbreakable spirit of goodwill—will undergird and help guarantee the highest possible human happiness.

The kind of love described in 1 Corinthians 13 is not limited to the emotions. It is primarily a matter of the intellect and the will of a Christian who has experienced the love of God through faith in Jesus Christ. The kind of love described here is the supreme gift of the Holy Spirit. If Christians are to achieve the highest possible happiness in marriage, they must recognize the indwelling presence of the Holy Spirit and respond to his leadership day by day. Then they will develop a relationship as husband and wife that will be mutually creative, stimulating, and helpful. To make marriage abundantly happy, Christian love should be practiced by both members of the new partnership who come together to establish a home.

The minister may now inquire, "Who gives this woman to this man in marriage?" The father may reply, "I do," or he may reply, "Her mother and I."

If you, then, _____ and _____, have freely and deliberately chosen each other as partners in this holy estate and know of no just cause why you should not be so united, in token thereof you will please join your right hands.

Groom's Vow

_____, in taking the woman you hold by the right hand to be your lawful and wedded wife, before God and the witnesses present you must promise to love her, to honor and cherish her in that relation, and leaving all others cleave only unto

380

her, and be to her in all things a true and faithful husband so long as you both shall live. Do you so promise?

Groom's Answer: I do.

Bride's Vow

_____, in taking the man you hold by the right hand to be your lawful and wedded husband, before God and the witnesses present you must promise to love him, to honor and cherish him in that relation, and leaving all others, cleave only unto him, and to be to him in all things a true and faithful wife so long as you both shall live. Do you so promise?

Bride's Answer: I do.

Pastor's Response

Then are you given to the other in advances or reverses, in poverty or in riches, in sickness and in health, to love and to cherish, until death shall part you.

The Rings

For unnumbered centuries, the ring has been used on important occasions. It has reached its loftiest prestige in the symbolic significance that it vouches at the marriage altar. It is a perfect circle, having no end. It symbolizes your desire, and our desire, and God's desire that there be no end to the happiness and success for which your heart hungers. It is thus a symbol of the unending plan and purpose of God for your happiness and well-being.

Pastor's Question: Do you give these rings to each other as a token of your love for each other?

Couple's Answer: We do.

Pastor's Question: Will both of you receive these rings as tokens of your companion's wedded love for you, and will you wear them as tokens of your love for your companion?

Couple's Reply: We will.

Closing Proclamation

Here in the presence of your parents, your relatives, your friends, your pastor, and the living God, you have made vows. These vows are binding upon you by the laws of this state. They are binding upon you by the law of God. And they are binding upon you by the law of your own love for each other. You have sealed these vows by the giving and receiving of rings. Acting in the authority vested in me as a minister of the gospel by this state, and looking to heaven for divine sanction, I now pronounce you husband and wife. What therefore God hath joined together do not let anything put asunder.

The pastor may now request the relatives and friends to join with him in a prayer for the Lord's blessing on the couple.

Following the prayer, the minister may speak to the groom and say, "You may now claim your bride with a kiss."

Following the kiss, the minister may instruct the couple to face their friends or the congregation and then say, "I now introduce to you Mr. and Mrs. _____."

Title: A Marriage Ceremony

The Holy Scriptures tell us that at the very dawn of human history, God saw that it was not good for the man to be alone. Marriage is God's first institution for the welfare and happiness of the human race. The divine Creator made for man a helpmate suitable for him and established the rite of marriage while heavenly hosts witnessed this wonderful scene in reverence.

Our Lord sanctioned the contract of marriage and honored it with his presence and power at a marriage in Cana of Galilee. It was on this occasion that he demonstrated his glory and rendered a ministry to the family that prevented them from being embarrassed.

The relationship of a man and a woman in marriage is declared by the apostle Paul to be honorable among all. It is ordained by God that a man shall leave his father and mother and cleave to his wife and they twain shall be one flesh, united in hopes and aims and sentiments until death alone shall part them.

The minister may now ask, "Who gives this woman to this man in marriage?" The father may reply, "I do." Or he may reply, "Her mother and I."

The minister may then address the couple and present to them the vows as follows:

If you, then, _____ (Groom), and _____ (Bride), after careful consideration, and in the fear of God, have deliberately chosen each other as partners in this holy estate, and know of no just cause why you should not be so united, in token thereof you will please join your right hands.

Groom's Vow

_____, will you have this woman to be your wedded wife, to live together after God's ordinance in the holy estate of matrimony? Will you love her, comfort her, honor and keep her in sickness and in health, and forsaking all others keep yourself only unto her so long as you both shall live?

Groom's Answer: I will.

Bride's Vow

_____, will you have this man to be your wedded husband, to live together after God's ordinance in the holy estate of matrimony? Will you love him, honor him, and keep him in sickness and in health, and forsaking all others keep yourself only unto him so long as you both shall live?

Bride's Answer: I will.

Vows to Each Other

I, _____ (Groom), take thee, _____ (Bride), to be my wedded wife, to have and to hold from this day forward, in prosperity or adversity, in sickness or in health, in advances or reverses, to love and to cherish till death do us part, according to God's holy ordinance, and thereto I pledge thee my faith.

I, _____ (Bride), take thee, _____ (Groom), to be my wedded husband, to have and to hold from this day forward, in prosperity or adversity, in sickness or in health, in advances or reverses, to love and to cherish till death do us part, according to God's holy ordinance, and thereto I pledge thee my faith.

Pastor's Response: Then are you each given to the other for richer or poorer, for better or worse, in sickness and in health, till death alone shall part you.

The Rings

From time immemorial the ring has been used to seal important covenants. The golden circlet, most prized of jewels, has come to its loftiest prestige in the symbolic significance that it vouches at the marriage altar. Its untarnishable material is of the purest gold. Even so may your love for each other be pure and may it grow brighter and brighter as time goes by. The ring is a circle, thus having no end. Even so may there be no end to the happiness and success that come to you as you unite your lives together.

Pastor's Question: Do you, _____ (Groom), give this ring to your wedded wife as a token of your love for her?

Groom's Answer: I do.

Pastor's Question: Will you, _____ (Bride), receive this ring as a token of your wedded husband's love for you, and will you wear it as a token of your love for him?

Bride's Answer: I will.

Pastor's Question: Do you, _____ (Bride), give this ring to your wedded husband as a token of your love for him?

Bride's Answer: I do.

Pastor's Question: Will you, _____ (Groom), receive this ring as a token of your wedded wife's love for you, and will you wear it as a token of your love for her?

Groom's Answer: I will.

Pastor's Response: Having pledged your faith in and love to each other in the sight of God and these assembled witnesses, and having sealed your solemn marital vows by giving and receiving the rings, acting in the authority vested in me as a minister of the gospel by this state, and looking to heaven for divine sanction, I pronounce you husband and wife. Therefore, what God hath joined together, let no man put asunder.

The minister should then pray for the couple that God might unite them in an indissoluble manner and that their lives might ever be a blessing to each other and to those about them.

The minister may then say to the groom, "You may now claim your bride with a kiss."

If the wedding ceremony was rehearsed, the minister may have instructed the couple at this point to turn and face the congregation and pause before the recessional. At this point the minister could introduce the new couple as Mr. and Mrs. _____.

Sentence Sermonettes

If you live a Christless life, you will die a Christless death.

Prayer is the key to the day and the lock to the night.

Time will not tarry.

The life of a Christian is like breathing in and out: in for strength and training, and out for ministry and service.

Conditions are changed only as people are changed.

Walk your talk.

To step out of God's will is to step down, never up, in quality of life.

The love of God never dims or dies.

The most costly thing God ever did was to love you and me.

People were made for God like notes were made for music.

All spiritual life begins with a birth.

The love of God never fades or fails.

The Bible is not the book of the month, rather it is the Book of the Ages.

God feeds the sparrow, but he never throws the food into the nest.

Prayer is the greatest power we have on earth.

Prejudice melts in the face of compassion.

We are a product of our thoughts.

When it comes to giving, some folks stop at nothing.

The smallest deed is better than the grandest intention.

Life does not give you a dress rehearsal. There is one try; either you succeed or fail.

God operates on eternal standard time.

God always raises a solution in the midst of the pollution.

Eternity is in the tiny minute that is yours right now.

The Bible is from everlasting to everlasting.

There is no ignorance like an educated ignorance.

The heart of God is filled with love for all people.

Subject Index

New covenant, the, 222
Outreach, 192
Parables, 93, 239, 254, 261, 268, 275, 313
Patience, 250
Peace, 243
Prayer, 62, 195
Pride, 204
Purity in religion, 229
Purpose of God, 347
Rebellion, 139
Reflecting on the past, 363
Regeneration, 42
Relationships, 55, 127, 136
Resurrection, the, 122, 306
Revelation, divine, 219
Salvation, 226
Second Coming, the, 90, 356

Self-love, 157
Sermon on the Mount, the, 288
Sinfulness, 198
Sloth, 241
Sorrow, 376
Stewardship, 163, 309, 320, 326
Teenagers, 139, 147, 152, 159, 167, 174, 181, 188, 195
Temptation, 27, 267, 370
Thankfulness, 326
Tithing, 309, 314
Victory, spiritual, 293, 311, 329
War, 147
Way, Jesus as the, 302
Will of God, 108, 188
Wise men, the, 11
Worship, 131
Youth, 370, 372, 374. *See also* Teenagers

Index of Scripture Texts

Folly, Grace, and Power
The Mysterious Act of Preaching

John Koessler

When you stand before your congregation, what do you hope to accomplish when you preach the Word? If people have Bibles and the freedom to read and pray on their own—why do they need you? In short, what do you bring to the table?

Author, pastor, and professor John Koessler answers those questions and many more.

Why does one sermon have a powerful effect on the audience while another falls flat? Why should listeners heed what the preacher says? Is human language adequate for facilitating an encounter with God? What is the point of preaching a sermon?

Folly, Grace, and Power is a must-read for pastors, seminarians, and lay leaders charged with the task of preaching God's Word. It was named one of 2011's "Best Books" of the year by *Preaching Magazine*, and also won a Preaching Today Book Award in 2012. This essential book is both a stern reminder of the sacredness of the awesome "job" of being a preacher as well as a how-to that reveals the key to speaking powerfully on God's behalf.

Available in stores and online!

ZONDERVAN®
.com

The Hardest Sermons You'll Ever Have to Preach

Help from Trusted Preachers for Tragic Times

Editor: Bryan Chapell

Contributors: Dan Doriani, Tim Keller, George Robertson, John Piper, Wilson Benton, Robert S. Rayburn, Bob Flayhart, Jack Collins, Mike Khandjian, Michael Horton, and Jerram Barrs

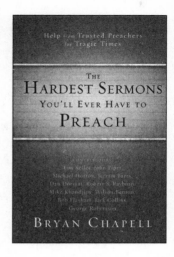

Cancer. Suicide. The death of a child. As much as we wish we could avoid tragedies like these, eventually they will strike your church community. When they do, pastors must be ready to offer help by communicating the life-changing message of the gospel in a way that offers hope, truth, and encouragement during these difficult circumstances. Those asked to preach in the midst of tragedy know the anxiety of trying to say appropriate things from God's Word that will comfort and strengthen God's people when emotions and faith are stretched thin.

The Hardest Sermons You'll Ever Have to Preach is an indispensable resource that helps pastors prepare sermons in the face of tragedies. It provides suggestions for how to approach different kinds of tragedy, as well as insight into how to handle the theological challenges of human suffering. For each type of tragedy, a specific description of its context is provided, the key concerns that need to be addressed in the message are highlighted, and an outline of the approach taken in a sample sermon follows.

Topics addressed include abortion; abuse; responding to national and community tragedies; the death of a child; death due to cancer or prolonged sickness; death due to drunk driving; drug abuse; and suicide. In addition, further suggestions of biblical texts for addressing various subjects as well as guidance for conducting funerals are provided in appendices.

Bryan Chapell, author of *Christ-Centered Preaching*, has gathered together messages from various contributors who are some of today's most trusted Christian leaders.

The Zondervan Encyclopedia of the Bible

Revised Full-Color Edition

Merrill C. Tenney and Moisés Silva, General Editors

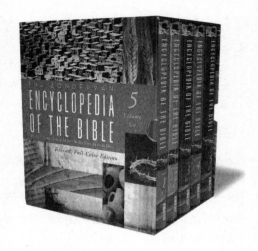

The Zondervan Encyclopedia of the Bible has been a classic Bible study resource for more than thirty years. Now thoroughly revised, this five-volume edition provides up-to-date entries based on the latest scholarship. Beautiful full-color pictures supplement the text, which includes new articles in addition to thorough updates and improvements of existing topics. Different viewpoints of scholarship permit a well-rounded perspective on significant issues relating to doctrines, themes, and biblical interpretation.

> *"The best Bible encyclopedia just got better. This resource is essential for anyone who wants to study the Bible."*
>
> — Mark Driscoll, Mars Hill Church in Seattle

> *"Pastors or teachers will be hard-pressed to find a topic that is not covered in* The Zondervan Encyclopedia of the Bible. *It can save a thoughtful pastor and teacher many hours of work in their study of the Scriptures."*
>
> — Haddon Robinson, Gordon-Conwell Theological Seminary

- More than 5,500 pages of vital information on Bible lands and people backed by the most current body of archaeological research
- More than 7,500 articles alphabetically arranged for easy reference
- Nearly 2,000 colorful maps, illustrations, charts, and graphs
- Over 250 contributors from around the world, including Gordon D. Fee, John M. Frame, and Tremper Longman III

Available in stores and online!

Share Your Thoughts

With the Author: Your comments will be forwarded to the author when you send them to *zauthor@zondervan.com*.

With Zondervan: Submit your review of this book by writing to *zreview@zondervan.com*.

Free Online Resources at
www.zondervan.com

Zondervan AuthorTracker: Be notified whenever your favorite authors publish new books, go on tour, or post an update about what's happening in their lives at www.zondervan.com/authortracker.

Daily Bible Verses and Devotions: Enrich your life with daily Bible verses or devotions that help you start every morning focused on God. Visit www.zondervan.com/newsletters.

Free Email Publications: Sign up for newsletters on Christian living, academic resources, church ministry, fiction, children's resources, and more. Visit www.zondervan.com/newsletters.

Zondervan Bible Search: Find and compare Bible passages in a variety of translations at www.zondervanbiblesearch.com.

Other Benefits: Register to receive online benefits like coupons and special offers, or to participate in research.

ZONDERVAN®

ZONDERVAN.com/
AUTHORTRACKER
follow your favorite authors